Everyman, I will go with thee,
and be thy guide

Émile Zola

POT-BOUILLE

Edited by
ROBERT LETHBRIDGE
University of London

Based on a translation by
PERCY PINKERTON

Consultant Editor for this Volume
TIMOTHY MATHEWS
University College London

EVERYMAN
J. M. DENT · LONDON
CHARLES E. TUTTLE
VERMONT

Introduction and other critical apparatus
© J. M. Dent 2000

This edition first published in Everyman in 2000

J. M. Dent
Orion Publishing Group
Orion House,
5 Upper St Martin's Lane, London WC2H 9EA
and
Charles E. Tuttle Co. Inc.
28 South Main Street, Rutland,
Vermont 05701, USA

Typeset in Sabon by SetSystems Limited, Saffron Walden, Essex
Printed in Great Britain by
The Guernsey Press Co. Ltd, Guernsey, C.I.

British Library Cataloguing-in-Publication Data
is available upon request.

ISBN 0 460 87579 5

CONTENTS

NOTE ON THE AUTHOR AND EDITOR

ÉMILE ZOLA was born in Paris on 2 April 1840. His father was an Italian engineer who had settled and married in France. In 1843 the family moved to Aix-en-Provence, but the death of Zola's father four years later left them in straitened circumstances. Zola was educated at the Collège Bourbon in Aix and completed his studies at the Lycée Saint-Louis in Paris, to which he and his mother returned in 1858.

As an only child, Zola would remain responsible for his mother until her own death in 1880. Having failed the *baccalauréat*, he was briefly employed in the customs offices of the Paris docks before bringing to an end a life of Bohemian poverty by obtaining, in 1862, a post in the publicity department of the publisher Hachette. His early writings included *Contes à Ninon* (1864) and a number of novels. At the same time he began a career as a journalist, initially as a book-reviewer and art-critic, and then, towards the end of the Second Empire, in the opposition press. It was partly this experience which resulted in his ambition to produce a vast fictional panorama of the period. By 1868–9 Zola had drawn up a plan for a series of ten novels, which was to become the twenty-volume *Les Rougon-Macquart*, finally completed in 1893. He went on to write the trilogy of *Les Trois Villes* and three of *Les Quatre Évangiles*.

During his lifetime, Zola was considered one of the greatest European novelists of his generation. But he was also an exceptionally controversial figure, from his championing of the early Impressionists to the uncompromising portrayals of contemporary life found in his writing. This reputation was consecrated in his public defence of Alfred Dreyfus, the Jewish army officer wrongly accused of spying for the Germans. Zola's open letter to the President of the Republic, J'Accuse (13 January 1898), led to his being put on trial and fleeing to England where he spent a year in exile. Zola died in 1902.

ROBERT LETHBRIDGE is Professor of French Language and Literature in the University of London at Royal Holloway. He is a leading authority on French Naturalism and has written extensively on Zola and Maupassant, as well as on the relationship between literature and the visual arts in nineteenth-century France.

CHRONOLOGY OF ZOLA'S LIFE

Year   *Age*   *Life*

1840   2 April: birth of Émile Zola in Paris, the only child of Émilie Aubert and François Zola, an Italian engineer

1843   3   Zola's family moves to Aix-en-Provence

1847   7   Death of Zola's father, leaving his family with financial problems, forced to move to ever more modest accommodation

1852   12   Zola a pupil at the Collège Bourbon in Aix. Friendship with Cézanne

1858   18   Returns to live in Paris. Writes much poetry around this period, most of which has been lost

Year	Intellectual Events	Historical Events
1839	Stendhal, La Chartreuse de Parme	
1848		February Revolution. Fall of the July Monarchy; Second Republic declared. Louis Napoléon Bonaparte elected President
1849	Dickens, David Copperfield	
1850	Death of Balzac	
1851		2 December: coup d'état
1852	Gautier, Émaux et Camées	2 December: proclamation of the Second Empire
1853	Hugo, Les Châtiments	Marriage of Napoléon III with Eugénie de Montijo. Haussmann becomes Prefect of the Seine; beginning of the reconstruction of Paris
1854–6		Crimean War
1857	Baudelaire, Les Fleurs du mal Flaubert, Madame Bovary	

Year   Age   Life

1859   19   Fails the *baccalauréat*. Leads a Bohemian existence in the company of his artist friends

1862   22   Finds modest employment with the publisher Hachette and rapidly becomes head of the publicity department. Becomes a naturalized French citizen

1863   23   Begins a career as a journalist writing for several newspapers

1864   24   *Contes à Ninon*

1865   25   Meets his future wife, Alexandrine Meley. *La Confession de Claude*, his first novel

1866   26   Leaves Hachette to live (with great difficulty) as a writer. Meets Manet. *Mes haines. Mon salon*

1867   27   *Les Mystères de Marseille. Thérèse Raquin. Édouard Manet*

1868   28   *Madeleine Férat*. Formulates a plan for a series of ten novels, which will become the twenty-volume series: *Les Rougon-Macquart*

1870   30   Marries Alexandrine Meley

1871   31   *La Fortune des Rougon*, first of the *Rougon-Macquart* novels

Year	Intellectual Events	Historical Events
1859	Hugo, *La Légende des siècles*	Italian War
1860		Beginnings of the 'liberal Empire'
1862	Flaubert, *Salammbô* Hugo, *Les Misérables*	Mexican War
1863	Salon des Refusés Manet, *Le Déjeuner sur l'herbe*	
1864		The First International Working Men's Association founded in London
1865	Claude Bernard, *Introduction à l'étude de la médecine expérimentale* E. & J. de Goncourt, *Germinie Lacerteux*	
1866		French troops evacuate Mexico
1867	Baudelaire, *Petits Poèmes en prose* Marx, first published volume of *Das Kapital*	Constitutional reforms announced. Universal Exhibition in Paris
1869	Flaubert, *L'Éducation sentimentale*	
1870		Franco-Prussian War. 2 September: defeat at Sedan; 4 September: fall of the Second Empire; 19 September: Siege of Paris
1871		18 March–28 May: Paris Commune. 31 August: Thiers elected President of the Third Republic

Year	Intellectual Events	Historical Events
1873		7 January: death of Napoleon III; 24 May: Mac-Mahon becomes President of the Republic after the resignation of Thiers. German troops leave France
1874	First Impressionist exhibition	
1876	Mallarmé, *L'Après-Midi d'un faune*	
1877	Hugo, *La Légende des siècles* Flaubert, *Trois Contes* Edmond de Goncourt, *La Fille Elisa*	October: legislative elections; republican victory
1879	Edmond de Goncourt, *Les Frères Zemganno*	Grévy elected President of the Republic
1880	Death of Flaubert	Amnesty for the Communards. First Ferry Ministry
1881	Céard, *Une belle journée* Flaubert, *Bouvard et Pécuchet* Huysmans, *En ménage* Verlaine, *Sagesse*	Ministry of Gambetta
1882		Union Générale crash. Fall from power and death of Gambetta
1883	Maupassant, *Une vie*	Death of the comte de Chambord, the legitimist pretender
1884	Huysmans, *À rebours*	Trade unions legalised

Year	Age	Life
1885	45	*Germinal*
1886	46	*L'Œuvre*
1887	47	*La Terre*
1888	48	*Le Rêve*. Start of liaison with Jeanne Rozerot
1889	49	Birth of Denise, daughter of Jeanne Rozerot and Zola
1890	50	*La Bête humaine*
1891	51	*L'Argent*. Birth of Jacques, son of Jeanne Rozerot and Zola
1892	52	*La Débâcle*, novel about the Franco-Prussian War and the Paris Commune (and thus the close of the Second Empire)
1893	53	*Le Docteur Pascal*, concluding the *Rougon-Macquart* series. Triumphant visit to London

Year	Intellectual Events	Historical Events
1885	Maupassant, *Bel-Ami* George Moore, *A Mummer's Wife* Death of Victor Hugo	Grévy re-elected President
1886		Boulanger Minister of War
1887		Resignation of Grévy; Sadi Carnot elected President
1888	Maupassant, *Pierre et Jean*	Boulangist campaign
1889		Universal Exhibition in Paris. Eiffel Tower completed. Flight of Boulanger
1891	J. Huret, *Enquête sur l'évolution littéraire,* including one of Zola's many interviews Hardy, *Tess of the d'Urbervilles* Huysmans, *Là-bas* Death of Rimbaud	
1892	Maeterlinck, *Pelléas et Mélisande*	
1892–3		Anarchist attacks. Panama scandal
1893	Death of Taine	
1894	George Moore, *Esther Waters*	June: assassination of Sadi Carnot. Casimir-Périer President. Arrest and conviction of Dreyfus
1895		January: Félix Faure elected President
1896	Jarry, *Ubu Roi*	
1897	Barrès, *Les Déracinés* Gide, *Les Nourritures terrestres*	Campaign in favour of Dreyfus

Year   Age Life

1898   58   13 January: publishes 'J'Accuse' in *L'Aurore*. Condemned to a
            year in prison. 18 July: returns to England, this time
            incognito. *Paris*, last novel of the trilogy *Les Trois Villes*
            (*Lourdes, Rome, Paris*)

1899   59   Returns to Paris. *Fécondité*, first of the uncompleted series,
            Les Quatre Evangiles (*Fécondité, Travail, Vérité,* [*Justice*])

1902   62   Night of 28–9 September: dies 'accidentally', choked by fumes
            from a blocked chimney in his Paris home

1908   Zola's remains are transferred to the Panthéon

Year	Intellectual Events	Historical Events
1898	Huysmans, *La Cathédrale*	11 January: acquittal of Esterhazy. 31 August: suicide of Major Henry. Fashoda incident
1899		Loubet elected President. Return of Dreyfus from exile to face trial; found guilty with extenuating circumstances, then pardoned
1902	Gide, *L'Immoraliste*	

INTRODUCTION

Pot-Bouille was serialised in *Le Gaulois* between 23 January and 14 April 1882, and was published in volume form on 29 April of the same year. As it shocked its contemporary reading public, so it continues to surprise those for whom Émile Zola enjoys a literary reputation, above all, as the author of *L'Assommoir* (1877) and *Germinal* (1885), those classic French novels of nineteenth-century working-class experience. In *Pot-Bouille*, by contrast, we have a picture of the Parisian bourgeoisie; and that is not unrelated to the outrage it provoked among so many middle-class readers who suddenly found their own lives subject to Zola's uncompromising scrutiny. The violence of its critical reception (outlined under 'Zola and his Critics' later in the present edition) is particularly telling in this respect. And there is no doubt that *Pot-Bouille* was conceived by Zola as complementary to both *L'Assommoir* and *Nana* (1880), and designed to explode the impression left by such works that misery and promiscuity might be the preserve of the proletariat. But it is also surprising in another sense: for *Pot-Bouille* reveals a quite different Zola from the one habitually included in literary histories stressing his black poetry, epic sweep and tragic vision. Instead, *Pot-Bouille* is a book notable for its ironic crafting and savage comedy, to the extent that it remains (in George Steiner's words) 'one of the best novels of the nineteeth century – great in its comic ferocity and tightness of design'.

Pot-Bouille was the tenth novel of Zola's twenty-volume series, *Les Rougon-Macquart*. The plan for the latter had been drawn up in 1868–9, initially as ten novels before being expanded to its definitive shape and size. The presiding genius of the project is Honoré de Balzac (1799–1850) whose *Comédie humaine*, re-read by Zola at exactly the moment he was formulating his own ambitions, provided the model for a vast historical panorama of an age. Marie Pichon (in *Pot-Bouille* itself) finds Balzac incompatible with her sentimental tastes: 'it's far too lifelike' (p. 210). Ironising such objections, Zola thereby signals once again a debt he was the first to acknowledge in his literary criticism throughout his career, and not least in those preliminary work-notes for his own series protestingly headed 'Differences between Balzac and myself'. Both there and in the *Rougon-Macquart*'s subtitle ('The natural and social history of a family under the Second Empire'), Zola spelled out his aim to do for the later period what Balzac had done for the Restoration (1815–30) and the July Monarchy (1830–48). Each of the novels of his cycle would explore a different social world, but would be bound together by the members of the Rougon and Macquart families and their descendants whose destinies would provide a microcosm of France under the reign of the Emperor Napoléon III (1852–70).

The future *Pot-Bouille*, however, figured neither in the original outline of 1868–9 nor in the revised master-plans Zola elaborated between 1872 and 1878. Its protagonist, Octave Mouret, does make a brief appearance in *La Conquête de Plassans* (1874), as the eldest son of François Mouret who marries into the Rougon family; but it is clear that he was being prepared there for his major role in *Au Bonheur des Dames* (1884) rather than the one he is given in *Pot-Bouille*. Indeed, at the point Zola started work on the latter, in February 1881, Octave was only going to make an episodic entry as one of the cuckolded husbands of the novel rather than the fancy-free young man who is central to the narrative. It was in response to problems with his plot that Zola brought him centre-stage, thus confirming the extent to which the reappearing characters of his series, whatever illusions of continuity their ancestry may provide, are always defined by the imperatives of the novel in hand. So too, while the cycle as a whole inserts each frame of the family saga into an overarching design, the individual novels of the *Rougon-Macquart* retain their autonomy.

What is more, and this is exemplified by *Pot-Bouille*, such novels are often generated by, or cast in particular ways as a result of, factors independent of Zola's original plans for his series. In the case of this particular novel, both its belated inclusion and its informing themes are inseparable from the author's public and private concerns in 1880. It was in that year that he published *Nana*, his study of the world of prostitution. And *Pot-Bouille* was an almost conscious act of revenge against a readership which had transformed *Nana* into a bestseller while castigating its author for obscenity in his portrayal of the sexual mores of courtesans who leave behind their street-walking origins by selling themselves to degenerate aristocrats. *Pot-Bouille*'s insistence on a hypocritical respectability is itself an attack *on* the hypocrisy of such readers.

But there were other reasons too why Zola, in 1880–81, inserted into his series a novel of such grim humour and acerbic disenchantment. He had been deeply affected by three deaths during 1880: those of Flaubert (8 May), another writer and friend, Edmond Duranty (9 April), and his own mother (17 October). In this respect, the repeated death scenes and funerals of *Pot-Bouille* are hardly a coincidence. But there is also ample testimony, in his correspondence and in eye-witness accounts, that Zola's general mood at this time was bleak. And *Pot-Bouille*'s devastating critique of marriage is undoubtedly linked to the parlous state of Zola's own. Little could he have imagined, however, that, towards the end of the decade, he would start an affair (and family) with his wife's maid, breaking out of childless tensions to establish a 'double' domestic life more painfully complicated than any in *Pot-Bouille*.

Zola's biographers are also agreed that, as well as being depressed, he was also exhausted. This resulted in the postponement (until 1883) of *La Joie de vivre*, a novel too despairingly close to his own emotional anguish. Having reached forty years of age and barely the halfway stage of his gigantic project, his portrait of the fictional Monsieur Vabre's interminable labours is not entirely devoid of sympathy. The writing of *Nana* had involved a huge amount of research. The novel next on the 'production line' was originally meant to be *Au Bonheur des dames*, a study of the new phenomenon of the department store, which would require major documentation of another background with which he was unfamiliar. With its limited scale and self-contained setting, and needing neither technical nor historical substantiation, the subject of *Pot-Bouille* seemed an easier option.

That the preparation of this novel nevertheless needed some such documentation, and that it was greeted with the charge that Zola was writing in ignorance of bourgeois realities, serves to remind us of the true function of such research within Zola's habits of composition. It was to accusations of the gross exaggerations of *L'Assommoir* and *Nana* that Zola mounted a defence based on the argument that the veracity of his descriptions was supported by published sources and his own empirical observations of the social worlds represented in his novels. Polemical pressures so vitiated Zola's accounts of his own achievement (with the strategic analogy of the novelist and natural scientist hardening into a militant Naturalism) that by 1880, in his best-known theoretical work, *Le Roman expérimental*, he was going so far as to claim that the documents assembled by Naturalist writers like himself were entirely responsible for the structure and content of their work: they both preceded the elaboration of character and plot, and were transposed so directly that the creative imagination was virtually redundant. Scholars with access to the preparatory notes for his novels have since shown the more dogmatic statements to be highly misleading, and intelligible only in a climate in which Zola was violently attacked for his depiction of unaesthetic physical appetites and social conditions. For as his opponents insisted that obscenity and bias resulted from a perverse and politically motivated representation of reality, so Zola found himself denying that any such distortion had taken place; quasi-scientific evidence, he asserted, was the cornerstone of his objective realism.

As far as the documentation of *Pot-Bouille* is concerned, we know (from the preparatory dossier of the novel preserved in the Bibliothèque Nationale in Paris) that Zola had recourse to various sources only once its outline was in place. He consulted accounts of the historical and political context of the period 1860–64; he visited the church of Saint-Roch notebook in hand; he secured information about the education of women, the duties and salaries of various officials, and the terms and conditions of ecclesiastical architects. Above all, he relied on the specialist knowledge of friends and colleagues who patiently replied to each and every one of his enquiries. Two of them, in particular, Joris-Karl Huysmans and Henri Céard, filled out details on subjects as diverse as commission agencies (see note to p. 30) and the precise medical constraints on Madame Campardon's 'conjugal duties'. These two men were also, compared to Zola's orderly virtue, worldly wise: they regaled him with extraordinary permutations of marital infidelity, their gossipy conversations recorded in sketches and anecdotes which in turn generated some of *Pot-Bouille*'s scenarios.

The novel's major concerns, however, had already been articulated in an article Zola published in *Le Figaro* on 28 February 1881, entitled 'Adultery among the Bourgeoisie', in which he compared middle-class infidelity with proletarian prostitution, stressing the determinants in both of milieu and education. It was intended as a serious analysis of marriage and adultery, contextualised by the wider debate leading, in 1884, to the law which restored the right to divorce. And that it struck a chord is confirmed by the presence, in the dossier of *Pot-Bouille*, of a letter from one of the newspaper's readers plaintively identifying with Zola's hypothetical examples of marital disharmony. However abstract, these usher in the figures of Valérie Vabre, Berthe Josserand and Marie Pichon in *Pot-Bouille*. For, as in the novel itself, Zola's article sets up a taxonomy of female adultery, its variants calculated in equations factoring in the parts played by physiology and ignorance.

In particular, in this article which coincides exactly with Zola's first notes for *Pot-Bouille*, he analyses three forms of upbringing: the neurotic effect of spatial enclosure on incipient degeneracy seeking a sexual outlet; mothers' roles in instructing their daughters, perverted to the extent that the goal of 'catching a man' both makes marriage synonymous with legalised prostitution and encourages subsequent adultery in exchange for further material reward; and the perpetuation of girlhood innocence *within* marriage, thus encouraging the most prevalent of adulterous escapisms, driven less by frustrated physical needs than by the attractions of living out amorous illusions fostered by an educational diet of romantic novels. Such a cynical analysis is also testimony to Zola's inability to conceive of the destinies of women outside the misogynistic stereotypes of his age, notably those grounded in domestic values overlaid on perceptions of the physiological mysteries in female sexuality. But that is not to dismiss either the originality or the sincerity of his critique of bourgeois marriage, in which women are the victims of ignorance, imprisonment and inherited cupidity. The misery of the female characters of *Pot-Bouille* is nowhere more starkly paraded than in their literal proximity to, but ironic figurative distance from, the emblematically named 'Au Bonheur des Dames' apparently catering (as such a shop title suggests) for their happiness.

The education of young women, which is integral to Zola's

explanation of such conjugal misery, was a long-standing concern. As early as 1868–9, he had deplored a convent apprenticeship and enforced female idleness leavened by sentimental
reading as a recipe for marital disaster; in a series of short tales,
under the heading *How one gets married*, published in *Le
Messager de l'Europe* in 1876, he had returned to the same
idea; and, in his literary criticism, castigation of romantically
unreal texts (from Walter Scott to George Sand) is inseparable
from their insidious social and moral effects on the expectations
of a female readership. As Flaubert's *Madame Bovary* (1857)
immortalises the theme, so *Pot-Bouille*, too, will lay a particular
emphasis on such reading as one of the causes of the disenchantment with the constraints of adult life. And Zola's novel, no less
than Flaubert's, brutally situates itself in opposition to such a
tradition.

The closely focused analysis of bourgeois marriage and adultery in *Pot-Bouille*, however, is part of a much wider satirical
perspective which runs through Zola's writing, whether as a
polemical journalist or in the *Rougon-Macquart* series itself. In
an article on Balzac (*Le Rappel*, 13 May 1870), Zola had
underlined the justified ferocity of his predecessor's portrayal of
the bourgeoisie's material greed and moral duplicity. And,
during the early years of the Third Republic, these were themes
to which Zola consistently returned in newspaper articles bringing him to the attention of displeased authorities. Although they
are explicitly set in the period of the discredited Second Empire,
the opening novels of the *Rougon-Macquart* are savage indict-
ments of values more permanent than régimes. For, over and
above their historical and political specificity, these novels catalogue principles and public virtue endlessly betrayed by ruthless
self-interest and vicious hypocrisy. *Pot-Bouille* is the *summa* of
those preoccupations, the most sustained exploration of such
themes in the whole of his work; and, in his preparatory notes
for the novel, Zola reveals himself to be perfectly aware that to
denounce the bourgeoisie is to engage in 'the most violent
possible indictment of French society'.

To accommodate such a sweeping satire within the economies
of a single text, Zola has recourse to a technique used before
and since. As Balzac's *Le Père Goriot* (1834–5) exploits the
Pension Vauquer as a microcosm of Parisian society (in which

Rastignac, its conquering hero, will seek his fame and fortune), and as pragmatic playwrights and film directors often choose to focus on a single location in order to organise an exemplary cross-section, so Zola places within one building, in the Rue de Choiseul, his own cast of characters. And contemporary caricaturists quickly portrayed him as Asmodeus, the mythical limping devil who raised the roofs of houses to reveal the domestic secrets beneath.

For, as well as satisfying demands of scale and typicality, Zola's choice of a bourgeois apartment-house allows him both to explore the hierarchies of social class correlated to its internal topography and to peer into the private lives of its occupants. Indeed, the entire book plays on the ironic contrast between inner and outer: between visible respectability and hidden vices; solid appearances and disintegrating fabrics; public façades and closeted putrefaction; receptions for collective viewing and the mess behind the scenes; marital bliss and promiscuity; the rhetoric of courtship and the animality of sex; surface well-being and penury too shameful to admit; family contentment and internecine strife; piety and selfishness; the language of the front drawing-room and the obscenities of the courtyard. Not even *Pot-Bouille*'s most fervent admirers would claim that such a strategy is a subtle one. But this relentless stripping away of the outward signs of bourgeois self-definition and hypocritical posturing undoubtedly accounts for the novel's satirical force and sardonic humour.

At the same time, there are many aspects of *Pot-Bouille* that are potentially more disconcerting, not least its oblique relationship to what is, in effect, the tradition of the novel of adultery. For *Pot-Bouille* does not quite correspond to the accepted cultural template; instead, it positions itself *against* that most pervasive of narrative models, as irresistible a temptation for the nineteeth-century novelist as for the legendary 'bored housewife'. As the poet Charles Baudelaire famously put it, in his review of *Madame Bovary*, adultery was, by then, the most hackneyed of subjects. Nor had much changed by the time Huysmans wrote (in a late preface added to his *A Rebours*, 1884), that the plot of each and every novel of the day could be distilled into the question of whether Mr X would, or would not, commit adultery with Mrs Y. At first sight, *Pot-Bouille* reinforces Huysmans's lament ('endless seduction and no less endless adultery'), to the extent that Zola seems to have transposed to 'twenty' apartments (figuratively speaking), Flaubert's generalising remark that 'my poor Bovary is weeping in twenty villages across France'. And if, as long ago as 1857, Flaubert was already (in Baudelaire's formulation) the 'latecomer', Zola too could not but be himself, in this respect, 'the writer following on from everybody else'.

But if *Pot-Bouille* is written in the shadow of other texts, there is another sense in which it also more deliberately *shadows* other texts, and, in particular, those that remained Zola's favourite (and often re-read) novels: Balzac's *La Cousine Bette* (1846), with its portrait of lustful senility anticipating Uncle Bachelard's, its myriad liaisons and *in flagrante* scenarios; *Madame Bovary* itself, inevitably, and not just in its general proposition but in many specific echoes; but also, and even more self-consciously, Flaubert's *L'Éducation sentimentale* (1869). The reworkings are insistent: Frédéric Moreau and Madame Dambreuse on the one hand, Léon Josserand and Madame Dambreville on the other; Frédéric's 'fear of incest' with the maternal Madame Arnoux, and Octave's similar scruples on being granted access to Madame Campardon's bedroom. To read the two novels side by side is to be struck by quite remarkable parallels. More significally, reworkings are almost perverse. In juxtaposing Rosanette (the available prostitute) and Marie Arnoux (the inaccessible wife), Flaubert problematises the binary opposition of sacred and profane (only because Marie is fortuitously prevented from coming to the bed Frédéric had arranged is Rosanette substituted for her). Zola's ironic inversion, on the other hand, has Valérie (whom Octave treats like a whore) refuse him while the Marie (Pichon) of *Pot-Bouille* takes her place.

To note such traces of other texts is better to understand Zola's remark that *Pot-Bouille* would be 'my own *Éducation sentimentale*', thus situating his novel in relation to, but at a subjective distance from, the Flaubertian masterpiece he had admired in an 1879 essay as 'the very negation of the novelistic'. In that light, *Pot-Bouille* is, in some ways, halfway between the generic model of *L'Éducation sentimentale* and the *reductio ad absurdum* of Henri Céard's *Une belle journée* (1881), in which adultery is planned but, as a result of mutual boredom, never consummated. Published in the year Zola was working on *Pot-*

Bouille, Une belle journé parodies the novel of adultery to the
extent of resisting the impulse towards closure which directs the
traditional plotting of such fiction.

Like so many other novels by Zola (characterised by their
strongly directed plots), *Pot-Bouille* is full of plotters in the
other sense: not just those plotting marriages and love affairs,
but also those like Madame Hédouin with commercial strategies
for her shop's departments, and the architect and priest organising perspectival designs in Saint-Roch. It is, nevertheless,
Octave's repeated schemes and plans that punctuate the novel,
dreaming of his future success, organising his life and loves, and
the love lives of other characters too (conceiving the Pichons'
reunited bliss, for example, in the very terms of Zola's own
planning). But if *Pot-Bouille* is planned essentially as a series of
sexual conquests, the reader cannot fail to notice the curious
fact that the novel is elaborated as a series of *failed* seductions.
The rake's proverbial progress – or 'sentimental education' – is
more a dismal regression: the initial energy of Octave's Balzac-
ian arrvial is dissipated; the archetypal Don Juan 'possesses'
Marie Pichon with neither seductive strategy nor satisfaction;
his is a 'triumph' over a passivity no more resistant than the fall
of an object from the table on which Marie indifferently
becomes his first mistress within the house. And there is no
more comic episode in the novel than the epilogue (in chapter
14) of this desultory affair: on his way up the stairs to a longed-
for rendezvous with Berthe, Octave (almost by accident) makes
love to Marie and is so exhausted by his exertions that he
spends the next few hours yawning away in his bedroom
desperately hoping that Berthe won't come after all. In other
words, this is a novel of adultery that too often seems to go
wrong, diverting its virile protagonist down impotent dead-
ends.

Pot-Bouille has been described as having only 'a ghost of a
plot'. What it has, in practice, are the threads of a number of
plots. Octave's potential conquests include Madame Juzeur,
Madame Campardon, Valérie Vabre and Madame Hédouin,
each of these offering the possibility of a story-line. But in spite
of Octave's machinations and fevered hypotheses, none of them
leads anywhere. These threads of plots are never interwoven
sufficiently to conjure a dénouement, let alone invested with the
tensions necessary to the reader's pleasure in the plotting of a

novel of adultery. Instead, and thus mirroring Octave's own confusion about the rules, we have the semblance of an involved literary game fleshed out in an endless series of substitutions: Octave is not only deprived of heroic presence, but is ultimately reduced to the status of yet another onlooker at a vaudevillesque roundabout.

This dynamic of substitution works within and across the simplified oppositions, set up by the novel, of inner and outer, surface and depth, appearance and reality. For alongside all the contrasts mentioned earlier, this is a fictional universe character-ised by the erosion of difference; its series of substitutions is at odds with distinctiveness. On a spatial level, for example, *Pot-Bouille* seems a novel apparently tightly organised according to the floors in the building, with the inhabitants categorised by class, occupation and prosperity; in fact, this is a world of interchangeable beds and tables, of only superficially differenti-ated spaces and décors that are reduplicated as frequently as their habitués. For the characters move across thresholds and invert the protocols of *chambre* and *anti-chambre* as surely as noise seeps through the partitions of rooms nominally reserved for distinct groups (male or female, family or guests, servants and masters). As this permeability wafts underfloor heating up into the primmest skirts, so architectural commissions take Campardon into the church of Saint-Roch and the Abbé Mau-duit back into Campardon's secular *salon*. *Pot-Bouille* is a novel of interpenetrating conversations, of superimposed narrative spaces too, with the story of a wedding and the story of an adultery within the same frame. Sectioned though the apart-ment-building may appear to be, with its vertical gradations of individual destinies, on closer scrutiny there is topological level-ling between private chambers and inner courtyard, grand entrance and back stairs. Connecting doors are at the interface not of a distinction between appearance and reality, but of further dissolutions. Falsity emerges from behind the falsity, a cardboard world from behind the phoney marble, and within one performance merely another. And facing the window, appropriately enough, there is a painted window (p. 7).

At the heart of this novel, so often praised for its brilliant organisation, there is disorder: of jumbled clothes and port-folios; of elegant gloves in servants' beds or chamberpots; but also that of sexual intercourse and the disarray of chairs, apartments and buffet suppers. More critically, Zola goes one stage further than Flaubert takes Emma Bovary as she rediscovers 'in adultery all the platitudes of marriage'; for his own substitutions serve to erode the distinctions between innocence and guilt, marriage and adultery, to the extent that marriage itself is seen as another form of adultery. Affective transpositions know no bounds: Bachelard's adopted waif is his child-mistress; Saturnin's feelings for his sister speak of incestuous jealousy; in the Campardon *ménage-à-trois*, the wife is coddled like a sickly daughter. But not the least irony of the ever-multiplying sexual encounters in this *maison close* (i.e. 'house of ill-repute', but with the claustral emphasis of the original French term) is that there is less and less sex; instead there is conjugal sublimation in music or books; or Madame Juzeur's teasingly restored virginity; or the insuperable obstacles placed in the way of Octave's physical relationship with the woman who is supposed to be his mistress. What is more, the final differentiation eroded in *Pot-Bouille* is that of gender itself: the inversion in the so-called 'seduction' of Berthe gives to Octave the woman's role; more radically, the manly Madame Hédouin is as sexless as Madame Campardon; and Valérie is less androgynous than neutered, described as being devoid of both resistance and desire.

All this is to suggest, certainly, that *Pot-Bouille* is thematically consistent with the *Rougon-Macquart*'s vision of a world falling apart, of definitions subject to erosion and indeterminacy, of corruption blurring the outline of identifiable norms. But more than this, in its own formal design, *Pot-Bouille* is a novel that dramatises the paradox of organising that decomposition in intelligible fictional structures. In other words, those superimposed relativities which reveal yet another surface beneath the surface militate against a declared authorial ambition to unmask the truth behind appearances. Quite apart from the overlaid ironies of its dissolute characters engaging in a critique of dissolution, *Pot-Bouille* is itself a dissolving novel, one in which Zola seems to have been aware of the difficulties of saying anything with any clarity, precisely because of the absence of contrasting planes he is working with. At one point in its preparation, he writes to a colleague: 'Up to now, I still can't find a central idea holding it all together. Perhaps, in order to resolve the problem, I should invent a worker and use him as a contrast.' It is as if argument and synthesis cannot function without some oppositional structure which would generate a fixed point of judgement within the essential sameness revealed by dissolving boundaries.

If *Pot-Bouille* is, indeed, a *catalogue* of bourgeois vices, then its mirror-image is perhaps less those novels of adultery deplored by its characters than the catalogue worked on by Monsieur Vabre within this novel itself. For his referencing of scenes he has not experienced is vitiated by nominal changes of identity which unstructure his attempts to organise or 'plot' some linearity in the pictorial fictions framed and displayed at successive Salons. Vabre's project provides us with all sorts of forceful analogies: with Zola's own arbitrary substitution of names; with his own sense of unwitnessed scenes. Vabre's despair that his work will never be complete testifies to Zola's own mood in 1881. For Vabre's inconclusive activities speak of the absence of an intellectual order that would allow conclusion, and of a tension between formless openness and a will to closure that reflects the conflicting demands of narrative and the representation of ongoing history which in turn provide the *Rougon-Macquart* as a whole with so much of their dynamism.

There is, of course, a semblance of closure at the end of *Pot-Bouille*: in the words of Julie, the maid endowed with omniscience within the building and within the novel, and who is about to leave this particular service, but clearly resigned to the sameness of bourgeois spaces: 'once you've seen one, you've seen them all' (p. 379). That doubling of the present mutes the voice of a transformed future; and if the novel closes with the maid's last word of unhappy families infinitely repeated, *Pot-Bouille* itself risks restating no more than that in a banal coda tying up its loose ends and narrative threads.

At one level, the novel is saved from decomposition by what has been called its 'cumulative sense of circular monotony' – a recuperative circularity which allows a daughter to be like her mother and lover to become husband, justifying Octave's 'strange feeling as if all were beginning again' (p. 375); and which also allows (on Zola's part) a formal re-composition paradoxically related to the experience of sameness. But, at another level, this circularity becomes an obtrusive, somewhat mechanical and artificial criss-crossing of plots. Put another way, the foregrounded stitching of what Zola's friend, Paul

Alexis, termed *Pot-Bouille*'s 'multiple threads' is no more than a 'stitching-up' of a novel moving fitfully from space to space – energyless or threatening to peter out – as its latter-day Rastignac works his way through the daughters of the house. In this 'reading for the plot' (to cite the seminal title of Peter Brooks's 1984 study), there is a singular absence of narrative desire, that driving curiosity which impels us to want to know how the story works out in the end. As Octave himself reflects, in the final chapter, looking back on his life since the novel started: 'the two years of life in the Rue de Choiseul were a blank . . . his life hadn't changed; today was like yesterday, seamlessly the same' (p. 375), without (as the original French puts it) any *dénouement*.

Bracketed out of *Pot-Bouille*'s dissolving, inward-looking, fetid little world, there is (we should also remember) a real nineteenth-century context: there are taxonomies which try to distinguish between class and *quartier*, between *arrondissements*, between train compartments reserved for certain social types, between *maison close* and unregulated vice, between the hierarchies of genre, grammar and art, the borders and the boundaries of legitimation. *Pot-Bouille*, by contrast, is a novel of dissolution – ethical, political and social; of dissolving structures exemplifying the thematics of entropy. But it can also be argued that the novel's formal design enacts the unmaking of a certain kind of novel plotted to make sense; and the unmaking of a certain kind of sense plotted in the great tradition of nineteenth-century narrative explanations of reality.

The richness of *Pot-Bouille* is inseparable from the very different ways in which it can be read and re-read: as a slice of Parisian life in the 1860s; as a timeless social comedy built on human foibles, with a register moving from pathos to farce, and from the sardonic to the horrifically grotesque; and as a parody of those innumerable dramas of adultery which are the residual staple of our reading pleasures (even reconfigured in the scripts of stage and screen), with far-reaching implications for both our habits of reading and the art of the novel itself.

ROBERT LETHBRIDGE

EDITOR'S NOTE

I would like to thank Julie Mead for her help in revising the original translation of the novel. Timothy Mathews has been the most patient of commissioning editors. Hilary Laurie and her colleagues at Everyman Paperbacks have been equally supportive. I am also grateful to Nicholas White, both for being able to use, as the basis for my own, the Chronologies in his edition of Zola's *L'Assommoir* (Everyman, 1995), and for many discussions about *Pot-Bouille* grounded in the critical and scholarly expertise he has brought to this particular novel in recent years.

NOTE ON THE TEXT

The text is a modernised version of Percy Pinkerton's translation of *Pot-Bouille*. This was first published by the Lutetian Society in 1895. Inspired by the Latin name for Paris (Lutetia), the Society's mission was to make available in translation 'the master-pieces of fiction by Continental authors'. Six of Zola's novels appeared under its auspices. But, given Victorian sensitivities, these were privately published in limited editions of 300 copies. We do not know very much about Percy Pinkerton himself, except that he was a prolific translator (from German, Russian and Italian, as well as French), the editor of the works of Christopher Marlowe, and the author, in his own right, of some minor poetry and lyrical drama. His 1895 version of *Pot-Bouille* continued to be reprinted right up until the 1950s. It has the great merit of being neither bowdlerised nor mutilated, unlike so many early English translation of Zola. In the preface he provided to a 1953 reprinting of the novel, Angus Wilson was content to endorse Pinkerton's 'admirable' version. Graham King, however, subsequently noted that 'it lacks style and annoys with unnecessary antiquated colloquialisms' (*Garden of Zola: Emile Zola and his Novels for English Readers* (London, Barrie & Jenkins, 1978), p. 393). And, indeed, on closer and prolonged scrutiny, one would go rather further and conclude that while it is broadly 'faithful', Pinkerton's 1895 translation is serviceable at best: it is not only exceptionally awkward; its often flowery prose is incompatible with Zola's directness; its rearrangement of the original punctuation and paragraphing alters the rhythm of the text; it is occasionally careless, missing out the odd sentence or phrase; and it is sometimes so inaccurate that Pinkerton comes up with the exact opposite of the meaning of the French! The present edition's debt to Percy Pinkerton is qualified by the scale of its revision to his translation.

NOTE ON THE TITLE

Literally, *pot-bouille* is a culinary term; its nearest English equivalent is a stockpot containing left-overs bubbling on the stove. It derives from *bouiller le pot*, to boil the pot, and is to be found in the working-class slang Zola included in *L'Assommoir* when its characters put together a cheap meal. Although it is seldom used in modern French, in nineteenth-century France it also meant, by association, the ordinariness of everyday life. And two of its further associations are similarly exploited by Zola in his choice of title for his novel of 1882: *Faire pot-bouille avec quelqu'un* meant 'to shack up with somebody'; and *faire sa pot-bouille* had the sense of 'feathering one's nest'. Zola's title therefore has a symbolic value which accommodates many of the central features of *Pot-Bouille*: its kitchens and parsimonious meals; its simmering discontents and passions 'under the lid' of respectable domesticity; its legal and transgressive versions of 'living together'; its selfishness and self-interest; and, of course, the pervasively boring routines of middle-class life represented by the novel. *Pot-Bouille* has been variously translated as *Piping Hot* (London, Vizetelly, 1885), *Lessons in Love* (New York, Pyramid Books, 1953) and *Restless House* (London, Weidenfeld & Nicolson, 1953). As a title, it remains untranslatable.

POT-BOUILLE

CHAPTER I

In the Rue Neuve-Saint-Augustin,* the sheer number of cabs brought to a halt the one that was bringing Octave and his three trunks from the Gare de Lyon.* The young man lowered a window, although the cold on that gloomy November late afternoon was already intense. In this quartier of narrow streets, swarming with people, it was suddenly dusk. The drivers' oaths, as they thrashed their snorting horses, the endless jostling on the pavements, the serried row of shops full of attendants and customers made him almost dizzy; for, if he had imagined Paris to be cleaner than this, he had never expected to find such a commercial bustle and it seemed as if, for the able-bodied with healthy appetites, the city was there for the taking.

The cabman leaned back towards him. 'It's the Passage Choiseul you said, didn't you?'

'No, no; the Rue de Choiseul. A new building, I think.'

And there it was: the cab had only to turn the corner, the building in question, a big, four-storeyed one, being the second one in the street. Its stonework was hardly discoloured, in the middle of the faded plaster of the adjoining façades. Octave, who had stepped down on to the pavement, measured it and studied it with a mechanical glance, from the silk warehouse at street level to the windows on the fourth floor, slightly set back from a narrow terrace. On the first floor, carved female heads supported a cast-iron balcony of intricate design. The framework of the windows, roughly chiselled in soft stone, was equally elaborate and lower down, over the even more heavily ornamented doorway, were two Cupids holding a scroll bearing the number, illumined at night by a gas lamp behind it.

A stout, fair-haired man, who was coming out of the entrance hall, stopped short when he caught sight of Octave.

'What are you doing here already?' he cried. 'I didn't expect you until tomorrow.'

'Well, you see,' replied the young man, 'I left Plassans* a day earlier than I planned. Is the room not ready?'

'Oh, yes! I leased it a fortnight ago and had it furnished right

away, just as you asked me to. Wait a moment, and I'll take
you up there.'

And, despite Octave's entreaties, he went back inside. The
cabman had brought in the three trunks.

In the concierge's lodge a dignified-looking man, with a clean-
shaven face, stood gravely reading the *Moniteur.** However, he
condescended to display some concern about this luggage now
deposited at his door, and, coming forward, he asked his tenant,
the architect of the third floor, as he called him: 'Is this the
person, Monsieur Campardon?'

'Yes, Monsieur Gourd, this is Monsieur Octave Mouret, for
whom I took the room on the fourth floor. He will sleep there
and take his meals with us. Monsieur Mouret is a friend of my
wife's family, and I should be grateful if you could treat him
accordingly.'

Octave was examining the entrance with its sham marble
panelling and its vaulted ceiling decorated with rosettes. The
paved and cemented courtyard visible beyond looked impos-
ingly clean and cold; at the stable door a groom stood polishing
a bit with a piece of leather. Surely the sun never reached there.

In the meantine, Monsieur Gourd was taking stock of the
luggage. He pushed the trunks with his foot and, impressed by
their weight, talked of fetching a porter to carry them up the
servants' staircase.

Putting his head round the door, he called out to his wife:
'Madame Gourd, I'm going out.'

The room was like a little parlour, with its gleaming mirrors,
rosewood furniture, and a red-flowered carpet.

Through the half-opened door, you could just see a corner of
the bedroom, and the dark red bedlinen. Madame Gourd, a
very fleshy woman with yellow ribbons in her hair, was
stretched out in an armchair, her idle hands firmly together.

'Well, let's go up,' said the architect. Seeing the impression
made upon the young man by Monsieur Gourd's black velvet
cap and sky-blue slippers, he added, as he pushed open the
mahogany door of the lobby: 'You know, at one time he was
valet to the Duc de Vaugelade.'

'Really!' said Octave, simply.

'Yes, indeed; and he married the widow of some bailiff from
Mort-la-Ville.* They even own a house there. But they're waiting until they've got three thousand francs a year from their

savings before they settle back there. Oh, they're most respectable people!'

About the lobby and staircase there was a certain gaudy splendour. At the foot of the stairs a gilt figure of a Neapolitan woman supported a jar on her head, from which protruded three gas jets in ground-glass globes. The sham marble panelling, white with pink edges, went right up the stairway at regular intervals, while the cast-iron balustrade, with mahogany handrail, was meant to look like wrought silver, with flourishes of gold leafwork. A red carpet with brass rods covered the staircase. But what first struck Octave as he went in was the hothouse temperature, hitting him in the face as if blown towards him by some warm mouth.

'Am I right in thinking the staircase is heated?' he asked.

'Of course,' replied Campardon; 'all self-respecting landlords go to that expense, nowadays. The house is a very fine one – very fine.'

He looked around him as though testing the solidity of the walls with his architect's eyes.

'And as you see, my dear chap, it's both very comfortable, and only lived in by thoroughly respectable people.'

Then, as they slowly went up, he named the various tenants. On each floor there were two sets of apartments, one looking out on to the street, and the other the courtyard, with their polished mahogany doors facing each other. Monsieur Auguste Vabre was the first to get a mention. He was the landlord's eldest son: that spring he had taken the silk warehouse on the ground floor, as well as having the whole of the first-floor landing to himself. Then, on the first floor, there was the landlord's other son, Théophile Vabre, and his wife who lived on the courtyard side, while overlooking the street there was the landlord himself, formerly a Versailles notary, but now living with his son-in-law, Monsieur Duveyrier, a counsellor at the Court of Appeal.

'A fellow who is not yet five-and-forty,' said Campardon, as he paused on the way up. 'That's not bad, is it?'

Two steps further on he looked quickly back over his shoulder and added: 'Water and gas on every floor.'

Under each high window on the landing, whose panes, with the Grecian border, lit up the staircase with a white light, there was a narrow velvet-covered bench. Here, as the architect pointed out, elderly folk could sit down.

Then, as he went past the second floor without mentioning the occupants, Octave asked: 'And who lives there?' pointing to the door of the apartment on the street.

'Oh, there!' he said. 'Tenants one never sees, and never gets to know. The house could well do without such people. However, there are blemishes to be found everywhere, I suppose.'

He sniffed disdainfully.

'The gentleman writes books, I believe.'

But, on reaching the third floor, his complacent smile returned. The apartments facing the courtyard were subdivided. Madame Juzeur lived there, a little woman who had seen much misfortune, and a very distinguished gentleman, who had rented a room, to which he came on business once a week. While continuing his commentary, Campardon opened the door immediately opposite.

'This is where I live,' he said. 'Wait a minute; I just have to get your key. We'll go up to your room first, and afterwards you can come in and say hello to my wife.'

In those two minutes that he was left alone, Octave felt penetrated by the awesome silence of the staircase. He leaned over the banisters in the tepid air which came up from the hall below; then he raised his head, to hear if any noise came from above. There was a deadly calm, the peace of a middle-class drawing-room, carefully shut in, admitting no whisper from without. Behind those fine doors of lustrous mahogany there seemed to be veritable abysses of respectability.

'You will have excellent neighbours,' said Campardon, as he reappeared with the key; 'the Josserands at the front – the entire family; the father is cashier at the Saint Joseph glassworks, with two marriageable daughters. Next to you are the Pichons; he's a clerk. They're not exactly rolling in money, but are impeccably well-bred. Everything has to be let, hasn't it? Even in a building of this sort.'

After the third floor the red carpet came to an end, and was replaced by a plain grey covering. Octave's sense of dignity was slightly wounded by this. Little by little the staircase had filled him with awe; he felt quite flattered at the thought of living in such a thoroughly well-appointed house, as the architect had termed it. As he followed the latter along the passage to his room, through a half-opened door he caught sight of a young woman standing beside a cradle. Hearing a sound, she looked up. She was fair with light, expressionless eyes; and all that he got was this singular gaze, for the young woman, blushing, suddenly pushed the door to with the bashful manner of some-one taken by surprise.

Campardon, turning round, repeated: 'Water and gas on every floor, my dear boy.'

Having pointed out a door opening on to the servants' staircase whose rooms were overhead, he then stopped at the end of the passage: 'Here we are at last.'

The room was quite large and square-shaped, with wallpaper of blue flowers on a grey background. It was simply furnished. Near the alcove there was a washstand just big enough to rinse your hands. Octave went straight to the window, through which a greenish light entered. The courtyard loomed below, depress-ingly clean, with its symmetrical paving, and its cistern with a shining copper tap. Not a soul, not a sound; nothing but rows of windows, devoid of a birdcage or a flower-pot, displaying all the monotony of their white curtains. To hide the great bare walls of the house on the left, which shut in the quadrangle, fake windows had been painted on to it with shutters eternally closed, behind which the walled-in life of the adjoining apart-ments seemed to be going on.

'This will suit me perfectly,' cried Octave, delighted.

'I thought it would,' said Campardon. 'I certainly took as much trouble as if it were for myself, and I carried out all of your written instructions. So you like the furniture, do you? It's all that a young fellow wants. You can see about other things later on.'

And as Octave shook him by the hand and thanked him, while apologising for having given him so much trouble, he added in a more serious tone: 'Only, my good fellow, there must be no rowdiness here, and, above all, no women. Believe me that if you were to bring a woman here, there would be an almighty revolution.'

'Don't worry,' muttered the young man, somewhat uneasy.

'No, let me tell you, for I would be the one who would be compromised. You've seen who lives here. All middle-class people, and so awfully moral. Between ourselves, I think they rather overdo it. Ah, well! Monsieur Gourd would at once fetch

Monsieur Vabre, and we should both be in a true mess. So, my
dear chap, for my own peace of mind's sake, I ask you, do
respect the house.'

Overcome by so much virtue, Octave declared on oath that
he would.

Then Campardon, looking round him warily and lowering
his voice, as if fearful of being overheard, added, with shining
eyes: 'Elsewhere, it's nobody business, eh? Paris is so big; there's
plenty of room. I myself am an artist at heart, and personally I
don't care a damn about such things.'

A porter brought up the luggage. When everything had been
put straight, the architect watched with fatherly interest as
Octave cleaned himself up and changed his clothes. Then, rising,
he said: 'Now let's go down and see my wife.'

On the third floor the maidservant, a slim, dark, coquettish-
looking girl, said that Madame was engaged. In order to put his
young friend at ease, Campardon showed him over the apartment. First of all, there was a big white and gold drawing-room,
excessively decorated with reproduction mouldings. This was
placed between a little green parlour, which had been turned
into a study, and the bedroom, into which they could not go,
but the architect described its narrow shape and the mauve
wallpaper. When he took him into the dining-room, all in
imitation wood, with its strange combination of beading and
panels, Octave was enchanted.

'It's very handsome!'

There were two great cracks right through the panelling of
the ceiling, and in one corner paint had peeled off and showed
the plaster.

'Yes, it does create an effect,' said the architect, slowly, with
his eyes riveted to the ceiling. 'Indeed, these kind of houses are
only built for effect. That's not been up twelve years yet, and
it's already cracked. They build the frontage of handsome stone,
with all sorts of sculptural flourishes, give the staircase three
coats of varnish, touch up the rooms with gilt and paint; that's
what flatters people, and makes them think a lot of it. Oh, it's
solid enough yet! It'll last our lifetime.'

He led Octave through the ante-room again, with its ground-
glass windows. To the left, overlooking the courtyard, there was
another bedroom, where his daughter Angèle slept; all its whiteness, on this November afternoon, made it seem as mournful as

a tomb. Then, at the end of the passage, there was the kitchen, which he insisted on showing to Octave, saying he must see everything.

'Do come in,' he repeated, as he pushed the door open.

A hideous noise assailed their ears. Despite the cold, the window was wide open. Leaning over the rail, the dark maidservant and a fat, jolly old cook were looking down into the narrow well of an inner courtyard, lit up by the kitchens opposite one another on each floor. Bent forwards, they were both shouting at the top of their voices; while from the pit below came the sound of raucous laughter, and filthy swearing. It was as if a sewer had brimmed over. All the domestics of the house were there, letting off steam. Octave thought of the middle-class majesty of the grand staircase.

As if warned by some instinct, the two women turned round. At the sight of their master with a gentleman they looked startled. There was a slight hissing noise, windows were shut, and the silence of the dead was restored.

'What's the matter, Lisa?' asked Campardon.

'If you please, sir,' said the maid, in great excitement, 'it's just that dirty Adèle again. She's thrown a rabbit's guts out of the window. You should speak to Monsieur Josserand, sir.'

Campardon looked serious, but would not commit himself. He withdrew to the study, saying to Octave: 'You've seen everything now. The rooms are the same on each floor. Mine costs me two thousand five hundred francs; on the third floor, too! Rents are going up every day. Monsieur Vabre must make about twenty-two thousand francs a year out of his house. That will go on increasing, for there is a talk of making a broad thoroughfare from the Place de La Bourse to the new opera house.* And the ground on which this is built he got for virtually nothing, about twelve years ago, when there was that big fire, started by some chemist's maid.'

As they entered, Octave noticed, above a drawing-table, and with the light from the window full upon it, a handsomely framed picture of the Virgin Mary, showing at her breast an enormous flaming heart. He could not conceal his surprise, and looked at Campardon, whom he remembered as having been a bit of a rake in Plassans.

'Oh!' said the latter, blushing somewhat. 'I forgot to tell you I have been appointed architect to the diocese – at Evreux,* it

is. A mere trifle financially – barely two thousand francs a year.
But there's nothing to do – a journey now and again; besides,
I've got a surveyor down there. Then, you see, it's rather a good
thing if one can put on one's card, "Architect to the Government". You can't imagine what a lot of work that brings me
from high society.'

As he spoke, he gazed at the Virgin with her fiery heart.

'To tell you the truth,' he added, in a sudden fit of candour,
'I couldn't care less about all their nonsense.'

But when Octave burst out laughing, the architect felt certain
misgivings. Why confide in this young man? He looked at him
sideways, assumed a contrite air, and tried to qualify his last
remark.

'Well, I don't care and yet I do somehow. That's about it.
Just you wait, my friend; when you're a little older you'll do the
same as everybody else.'

He spoke of his age – forty-two – of the emptiness of
existence, and hinted at a melancholy at odds with his robust
health. Under his flowing hair and beard, trimmed *à la* Henri
VI,* there was the flat skull and square jaw of a middle-class
man of limited intelligence and animal appetites. In his younger
days he had been happy-go-lucky to the point of being tiresome.

Octave's eyes fell on a copy of the *Gazette de France*,* which
was lying among some plans. Then Campardon, becoming more
and more embarrassed, rang for the maid, to know if Madame
was now available. Yes, the doctor was going, and Madame
would come directly.

'Is Madame Campardon not well?' asked the young man.

'Just her normal self,' said the architect, with a touch of
annoyance in his voice.

'Oh, what's the matter with her?'

Once again uneasy, he answered evasively: 'Women, you
know, have always got something the matter with them. She's
been like that for thirteen years – ever since her confinement. In
other respects she's flourishing. You'll even find that she's filled
out.'

Octave sensed that further questions would be unwelcome.
Just then, Lisa came back, holding a calling-card, and the
architect, apologising, hurried into the drawing-room, begging
the young man to talk to his wife meanwhile. As the door
quickly opened and shut, in the centre of the spacious white and

gold apartment Octave caught sight of the black stain of a cassock.

At the same moment Madame Campardon came in from the ante-room. He didn't recognise her. Years ago when, as a lad he'd known her in Plassans, at the house of her father, Monsieur Domergue, who had been in charge of building bridges and roads, she was thin and plain, and for all her twenty years, as puny as a girl on the verge of puberty. Now, he found her plump, with clear complexion, and as composed as a nun: soft-eyed, dimpled, and sleek as a fat tabby cat.

Though she had not become pretty, her thirty summers had ripened her, giving her a sweet savour, a pleasant, fresh odour like that of autumnal fruit. He noticed, however, that she walked with difficulty, her hips swaying in a long loose gown of pale yellow-coloured silk, which gave her a languid air.

'Why, you're quite a man now,' she said, gaily holding out both hands. 'How you've grown since we last travelled south!'

And she surveyed this tall, tanned, good-looking young man with his carefully trimmed beard and moustache. When he told her his age, twenty-two, she would not believe it – declaring that he looked at least twenty-five. Octave – whom the very presence of a woman, even of the lowest maidservant, enraptured – laughed a silvery laugh as he gazed at her with eyes the colour of old gold and soft as velvet.

'Yes,' he repeated, gently, 'I've grown, I've grown. Do you remember when your cousin, Gasparine, used to buy me marbles?'

Then he gave her news of her family. Monsieur and Madame Domergue were happily retired; their only complaint was that they were alone, still not having forgiven Campardon for carrying off their little Rose when he had come down to Plassans on business. Octave then tried to turn the subject of the conversation to cousin Gasparine to clear up a mystery which had intrigued him as a curious adolescent – the architect's sudden passion for Gasparine, a tall, beautiful girl without a penny, and his hasty marriage to the skinny Rose, with her thirty thousand francs dowry, a whole drama of tears and recrimination resulting in the abandoned Gasparine fleeing to her dressmaker aunt in Paris. But Madame Campardon, though her calm face flushed slightly, appeared not to understand. She gave absolutely nothing away.

'And your own parents, how are they?' she enquired, in her turn.

'Thank you, they're very well,' he replied. 'My mother never stirs out of her garden now. You would find the house in the Rue de la Banne just the same as when you left it.'

Madame Campardon, who seemed to be unable to remain standing for any length of time without fatigue, was sitting in a high easy-chair, her limbs extended beneath her gown, and Octave, taking a low chair, raised his head towards her, adopting an adoring pose as he talked – with his wide shoulders, there was something feminine about him, something appealing to women, that touched them and made them instantly take him to their heart. Thus, in no time at all they were both chatting away like two old friends.

'Well, here I am, taking up your offer of room and board,' he said, stroking his beard with a shapely hand, the nails of which were carefully trimmed. 'We're sure to get on famously together, you'll see. It was awfully nice of you to think of the little lad from Plassans, and to deal with everything the minute I asked you.'

'No, no, don't thank me,' she protested. 'I'm far too lazy; I never move a finger. It was Achille who arranged everything. After all, when my mother told us that you wanted to board with a family, inviting you here was the obvious solution. You won't be among strangers, and it will be company for us.'

Then he brought her up to date as far as his own life was concerned. After getting his bachelor's diploma, to please his family, he had just spent three years in Marseilles, in a large calico print firm which had a factory near Plassans. He had a passion for trade, for the trade in luxury goods for women, in which there was something of the pleasure of seduction, of slow possession achieved by gilded phrases and flattering looks. And with the laugh of a conqueror, he told her how with the prudence of a Jew behind this appearance of a likeable scatter-brain, he had made the five thousand francs without which he would never have risked coming to Paris.

'Would you believe it; they had a Pompadour calico, an old design – quite marvellous. Nobody jumped at it; it had been lying around in the warehouse for two years. So, as I was going to travel through the Var and the Basses-Alpes,* I suddenly thought of buying up the whole stock and selling it on my own account. It was an overwhelming success. Women virtually fought over the remnants, and today every one of them has got some of my calico next to their skin. I must say, I sweet-talked them so well! They were like putty in my hands; I could have done what I liked with them.'

And he laughed, while Madame Campardon, fascinated and somewhat excited, in spite of herself, at the thought of that Pompadour calico, kept asking him questions. Little bunches of flowers on a light-brown background – was that the pattern? She had been looking everywhere for something similar, for her summer dressing-gown.

'I've been travelling for two years,' he went on, 'and that's enough. Now there's Paris for me to conquer. I must look out for something at once.'

'Why, didn't Achille tell you?' she exclaimed. 'He's got a position for you, and close by, too.'

He thanked her, as astonished as if he were in fairyland, and asked, jokingly, if he would find a wife with a hundred thousand francs a year in his room that evening, when the door was pushed open by a plain, lanky girl of fourteen with straw-coloured hair, who uttered a slight cry of alarm.

'Come in, and don't be shy,' said Madame Campardon. 'This is Monsieur Octave Mouret, of whom you have heard us speak.'

Then, turning to Octave, she said: 'My daughter, Angèle. On our last journey we didn't take her with us; she was so delicate. But she's less fragile now.'

Angèle, with the awkwardness of girls at this ungraceful age, took up her stand behind her mother and stared at the smiling young man.

Almost immediately Campardon came back, looking excited, unable to resist hurriedly telling his wife of his piece of good luck. Abbé Mauduit, the vicar of Saint-Roch, had come about some work – merely repairs, but it might lead to other things. Then, vexed at having talked of this in front of Octave, yet still trembling with excitement, he struck both hands together, and said: 'Well, what shall we do?'

'Why, you were about to go out,' said Octave. 'Please don't change your plans on my account.'

'Achille,' murmured Madame Campardon, 'that job, at the Hédouins.'

'Why, of course,' exclaimed the architect, 'I had forgotten

that. My dear fellow, it's the job of head assistant at a large haberdasher's. I know somebody there who's put in a word for you. They are expecting you. As it's not four o'clock yet, would you like me to take you round there now?'

Octave hesitated, and, in his obsession with being correctly dressed, felt nervous about whether his necktie was done up exactly right. However, when Madame Campardon assured him that he looked very neat, he decided to go. With a languid gesture, she offered her forehead to her husband, who kissed her with effusive tenderness, as he repeated: 'Bye, my pet; bye, my treasure.'

'Remember, we dine at seven,' she said, as she accompanied them across the drawing-room to get their hats. Angèle awkwardly followed. Her music master was waiting for her, and she began to tinkle on the keys with her skinny fingers. Octave, who loitered in the ante-room repeating his thanks, could hardly hear himself speak. And as he went down the staircase the sound of the piano seemed to pursue him. In that lukewarm silence other pianos, Madame Juzeur's the Vabres', and the Duveyriers', seemed to respond, each in its own way, from every floor; tunes that sounded half remote, half religious, as they reached him from behind those chastely solemn walls.

When they got downstairs Campardon turned up the Rue Neuve-Saint-Augustin. He was silent, like a man waiting to broach a subject.

'Do you remember Mademoiselle Gasparine?' he asked, at length. 'She's head saleswoman at the Hédouins. You will see her.'

Octave thought this a good chance of satisfying his curiosity.

'Oh!' he said. 'Does she also take room and board with you?'

'No, no!' exclaimed the architect hastily, and as if stung at the suggestion.

Then, as Octave seemed taken aback by his brusque response, he added, in a gentler tone of embarrassment: 'No, my wife and she no longer see each other. In families, you know ... I've bumped into her myself, and I couldn't very well refuse to shake hands, could I? More especially as the poor girl's badly off. So now the two of them get news through me. In old quarrels of this sort only time can heal the wounds.'

Octave was just about to ask him straight out about the

circumstances of his marriage, when the architect cut matters short by saying: 'Here we are!'

It was a linen draper's, on the corner of the Rue Neuve-Saint-Augustin and the Rue de la Michodière, facing the triangle of the Place Gaillon. On a signboard, just above the store, were the words in faded gilt lettering, 'Au Bonheur des Dames'* Established 1822', while the shop windows bore the name of the firm, in red: 'Deleuze, Hédouin and Co.'

'In style it's not quite up to date, but it's a sound, straight-forward concern,' explained Campardon, rapidly. 'Monsieur Hédouin, at one time a clerk, married the daughter of the elder Deleuze, who died two years ago, so that the business is now managed by the young couple – old Deleuze and another partner, I think, both keep out of it. You'll see Madame Hédouin. Ah, she's got a head on her shoulders! Let's go in.'

As her husband was away, in Lille buying linen, it was in fact Madame Hédouin who received them. She was standing, with a pencil behind her ear, giving orders to two male assistants, who were putting pieces of material in order on the shelves. Octave thought her so tall and attractive-looking, with her regular features and neatly plaited hair, black dress, turn-down collar, and man's tie. As she smiled at him, the young man, who was normally far from shy, could hardly stammer out a reply. In a few words everything was settled.

'Well,' she said, with the quiet and graceful manner of a professional salesperson, 'as you've got a moment, perhaps you might like to look over the premises.'

Calling a clerk, she entrusted Octave to his care, and then after politely replying to Campardon that Mademoiselle Gaspar-ine was out, she turned her back and went on with her work, giving orders in the same gentle, firm voice.

'Not there, Alexandre. Put the silks up at the top. Look out! Those are not of the same make.'

After some hesitation, Campardon said he would come back for Octave in time for dinner. So for two hours the young man explored the shop. He found it badly lit, small, over-laden with stock, which, as there was no room for it in the basement, had to be piled up in corners, leaving only narrow passages between high walls of bales. Several times he met Madame Hédouin tripping busily along the narrowest of the passages without ever catching her dress on anything. She seemed to be the life and soul of the place, obeyed at the slightest indication of a white hand. Octave was rather hurt that she didn't take more notice of him. About a quarter to seven, just as he was coming up from the basement for the last time, he was told that Campardon was on the first floor, with Mademoiselle Gasparine, who was in charge of the hosiery counter there. But, at the top of the winding staircase, Octave stopped short behind a pyramid of calico bales, symmetrically arranged, as he heard the architect obviously engaged in an intimate conversation with Gasparine.

'I swear I haven't,' he cried, forgetting himself so far as to raise his voice.

There was a pause.

'How is she now?' asked the young woman.

'Oh, good Lord! She's always the same. One day better; one day worse. She knows she'll never be completely right again.'

'It's you, my poor friend, who are to be pitied. However as you've managed to make alternative arrangements, do tell her how sorry I am to hear that she is still so poorly.'

Without letting her finish her sentence, Campardon caught her by the shoulders and kissed her roughly on the lips in the gas-heated room where the fumes already hung heavy in the air beneath the low ceiling.

She returned his kiss, murmuring: 'Tomorrow morning, then, at six, if you can come. I'll stay in bed. Knock three times.'

Octave, astounded, but beginning to understand, coughed first and then came forward. Another surprised awaited him. Gasparine had become shrivelled, lean and angular, with projecting jaws and coarse hair. All that she had kept in this cadaverous face of hers were her great, splendid eyes. Her envious brow and sensuous, stubborn mouth distressed him as much as Rose had charmed him by her late blossoming into an indolent blonde.

Gasparine, if not effusive, was polite. She remembered Plassans, and she talked to the young man of old times. As Campardon and he took their leave she shook them by the hand.

Downstairs Madame Hédouin simply said to Octave: 'Well, then, we shall see you tomorrow.'

When he got into the street, deafened by cabs and hustled by passers-by, he couldn't help observing that the lady was certainly very attractive, if not particularly affable. The lustrous windows of newly painted shops, ablaze with gas lamps, cast squares of bright light across the black, muddy paving, while the older shops, with their dim interiors half lit by smoking lamps, like distant stars, only made the streets more gloomy with their broad patches of shadow. In the Rue Neuve-Saint-Augustin, just before turning into the Rue de Choiseul, Campardon raised his hat as he passed one of these shops.

A young woman, slim and elegant, wearing a silk mantle, stood at the door, holding a little boy of three close to her and away from the traffic. She was talking familiarily to an old, bare-headed woman, evidently the shopkeeper. It was too dark for Octave to distinguish her features, but, in the flickering gaslight, she seemed to him to be pretty, with two bright eyes, fixed for a moment upon him like two flames. Behind her the shop seemed like a damp cellar, indistinct save for a faint odour of saltpetre.

'That's Madame Valérie, the wife of Monsieur Théophile Vabre, the landlord's younger son, you know – the people on the first floor,' said Campardon, after they had gone a little further.

'She's a most charming person – born in that very shop, one of the best-paying linen drapers of the neighbourhood, which her parents Monsieur and Madame Louhette still manage, just to have something to do. They've made a pile of money you can be sure!'

But Octave was totally ignorant of the kind of trade carried on in the Paris of yesteryear, where, once upon a time, a single piece of cloth displayed in the window served as a shop sign. He vowed that nothing on earth could ever make him agree to live in such a dingy hole which would certainly be bad for your health.

Thus chatting, they reached the top of the stairs. Dinner was waiting for them. Madame Campardon had put on a grey silk gown, and had dressed her hair most coquettishly, paying great attention to her toilette. Campardon kissed her on the neck, with all the emotion of a dutiful husband.

'Good-evening, my angel. How's my treasure?'

Then they went into the dining-room. The dinner was delightful. At first, Madame Campardon spoke of the Deleuzes and the Hédouins – families well known and respected throughout the neighbourhood. A cousin of theirs was a stationer in the Rue Gaillon; their uncle kept an umbrella shop in the Passage

Choiseul; while their nephews and nieces were, all of them, in business here and there. Then the conversation turned to Angèle, sitting bolt upright in her chair and eating listlessly. She was being brought up at home; it was safer, so her mother thought; without spelling it out, a mere wink suggested what awful things little misses learned at boarding-school. The child was slyly trying to balance her plate on her knife.

Lisa, as she was clearing away, almost broke it, and exclaimed: 'That was your fault, mademoiselle!'

Angèle struggled to hide her laughter, while her mother just shook her head. When Lisa had left the room to bring in the dessert, Madame Campardon sung the praises of her maid – very intelligent, very busy, a real Parisienne, never at a loss. They might easily do without Victoire, the ageing cook whose standards of hygiene left a lot to be desired; but, you see, she had been in the service of her master's father, when Campardon was a baby. In short, she was a family ruin that they respected.

Then, as Lisa came back with some baked apples: 'She's irreproachable,' continued Madame Campardon, in Octave's ear. 'So far, I have found out nothing against her. Only one day off a month, when she goes to look after her aunt, who lives a good way off.'

Octave looked at Lisa. Noticing how nervous, flat-bosomed, and bleary-eyed she was, he thought to himself what a high old time she must have at that aunt's. However, he entirely con-curred in the views of the mother, who continued to impart to him her ideas on education; a girl was such a heavy responsi-bility, she ought to be shielded from the very breath of the streets. All this time, whenever Lisa leaned across near Angèle's chair to change a plate, the child would pinch her thighs in a kind of obscene intimacy, though outwardly both remained utterly serious, neither of them moving a muscle.

'Virtue is its own reward,' said the architect, sagely, as if to put an end to thoughts that he did not express. 'For my part, I don't care a hang what people think; I'm an artist, I am.'

After dinner, they stayed in the drawing-room until midnight. It was a special occasion to celebrate Octave's arrival. Madame Campardon seemed dreadfully tired and gradually wilted on the sofa.

'Are you in pain, my darling?' asked her husband.

'No,' she replied, under her breath. 'It's the same as always.'

Then, looking at him, she said, softly: 'You saw her at the Hédouins?'

'Yes; she asked me how you were.'

Tears came into Rose's eyes.

'She's always so well, she is!'

'There, there,' said Campardon, as he lightly kissed her hair, forgetting that they were not alone. 'You'll make yourself worse again. Don't you know that I love you all the same, my poor sweet thing?'

Octave, who had discreetly moved to the window, and pretended to be looking into the street, once more proceeded to scrutinise Madame Campardon's features, for his curiosity was roused, and he wondered what could be the matter with her. But she wore her usual look, half doleful, half good-tempered, as she curled herself up on the sofa, like a woman who submits resignedly to her share of caresses.

At length Octave bade them good-night. Candlestick in hand, he was still on the landing when he heard the rustle of silk dresses as they brushed up the stairs. He politely stood back to let them pass. Evidently these were the ladies on the fourth floor, Madame Josserand and her two daughters, coming home from a party. As they went by, the mother, a stout, arrogant-looking woman, stared full in his face; the elder of the daughters stepped aside with a petulant air, while her sister, heedless, looked up at him an smiled in the bright light of the candle. She was charmingly pretty, with tiny features, fair skin, and shining auburn hair; she had a certain intrepid grace, the easy charm of a young bride returning from a ball, in an elaborate gown covered with bows and lace, such as maidens never wear. The trains of their dresses disappeared at the top of the stairs and a door closed behind them. Octave stood there enjoying the look he had seen in her eyes.

Slowly he went upstairs in his turn. Only one gas jet was alight; the staircase, in this heavy, heated air, seemed fast asleep. More than ever did it wear a modest mien, with its chaste portals of handsome mahogany, that enclosed so many respectable hearths. Not a whisper could be heard; it was a polite silence of well-mannered people conscious even of the sound of their breathing. But then he heard a slight noise. Leaning over the banister, he saw Monsieur Gourd, in velvet cap and slippers, turning off the last gas burner. Then the whole house was lost in darkness, as if obliterated by the refinement and absolute propriety of its slumbers.

However, Octave found it hard to get to sleep. He tossed about feverishly, his brain filled with all the new faces that he had seen. What on earth made the Campardons so civil to him? Did they think of offering him their daughter's hand later on? Perhaps the husband had taken him as a lodger just to amuse his wife and cheer her up. Poor woman! What could the extraordinary complaint be from which she was suffering? Then his ideas grew more confused; phantoms passed before him: Little Madame Pichon, his neighbour, with her vacuous look; handsome Madame Hédouin, calm and self-possessed, in her black dress; the fiery eyes of Madame Valérie, and the merry smile of Mademoiselle Josserand. In just a few hours, the streets of Paris had become a fertile terrain. This had always been his dream, that women would take him by the hand, and help him on in his business. Again and again the faces came back, tiring him out as they became superimposed on each other. He couldn't decide which to choose, while trying to let his voice remain tender and his gestures seductive. Then, all at once, weary and exasperated, he gave in to the brutal impulse within him, a ferocious disdain for women merely masked by his adoring poses.

'Are you ever going to let me sleep?' he exclaimed aloud, throwing himself violently on his back.

'I'll take the first one available and all of them at the same time, if that's what they want! To sleep! Tomorrow's another day.'

CHAPTER 2

When Madame Josserand, preceded by her daughters, left Madame Dambreville's party in the Rue de Rivoli, on the fourth floor at the corner of the Rue de l'Oratoire,* she slammed the street door in a sudden outburst of wrath that she had been suppressing for the last two hours. Her younger daughter Berthe had again just missed getting a husband.

'Well, what are you standing there for?' she angrily asked the girls, who had slipped under the arcade and were watching the cabs go by.

'Go on, start walking; for you needn't imagine that we're going to take a cab and spend another two francs!'

And when Hortense, the elder, grumbled: 'H'm! pleasant, walking in all this mud! It will finish off my shoes, that's for sure!'

'Go on, walk I said,' responded the mother, in a fury. 'When your shoes are done for, you'll have to stay in bed, that's all! A lot of good it is, taking you out!'

With bowed heads, Berthe and Hortense turned down the Rue de l'Oratoire. They held up their long skirts as high as they could above their crinolines, huddling up their shoulders, shivering in their opera cloaks. Madame Josserand walked behind them, wrapped in an old fur mantle that looked like shabby cat-skin. None of them wore bonnets, but had enveloped their hair in lace wraps, a headgear that made passers-by look round at them in surprise as they tramped along in single file past the houses, with backs bent and eyes fixed on the puddles. The mother grew more exasperated as she thought of many similar returns home during the last three winters, hampered by their smart gowns, in the black mud of the streets, a butt for the wit of those out late. No, she'd certainly had enough of this carting her daughters all around Paris, without ever daring to enjoy the luxury of a cab, for fear of having to make do with one less course for the next day's dinner!

'So she's a match-maker, is she?' she went on out loud, as she thought of Madame Dambreville, talking to herself by way of solace, not even addressing her daughters, who had gone along

the Rue Saint-Honoré. 'Fine matches she makes! A lot of pert
hussies from goodness knows where! Oh, if only one weren't
obliged to go through all this! That was her last success, I
suppose – that bride trotted out just to show us that it does
sometimes work. And what a fine specimen at that! Some
wretched girl who'd been seduced and who had to be sent back
to a convent for six months to get another coat of whitewash!'

As they crossed the Place du Palais Royal it started to rain.
This was the last straw. Slipping and splashing about, they
stopped and once again eyed the empty cabs rolling by.

'On you go!' cried the mother, ruthlessly. 'We're almost
home; it's not worth forty sous. And as for your brother Léon,
who wouldn't leave with us for fear of having to pay for the
cab! If he can get what he wants at that woman's so much the
better! But I have to say it's almost indecent. A frump, well past
fifty, who only invites young people to her house! A nobody
married off to that idiot Dambreville in exchange for the
promise of a head-clerkship!

Hortense and Berthe plodded along in the rain, one in front
of the other, without appearing to listen. When their mother let
herself go like this, oblivious of all the strict rules laid down for
their own delicate education, it was tacitly agreed that they
should be afflicted by deafness. But on reaching the dark and
deserted Rue de l'Échelle, Berthe rebelled.

'There!' she cried. 'There goes my heel! I can't go another
step!'

Madame Josserand's fury was unleashed.

'Walk on at once! Do I complain? Do you think it's fit for me
to be out on the streets at this time of night, and in such
weather, too? It would be different if you had a father like other
people. Oh, no, sir is sitting at home with his feet up! It's always
me who has to take you out to social functions; he'll never be
bothered to do so! I've had about enough of it. Your father can
do it in future; you're not going to find me dragging you about
any more to places I can't stand! I was completely taken in by
that man's apparent qualities and I have been disappointed time
and again. Good Lord! If I were to have my life again, I certainly
wouldn't get married to a man of *that* sort!'

The girls stopped grumbling. They well knew this oft-
recounted chapter in the story of their mother's blighted hopes.
With their lace mantillas sticking to their faces, and their ball

shoes soaked through, they hurried along the Rue Sainte-Anne.
But in the Rue de Choiseul, at the very door of her own house,
Madame Josserand had to undergo a final humiliation, for the
Duveyriers' carriage splashed her all over as it drove up.

Exhausted and furious, both mother and girls made a point
of seeming composed when they had to pass Octave on the
stairs. But, as soon as their door was shut, they rushed through
the dark drawing-room, bumping into furniture, to the dining-
room, where Monsieur Josserand was writing by the feeble light
of a little lamp.

'Another failure!' cried Madame Josserand, as she flopped
into a chair.

And she tore the lace covering from her head, flung her fur
cloak over the chair, revealing a gaudy red dress, trimmed with
black satin, and cut very low. She looked enormous, though her
shoulders were still attractive, and resembled the shining flanks
of a mare. In her square face, with its big nose and flabby
cheeks, you could sense the tragic fury of a queen checking her
desire to lapse into the language of the gutter.

'Ah!' said Monsieur Josserand, simply, thrown off balance by
this sudden entrance.

His eyelids blinked uneasily. It was positively overwhelming
when his wife displayed that mammoth bosom; it seemed as if
he felt its weight crushing the back of his neck. Dressed in a
seedy frock-coat that he was wearing out at home, his countenance washed out and dingy with thirty years of office routine,
he looked up at her with his large lacklustre eyes. Pushing back
his grey locks behind his ears, he was too disconcerted to speak,
and attempted to go on writing.

'But you don't seem to understand!' continued Madame
Josserand, in a harsh voice. 'I tell you, there goes another
marriage that hasn't come off – the fourth!'

'Yes, yes, I know – the fourth,' he murmured. 'It's annoying,
very.'

And to avoid that terrifying expanse of flesh, he turned
towards his daughters with a kindly smile. They also took off
their lace and their cloaks; the elder was in blue, the younger in
pink, and their dresses, too daring in cut and over-trimmed, had
something provocative about them. Hortense had a sallow
complexion; her nose spoiled her: it was like her mother's, and
gave her an air of stubborn disdain. She was only twenty-three,

but looked twenty-eight. Berthe, however, was two years
younger, and kept all her childlike grace, with similar features,
only more delicate, and a skin of dazzling whiteness, which
would defy an inherited coarseness until she was about fifty.

'When are you going to start taking any notice of us?' cried
Madame Josserand. 'For God's sake put your writing away; it
gets on my nerves!'

'But, my dear, I've got these wrappers to do!' he said gently.

'Oh, yes, I know your wrappers – three francs a thousand!
Perhaps, you think that with those three francs you'll be able to
marry off your daughters!'

In the faint light you could see that the table was strewn with
large sheets of greyish paper, printed wrappers on which Monsieur wrote addresses for a well-known publisher who had
several periodicals. As his cashier's salary didn't make ends
meet, he spent whole nights at this thankless task, doing it on
the quiet, lest anyone should find out how poor they were.

'Three francs are three francs,' he insisted in his slow, tired
voice. 'With those three francs you'll be able to add bows to
your gown, and get a cake for your guests on Tuesdays.'

He regretted the remark as soon as he had uttered it, for he
felt that it had gone straight to the open wound of Madame
Josserand's pride.

Her bosom flushed; she seemed just about to come out with
some vindictive reply, but, by a majestic effort, she only stammered: 'Heaven help us!' And she looked at her daughters,
shrugging those awesome shoulders, as if in masterful scorn of
her husband, and as much as to say: 'There! You hear the idiot,
don't you?'

The girls nodded. Seeing himself vanquished, he regretfully
laid down his pen and took up a copy of *Le Temps*,* which he
brought home with him every evening from the office.

'Is Saturnin asleep?' asked Madame Josserand, drily, referring
to her younger son.

'Yes, long ago; and I told Adèle she could go to bed, too. I
suppose you saw Léon at the Dambrevilles?'

'Of course. Why, he sleeps there!' she rapped out, in a sudden
paroxysm of spite.

The father taken aback, ingenuously asked: 'Do you really
think he does?'

Hortense and Berthe became deaf, smiling slightly; they pre-

tended to be examining their shoes, which were in a pitiable
state. By way of a diversion, Madame Josserand tried to pick
another quarrel with her husband. She begged him to take
away his newspaper every morning, and not to leave it lying
about all day long, as he had done last night, for instance. That
particular copy just happened to contain details of a scandalous
trial, which his daughters might easily have read. That kind
of carelessness showed what little concern he had for moral
values.

'So it's bedtime, is it?' yawned Hortense. 'I'm hungry.'

'What about me?' said Berthe. 'I'm simply starving.'

'What's that?' cried Madame Josserand. 'Hungry? Didn't you
get some *brioche* when you were there? What a couple of fools!
You're meant to eat at those occasions. I certainly did.'

But the girls kept on that they were dying of hunger, so their
mother at last went to the kitchen to see if there was anything
left. Their father furtively set to work on his wrappers again.
He was well aware that, without those wrappers of his, all the
little luxuries they allowed themselves would have disappeared;
and so, in spite of the unfair gibes and scorn heaped on his
head, he doggedly kept at this secret night-time drudgery
spurred on by the thought that just one more scrap of lace
might bring about a wealthy marriage. Though household
expenses were being pared down, they still didn't have enough
to pay for dresses and those Tuesday receptions, so he resigned
himself to his quill-driving like a martyr, dressed in tatters,
while his wife and daughters went flouncing through high
society with flowers in their hair.

'It smells foul in here!' cried Madame Josserand, as she
entered the kitchen. 'I can never get that slut Adèle to leave the
window open. She always says that in the morning it makes the
place as cold as ice.'

She went to open the window, and from the narrow yard
below there rose a stale coldness like that of some musty cellar.
Berthe's lighted candle threw dancing shadows of huge naked
shoulders on the opposite wall.

'And what a mess!' continued Madame Josserand, sniffing
about, poking around in every corner of filth. 'Those are the
dirty plates of two days ago. It's absolutely disgusting! And her
sink! Just smell her sink, if you please!'

She was gradually working herself up. She upset plates and

dishes with arms all white with rice powder and bedecked with
gold bracelets. She trailed her red skirts through the filth,
catching them in the pans shoved under the tables, soiling her
elaborate finery with greasy garbage. Finally, at the sight of a
ruined knife, she exploded.

'Tomorrow morning I'll send her packing!'

'What good will that do you?' asked Hortense, quietly. 'We
can never keep anybody. She's the first girl who's stayed even as
long as three months. As soon as they're trained and have
learned how to make a white sauce, off they go.'

Madame Josserand bit her lip. As a matter of fact, Adèle,
fresh from Brittany, a dim and grubby girl, had been the only
one to survive the abject poverty of this vain bourgeois household which took advantage of her dirt and ignorance to starve
her. Scores of times, when they had discovered a comb in the
bread, or when, after some nauseous stew they had had colic,
they talked of getting rid of her; but then, again, they preferred
to put up with her rather than bother finding another cook, for
even pilferers refused to work in such a hole, where the very
lumps of sugar were counted.

'I can't find anything at all,' muttered Berthe, as she ransacked
a cupboard.

The shelves had the mournful barrenness and sham display of
households where they buy inferior meat so as to be able to
have a show of flowers on the table. There were only a few
spotlessly clean china plates with gold edges, a crumb-brush
with some of the plated silver rubbed off its handle, a cruet-
stand, in which the oil and vinegar had dried up; but not a
solitary crust, not a scrap of fruit, pastry, or cheese. Obviously
Adèle's insatiable hunger made her lick the very gilt off plates,
in mopping up any drops of gravy or sauce left by her
employers.

'Why, she must have eaten up all the rabbit!' cried Madame
Josserand.

'Yes,' said Hortense, 'there was a bit of the tail left! No, here
it is! I should have been surprised if she'd dared to. I think I'll
have it. It's cold, but it's better than nothing.'

Berthe kept rummaging about, but without success. At last
she caught hold of a bottle in which her mother had diluted the
contents of an old pot of jam in order to make redcurrant syrup

for her evening parties. Berthe poured out half a glass, saying: 'I'll soak some bread in this, as there's nothing else.'

But Madame Josserand's anxiety barely masked her irony: 'Yes, why don't you fill up your tumbler to the brim while you're about it. Then, tomorrow, I can give our guests water to drink.'

Luckily, another of Adèle's crimes cut short her reprimand. Still hunting for evidence of misdemeanour she caught sight of a book lying on the table, which brought her rage to a climax.

'Oh, the slut! She's brought my edition of Lamartine* into the kitchen again!'

It was a copy of *Jocelyn.** Picking it up, she rubbed it, as if to clean it. How many times had she forbidden Adèle to take it around the apartment with her and to use it to do her accounts. Meanwhile Berthe and Hortense had divided the little piece of bread between them and went off with their supper saying that they would undress first. Their mother gave a parting glance at the ice-cold oven and went back to the dining-room, tightly holding her Lamartine under a fleshy arm.

Monsieur Josserand continued writing. He hoped that his wife would be satisfied with giving him a crushing look as she went past on her way to bed. But once again she sank into a chair facing him, and stared at him without speaking. This made him so uneasy that his pen spurted ink on the flimsy wrapper-paper.

'So it was you who prevented Adèle from making a custard for tomorrow evening,' she said, at last.

He looked up in amazement.

'What do you mean, my dear?'

'Oh, you'll deny it, just as you always do! In that case, why hasn't she made it as I told her to? You know very well that Uncle Bachelard's coming to dinner tomorrow; it's his saint's day, and, unfortunately, on the very day of our party, too! If there's no cream dessert, we must have sorbet which means another five francs down the drain.'

He didn't even attempt to plead his innocence. Not daring to go on with his work, he began to toy with his penholder.

'Tomorrow morning,' resumed Madame Josserand, after a long silence, 'I'd be grateful if you could call on the Campardons and remind them as politely as you can that we're expecting them in the evening. The young man, their friend, arrived this afternoon. Ask them to bring him, too. I hope that's clear, I wish him to come.'

'What young man?'

'Oh, just some young man; it would take far too long to explain. I've found out everything about him. I have to try every avenue as you've left it entirely to me to get rid of your two daughters, taking about as much interest in their marriage as you do in the Grand Turk's.'

At this thought her anger revived.

'Though I do my best not to show my real feelings, it's more than anyone can stand. Don't answer, sir; don't answer, or I shall positively explode!'

He didn't, but she exploded all the same.

'The long and the short of it is, I won't put up with it. I warn you that one of these fine days I shall go off and leave you with your two empty-headed daughters. Do you think I was born to lead such a beggarly life as this? Always splitting farthings into four, denying oneself even a pair of boots, while unable to entertain one's friends in decent fashion! And you're to blame for it all! Don't shake your head, sir; don't exasperate me further! Yes, your fault; I repeat, your fault! You tricked me, sir; basely tricked me. One ought not to marry a woman if one has resolved to let her want for everything. You bragged about your fine future, declaring you were the friend of your employer's sons, those Bernheim brothers, who then made such a fool of you. What! Are you trying to tell me that they didn't? Why, by this time you ought to be their partner! You were the one who made their glass business what it is – one of the finest in Paris, and what are you? Their cashier, a servant, an underling! You're useless! Hold your tongue!'

'I draw eight thousand francs a year,' murmured the hireling; 'it's a very good job.'

'A good job, indeed! After more than thirty years' service. They grind you down, and you're delighted. Do you know what I would have done, if it had been me? I should have seen to it that the business filled my pocket twenty times over. That was easy enough; I saw it when I married you, and I've been telling you ever since. But it needed initiative, intelligence; it meant not going to sleep like a blockhead on the office stool!'

'Come, come,' broke in Monsieur Josserand, 'are you going to upbraid me for being honest?'

She rose, brandishing her Lamartine in his face. 'What do you mean by honest? First of all, be honest towards me; others come second, I hope! And let me tell you that it's not honest to take a girl in by pretending to want to become rich some day, and then to lose your wits in looking after someone else's money! It's true, I was most beautifully swindled! I wish to goodness things could happen over again! Ah, if I'd only known what your people were like!'

She paced up and down the room in a rage. He couldn't refrain from a movement of impatience, despite his great desire for peace.

'You ought to go to bed, Eléonore,' he said. 'It's past one o'clock, and this work can't wait. My relatives have done you no harm, so why bring them into it?'

'And why shouldn't I? Your family is no more sacred than anybody else's, I presume? Everyone in Clermont* knows that your father, after selling his solicitor's practice, let a servant girl ruin him. You might have married off your daughters long ago if he hadn't picked up with a little slut when he was over seventy. He swindled me, too, he did!'

Monsieur Josserand turned pale, and replied in a trembling voice, which grew louder as he went on: 'Look here, don't let's start the old game of insulting each other's relations. Your father's still not paid me your promised dowry of thirty thousand francs.'

'What are you talking about? Thirty thousand francs!'

'Just so; don't pretend to be so astonished. And if my father fell on bad times, yours behaved most shamefully towards us. We never did get to the bottom of the matter as far as his will was concerned; all sorts of underhand moves led to your sister's husband getting the school in the Rue des Fossés-Saint-Victor – that good-for-nothing pawn, who no longer condescends to acknowledge us if he passes us in the street. We were robbed, and that's all there is to it!'

Madame Josserand grew livid with suppressed rage at this inconceivable outburst on the part of her husband. 'Don't say a word against Papa! For forty years he was a credit to the teaching profession. Just mention the Bachelard Institute around the Panthéon* and see what they say! And as for my sister and her husband, they are what they are. They swindled me, that I know; but it's not for you to mention it, and I won't put up with it; do you hear me? Do I ever bring up the subject of your sister from Les Andelys* who ran off with an officer? Oh! Your relations are wonderully respectable aren't they?'

'Yes, madame, but the officer married her. And while we're about it, let's not forget Uncle Bachelard, that crooked brother of yours.'

'Sir! Are you going mad? He's rich; he makes as much as he likes in his commission agency,* and he's promised to give Berthe a dowry. Have you no respect for anyone?'

'All very fine; give Berthe a dowry! I wouldn't mind betting he doesn't give her a penny, and that we shall have to put up with his revolting habits for nothing. Whenever he comes here I'm quite ashamed of him. A liar, a rake, an adventurer, who takes advantage of the situation; and who, seeing us grovel for the last fifteen years at the thought of his fortune, gets me to spend two hours every Saturday in his office, to check his accounts! That must save him at least five francs. We have yet to see the colour of his money!'

Breathless with emotion for a moment, Madame Josserand paused. Then she flung back this final taunt: 'And you, sir, have got a nephew in the police!'

There was another pause. The light from the little lamp grew dimmer; as Monsieur Josserand feverishly gesticulated, the wrappers fluttered about in all directions. As he confronted his spouse, looking her full in the face, with her sitting there in her low-cut dress, he resolved to say what he'd always wanted to say, trembling with admiration at his own courage.

'With eight thousand francs one can get by very well,' he went on. 'You're always grumbling. But you shouldn't have tried to do things on a scale above our means. It's your mania for entertaining and for paying visits, for having an "at home" day with tea and cakes—'

She didn't let him finish his speech. 'Oh! I understand what this is really about! You'd better shut me up in a box at once. Why don't you suggest I should go out stark naked? And how do you suppose your daughters will ever find husbands if we see nobody? To think that after all these sacrifices one is judged in this despicable way!'

'We must all of us make sacrifices. Léon had to give priority to his sisters, leave the house and support himself. As for

Saturnin, poor boy, he can't even read. And as for myself, I go without everything, and spend my nights—'

'Then, why did you ever have daughters? You're surely not going to begrudge them their education? Any other man, in your place would be proud of Hortense's certificate, and of Berthe's artistic talents. Everyone tonight was charmed with the dear girl's playing of that waltz, "The Banks of the Oise", and I'm sure her last watercolour sketch will delight our guests tomorrow. But you, sir, you've not even the instincts of a father; you'd rather have your daughters look after cows than send them to school!'

'Ah! And what about the insurance policy I took out for Berthe? Wasn't it you who by the time the fourth instalment was due, spent the money on chair covers for the drawing-room? And then you even got the premiums refunded as well.'

'Of course I did, because you left us all to die of hunger. You're the one who'll look ridiculous if your daughters became old maids!'

'And who do you suppose scares away all the likely men with those fine dresses and ridiculous parties? And you think *I* look ridiculous? God damn you!'

In all his life Monsieur Josserand had never gone so far. His wife, gasping, stuttered: '*Me* – ridiculous!' when the door opened. Hortense and Berthe came in wearing petticoats, camisoles and slippers with their hair down.

'Oh, it's so cold in our room!' said Berthe shivering. 'It freezes the very food in your mouth. Here, at least, there's been a fire this evening.'

And they both drew up their chairs and sat close to the stove, which still retained some heat. Hortense held the rabbit bone between her fingertips, and adroitely picked it. Berthe dipped bits of bread in her tumbler of syrup. But their parents hardly noticed them enter.

'Ridiculous, did you say, sir, ridiculous? Well, I shan't be in future. I'll be damned if I ever wear out another pair of gloves in trying to get them husbands! Now it's your turn; and try not to be more ridiculous than me!'

'What a hope, now that you've trotted them about and compromised them everywhere! Whether you get them married or whether you don't, I don't care one jot!'

'And I care less still, Monsieur Josserand! So little do I care, that if you get me any angrier I'll throw them out the front door. And you can go, too, if you like; the door's open. Lord! What a good riddance of bad rubbish that would be!'

The girls listened patiently. They were used to such rows. They went on eating, with their camisoles unbuttoned and revealing their shoulders, letting their bare skin gently touch the lukewarm earthen sides of the stoves. They looked charming in this state of undress, with their youth and healthy appetites, and their large eyes heavy with sleep.

'It's silly of you to quarrel like this,' said Hortense, at length, with her mouth full. 'Mamma's blood pressure will go up, and Papa will be ill at the office all day tomorrow. It seems to me that we're old enough to get husbands for ourselves.'

This created a diversion. The father, utterly worn out, pretended to go on with his wrappers, while the mother, who was pacing up and down the room like an uncaged lioness, came up to Hortense.

'If you're alluding to yourself, you're a precious fool! That Verdier of yours will never marry you!'

'That's my look-out,' replied Hortense, bluntly.

After having disdainfully refused five or six suitors – a clerk, a tailor's son, and other young men whom she also thought had no prospects, she set her sights on a lawyer, a man over forty, whom she had met at the Dambrevilles'. She thought him very clever, and bound to make a large fortune. But, in fact, for the last fifteen years, Verdier had been living with a mistress, who, in their neighbourhood, even passed as his wife. Hortense knew this, but didn't appear to be much troubled by it.

'My child,' said her father, looking up from his work, 'I have begged you to give up the very idea of such a marriage. You know what the situation is.'

She stopped sucking her bone: 'Well, what of it? Verdier's promised to give her up. She's only a fool.'

'You've no right to talk like that, Hortense. And if the fellow gives you up, too, one day, and goes back to the very woman you made him leave?'

'That's my look-out,' said the girl, drily.

Berthe listened, as she knew the whole story, and discussed each new development with her sister every day. Like her father, she sided with the poor woman, who, after fifteen years of housekeeping, was to be turned into the street.

But Madame Josserand interrupted: 'That's not the point. Wretched women of that sort always drift back to the gutter from which they came. It's Verdier, though, who will never have the strength of mind to leave her. He's leading you on nicely, my dear. If I were you I wouldn't wait another second for him, but I'd try and find somebody else.'

The girl's voice grew harsher still, and two livid spots appeared on her cheeks.

'You know me, Mamma. I want him, and I'm going to have him. I shall never marry anybody else, if I have to wait for him a hundred years!'

The mother shrugged her shoulders.

'And you're the one who calls other people fools!'

Hortense rose, trembling with anger.

'Now, then, don't start getting at me!' she cried. 'I've done eating my rabbit, and I'd rather go to bed. Since you can't manage to get us husbands, and must let us try and find them ourselves in whatever way we choose!'

And she went out, slamming the door behind her.

Madame Josserand turned majestically towards her husband with the profound remark: 'There, sir; that's how you have brought them up.'

Monsieur Josserand made no reply, but kept making little dots of ink on his fingernail, while waiting to continue his writing. Berthe, who had eaten her bread, was dipping her finger in the glass to finish her syrup. As her back was nice and warm, she felt comfortable, and was in no hurry to go back to her room, where she would have to put up with her sister's ill-temper.

'Yes, that's what one gets,' continued Madame Josserand, as she walked up and down the dining-room. 'For twenty years one wears oneself out for these girls, denying oneself everything, so that they may become accomplished, and then they won't even give you the satisfaction of making a marriage you approve of. If one had ever refused them anything it would be different. But I've spent my last centime on them, and have gone without proper clothes, to try to dress them as if our income were fifty thousand francs a year. No, it really is *too* much. When the minxes have got out of you a sophisticated education, learning just enough of religion and the manners of the rich, they turn their backs on you, and talk of marrying lawyers, debauched adventurers, and the like.'

Stopping in front of Berthe, she shook her finger at her: 'As for you, if you behave like your sister, you'll have me to deal with.'

Then she resumed her march, talking to herself, jumping from one idea to another, contradicting herself with the complacent effrontery of a woman who is always right.

'I did what I ought to have done, and if need be I'd do it again. In life it's only the most timid who go to the wall. Money is money, and if you haven't got any you'd better shut up shop at once. For my part, whenever I had twenty sous I always pretended I had forty, for the important thing is to command envy, not pity. It's no good having a fine education if one has shabby clothes, for then people only look down on you. It might not be right; but that's how it is. I'd rather wear dirty petticoats than a cotton gown. Eat potatoes if you like, but put a chicken on the table if you ask people to dinner. It's only fools who would deny that.'

She looked hard at her husband, for whom these last remarks were intended. But, utterly exhausted, he declined to renew the battle a second time, and was cowardly enough to say: 'Ah, too true! Money is everything nowadays.'

'You hear that,' said Madame Josserand, approaching her daughter. 'Get on with it and try and do us credit. How was it you managed to let this marriage slip through your fingers?'

Berthe felt that now it was her turn. 'I don't know, Mamma,' she faltered.

'An assistant manager,' continued her mother, 'not yet thirty, and with magnificent prospects. Money coming in every month – a regular income; there's nothing like it. I'm sure you did something stupid, some nonsense, like last time.'

'No, I am sure I didn't, Mamma. I expect he found out that I hadn't got a farthing.'

Madame Josserand's voice rose. 'And what about the dowry that your uncle is going to give you? Everyone knows about that. No, it must have been something else; he backed off too abruptly. After dancing with him you went in the parlour, and—'

Berthe started to get upset.

'Yes, Mamma, and, as we were alone, he tried to do all sorts of horrid things . . . caught me by the waist and kissed me. And I was frightened, and . . . I pushed him back against the furniture.'

Her mother, boiling over with rage, interrupted her. 'Pushed him back against the furniture! Oh, the idiot! She pushed him back, did she?'

'Well, Mamma, he caught hold of me.'

'So what? Caught hold of you? As if that mattered. A lot of good it is to send simpletons like you to school! Whatever did they teach you there, eh?'

Blushes covered the girl's cheeks and shoulders, while tears came into the eyes of the assaulted virgin.

'I couldn't help it. He looked so wicked; I didn't know what to do.'

'Didn't know what to do? She didn't know what to do! Haven't I told you a hundred times not to be so absurdly timid? You've got to live in the real world. When a man takes liberties, it means that he's in love with you, and there's always a way of gently keeping him in his place. Just for a kiss behind the door! Why, I'd be ashamed to mention such a thing. And you go pushing people back against the furniture ruining your chances of getting married?'

Then, assuming a learned air, she went on: 'I give up in despair; you're really so silly, my child. I'd need to coach you in every detail, and that would be a bore. As you have no fortune, do try and understand that you've got to catch men by some other means. One has to be sweet, give tender glances, let them have your hand now and then, and submit to a little hanky-panky without appearing to do so; in short, one should fish for a husband. Now, you needn't think it improves your eyes to cry like a great baby.

'Look here, you're getting on my nerves – do stop crying! Monsieur Josserand, tell your daughter not disfigure herself by crying like that. If she loses her looks, that will really be too much.'

'My child,' said her father, 'be good and listen to your mother's advice. You mustn't spoil your looks, my pet.'

'And what annoys me is that when she wants to be she can be agreeable enough,' continued Madame Josserand. 'Come, dry your eyes and look at me as if I were your suitor. You must smile and let your fan drop, so that, as he picks it up, his fingers

just touch yours. No, no, that's not the way! With your head
stuck up in the air like that, you look like a sick hen. Throw
back your head and show your neck; it's pretty enough to be
looked at.'

'Like this, Mamma?'

'Yes; that's better. And don't stand so upright; keep your
waist lissom. Men don't care for stiff boards. And, above all, if
they go a little bit too far, don't behave like an outraged maiden.
When a man goes too far, he's done for, my dear!'

The drawing-room clock struck two, and, excited as she was
by sitting up so late, and as her desire for an immediate marriage
grew frenzied, the mother, in her abstraction, began thinking
aloud as she twisted her daughter about like a Dutch doll.

Berthe, heavy at heart, submitted in a tame, spiritless fashion;
fear and confusion half choked her. Suddenly, in the middle of
a merry laugh that her mother was forcing her to attempt, she
burst into tears, exclaiming: 'No, no, it's no use; I can't do it!'

For a moment Madame Josserand remained speechless with
astonishment. Ever since leaving the Dambrevilles' party her
hand had been itching; and suddenly she slapped Berthe with all
her might.

'There, take that! You're absolutely impossible, you great
booby! Upon my word, I don't blame the men!'

The motion made her drop her Lamartine. Picking it up, she
wiped it and swept majestically out of the room without another
word.

'I knew it would end like that,' muttered Monsieur Josserand,
who was relieved when his daughter immediately went off to
bed, holding her cheek and sobbing louder than ever.

As Berthe felt her way across the ante-room she found her
brother Saturnin, barefooted and listening at the door. Saturnin
was a big hulking fellow of twenty-five, wild-eyed, and who had
remained infantile after an attack of brain fever. Without being
actually insane, he occasionally frightened the household by fits
of blind fury whenever anybody annoyed him. Only Berthe was
able to subdue him by a look. When she was still a little girl he
had nursed her throughout a long illness, obedient as a dog to
all her little caprices; and, ever since he had saved her life, he
adored her with a deep, passionate devotion.

'Has she been beating you again?' he asked, in a deep, tender
voice.

Surprised at meeting him, Berthe tried to send him back to his room.

'Go to bed; it's none of your business.'

'Yes it is. I won't let her beat you. She was shouting so loudly that she woke me up. She'd better not do it again, or else I'll give it her.'

Then she caught hold of his wrists, and talked to him as if he were a disobedient animal.

He immediately calmed down and whimpered like a little boy: 'It hurts, doesn't it? Where did she hit you? Let me kiss it better.'

And when he found her cheek in the dark, he kissed it, wetting it with his tears, as he repeated: 'Now it's all better; now it's all better.'

Meanwhile Monsieur Josserand, left alone, had put down his pen, too upset to go on writing. After a few minutes, he got up and went to listen. Madame Josserand was snoring. No sounds of weeping came from his daughters' room. Everything was dark and silent. Then, somewhat less heavy-hearted, he returned. He adjusted the lamp, which was smoking, and mechanically began writing again. Without him being even aware of it, two great tears rolled down his cheeks and dropped on to the wrappers, amid the profound silence of the sleeping household.

As soon as the fish had been served (some dubiously fresh skate, in brown butter sauce, which that incompetent Adèle had drowned in vinegar), Hortense and Berthe, seated on either side of their Uncle Bachelard, kept urging him to drink, taking turns to fill up his glass and repeating: 'Come on, have another drink; it's your saint's day, you know! Here's to your health, uncle!'

Their plan was to get twenty francs out of him. Every year, on this occasion, their thoughtful mother placed them on either side of her brother, leaving him to their tender mercies. But it was uphill work, needing all the cupidity of two girls spurred on by visions of Louis Quinze shoes* and five-button gloves. In order to get him to give them the twenty francs, they had to get him completely drunk. With his own relations he was brutally tight-fisted, though once outside the family he would squander in drunken debauchery the eighty thousand francs which he made through his commission agency. Fortunately, that evening he had arrived already half drunk, having spent the afternoon with a lady in the Faubourg Montmartre, a dyer, who used to get vermouth for him from Marseilles.

'Your good health, my lovelies!' he replied in his big, raucous voice, whenever he emptied his glass.

Sporting all manner of jewellery, and a rose in his buttonhole, he filled the centre of the table – the type of a huge, boozing, loud-mouthed tradesman who has wallowed in all sorts of vice. There was a lurid brilliancy about the false teeth in his ravaged face and his great red nose was poised like a beacon below his snow-white, close-cropped hair; now and again his eyelids dropped involuntarily over his rheumy eyes. Gueulin, the son of his wife's sister, declared that his uncle had never been sober during the whole ten years that he'd been a widower.

'Narcisse, can I serve you some skate? It's excellent,' said Madame Josserand, smiling at her brother's drunken condition, though inwardly nauseated.

She sat directly opposite him, with young Gueulin on her left, and on her right, Hector Trublot – to whom she was obliged to show some attention. She usually took advantage of this family dinner to pay back certain invitations; and so Madame Juzeur was also present, sitting next to Monsieur Josserand. As the uncle always behaved outrageously at table, only his fortune tempering their disgust, she restricted the guest-list to her closest friends or those she was no longer trying to impress. For instance, at one time she had thought of young Trublot as a son-in-law, as he was working for a stockbroker while waiting for his wealthy father to buy him a share in the business. But as Trublot had expressed a calm disdain for marriage, she didn't waste time on him, even putting him beside Saturnin, who had never learned how to eat decently. Berthe, who always had to sit next to her big brother, had the job of keeping him in order with a look whenever his fingers found their way too frequently into the sauce.

After the fish came a pastry dish, and the sisters thought the moment ripe for their preliminary attack.

'Do have another drink, uncle dear!' said Hortense. 'It is your saint's day after all; now aren't you all going to give us something to celebrate it?'

'Oh! Yes, that's true, isn't it,' added Berthe, with an innocent air. 'On saint's day it's normal to give us a present; so you could give us twenty francs.'

As soon as there was any mention of money, Bachelard pretended to be even more drunk. That was his usual trick. His eyelids drooped, and he stopped making any sense at all.

'Eh, what's that?' he stuttered.

'Twenty francs. You know very well what twenty francs are; it's no use pretending that you don't,' said Berthe. 'Give us twenty francs; and then we'll love you – oh, ever so much!'

They flung their arms about his neck, called him the most endearing names, and kissed his swollen red face, without being put off by the revolting odour of vile debauchery that he exhaled. Monsieur Josserand, disturbed by this nauseous smell – a mixture of absinthe, tobacco and musk – was shocked to see his daughters' virginal charms in such close contact with this lecherous old blackguard.

'Do leave him alone!' he cried.

'What for?' asked Madame Josserand, as she gave her husband a terrible look. 'They're only playing a game. And if Narcisse wants to give them twenty francs, he has a perfect right to do so!'

'Monsieur Bachelard is so good to them,' murmured little Madame Juzeur obligingly.

But their uncle refused to give in, slobbering like a drunken idiot.

''S funny,' he said, hiccuping, 'but I dunno, I really don't.'

Hortense and Berthe exchanged glances and then let him go. No doubt, he hadn't had enough to drink. So they filled up his glass once again, laughing like whores who mean to clean out a man. Their bare arms, delightfully plump and fresh, kept passing every moment under their uncle's bright red nose.

Trublot meanwhile, like a quiet fellow who prefers having his fun all to himself, kept watching Adèle as she clumsily waited on the guests. He was very short-sighted, and thought she looked pretty with her heavy Breton features and her hair the colour of dirty hemp. As she placed the roast veal on the table, she stretched right across him; and pretending to pick up his napkin, he gave her a good pinch on the calf of her leg. The maid, not understanding what was going on, looked at him as if he had asked her for some bread.

'What's the matter?' said Madame Josserand. 'Did she push against you? Oh, that girl! She's so clumsy! But she's only just started and needs proper training.'

'Of course she does; everything's fine,' replied Trublot, stroking his bushy black beard with an air as serene as that of some Indian god.

Conversation grew brisker in the dining-room, icy cold at first, but gradually being warmed by the steam from the various dishes. Once again Madame Juzeur confided in Monsieur Josserand the whole sad story of her thirty years of solitude. She raised her eyes to heaven, by way of a discreet allusion to the drama of her life. Her husband, after being married to her for only ten days, had left her – no one knew why, and that's all she'd say.

Now she lived in quiet, comfortable surroundings, often visited by priests.

'It's so sad, though, at my age!' she simpered, cutting up her veal in an affected manner.

'A most unfortunate little woman,' whispered Madame Josserand in Trublot's ear, with an air of profound sympathy.

But Trublot looked with indifference at the devotee, with her bright eyes and mysterious reserve. She was not at all his type.

Then they had a sudden scare. Saturnin, whom Berthe was no longer watching as she was so busy with her uncle, had begun playing with his food, making a revolting mess with it on his plate. To his mother the poor lad was a source of exasperation, for she was both afraid and ashamed of him. She couldn't imagine how she was going to get him off her hands; she felt guilty at the idea he should get some menial labouring job; her pride forbidding her, for she knew she had sacrificed him in favour of his sisters, by taking him away from a school where he had shown little sign of making any progress. All these years that he had lounged about the house, helpless and stupid, had been years of terror for her, especially when she had to introduce him to people. Her pride simply couldn't stand it.

'Saturnin!' she cried.

But Saturnin just grinned with delight at the nasty mess on his plate. He had no respect for his mother, treating her as a lying old hag, with the strange intuition of idiots who think aloud. The situation was going to get nasty, and he would have thrown the plate at her head if Berthe, recalled to her duty, had not fixed him with a look. He tried to resist; then his eyes dropped, and he leaned back in his chair, gloomy and depressed, as if in a trance, until dinner was over.

'Gueulin, I hope you've brought your flute?' asked Madame Josserand, trying to lighten the atmosphere.

Gueulin played the flute in amateur fashion, but only at houses where he felt quite at home.

'My flute? Of course I did,' he replied.

His red hair and whiskers seemed more tangled and bristly than usual as he looked on, utterly absorbed by the girls' manoeuvre to trick their uncle. Himself a clerk in an insurance office, he used to meet Bachelard directly after office hours and never left his side, doing the round of all the cafés and brothels in his wake. Behind the huge, ungainly figure of the one, you were sure to see the pale, wizened features of the other.

'That's it; keep at it; stick to him!' he urged on the two sisters, as if he were a spectator at a wrestling match.

Uncle Bachelard, as a matter of fact, was getting the worst of it. When, after the vegetables – green beans soaked in water – Adèle brought in a vanilla and currant ice, there was great rejoicing all round the table; and the young ladies took advantage of the situation to make their uncle drink half the bottle of

Champagne which Madame Josserand had brought at a grocer's round the corner for three francs. He was getting maudlin, and forgot to keep up the farce of appearing imbecile.

'Eh? Twenty francs! Why twenty francs? Oh, I see! You want me to give you twenty francs? But I haven't got any money with me! Ask Gueulin. Didn't I come out without my purse, Gueulin, and you had to settle up at the café? If I'd got them, my sweet things, you should have your twenty francs for being so nice to me!'

Gueulin, with a laugh that sounded like a badly greased cartwheel, muttered: 'Oh, the old devil!'

Growing excited, he cried: 'Why don't you search his pockets?'

Then, losing all restraint, Hortense and Berthe flung themselves on their uncle. Checked at first by their good breeding, this desire for the twenty francs suddenly got the better of them, and they lost control completely. While one searched his waistcoat, the other thrust her hands deep into the pockets of his frock-coat. Uncle Bachelard struggled to resist this double attack, but then started to laugh, a laughter broken by drunken hiccups.

'I really haven't got a penny on me. Leave me alone; you're tickling me!'

'Look in his trousers!' cried Gueulin.

So Berthe, suddenly resolute, thrust her hands into one of his breeches pockets. The girls trembled with excitement as they grew rougher and rougher, almost resorting to violence. Then Berthe uttered a cry of victory; from the depths of his pocket she pulled out a handful of money, which she scattered on a plate, and there, among copper and silver, was a gold twenty-franc piece.

'I've got it!' she cried, with hair undone and flushed cheeks, tossing the coin in the air and catching it.

All the guests clapped their hands; they thought it a great joke. There was a buzz of merriment, and it was the high point of the dinner. Madame Josserand smiled a smile of motherly solicitude as she watched her dear daughters. The old man, putting his money away, remarked sententiously that if one wanted twenty francs one ought to earn them. And the two girls, exhausted but content, sat panting on either side of him, their lips still quivering with desire.

A bell rang. They had lingered at the table, and after-dinner guests were now beginning to arrive. Monsieur Josserand, who had decided to laugh, like his wife, at what had occurred, would willingly have had them sing a little Béranger, but she silenced him; that sort of entertainment was not good enough for her poetic tastes. She hurried on the dessert, the more so because her brother Bachelard, vexed at having had to give the twenty francs as a present, was becoming quarrelsome, complaining that Léon, his nephew, had not even deigned to wish him many happy returns. Léon had only been invited for the later part of the evening. Then, as they rose from table, Adèle said that the architect from the floor below and a young gentleman were in the drawing-room.

'Ah, yes! That young man,' whispered Madame Juzeur, as she took Monsieur Josserand's arm. 'So you invited him? I saw him today in the concierge's lodge. He's very nice-looking.'

Madame Josserand took Trublot's arm. But then Saturnin, who alone remained at table, and whom all the fuss about the twenty francs had not roused from his torpor, with eyes rolling, threw his chair to the ground in a sudden paroxysm of fury, crying: 'I won't have it, by God! I won't!'

This was just what his mother feared. She motioned to Monsieur Josserand to go on with Madame Juzeur, while she disengaged her arm from that of Trublot, who took the hint to disappear. But, apparently by mistake, he followed Adèle into the kitchen. Bachelard and Gueulin, ignoring the 'crackpot', as they called Saturnin, stood chuckling and nudging each other in a corner.

'He was quite peculiar all evening; I feared something like this might occur,' muttered Madame Josserand, with alarm in her voice.

'Berthe, quick, come here!'

But Berthe was showing her booty to Hortense.

Saturnin was now clutching a knife, and kept repeating: 'By God! I won't have it. I'll rip their bellies open, I will!'

'Berthe!' shrieked her mother, in despair.

And when her daughter came rushing up, she only just had time to prevent Saturnin from going straight to the drawing-room, knife in hand.

She angrily shook him, while he, insanely logical, tried to explain. 'Let me do it; they deserve it. It will be all right, I tell you. I'm sick of their filthy goings-on. They'd sell our souls for money.'

'Stuff and nonsense!' cried Berthe. 'Why, what's the matter with you? What are you going on about?'

Confused and trembling with fury, he stared at her, as he stammered out: 'They've been trying again to get you married. I'm not going to let it happen. Do you hear? I won't let anybody harm you!'

His sister couldn't help laughing. How had he got hold of the notion that they were going to marry her off? He nodded his head, declaring that he knew it, that he was certain of it. And when his mother tried to soothe him, he gripped the knife so fiercely that she shrank back, appalled. It alarmed her, too, to think that others had witnessed the scene; and she hurriedly told Berthe to take him away and lock him in his room, while Saturnin kept gradually raising his voice as he became angrier and angrier.

'I won't have them marry you to anybody. I won't have them hurt you. If they do, I'll rip their bellies open!'

Then Berthe put her hands on his shoulders and looked him straight in the face.

'I'll tell you what,' she said; 'you just be quiet, or else I won't love you any more.'

He staggered back; his face wore a gentler, despairing look, and his eyes filled with tears.

'You won't love me any more? You won't love me any more? Oh, don't say that! Oh, say you'll love me still; say that you'll always love me, and never love anybody else!'

She caught him by the wrist and led him out, docile as a child.

In the drawing-room Madame Josserand, with exaggerated cordiality, addressed Campardon as her dear neighbour. Why hadn't Madame Campardon given her the great pleasure of her company too? When the architect replied that his wife was still ailing, she grew even more gushing and declared that she would have been delighted to welcome her in a dressing-gown and slippers. But her smile had lighted on Octave, who was talking to Monsieur Josserand; for her entire performance as welcoming hostess was meant to reach him over Compardon's shoulder. When her husband introduced the young man to her, she was so effusive that Octave was quite unnerved.

Other guests now came in – stout mothers with skinny daughters; fathers and uncles only just roused from a sleepy day at the office, driving before them their flocks of marriageable daughters. Two lamps, covered with pink paper shades, threw a subdued light over the room, hiding the shabby yellow velvet of the furniture, the dingy piano, and the three dirty prints of Swiss scenery, which formed black patches against the bare, chilly panels of white and gold. It also had the effect of making it hard to see the undistinguished features of the guests and, as one couldn't but be painfully aware, the effort they'd made to get dressed up. Madame Josserand wore her flame-coloured gown of the previous evening; only, in order to disguise the fact, she had spent the whole day sewing new sleeves on to the body and in embellishing it with a mantle of lace to hide her shoulders, while her daughters sat beside her in the their grubby camisoles, stitching away with all their might to put new trimmings on their only gown, which ever since the previous winter they had been patching up and altering in this way.

Each time the bell rang there was a sound of whispering in the ante-room. In the bleak drawing-room people talked in undertones, where every now and then the forced gigglings of some young woman struck a discordant note. Behind little Madame Juzeur, Bachelard and Gueulin kept nudging each other as they told dirty stories. Madame Josserand anxiously watched them, fearful that her brother might misbehave himself. But Madame Juzeur was ready to listen to everything, her lips trembling as she smiled angelically at all their anecdotes. Uncle Bachelard was reputed to be a ladies' man. His nephew, on the other hand, was chaste. However tempting the opportunity, Gueulin refused women's favours on principle; not because he despised them, but because he had doubts as to the sequel of such bliss. 'Sure to have some bother or other,' he would say.

At last Berthe came back. She hurriedly approached her mother.

'Well, that was a business,' she whispered. 'He wouldn't go to bed. I double-locked the door, but I'm afraid he'll break everything in his room.'

Madame Josserand tugged her daughter's frock furiously. At that moment Octave, close by, turned his head.

'My treasured daughter Berthe, Monsieur Mouret,' she said,

in her most gracious manner, as she introduced her to him. 'And this is Monsieur Octave Mouret, my dear.'

She gave Berthe a look. The latter well knew the significance of that look – an order, as it were, to commence action, a supplementary lesson to those of the previous night. She obeyed immediately, with the complacent indifference of a girl who no longer cares to pick and choose a suitor. She went through her part quite prettily, with the easy grace of a Parisienne, already a trifle bored, but completely at home on any subject, speaking enthusiastically of the South, where she had never been. Used as he was to the starched manner of provincial virgins, Octave was charmed by this talkative woman, who chattered away as if she were one of his friends.

Just then Trublot, who hadn't been seen since dinner, suddenly slipped in through the dining-room door, only for Berthe to ask him where he'd been. He didn't answer, which embarrassed her somewhat, and, to get out of her awkward position, she introduced the two young men to each other.

Her mother, meanwhile, never took her eyes off her, assuming the attitude of a commander-in-chief, and directing the progress of the campaign from her armchair. When satisfied that the first engagement had been thoroughly effective, she made a sign to her daughter, and whispered: 'Wait until the Vabres come before you play. And mind you play loud enough.'

Octave, finding himself alone with Trublot, began to question him.

'Charming, isn't she?'

'Yes, not half bad.'

'The young lady in blue is her elder sister, isn't she? She's not so pretty.'

'I agree, she's much skinnier.'

Trublot, short-sighted as he was, could really distinguish nothing, but he had the build of a strapping male who knew exactly what he liked. He had returned from the kitchen contented, chewing little black things, which to his surprise, Octave perceived were coffee-berries.

'I suppose,' he asked, bluntly, 'women in the South are generally plump, aren't they?'

Octave smiled, and immediately he and Trublot were on the best of terms. They saw eye to eye on things that mattered. Lolling back on the sofa, they proceeded to exchange confidences. The one talked of his manageress at 'Au Bonheur des Dames' – Madame Hédouin, a damned fine woman, but too frigid. The other said that he was employed writing letters from nine to five at Monsieur Desmarquay's, the money-changer's, where there was a delicious maid. Just then the door opened, and three people came in.

'Those are the Vabres,' whispered Trublot, as he leaned forward to his new friend. 'Auguste, the tall one, with a face like a diseased sheep, is the landlord's eldest son. He's thirty-three, and suffers continually from splitting headaches, which affect his eyesight, and at one time prevented him from learning Latin – a bad-tempered fellow, who's gone into trade. The other, Théophile, that sandy-haired horror with a weedy-looking beard, that little old man of twenty-eight, always coughing and suffering from toothache, first tried all sorts of jobs, and then married the young woman walking in front, Madame Valérie.'

'I've seen her before,' interrupted Octave. 'She's the daughter of a neighbouring haberdasher, isn't she? But how deceptive those little veils are. At first sight I thought her pretty, but she's only striking-looking, with her dried-up, leaden complexion.'

'Yes, there's another woman who's not my type at all,' replied Trublot, sententiously. 'She's got splendid eyes; some men are satisfied with that. But, my word, she's just skin and bones.'

Madame Josserand had risen to shake hands with Valérie.

'What?' she cried, 'Monsieur Vabre hasn't come with you? And Monsieur and Madame Duveyrier haven't honoured us by their presence either, though they promised to come. It's really most unfortunate!'

The young wife made excuses for her father-in-law on the grounds of his age, though he really preferred to stay at home and work in the evening. As for her brother-in-law and sister-in-law, they had asked her to send their apologies as they'd been invited to an official reception which they were obliged to attend. Madame Josserand bit her lip. She had never missed one of the Saturdays of those stuck-up first-floor people, who thought it beneath them to come up to the fourth floor for her Tuesdays. Certainly, her modest tea-party was not equal to their concerts with a full chamber orchestra. But, just let them wait! When her daughters were both married, and she had two sons-in-law and all their relatives to fill her drawing-room, she too would put on proper musical evenings.

'Get ready to begin,' she whispered in Berthe's ear.

There were about thirty guests, wedged in rather tightly, as they had not thrown open the little *salon*, which now served as a cloakroom for the ladies. The newcomers shook hands all round. Valérie sat next to Madame Juzeur, while Bachelard and Gueulin made remarks in a loud voice about Théophile Vabre, whom they thought it droll to describe as 'good for nothing'. Monsieur Josserand, so unobtrusive in his own drawing-room that he resembled a guest nobody could find even if he was standing right next to you, was listening, horrified, to a story told by one of his old friends. He knew Bonnaud, didn't he? Bonnaud, the chief accountant of the Chemin de Fer du Nord, whose daughter got married last spring? Well, Bonnaud, it seems, had just found out that his son-in-law, to all appearances a most respectable person, had once been a clown, who, for ten years, had been living off a female circus-rider!

'Hush, hush!' murmured several obliging voices. Berthe had opened the piano.

'Well, you know,' explained Madame Josserand, 'it's quite an unpretentious sort of piece – a simple little rêverie. You are fond of music, Monsieur Mouret, I dare say. Won't you come closer to the piano? My daughter plays this rather well – only an amateur, you know; but she plays it with feeling – a great deal of feeling.'

'You're in for it!' said Trublot, under his breath. 'That's the sonata trick.'

Octave was obliged to rise, and remained standing near the piano. To see the attentions that Madame Josserand lavished upon him, one would have thought that she was making Berthe play simply and solely for him.

' "The Banks of the Oise",' she went on. 'It's really very pretty. Now, my love, off you go, and don't be nervous. I'm sure Monsieur Octave will make allowances.'

The girl attacked the piece without the least sign of nervousness; even though her mother never took her eyes off her, looking like a sergeant ready to punish with a slap the least technical blunder. What mortified her was that the instrument, cracked and wheezy after fifteen years of daily scale-playing, didn't have the sonorous quality of tone of the Duveyriers' grand piano. And in Madame Josserand's view her daughter never played loud enough.

After the tenth bar Octave, with a rapt expression, and tilting his head at the more florid passages, was no longer listening. He watched the audience, noting the polite efforts to pay attention on the part of the men, and the affected delight of the women. He surveyed this collection of human beings left alone with their thoughts, free from their daily chores, which had deepened the gloom of their tired faces. The mothers, it was plain, cherished fond dreams of marrying off their daughters, as they stood there with mouths agape and ferocious teeth, unconsciously letting themselves go. This was the all-consuming passion of this drawing-room: these bourgeois women's ravenous appetite for sons-in-law, as they sat there listening to the piano's asthmatic utterances. Their daughters started to doze off, as their heads drooped and they forgot to hold themselves upright. Octave, who despised novices, took a greater interest in Valérie. Plain she certainly was, in that extraordinary yellow silk dress, trimmed with black satin; but she was strangely attractive and his eyes kept wandering back to her, noting her vaguely neurotic smile as she listened to the shrill music.

Then there was a catastrophe. The bell rang outside, and a gentleman entered without warning.

'Oh, doctor!' said Madame Josserand, barely able to hide her irritation.

Doctor Juillerat bowed his excuses, and remained stationary. At that very moment Berthe dwelled lingeringly on a phrase as it died away, which her listeners greeted with a buzz of approval. 'Charming!' 'Delightful!' Madame Juzeur assumed a languishing attitude, as though someone were tickling her. Hortense, sullenly turning over the score for her sister, remained unmoved by the surging torrent of notes, with one ear cocked for the sound of the door-bell; and when the doctor came in, her gesture of disappointment was so marked that she tore one of the pages. Then suddenly the piano trembled beneath the hammering of Berthe's frail fingers. The little rêverie had come to an end in a deafening crash of furious harmonies.

There was a moment's hesitation, before the audience came to life. Had it really finished? Then came a shower of compliments.

'Quite lovely!' 'Oh! What talent!'

'Mademoiselle really plays wonderfully well,' said Octave, no longer free just to watch the scene. 'No one has ever given me such pleasure before.'

'Yes, indeed! That's how we all feel,' purred Madame Josserand. 'She plays that really quite well, if I don't say so myself . . . But, then, anything she's ever wanted, any artistic skill she wished to develop, we've refused her nothing . . . Oh! Monsieur Octave, if only you were to get to know her better . . .'

Once more a confused sound of voices filled the room. Berthe coolly accepted the collective praise and remained at the piano, waiting for her mother to relieve her. The latter was just telling Octave of the astonishing brilliance with which her daughter played 'The Reapers', when a dull, far-off sound of knocking created some commotion among the guests.

Every minute the noise grew louder, as if someone were trying to break open a door. The guests were silent, and exchanged questioning glances.

'What ever can that be?' Valérie ventured to enquire. 'You could hear that knocking just a minute ago while the music was coming to an end.'

Madame Josserand had turned quite pale. She had recognised Saturnin's lusty blows. Wretched lunatic that he was. She had a vision of him rushing into the room among her guests. If he went on thumping like that, there was another marriage knocked on the head.

'It's the kitchen door that keeps banging,' she said, with a forced smile. 'Adèle always forgets to shut it. Just go and see will you Berthe.'

Her daughter, who had also understood the situation, got up and went out of the room. The knocking ceased at once, but she didn't immediately come back. Uncle Bachelard, not content with his loud remarks during the performance of 'The Banks of the Oise' now finally outraged his sister by shouting out to Gueulin that he was bored to death, and was going to get himself some grog. They both returned to the dining-room, slamming the door behind them.

'Dear old Narcisse – such a character!' said Madame Josserand to Valérie and Madame Juzeur, as she sat down between them. 'He's so busy with his financial affairs! You know, he's made nearly a hundred thousand francs this year!'

Free at last, Octave had hurried to rejoin Trublot, lolling

drowsily on a sofa. Near them a group surrounded Doctor Juillerat, the old physician of the neighbourhood, a man of mediocre ability, but who had gradually put together a thriving practice, having attended all the mothers in their confinements, and prescribed remedies for all their daughters' ills. He was known as a specialist in feminine complaints, so that when he was out socially he was besieged by husbands taking him into a corner to obtain some free medical advice. Théophile was just telling him that Valérie had had another attack yesterday; she always struggled for breath, complaining of a lump in her throat. Although he was not very well himself, his own symptoms were quite different. But that prompted him to start talking about himself and the terrible luck he'd had. First, he had begun to study law, then dabbled in industry at an iron-foundry, tried administrative work at the pawnbroker's. After taking up photography, he then believed he had discovered a patent for driverless cabs but while that was being developed he earned commission by selling piano-flutes, invented by one of his friends. Finally he returned to the subject of his wife; it was her fault if success always eluded them, her perpetual nervous seizures were enough to kill him.

'Do give her something, doctor,' he pleaded, with a malevolent light in his eye, coughing and moaning in his impotent rage.

Trublot scrutinised him, full of disdain, laughing inwardly as he looked at Octave. Doctor Juillerat, meanwhile, was uttering vague and soothing words; doubtless some efficacious remedy could be administered to the dear lady. At the age of fourteen she used to have similar attacks at the shop in the Rue Neuve-Saint-Augustin; he had treated her for fainting fits which had led to nose bleeds. And as Théophile recalled in despair her languid sweetness as a girl, while now he could hardly bear her flighty changes of mood twenty times a day, the doctor was content to nod his head. Marriage did not agree with every woman.

'Astonishing!' murmured Trublot. 'What with a father worn down by hawking needles and cottons for thirty years, and a mother whose face was always a mass of pimples, and living in that stuffy hole of a shop – how do you suppose such people could produce healthy daughters?'

Octave was taken aback. He had begun to lose some of his respect for this drawing-room, which he had entered with all

the awe of a provincial. But his curiosity was aroused when he
saw Campardon consulting the doctor in his turn, whispering,
however, like a person of some public importance who did not
wish anyone to know of his domestic disasters.

'By the way,' said Octave to Trublot, 'as you seem to know
everything, do tell me what's the matter with Madame Campardon. Whenever her ill-health is mentioned I notice that everyone
assumes an expression of profound pity.'

'Why, my dear fellow,' replied the young man, 'she's got . . .'

And he whispered in Octave's ear. At first his listener smiled,
then his face lengthened in profound amazement.

'Surely not!' he said.

Whereupon Trublot declared upon his word of honour that
that's what the problem was. He knew another lady who had
the same thing.

'Besides,' he added, 'after a confinement it does sometimes
happen that . . .'

And he began to whisper again. Octave, no longer in doubt,
felt sad. For a moment there, he had imagined the plot of a
whole novel: the architect busy elsewhere, and encouraging him
to console his wife! At any rate, he could feel sure that her
honour was safe. The young men pressed closer against each
other in the excitement of unveiling these feminine secrets,
oblivious of the risk of being overheard.

Just then Madame Juzeur was imparting to Madame Josserand her impressions of Octave. She certainly thought him most
agreeable, but she preferred Monsieur Auguste Vabre. The latter
stood, mute and insignificant, in a corner of the room, with his
usual evening headache.

'What I find surprising, my dear, is that you haven't thought
of him for your daughter Berthe. A young man already established in business and not the kind to take risks. He wants a
wife, too. I know that he's keen to get married.'

Madame Josserand listened in surprise. She had really never
thought of the haberdasher. Madame Juzeur, however, was
insistent, for whatever her own misfortune, all she wanted to do
was to work for the happiness of other women, so that she took
an interest in all the romantic goings-on in the house. She
declared that Auguste had never once taken his eyes off Berthe.
In short, she brought her own experience of men to bear upon
the subject; Monsieur Mouret would never let himself be caught,

whereas a match with the nice Monsieur Vabre would be both easy and advantageous. But Madame Josserand, weighing up Vabre with her eyes, felt quite sure that a son-in-law of that sort would never enhance her drawing-room.

'My daughter detests him,' she said, 'and I would never go against her feelings.'

A gawky young woman had just played a fantasia based on the *Dame Blanche*.* Uncle Bachelard having fallen asleep in the dining-room, Gueulin came back with his flute and started to imitate the noise of a nightingale. Nobody listened, however; the Bonnaud story was going the rounds. it had quite upset Monsieur Josserand; fathers held up their hands in horror, while mothers gasped for breath. What! Bonnaud's son-in-law was a clown! Who could you trust nowadays? These parents desperate to marry off their children were faced by the nightmare of finding a convict disguised in evening dress. As a matter of fact, Bonnaud had been so delighted to get rid of his daughter that the flimsiest of references had sufficed him, despite his attention to detail as a fussy accountant-in-chief.

'Mamma, tea is ready,' said Berthe, as she and Adèle opened the folding doors.

Then, as people slowly passed into the dining-room, she went up to her mother and whispered: 'I've had about enough of it. He wants me to stay and tell him stories, or else he says he'll smash up everything.'

On a grey cloth, too small for the table, one of those laboriously served teas was spread, with a *brioche* bought at a neighbouring baker's and flanked by sandwiches and little cakes. At either end of the table were flowers in profusion; roses of great beauty and great price prevented one from noticing the stale biscuits and rancid butter. The reaction was one of envy and spite; those Josserands were simply ruining themselves in their attempt to marry off their daughters. And the guests, throwing sidelong glances at the flowers, imbibed the weak tea and gorged themselves on the stale buns and badly baked *brioche*; for they had only had a small bite to eat before going out, and their one thought was to go to bed with their bellies full. For those who did not like tea, Adèle handed round redcurrant syrup in glasses. This was pronounced excellent.

Meanwhile the uncle slumbered in a corner. Far from waking him, they politely pretended not to see him at all. One lady spoke of how tiring business was. Berthe was most attentive, handing round sandwiches, carrying cups of tea, asking the men if they would like any more sugar. But she couldn't attend to everybody, and Madame Josserand kept looking for Hortense, until she suddenly spotted her in the centre of the empty drawing-room talking to a gentleman whose back alone was visible.

'Ah! Yes, I see,' her mother blurted out angrily, 'he's come at last!'

The guests began to whisper. It was that Verdier, who had been living with a woman for fifteen years, while waiting to marry Hortense. Everybody knew the story, and the young women exchanged significant glances; but for propriety's sake they remained tight-lipped. When Octave had been put in the picture, he watched the gentleman's back with interest. Trublot knew the woman involved, a good soul, a reformed prostitute, now as clean-living as the best of wives, looking after her man and keeping his shirts in order. He was full of fraternal sympathy for her. In the line of sight those in the dining-room, Hortense was rebuking Verdier for being so late, with the peevishness of the well-bred maiden.

'Ah! Redcurrant syrup,' said Trublot, observing Adèle in front of him, tray in hand. Sniffing at it, he declined. But, as Adèle turned round, a corpulent lady's elbow pushed her against him, and he squeezed her hips with some pressure. She smiled, and came back with the tray.

'No, thanks,' he said. 'Later on, perhaps.'

The ladies sat round the table, while the men stayed on their feet behind them, eating. Enthusiastic comments could be heard, stifled as mouths were filled. The men were asked for their opinion.

Madame Josserand exclaimed: 'True; I was forgetting. Come and look, Monsieur Mouret, as you are fond of art.'

'Ah, watch out! That's the watercolour trick,' muttered Trublot, who knew the ritual. But it was even better than a watercolour. As if by chance, there was a porcelain bowl on the table, and inside it, in a mount of newly varnished bronze, there was a copy of Greuze's *Girl with Broken Pitcher** painted in washy tints varying from lilac to blue. At the chorus of praise, Berthe smiled.

'Mademoiselle possesses every gift,' said Octave, putting on his best manners. 'How well the colours are blended. And an exact likeness, too.'

'Well, at least, as far as the detail of the composition is concerned,' said Madame Josserand, exultant. 'There's not a hair too many or too few. Berthe copied it at home from an engraving. At the Louvre, you know, there are really too many nudes and all sorts of people you wouldn't normaly mix with.' She lowered her voice during this running commentary, anxious to assure the young man that although her daughter was artistic that didn't mean she embraced the moral values of artists. However, Octave, she thought, seemed indifferent; she felt, somehow, that the bowl had not made its mark, and she watched him anxiously, while Valérie and Madame Juzeur, who had got to their fourth cup of tea, were twittering with admiration as they examined Berthe's masterpiece.

'You're looking at her again,' said Trublot to Octave, whose eyes were riveted on Valérie.

'So I am,' he replied, somewhat embarrassed. 'A funny thing, but just at this moment she looks quite pretty. You can spot a passionate woman when you see one. What do you reckon? Do you think one might risk having a go?'

Trublot puffed out his cheeks. 'Who knows whether she's passionate. Strange you should be tempted. But, anyway, I suppose it's better than marrying the young miss.'

'What young miss?' cried Octave, forgetting himself. 'Do you really think I'm going to let myself be trapped? Never. We don't go in for marriage down in Marseilles.'

Madame Josserand, standing close by, overheard that last phrase. It stabbed her like a knife. Another fruitless campaign, another evening wasted on entertaining. The blow was such that she had to lean against a chair as she ruefully surveyed the table, swept clean of every morsel of food except the burned top of the *brioche*. She no longer counted her defeats; but this one was going to be the last. And she swore a terrible oath that never again would she feed folk who simply came to her home to stuff themselves. And, in her exasperation, she looked round the room to see if there was a man at whom she could hurl her daughter, when she spied Auguste leaning against the wall, looking miserable and having had nothing to eat.

Just then Berthe, all smiles, was moving towards Octave with a cup of tea in her hand. She was carrying on the campaign according to her mother's instructions. But the latter seized her roughly by the arm, and spoke to her under her breath as if she were some disobedient animal. Then she said out loud, in her most gracious manner: 'Take that cup to Monsieur Vabre, who has been waiting a whole hour.'

Then she took her aside again, threateningly. 'Make yourself agreeable,' she whispered, 'or you'll have me to deal with!'

Berthe, disconcerted for a moment, regained her composure. This change of attack occurred as often as three times an evening. She took the cup of tea to Auguste, together with the smile that she had begun to wear for Octave. She made herself most agreeable, talked about Lyons silks* and played the role of an engaging young lady who would look charming behind a counter. Auguste's hands trembled somewhat, and his face flushed, as that evening he had a worse headache than usual.

Out of politeness, some of the guests went and sat down again for a moment in the drawing-room. They had had their food, and now it was time to go. When they looked for Verdier he had already left, and the young women, in their merriment, could only take away with them the blurred impression of his back. Without waiting for Octave, Campardon made his way out with the doctor, keeping him in conversation on the staircase to ask if there was really no hope. During tea one of the lamps had gone out, giving off an odour of rancid oil; the other lamp, with its burned wick, gave such a lugubrious light that even the Vabres rose to go, despite the profuse attentions of Madame Josserand. Octave, preceding them, had reached the ante-room, where a surprise was in store for him. Trublot, who was looking for his hat, suddenly disappeared. He could only have made his exit by the passage leading to the kitchen.

'Where's he gone? Does he use the servants' staircase?' murmured Octave to himself.

However, he thought no more about it. Valérie was there, looking for her Chinese crepe shawl. The two brothers, Théophile and Auguste, without waiting for her, were going downstairs. Having found the shawl, the young man presented it to her with the air of rapture with which he served pretty customers at 'Au Bonheur des Dames'. She looked at him, and he felt certain that her eyes, as they met his, were glowing.

'You are too kind, sir,' she said simply.

Madame Juzeur, who was the last to leave, enveloped them

both with a smile at once tender and discreet. And when Octave, his interest kindled, had got back to his cold bedroom, he glanced at himself in the mirror, and determined to have a go!

Meanwhile, mute, and storming about like a gale, Madame Josserand paced up and down the deserted room. She shut the piano with a bang, put out the last lamp, and then going into the dining-room, began to blow out the candles with such vehemence that they shook in their holders. The sight of the empty table, with its disarray of plates and empty teacups, only enraged her further, and, as she walked round, she flung terrible glances at her daughter Hortense, who sat calmly crunching the burned top of the *brioche*.

'You're working yourself up into a rage again, Mamma,' said the latter. 'Is something wrong? I'm quite happy. He's going to buy her some chemises so as to get rid of her.'

The mother shrugged her shoulders.

'Ah!' continued Hortense. 'You'll say that that proves nothing. All right, you do it your way and I'll do it mine. Now that's what I call a vile *brioche*. People who eat such filth can't be accused of squeamishness.'

Worn out by his wife's social occasion, Monsieur Josserand leaned back in his chair, dreading another argument, or that Madame Josserand might sweep him away in her tempestuous rounds of the apartment; so he joined Bachelard and Gueulin, who were sitting at the table opposite Hortense. On waking, the uncle had found a flask of rum, and, while emptying it, returned to the bitter subject of the twenty francs.

'It's not the money I mind,' he kept repeating to his nephew, 'but it's the way they did it. You know how I am with women; I'd give them the very shirt off my back, but I don't like them to ask like that. As soon as they begin asking, it annoys me, and I wouldn't give them a farthing.'

And when his sister began reminding him of his promises: 'Hold your tongue, Eléonore!' he rapped out. 'I know what my duty is as far as that child is concerned. But when a woman asks like that, it's more than I can stand. I've always got rid of them, haven't I, Gueulin? And besides, people are so disrespectful! Why, Léon has not even condescended to wish me many happy returns of the day!'

With clenched fists, Madame Josserand resumed her march. It was true; Léon had promised to come, but, like the others, had let her down. There was someone who wouldn't give up an evening even to get one of his sisters married! She had just found a little cake, which had fallen behind one of the vases, and was locking it up in a drawer, when Berthe, who had gone to set Saturnin free, brought him back with her. She was trying to soothe him, as, with a haggard look of mistrust in his eyes, he feverishly hunted about the corners of the room like a dog shut up for too long.

'How silly he is!' said Berthe; 'he thinks that I've just been married, and he's looking for the husband! There, there, dear Saturnin, look as much as you like! Didn't I tell you that it had all come to nothing. You know very well that it never *does* come to anything!'

Then Madame Josserand exploded: 'Ah, but it shan't come to nothing this time, that I swear! Even if I have to hook him on to you myself! He's the one who's going to pay for all the others. Yes, yes, Monsieur Josserand, you may stare, as if you didn't understand. The wedding will happen and, if you don't approve it, you can stay away. So, Berthe, just get on with it, do you hear?'

Saturnin didn't seem to be aware of what was going on. He was looking under the table. The girl pointed to him, but Madame Josserand made a sign as if to say that they would get rid of him.

And Berthe murmured: 'So it's settled, is it, that it's to be Monsieur Vabre? It's all the same to me. But I do think you might have managed to save me just one sandwich!'

Next day Octave began his campaign to get Valérie. He took note of her movements, and found out the time when he was likely to meet her on the staircase, managing to go up frequently to his room, either when lunching at the Campardons' or when he could find a pretext to get away from 'Au Bonheur des Dames'. He soon noticed that every day, about two o'clock, when taking her child to the Tuileries Gardens, the young woman went down the Rue Gaillon. Accordingly, he used to stand at the door and wait for her, greeting her, like a handsome shop assistant with a gallant smile. Every time they met, Valérie politely nodded her head, but never stopped, though he reckoned that her dark glance was smouldering with passion, and he found encouragement in her unhealthy complexion and the supple undulation of her hips.

He had already made his plan – the bold one of a seducer used to the cavalier conquest of a shop-girl virtue. It was merely a question of luring Valérie into his room on the fourth floor; the staircase was always quiet and deserted, and up there nobody would ever catch them. He laughed inwardly as he thought of the architect's moral advice; for having a woman who lived in the house was not the same as bringing one into it.

There was one thing, however, that made him uneasy. The Pichons' kitchen was separated from their dining-room by the corridor which meant their door was often open. At nine in the morning Pichon went off to his office, not returning until about five o'clock. Every other night of the week he went out after dinner, from eight to twelve, to do some book-keeping. Moreover, as soon as she heard Octave coming, his wife, who was shy and reserved, would push the door to, so that he only got a glimpse of her disappearing back and her light hair in its tight little knot.

Through the half-opened door so far he'd only seen a few corners, some spotless but sad-looking furniture, a pile of off-white linen lying in a pool of grey light from a window out of sight, the edge of a cot, at the back of an inner room – in fact, all the banal signs of a lonely woman busying herself from morning till night with the petty cares of a clerk's household. But not a sound was to be heard; the child seemed as silent and apathetic as its mother. Sometimes one could just hear her humming some tune for hours on end in a feeble voice. Octave, however, was none the less furious with 'Miss High and Mighty', as he called her. Perhaps she was playing the spy. In any case, Valérie could never come up to his room if the Pichons' door was always being opened in this way.

He had just begun to think that progress was being made. One Sunday, in the husband's absence, he had managed to be on the first-floor landing just as Valérie, in her dressing-gown, was leaving her sister-in-law's to return to her own apartment. She was obliged to speak to him, and they had exchanged a few polite remarks. Next time he hoped that she might ask him in. With a woman of her temperament the rest would follow as a matter of course.

During dinner that evening at the Campardons', they started talking about Valérie, so Octave tried to draw them out. But as Angèle was listening, and looking slyly at Lisa, who gravely handed round the roast mutton, the parents at first were lavish with praise. Besides, the architect was always going on about how respectable the house was, with the conceited assurance of a tenant who appeared to derive from this a certificate of his own moral probity.

'Most respectable people, my dear boy! You met them at the Josserands. The husband is no fool – a man full of ideas. Some day he'll make some great discovery. As for the wife, she's got class, as we artists might say.'

Then Madame Campardon, rather worse today and half recumbent, though her illness did not prevent her from eating great slices of red meat, languidly murmured, in her turn: 'Poor Monsieur Théophile! He's like me; he just drags himself around. And Valérie deserves a lot of credit, for it can't be much fun for her to be tied to a man who's always shaking with fever, and whose ailments make him peevish and difficult.'

During dessert Octave, seated between husband and wife, got to know more than he'd asked. They forgot Angèle's presence, and started to play with words, winking to underline their double meaning; and if these failed them, they whispered to him, confidentially, spelling out the crude facts of the matter. In short, Théophile was an impotent idiot, who deserved to be what his wife had made him. As for Valérie, she was pretty worthless and would have behaved just as scandalously, even if her husband had been able to satisfy her, unable as she was to resist her natural impulses. What's more, it was common knowledge that, two months after her marriage, and realising that she could never have a child by her husband, which meant she would lose her share of old Vabre's fortune if Théophile happened to die, she had her little Camille made for her by a brawny young butcher's assistant from the Rue Sainte-Anne.

Finally, Campardon whispered in Octave's ear: 'In short, you know, my dear fellow, a case of female hysteria!'

He pronounced this word meaningfully, revelling in the scandalous suggestion of middle-class indecency, all the time grinning like a family man whose imagination, suddenly unleashed, conjures up pictures of lascivious orgies. Angèle looked down at her plate, fearing to catch Lisa's eye in case she laughed. The conversation then moved on to the Pichons, for whom they had nothing but praise.

'Oh, what fine people!' repeated Madame Campardon. 'Sometimes, when Marie takes her little Lilitte out for a walk, I let Angèle go with her. And I can assure you, Monsieur Mouret, I wouldn't trust my daughter to just anybody. I have to be absolutely certain that their morals are unquestionable. You're very fond of Marie, aren't you, Angèle?'

'Yes, Mamma,' she replied.

But that wasn't all. It would be impossible to find a woman who was better bred, or who had stricter principles. And how happy her husband was! What a lovely sweet couple; they adored each other, and never had a cross word to say!

'Besides, if they weren't exemplary, they wouldn't be allowed to stay here,' declared the architect gravely, forgetting what he'd just said about Valérie. 'We only want decent folk in this building. I would give my notice the same day if my daughter ran into anybody disreputable on the stairs.'

That very evening he had made secret arrangements to take cousin Gasparine to the Opéra-Comique.* So off he went to fetch his hat, saying something about a business arrangement, which might detain him until very late. However, Rose must have been in the know, for Octave heard her murmur, in her resigned, motherly way, as Campardon stooped to kiss her with his usual effusive tenderness: 'Have a good time and don't catch cold after the performance.'

Next morning Octave had an idea. It was to make Madame Pichon's acquaintance by doing her some trifling neighbourly service; and thus, if she ever caught Valérie, she would keep her eyes shut. That very day an opportunity presented itself. She was in the habit of taking out her Lilitte, aged eighteen months, in a wicker pram, a process that infuriated Monsieur Gourd, adamant that it shouldn't be brought through the main staircase, so that Madame Pichon had to use the servants' entrance. Moreover, as the door of her apartment was too narrow, she had to take off the wheels every time, which was quite a business. On this particular day, as Octave was coming home, he found Marie with her gloves on having trouble unscrewing the wheels. When she sensed him standing behind her, waiting to get by, her hands trembled, and she quite lost her head.

'But why go to all that trouble?' he asked, at length. 'It would be far simpler to leave the pram at the end of the passage, behind my door.'

She didn't reply, but remained in a squatting position, excessive timidity preventing her from standing up, and under the flaps of her bonnet he noticed that her neck and ears were flushed.

Then he insisted: 'I assure you, madame, that it will not inconvenience me in the least.'

Without more ado, he got hold of the pram and carried it off. She had no choice but to follow him, so astounded by this startling event in her humdrum existence that all she could do was stammer out a few disjointed phrases: 'Dear me, I didn't meant to cause you such inconvenience . . . I'm so embarrassed . . . It'll be in your way . . . My husband will be so pleased . . .'

And she went back in to her apartment, almost half-ashamed, this time tightly fastening the door behind her. Octave thought she must be stupid. The pram was very much in his way, for it prevented him from fully opening his own door, and he had to get through it sideways. But he seemed to have won over his neighbour not least because Monsieur Gourd, thanks to Campardon's influence, had graciously consented to sanction this obstruction at the end of this out-of-the-way passage.

Every Sunday Marie's parents, Monsieur and Madame Vuillaume, used to come and spend the day with her. On the following Sunday, as Octave was going out, he noticed the whole family just about to have their coffee, and was discreetly hurrying past, when the young wife hastily whispered something to her husband. The latter immediately came to the door.

'Do forgive me, sir. I'm always out, and haven't yet had an opportunity of thanking you; but I did want to tell you how pleased I was . . .'

Octave, protesting, was obliged to go in, and, though he had already had some, to accept a cup of coffee, and the place of honour between Monsieur and Madame Vuillaume. Facing him on the opposite side of the round table, Marie had one of her sudden fits of embarrassment, which for no apparent reason sent all the blood from her heart to her face. She never seemed at her ease, and Octave agreed with Trublot that she was certainly not his ideal; she looked so weak and washed-out, with her flat chest and scanty hair, though her features were delicate, even pretty. When she had somewhat regained her composure, she began giggling, as she went on and on about the pram incident.

'Jules, if you could just have seen the way that Monsieur Mouret whipped it up in his arms! My goodness, it was done in a flash!'

Pichon reiterated his thanks. He was tall and thin, with a mournful expression, already crushed by the dull routine of office life, and his lacklustre eyes had the dumb resignation of a broken-down cab-horse.

'Oh! Please let's not talk about it any more,' Octave said at last. 'It's really not worth mentioning. Your coffee, madame, is delicious; it's the best I've ever had.'

Marie blushed again, so violently this time that even her hands grew rosy pink.

'Don't flatter her,' said Monsieur Vuillaume, gravely. 'Her coffee's good enough, but I've had better. You see how conceited she's grown all of a sudden.'

'Pride had a fall,' observed Madame Vuillaume, sententiously. 'We've always taught her to be modest.'

They were both little, shrivelled, grey-faced old people – the mother squeezed into a black gown, and her husband wearing an undersized frock-coat, with a large red ribbon at his buttonhole.

'Just look at me,' he said. 'I was decorated at the age of sixty, the day I got my pension, after thirty-nine years' service as a senior clerk at the Ministry of Education. Well, let me tell you, that day I dined just as usual, without letting my pride interfere with my ordinary habits. The Legion d'Honneur* was my due; of that I was well aware. I simply felt profoundly grateful.'

His record was untarnished, and he didn't want to keep it a secret. After twenty-five years' service his salary had been raised to four thousand francs. His pension amounted to two thousand. But he'd been obliged to re-enter the service on a lower grade, with a salary of fifteen hundred, as little Marie had been born to them late in life, when Madame Vuillaume had given up all hope of having either a girl or a boy. Now that the child had got a home of her own, they lived in a smaller place on the Rue Durantin, in Montmartre, where their pension went rather further.

'And I'm seventy-six years old,' he said, by way of conclusion. 'So there, my dear son-in-law, think of that.'

Pichon, tired and silent, just looked at the decoration in the old man's buttonhole. Yes, that would be his life story too if fortune favoured him. He was the youngest son of a green-grocer's widow who'd spent everything she'd had on his education, all her neighbours having pronounced him to be such an intelligent lad, and who had died penniless a week before he triumphantly got his degree at the Sorbonne. After three years of surviving all that his uncle could throw at him, he'd had the good luck to get a government appointment, which ought to lead to great things. He had already married on the strength of it.

'We do our duty, and the government do theirs,' he murmured, as he mechanically calculated that he would have another thirty-six years to wait before he could be decorated and obtain a pension of two thousand francs.

Then, turning to Octave, he said: 'It's children, you know, that are such a burden.'

'Of course they are,' remarked Madame Vuillaume. 'If we had had another, we should certainly never have been able to make ends meet. Don't you remember, Jules, what I made you promise when I gave you our Marie; one child and no more, or else we shall fall out. It's only the working classes that have as many children as a hen lays eggs, regardless of their cost, and then let them roam the streets like animals. I find it disgusting.'

Octave looked at Marie, thinking that so sensitive a subject would have brought rosy blushes to her cheeks. But her face was innocently pale, as she serenely agreed with her mother's remarks. He was bored to death and didn't know how to escape. There, in their chilly little dining-room, these people would spend the whole afternoon, chatting desultorily about nothing very much except their money. Even dominoes were too much of a distraction.

It was now Madame Vuillaume's turn to air her views. After a long silence which was the natural pause for reflection characteristic of their discussions, she began: 'You don't have any children; Monsieur Mouret? Ah, that'll come later. Oh, it's a great responsibility, especially for a mother! When my little girl was born I was forty-nine, an age when life's lessons have been learned. A boy, you know, can fend for himself, but a girl! And for her I was certainly able to do my duty!'

Then, in clipped sentences, she declared her educational principles. Propriety first of all. No playing about on the staircase, the child always at home and closely looked after her, for kids are always up to mischief. Doors and windows tightly shut; keep out nasty draughts from the street. Out of doors, never let go of a little girl's hand, and get her used to casting her eyes downwards so as to avoid seeing anything improper. Religion, useful as a moral check, ought not to be overdone. As she grows up, governesses must be engaged for she should never be sent to a boarding-school, where innocent children are corrupted. Then one should be present during her lessons, to see that she stays ignorant of certain things; all newspapers to be hidden, of course, and the bookcase locked.

'A girl always know too much,' declared the old lady, in conclusion.

While her mother was talking, Marie looked dreamily into space. In her mind's eye, she was back in the narrow cloistered rooms in the Rue Durantin, where she wasn't even allowed to look out of the window. Hers was a dreary childhood; all sorts of precautions that made no sense; lines in their fashion journal which her mother had scratched out, lines of black ink that made her blush; pieces cut out of her lessons which proved embarrassing even to her governesses when she asked them questions. But, on the whole, there was a sweetness about her childhood, a soft tepid greenhouse growth, a waking dream in which everyday words and deeds assumed a distorted, uninformed significance. And, even now, as all those memories came back to her, the distant smile on her face was that of a child, as ignorant after marriage as she had been before.

'You may not believe it,' said Monsieur Vuillaume, 'but when my daughter turned eighteen, she hadn't read a single novel. Had you, Marie?'

'No, Papa.'

Then he continued: 'I do have a very nicely bound edition of George Sand,* and, despite her mother's fears, I did allow her, some months before her marriage, to read *André*, a harmless work, uplifting and not based on reality. I'm all for a liberal education, you know. Literature certainly has its claims. Well, the book had a most extraordinary effect upon her. She used to cry at night in her sleep – proof that there's nothing like having a pure, unsullied imagination, in order to understand genius.' ·

'It's such a beautiful book,' murmured Marie with sparkling eyes.

But when Pichon expounded his own theory, no, no novels at all before marriage and every kind of novel after it, Madame Vuillaume gave a nod of dissent. She never read at all, and was quite happy. Marie gently alluded to her loneliness.

'Dear me! I sometimes get hold of a book to read. But Jules, you know, chooses one for me from the lending library in the Passage Choiseul. If only I could play the piano.'

For some time Ocatve had been looking for an opportunity to say something.

'Why, how can it be that you don't?'

The question was an embarrassing one. The parents spoke of unfortunate circumstances, not wishing to admit that they had been afraid of the expense. However, Madame Vuillaume was anxious to make it clear that Marie had sung ever since she was born, while as a little girl she knew all sorts of pretty songs by heart. She had only to hear a tune once in order to remember it; there was that song about Spain and the lady in the tower mourning for her paramour which the child sang with such expression that she drew tears from the hardest of hearts.

But Marie remained disconsolate. Pointing to the adjoining room where her baby was sleeping, she cried: 'Ah, I swear that Lilitte will learn how to play the piano, whatever sacrifices I have to make.'

'First of all, think of bringing her up as we did you,' said Madame Vuillaume, severely. 'Of course, I've got nothing against music; it develops feelings. But, above all, keep a close eye on your daughter; make sure she breathes only the purest air and see to it that she remains ignorant.'

Then she began all over again, this time laying further stress on religion, the requisite number of confessions to go to each month, what Masses it was unthinkable to miss – all such rules being dictated by propriety. Octave could bear it no longer; he was very sorry, he had an appointment. His ears buzzed from sheer boredom and it was clear that they would go on talking like this until the evening. So he made an escape, leaving the Vuillaumes and Pichons chatting, slowly emptying their coffee cups, just as they did every Sunday. As he made his final bow, Marie, for no reason whatever, suddenly blushed violently.

After this experience, on Sundays Octave would always hurry past the Pichons' door, especially if he heard the rasping voices of the Vuillaumes. Besides, his main goal was the conquest of Valérie. Despite the burning glances, apparently directed at him, she was mysteriously reserved; she seemed to be leading him a merry dance. One day, he met her by chance in the Tuileries Gardens, and when she began to talk calmly about the storm the previous night, this confirmed him in his view that she was supremely good at playing the coquette. He seemed to spend his life going down the staircase, waiting for the moment to get inside her apartment, determined as he now was to force the issue if necessary.

Every time he went by, Marie blushed and smiled at him. They nodded to each other in neighbourly fashion. Late one morning, shortly before lunch, as he was bringing her a letter to save Monsieur Gourd the long haul up to the fourth floor, he found her distraught. She had just placed Lilitte on the round table in her underwear and was trying to put the child's clothes back on.

'What's the matter?' he asked.

'Oh, it's just that I was silly enough to undress Lilitte because she was fretful. And I don't know what to do next.'

He looked at her in astonishment. She kept turning the child's petticoat over and over, trying to find the hooks and eyes.

Then she added: 'You see, her father always helps me to dress her in the morning, before he goes off. I never have to see to it all by myself. It's such a bother and it gets me so upset!'

The little girl, tired of being in her chemise, and frightened at seeing Octave, struggled and fell backwards on the table.

'Look out,' he cried, 'she's going to fall.'

A catastrophe seemed imminent. Marie seemed frightened to touch the naked limbs of her child. She gazed at her in maidenly wonderment, amazed at having been able to produce such a thing. Besides the fear of harming the child, there was in her awkwardness a certain vague repugnance towards its living flesh. However, helped by Octave, who soothed Lilitte, she was able to dress her again.

'How will you manage when you have a dozen?' he laughed.

'But we're never going to have any more!' she replied in a frightened tone.

Then he teased her, telling her you could never be sure; it was easy to make a little baby!

'No, no,' she repeated obstinately. 'You heard what Mamma said the other day. She told Jules that it was out of the question. You don't know her, but I can tell you that there would be endless squabbles if I had another baby.'

Octave was amused at the calm way in which she discussed the matter. He couldn't even succeed in embarrassing her. Whatever her husband wished, she would do. She was fond of children, of course, and if he wanted any more, she wouldn't say no. And yet what came through this compliance with her mother's orders was the indifference of a woman whose maternal instincts had not yet been roused. Lilitte had to be looked after in the same way as her home, a mere duty to be done. When she had washed up the crockery, and had taken the child for a walk, she reverted to her former life: a somnolent, empty existence, lulled by adolescent expectations of bliss. When Octave observed that she must find it very dull always being alone, she seemed surprised. Oh, no, it was never dull! The days slipped by somehow. Then on Sundays she either went out with her husband, or her parents came or else she had a book to read. If reading had not been responsible for her headache, she would have read from morning till night, now that she was allowed to read every sort of book.

'The annoying thing is,' she continued, 'that they have got nothing at the lending library in the Passage Choiseul. I wanted

to read *André* again, for instance, just because it made me cry
so much when I first read it. Well, that's the very volume that
has been stolen; and my father won't lend me his copy because
Lilitte might tear out the pictures.'

'It so happens that my friend Campardon has got all George
Sand's works,' said Octave. 'I'll ask him to lend me *André* for
you.'

She blushed again, and her eyes sparkled. It was really too
kind of him! And when he left her, she remained there standing,
looking at Lilitte, without an idea in her head, as she would do
this, and every other, afternoon. She hated sewing, but used to
crochet which explained why the same little scrap of wool was
always lying about.

The following day, which was a Sunday, Octave brought her
the book. Pichon had been obliged to go out to make a brief
visit to one of his superiors. Finding her dressed as if she'd just
come in from doing something in the neighbourhood, Octave,
just for curiosity's sake, asked her if she'd been to Mass,
thinking that possibly she was very religious. She said no. Before
her marriage her mother used to take her to church regularly.
And for six months after her marriage she used to go from sheer
force of habit, always afraid of getting there late. Then, she
hardly knew why, after missing two or three times, she stopped
going altogether. Her husband couldn't bear priests, and her
mother no longer mentioned the subject. Octave's question,
however, was a disturbing one, as if it had woken within her
emotions long since buried beneath the indolence of her present
existence.

'I must go to Saint-Roch* one of these days,' she said. 'When
you stop doing something you've got used to, you always miss
it.'

And over the pallid features of this child of elderly parents
there came an expression of sickly regret, of longing for some
other life, dreamed of long ago. Her face could hide nothing,
with her skin as tender and as transparent as that of some
chlorotic patient. Then she impulsively caught hold of Octave's
hand.

'Oh, I must thank you so much for bringing me this book!
Come in tomorrow, after lunch. I'll give it back to you, and tell
you what effect it had on me. I'd like that.'

There was something droll about the woman, thought

Octave, as he left. He had begun to feel interested in her, and he thought of speaking man to man to Pichon, so as to get him to wake her up a bit, for there was no doubt that she only wanted rousing. In fact, he met Pichon the very next day as he was going out, and he walked a part of the way with him, though he himself risked being a quarter of an hour late at 'Au Bonheur des Dames'. Pichon, however, appeared to be even more comatose than his wife, full of incipient manias, and overcome by a dread of dirtying his boots, as it was raining. He walked along on tiptoe, talking incessantly about his sub-director. Octave, whose motives were purely honourable, finally parted company with him in the Rue-Saint-Honoré, after advising him to take Marie as often as possible to the theatre.

'Whatever for?' asked Pichon, in amazement.

'Because it does women good. It makes them nicer.'

'Do you really think so?'

He promised to think about it, and crossed the street, terrified at the thought he might get splashed by a passing cab, this being the main fear in his life.

At lunch-time Octave knocked at the Pichons' door to fetch the book. Marie, with her elbows on the table, her hands in her dishevelled hair, was reading. She had just been eating an egg, cooked in a tin pan which was now lying on the messy table. Lilitte, neglected, was asleep on the floor, her nose touching the fragments of a plate she had no doubt herself smashed.

'Well?' said Octave, enqiringly.

Marie did not immediately reply. She was still in her dressing-gown, which had lost a button, gaping open to reveal the disorder of a woman who has just got out of bed.

'I've only read about a hundred pages,' she said, at last. 'My parents were here yesterday.'

Then she talked in a bitter, mournful way, When she was young, she'd longed to live in the depths of the forest, where she would meet a huntsman sounding his horn. In her dream, he approached and knelt down before her. All this happened in a clearing far, far away, where roses bloomed as in a park. Then in a trice, they were married, and lived on there, wandering about together forever after. She, in her perfect happiness, desired nothing more; while he, both tender and as submissive as a slave, was always at her feet.

'I had a chat with your husband this morning,' said Octave.

'You don't go out enough, and I've persuaded him to take you to the theatre.'

But she shook her head, pale and trembling. There was a silence. The narrow, chilly dining-room was all too real and the dull, decorous figure of Jules suddenly blotted out the huntsman of her romance, the distant sound of whose horn still rang in her ears. At times she would listen; perhaps he was coming. Her husband had never taken her feet in his hands and kissed them, nor had he ever knelt down to tell her that he adored her. She was very fond of him, of course, but it amazed her that love was not more tender.

'The parts that move me in novels,' she said, coming back to the book, 'are the parts where lovers tell each other of their love.'

Octave at last sat down. He wanted to treat the matter as a joke, caring little for such sentimental stuff.

'I can't stand those sweet nothings,' he said. 'If two people adore each other, the best thing is for them to prove it there and then.'

But apparently she didn't understand, as she looked at him with lacklustre eyes. Stretching out his hand, he just touched hers, and leaned close to her to look at a passage in the book, so closely that his breath warmed her bare shoulder. But she remained impassive, cold as a corpse. Then he got up to go, full of a contempt touched with pity.

As he was leaving, she said: 'I read very slowly; I won't have finished it until tomorrow. So it would nice if you could come in the evening.'

Octave certainly had no designs on the woman; and yet, somehow, he was angry with her. He had felt a curious sort of attachment for this young couple, who exasperated him in their stupid contentment. And he resolved to do them a service, in spite of themselves. He would take them out to dinner, get them drunk, and then happily watch them fall into each other's arms. Normally loath to lend anyone even ten francs, Octave took a generous pleasure in squandering money on bringing lovers together and in giving them joy.

However, this coldness on the part of little Madame Pichon led Octave to compare her with the passionate Valérie. Just one nuzzling breath would be enough for her. He was surely making progress as far as Valérie was concerned. One day, as she was

going upstairs ahead of him he had ventured to compliment her
upon her legs without provoking her displeasure.

Finally the long-awaited opportunity came. It was the evening
that Marie had made him promise to come and talk about the
novel when they would be alone, as her husband was not
coming home until very late. But Octave would have preferred
to go out; the mere thought of this literary treat appalled him.
However, about ten o'clock, he thought he might as well go,
when, on the first-floor landing, he met Valérie's maid in quite
a state.

'Madame is in hysterics, master is out, and all the neighbours
have gone to the theatre. Please come and help, as I'm all alone,
and I don't know what to do.'

Valérie was in her bedroom, stretched out in an armchair, her
limbs rigid. The maid had unlaced her stays to ease her breathing. The attack was over almost immediately. She opened her
eyes, seemed surprised to see Octave there, and behaved just as
if he were the doctor.

'I do apologise,' she murmured, in a choking voice. 'This girl's
only been working here since yesterday, and she lost her head.'

Her perfect composure, in taking off her stays and then
buttoning up her dress, disconcerted the young man. He
remained standing, resolved not to lose this opportunity, and
yet not daring to sit down. She had dismissed her maid, the
sight of whom seemed to irritate her, and she went to the
window, inhaling the cool night air in long, nervous gasps, with
her mouth wide open. After a pause, they began to talk. She
first had these attacks when she was fourteen, and Doctor
Juillerat was tired of prescribing drugs for her; sometimes it was
her arms that were affected, and sometimes her loins. However,
she was getting used to them; as well suffer from them as from
anything else, for nobody had perfect health, you know. And as
she talked, the sight of her passive body roused his sensual
appetites, drawn to that disorder, with her leaden complexion
and her features drawn, as if by the exhaustion of a long night
of love. Behind the dark tresses of hair falling on her shoulders,
he thought he could see the puny, beardless face of her husband.
Then, with outstretched arms, he roughly caught her round the
waist, as he would have grabbed some whore.

'What do you think you're doing?'

Now it was her turn to look at him; and, with her cold eyes

and impassive limbs, he felt frozen and awkwardly dropped his hands to his side. The absurdity of his gesture did not escape him.

Then, stifling a last nervous yawn, she slowly murmured: 'Ah, my dear sir, if you only knew!'

And she shrugged her shoulders, showing no sign of anger, but merely a weary contempt for all men. Octave thought she was about to have him thrown out when he saw her go towards the bell-rope, trailing her skirts as she went. But she only wanted some tea, very weak and very hot.

Utterly nonplussed, he muttered some excuse and made for the door, while she lay back in her armchair, like some feverish woman in absolute need of sleep.

As he went upstairs, Octave stopped on each landing. So she wasn't very keen on that, then? He had felt the weight of her indifference without a trace of either desire or resistance, as sexless as his employer Madame Hédouin. Why, then did Campardon say that she suffered from hysteria? How absurd that he'd been taken in by such nonsense! But for the architect's lie he would never have tried it on. And he was so bewildered by the outcome that he was no longer sure he knew anything about female hysteria, whatever he might have been told. But he remembered Trublot's remark: you never knew what to expect from unhinged women of that kind with eyes burning like coals.

On reaching his own floor, Octave, furious at women in general, tried to make as little noise as possible as he passed the Pichons' door. But it opened, and he resigned himself to his fate. Marie stood waiting for him in the little dimly lit room. She had drawn the cot close to the table, and Lilitte lay asleep in the yellow circle of light made by the lamp. The same plates that had done duty at lunch-time must have been used for dinner, for the closed book lay close to a dirty plate filled with the remains of some radishes.

'Have you finished it?' asked Octave, surprised at her silence.

She looked like someone who was intoxicated, with puffy cheeks, as if awaking from a heavy sleep.

'Yes, yes!' she exclaimed with difficulty. 'Oh, I've spent the whole day poring over it! When one is absorbed like that, one hardly knows where one is. Oh, my neck *does* ache!'

She was so exhausted that she had nothing more to say about

the novel; the emotions and confused images that it had provoked in her had almost overwhelmed her. Still ringing in her
ears, she heard the faint clarion notes of her ideal huntsman,
wafted to her across the dim blue landscape of her dreams.
Then, all of a sudden, she mentioned that she'd attended nine
o'clock Mass at Saint-Roch that morning. Ah! How she had
wept; in religion lay the one substitute for all other things.

'But I'm much better now!' she said, sighing deeply as she
stood facing Octave.

There was a pause. She smiled at him with her innocent eyes.
Never had she seemed to him so utterly spineless, with her thin
hair and wishy-washy complexion. Then, as she continued to
gaze at him, her face grew very pale, and she tottered forward,
so that he had to hold out his hands to save her from falling.

'My God! My God!' she sobbed out.

He looked at her in embarrassment.

'You ought to drink a little mint tea to give you back your
strength. This comes of reading too much.'

'Yes, it upset me when, on closing the book, I found myself
alone. How good you are, Monsieur Mouret! Without you, I
should have come to some harm.'

Meanwhile, he looked about for a chair on which to place
her.

'Would you like me to light a fire?'

'No, thank you; it would make your hands dirty; I've noticed
that you always wear gloves.'

The idea brought back that choking sensation at her throat,
and, as she sank down, half swooning, she clumsily launched a
kiss into the air, vaguely, as if in her dream. It just touched
Octave's ear.

The kiss astonished him. The young woman's lips were as
cold as ice. Then, as she fell forward against his chest, offering
herself, he felt a sudden rush of desire, and started to move her
towards the bedroom. But this abruptly checked Marie's surrender. Struggling to resist, her first thought was for her mother
rather than her husband, who would soon come home, and her
daughter asleep at her side.

'No, no, not that! No, it's wrong.'

But he kept saying in his excitement: 'Nobody will ever know;
I shall never tell.'

'No, no, Monsieur Octave! You will spoil our friendship. I'm sure it won't do us any good, and I had dreamed of – oh, other things!'

But he didn't respond, driven by the revenge he was going to take on all women, muttering to himself crudely under his breath: 'I'm going to have you!' And as she wouldn't go into the bedroom with him, he brutally spread her backwards across the table. She gave in, and he enjoyed her there, between the dirty plate and the novel, which fell to the floor when the table shook. The door had stayed open and the solemn silence of the staircase was unbroken. Lilitte lay sleeping peacefully in her cot. When Marie and Octave got up, she with her rumpled petticoats, neither of them spoke. Mechanically she went and looked at her daughter, picked up the plate, and then put it down again. He, too, had nothing to say, feeling equally ill at ease, for this had happened so unexpectedly. And he remembered his unselfish plan to make husband and wife fall into each other's arms.

He finally broke this unbearable silence: 'Why, you didn't even shut the door!'

She looked out on to the landing and stammered: 'No, I didn't, did I. It was open.'

She seemed to walk with difficulty, and on her face there was a look of disgust. Octave reflected that there wasn't much to be said for forcing himself on a helpless, lonely woman. She hadn't even got any pleasure out of it.

'Oh, look! The book's on the floor!' she continued, as she picked the volume up. One of the corners of the binding was crushed and bent. This gave them something to talk about, much to their relief. Marie was visibly upset.

'It wasn't my fault. You see how I'd put a paper cover on it to prevent it getting dirty. We must have knocked it off the table by mistake.'

'I didn't realise it was there,' said Octave. 'It doesn't matter a bit to me; but Campardon looks after his books so carefully.'

Each kept handing the book to the other, and trying to bend the corner straight. Their fingers touched, yet neither felt any emotion. As they thought of the consequences of what had happened, they were both dismayed at the accident which had befallen the beautiful volume of George Sand.

'It was bound to end badly,' said Marie, with tears in her eyes.

Octave felt obliged to console her. He would invent some story or other. Campardon wouldn't savage him. And, as they were about to separate, the feeling of uneasiness returned. One kind word, at least, they would like to have said to each other, but somehow it stuck in their throats. Fortunately, just then they heard a step; it was the husband coming upstairs. Silently Octave put his arms around her again, kissing her on the mouth. And once again she made no effort to resist, her lips as icy cold as before. When he had noiselessly got back to his room, he remarked to himself, as he took off his coat, that apparently here was another woman who didn't like that either. Then what on earth had Marie wanted? And why did she fall into a man's arms? Women were really very strange creatures.

Next day, after lunch at the Campardons', as Octave was again explaining how he had clumsily damaged the book, Marie came in. She was going to take Lilitte to the Tuileries Gardens, and had called to ask if they would let Angèle go with her. She smiled at Octave with perfect self-possession, and glanced innocently at the book lying on a chair.

'Why, of course,' said Madame Campardon. 'I should be delighted. Angèle, go and put on your hat. With you she's quite safe.'

Looking like modesty personified in her simple dark woollen dress, Marie referred to her husband, who had come home late last night and had caught cold. She also mentioned the price of meat; soon people wouldn't be able to afford any at all. Then, after she had left, taking Angèle with her, they all leaned out of the window to see them set off. There was Marie leisurely pushing Lilitte's pram along with her gloved hands, while Angèle, who knew that she was being watched, walked beside her, with downcast eyes.

'Doesn't she look nice!' exclaimed Madame Campardon. 'So ladylike, so respectable!'

Then, slapping Octave on the back, her husband said: 'In a family, education is everything, my dear boy – everything!'

At the Duveyriers' that evening there was a reception and a concert. Octave had been invited for the first time, and about ten o'clock he was just finishing dressing. He was in a serious, half-irritable mood. How was it that he'd got nowhere with Valérie, a woman with so many good connections? And as for Berthe Josserand, hadn't he been a bit hasty in turning down *that* opportunity? Just as he was tying his white tie, the thought of Marie Pichon became positively unbearable to him. Five months in Paris, and only that affair to his credit! He felt ashamed of himself, all too aware of its emptiness and pointlessness. And as he drew on his gloves, he vowed that he was no longer going to waste his time in that way. Now that he'd finally gained entry to high society, he was going to take advantage of the many chances which would come his way.

Marie was looking out for him at the end of the passage. As Pichon was not there, he had to go in for a moment.

'How smart you are!' she whispered.

The Pichons had never been invited to the Duveyriers', so that first-floor world filled her with awe. But she was jealous of no one, having neither the strength nor the will.

'I shall wait up for you,' she said, offering her forehead. 'Don't stay too late; and you must tell me whether you enjoyed yourself.'

Octave had no option but to kiss her hair. Though they had a relationship of sorts, sustained, from his point of view, entirely by the degree of his lust or boredom, they still addressed each other quite formally. At last he went downstairs, and, leaning over the banisters, she followed him with her eyes.

At the same moment quite a drama was being enacted at the Josserands'. According to the mother, the evening at the Duveyriers' was to decide the match between their daughter Berthe and Auguste Vabre. Despite being the object of a rigorous campaign during the past fortnight, the latter was still hesitating, evidently exercised by doubts about the size of the dowry. With a view to striking a decisive blow, Madame Josserand had written to her brother, announcing the projected marriage, and reminding him of his promises, hoping that his reply might provide her with further ammunition. And, at nine o'clock, as the whole family stood round the dining-room stove, already dressed to go downstairs, Monsieur Gourd brought up a letter from Uncle Bachelard, which had been left lying under Madame Gourd's snuff-box ever since the last delivery.

'Ah, at last!' cried Madame Josserand, as she tore open the envelope.

The girls and their father anxiously watched her as she read. Adèle, who had helped the ladies dress, was moving about clumsily as she cleared the dinner table. Madame Josserand turned very pale.

'Not a word!' she stuttered. 'Not a single unambiguous sentence! He says that he will think about it later on, at the time of the marriage. And he sends his love to us all! The crafty bugger!'

Monsieur Josserand, in evening clothes, sank backwards into a chair. Hortense and Berthe, whose legs ached, sat down as well; the one in the blue, the other in pink; those same frocks of theirs refurbished one more time.

'Bachelard is an imposter; I've always said so,' murmured the father. 'He'll never part with a penny.'

Standing there in her flaming red gown, Madame Josserand reread the letter over again. Then she exploded: 'Oh, men! Take my brother, for instance. You'd think he was an idiot, to judge by the life he leads. But no, not a bit of it! He may look like a fool, but he's wide awake enough as soon as you mention money. Oh, men!'

Then she turned towards her daughters, to whom this lesson was addressed.

'I sometimes wonder why you girls are so anxious to get married! Ah, if only you knew how little I've got out of it! I'll tell you what's out there: certainly not a man who'll both love you and bring you a fortune! Oh, no . . . Just millionaire uncles who eat you out of house and home for twenty years, and then refuse to give their nieces a dowry! And totally inadequate husbands, do you hear me, sir, totally inadequate!'

Monsieur Josserand hung his head.

Adèle, not even listening, was finishing clearing away the things. Madame Josserand swerved round furiously at her.

'And what do you think you're doing here, hanging about eavesdropping! Go back to the kitchen at once!'

Then came her summing-up.

'So we women get nothing, not even a crust if we're starving! The only thing men are fit for is to be taken in! So just mark my words!'

Hortense and Berthe nodded as though profoundly impressed by such wisdom. Their mother had long since convinced them of the inferiority of men whose sole fucntion was to take a wife and pay up. There was a long silence in the fusty dining-room, still smelling of the stale food Adèle had left on the table. Sitting about in their finery, the Josserands forgot the Duveyriers' concert as they mulled over life's disappointments. From the adjoining room came the sound of Saturnin, whom they had sent to bed early, snoring.

At last, Berthe spoke. 'So that's the end of that! As there's no point, shouldn't we get out of this lot?'

In an instant Madame Josserand's energy returned. What! Get out of those clothes! Why? Was their family not as good enough to marry into as any other? She would die rather than have this marriage not come off. And she hastily gave them each their parts. The girls were told to make themselves particularly agreeable to Auguste, and not to let go of him until he had taken the plunge. The father was given the task of winning over old Vabre and Duveyrier, by always agreeing with everything they said, if that wouldn't be too great a strain on his intellect. As for herself, she would tackle the women, and she knew exactly how to get them on her side. Then, collecting her thoughts, and glancing round the dining-room once more, as if to make sure that no weapon had been overlooked, she assumed the bearing of a warrior leading forth his daughters to be massacred, with the battle-cry: 'Let us go down!'

And down they went. In the solemn atmosphere of the staircase, Monsieur Josserand felt thoroughly uneasy. He foresaw many things, all too unpleasant for so strait-laced, well-meaning a man as himself.

The Duveyriers' apartment was already crowded as they entered. The huge grand piano filled one side of the panelled drawing-room; the ladies were seated before it in rows, as if at a theatre, with a dense black background of men in evening dress, which extended to the dining-room and parlour beyond.

The chandelier and six wall-lamps gave a dazzling brilliance to the white and gold décor, forming a violent contrast with the red silk of the drapes and furnishings. The ladies' fans, fluttering in the heat, filled the air with the heavy scent of the bosoms on display.

Just at that moment Madame Duveyrier was about to sit down at the piano. With a gesture, Madame Josserand smilingly reassured her hostess that they didn't need looking after. Leaving her daughters among the men, she took a chair between Valérie and Madame Juzeur. Monsieur Josserand found his way to the parlour, where Monsieur Vabre, the landlord, was asleep in his customary corner of the sofa. Here too, in a group, were Campardon, Théophile and Auguste Vabre, Doctor Juillerat, and the Abbé Mauduit; while Trublot and Octave had just fled together from the music to the back of the dining-room. Near them, behind the sea of black coats, stood Duveyrier, tall and thin, watching his wife at the piano, and waiting for silence. At his buttonhole, in a neat little rosette, he wore the ribbon of the Légion d'Honneur.

'Hush! Hush! Be quiet!' murmured many sympathetic voices. Then Clotilde Duveyrier attacked one of Chopin's most difficult nocturnes. Tall and fine-looking, with splendid auburn hair, she had a long face which was as pale and cold as snow. In her grey eyes, only music kindled a passion so great that it satisfied her every spiritual and physical need. Duveyrier continued looking at her; then, after the first few bars, his lips twitched nervously, and he withdrew to the far end of the dining-room. On his clean-shaven face, with its pointed chin and crooked eyes, angry red patches mottled the healthy smoothness of the skin.

Trublot, scrutinising him, quietly remarked: 'He doesn't like music.'

'Nor do I,' replied Octave.

'Ah! But for you it hasn't got the same unfortunate implications. And to think that Duveyrier seemed to have all the luck. No cleverer than anyone else, but always given a helping hand. Comes from an old middle-class family; his father, an ex-chief justice. Called to the bar as soon as he had passed his exams; appointed assistant judge at Rheims; transferred from there to Paris, to the High Court of Appeal; gets decorated, and made counsellor before he is forty-five. Not bad, eh? But he does hate music; the piano has proved the bane of his life. Well, one can't have everything!'

Meanwhile, Clotilde was rattling away in the coolest manner possible. She managed her piano as a circus-rider would her horse. Octave was hypnotised by her frenetic hands moving across the keyboard.

'Just look at her fingers,' he said in wonderment. 'After a quarter of an hour of that, I should think she must feel it.'

Then they both began talking about women, without taking any further notice of the performance. On seeing Valérie, Octave felt rather embarrassed. How should he behave? Speak to her, or pretend not to see her?

Trublot put on an air of fine disdain; not a woman there took his fancy; and, in reply to his companion's protest that there was surely somebody to suit his taste, he said with equanimity: 'Well, go ahead and pick one, and then you'll soon discover what's under the wrapping. But don't go for that one at the back over there, with feathers; nor that little blonde in mauve; nor that rather older woman, although she has the merit of being plump. In high society you'll never find what you want. Lots of airs and graces, but what about pleasure?'

Octave smiled. He had to make his way in the world; he couldn't afford merely to pander to his tastes, like Trublot, whose father was so rich. Those long rows of women set him thinking, and he asked himself which he would choose for his future wealth and happiness if his hosts were to give him permission to take one of them home. Suddenly, as he was weighing up their respective charms, he exclaimed in surprise: 'Look! There's my employer's wife! Is she normally invited here?'

'Yes; didn't you know?' rejoined Trublot. 'In spite of the difference in age, Madame Hédouin and Madame Duveyrier have been inseparable since they were at school together where they were known as the Polar Bears, as they were always twenty degrees below zero. What a grand pair! I pity Duveyrier, if that's the only hot-water bottle he's got to warm his feet in winter!'

Octave, however, had grown serious. It was the first time he'd seen Madame Hédouin in an evening gown, cut low, showing her neck and arms, with her dark hair plaited across her forehead, and under the hot lights she was like a vision of his every desire. A superbly healthy and good-looking woman who was everything a man could need. He was turning over in his mind all sorts of convoluted schemes, when a loud noise of clapping woke him from his daydream.

'What a blessing! It's over!' said Trublot.

Everyone was congratulating Clotilde. Rushing forward, Madame Josserand seized both her hands, while the men were happy to start talking again, and the women plied their fans with great vigour.

Duveyrier then felt able to retreat to the parlour, followed by Trublot and Octave. Hemmed in by skirts on every side, the former whispered: 'Look, there, on your right! The reels are out.'

It was Madame Josserand launching Berthe in the direction of young Vabre, who imprudently had gone up to them to pay his respects. That evening his headache was better, and he only felt a slight touch of neuralgia in the left eye; but the end of the evening filled him with dread as there was going to be singing, the very worst thing for his health.

'Berthe, tell Monsieur Auguste about the remedy that you copied out of that book for him which apparently cures headaches once and for all!'

And, having got them going, Madame Josserand left them standing near the window.

'Ah! They're already on to prescriptions,' whispered Trublot.

In the parlour, Monsieur Josserand, anxious to please his wife, sat facing Monsieur Vabre but not quite knowing what to do, for the old fellow was asleep, and it seemed rude to wake him. But when the music stopped, Monsieur Vabre opened his eyes. He was a portly little man, totally bald, with two tufts of white hair on his ears, a red face, thick flabby lips, and goggle eyes. After politely enquiring as to his health, Monsieur Josserand got him talking. The ex-notary, whose four or five topics of conversation always came out in the same order, began by mentioning Versailles, where, for forty years, he'd worked as a lawyer. Then he spoke of his sons, lamenting their incapacity to take over his practice, so that he had decided to sell it and live in Paris. Then came the whole history of the house, the building of which had been the romance of his life.

'I sank three hundred thousand francs into it. A magnificent speculative venture, so my architect said. But now I find it hard work to get my money back, especially as all my children have come to live here, hoping to do so free of charge. In fact, I should never get a quarter's rent out of them if I didn't make a point of asking for it myself on the fifteenth of every month. However, my work is a source of consolation, I'm glad to say.'

'Do you still have a lot of work to do?' asked Monsieur Josserand.

'Still and always!' replied the old man, with desperate energy. 'Work, to me, is life.'

Then he proceeded to explain his colossal work. For the past ten years he had gone through the official catalogue of the annual Salon,* filing the names of the pictures exhibited by each painter. He alluded to this wearily; he could hardly keep up to date, he complained; sometimes it proved too much for him. For instance, when a women artist got married and exhibited under her husband's name, how could he possibly be expected to know?

'My work will never reach completion; that's what is wearing me out,' he murmured.

'I suppose you take a great interest in art?' said Monsieur Josserand to flatter him.

The old man stared at him in surprised. 'Oh, certainly not! Not at all! There's no need for me actually to see the pictures, it's merely a matter of statistics. Well, well! I'd better go to bed so that my head will be clearer in the morning. Good-night to you.'

He leaned on a stick, which he used even indoors, and hobbled off, evidently suffering from partial paralysis of the spine. Monsieur Josserand was perplexed; he hadn't really understood. And he was afraid that he hadn't discussed the catalogue slips with sufficient enthusiasm.

Just then something was going on in the drawing-room, which brought Trublot and Octave back to the door. They saw a lady of about fifty coming in. She was powerfully built and still attractive, and was accompanied by a serious-looking, carefully dressed young man.

'Oh, they arrive as a couple now, do they?' murmured Trublot.

'Well, why not; what's the point of hiding it?'

The newcomers were Madame Dambreville and Léon Josserand. She had agreed to find him a wife, but meanwhile had reserved him for her own personal use, and now, as their romance was in full swing, they advertised their *liaison* in every middle-class drawing-room.

There was much whispering among mothers with marriage-able daughters. Madame Duveyrier, however, rushed to welcome Madame Dambreville, who was useful in providing her with young men to sing in her choruses. Then Madame Josserand, in turn, was as friendly as could be, thinking that some day she might make use of her son's friend. Léon drily exchanged a word or two with his mother, who began to believe that he might really make something of himself, after all.

'Berthe hasn't spotted you,' she said to Madame Dambreville. 'Please excuse her, but she's just telling Monsieur Auguste about a cure for his headache.'

'Of course. Why, they look quite happy where they are; don't disturb them,' she replied, with a meaningful glance. She had understood.

With maternal solicitude, they both watched Berthe. She had ended up by manoeuvring Auguste into the window recess, and had prettily hemmed him in there. He was growing so vivacious that a headache might not be too far off.

Meanwhile, in the parlour, a group of men were discussing politics with the utmost seriousness. The day before, there had been a stormy sitting in the Senate, over the Roman question.* Doctor Juillerat, an atheist and a revolutionary, was for giving Rome up to the King of Italy, while the Abbé Mauduit, one of the leading lights in the Ultramontane party, prophesied the direst catastrophes if France did not shed the last drop of her blood to protect the temporal power of the Pope.

'Perhaps some *modus vivendi* may be found acceptable to both parties,' said Léon Josserand, who had joined the group.

He was acting then as secretary to a famous barrister, one of the deputies of the Left. For two years, expecting no financial help from his parents, whose mediocrity exasperated him, he had posed in the Latin Quarter as a red-hot radical. But since he had got to know the Dambrevilles, where he had taken the edge off his appetites, he had grown calmer and was gradually becoming a principled Republican.

'No,' said the priest; 'no agreement is possible. The Church cannot compromise.'

'Then it will not survive,' cried the doctor.

And though most attached to each other, having met at every death-bed in the Saint-Roch district, they now seemed irreconcilable – the thin, nervous physician, and the portly, affable priest. The latter smiled politely, even when making the most absolute statements, like a man of the world who tolerates the ills of life, but also like a good Catholic with not the slightest intention of abandoning a single one of his beliefs.

'The Church not survive? Bah!' said Campardon, with a show of anger, for he wanted to make up to the abbé, from whom he expected to get work.

Moreover, all those present agreed with him; the Church would always survive. Théophile Vabre, as he coughed and spat and shivered with fever while dreaming of universal happiness as the goal of a humanitarian republic, was the only one to express the view that the Church might have to undergo some changes.

Then, in his gentle voice, the priest continued: 'The Empire is committing suicide. Wait and see next year, at election time.'

'Oh! As far as the Empire is concerned, you're quite at liberty to rid us of that,' said the doctor, bluntly. 'That will be doing all of us a great favour.'

But, at that, Duveyrier, who appeared to be listening intently, shook his head. He belonged to an Orléanist family,* but he owed everything to the Empire, and thought himself bound to defend it.

'Believe it,' he said, at last, severely, 'if you undermine the basis of society, everything else will collapse. We're the ones who suffer when there's a catastrophe of that kind.'

'That's very true,' remarked Monsieur Josserand, who had no opinion of his own, but who remembered his wife's instructions.

Then everybody spoke at once. None of them supported Napoléon III's policies. Doctor Juillerat condemned the Mexican Expedition,* the Abbé Mauduit censured the recognition of the Kingdom of Italy. Yet Théophile Vabre, and even Léon, felt anxious when Duveyrier threatened them with another '93. What was the point of all these revolutions? Hadn't liberty already been won? And this hatred of new ideas, this fear of the workers claiming their share, soothed the liberalism of these self-satisfied bourgeois. They were all unanimous, however, that they would vote against the Emperor. He had to be taught a lesson.

'Oh, God! How they bore me,' said Trublot, who had momentarily been trying to follow the discussion.

Octave induced him to return to the ladies. In the window recess, Berthe was dizzying Auguste with her bursts of laughter. The big, sickly man was forgetting his dread of women, and had grown quite flushed under the attacks of his bewitching companion, whose warm breath touched his face. But Madame Josserand considered that the campaign was not being conducted with sufficient dispatch, for she looked hard at Hortense who obediently went to her sister's aid.

'I hope you have quite recovered, Madame,' said Octave to Valérie.

'Entirely, thank you,' she coolly replied, as if she remembered nothing of what had occurred.

Madame Juzeur asked the young man about some old lace which she wanted to show him and get his opinion on, and he had to promise to call on her the next day for a minute or two. Then, seeing the Abbé Mauduit coming back to the drawing-room, she called over to him and made him sit beside her, with a look of rapture on her face.

Everybody continued to chat. The ladies were discussing their servants.

'Well, yes,' said Madame Duveyrier, 'I'm quite satisfied with Clémence; she's a very clean and lively girl.'

'And your footman, Hippolyte?' asked Madame Josserand. 'I believe you were thinking of dismissing him?'

Just then Hippolyte, the man-servant, was handing round ices. He was tall and strong, with a ruddy complexion, and when he had passed, Clotilde replied, with some embarrassment: 'No, we're going to keep him after all; changing them is such a nuisance. Servants get used to each other, you know, and I like Clémence so much . . .'

Madame Josserand quickly agreed, feeling they were on delicate ground. It was hoped to arrange a marriage between them some day; and the Abbé Mauduit, whom the Duveyriers had consulted about this, gently nodded his head, as if to hide a scandal well known to the whole house, but to which no one alluded. However, the ladies unburdened themselves of other secrets. Valérie that very morning had sacked another maid, the third within a week. Madame Juzeur had decided to get a fifteen-year-old from the children's home and train her herself.

As for Madame Josserand, she could have gone on all night about Adèle, that slut, that good-for-nothing, whose outlandish habits she recounted in detail. Sitting there languishing in the glare of the candles and the scent of the flowers, they wallowed in all this scullery gossip, as they eagerly discussed the insolence of a coachman or a parlourmaid.

'I say, have you seen Julie?' asked Trublot suddenly, in a mysterious voice.

As Octave looked at him in amazement, he added: 'My dear fellow, she's stunning. Go and have a look at her. Just pretend that you want to leave the room for a minute and then slip through into the kitchen . . . She's simply stunning.'

He was referring to the Duveyriers' cook. The ladies' conversation had taken another turn. Madame Josserand, in the most gushing manner, was praising the very modest property which the Duveyriers owned near Villeneuve-Saint-Georges, and which she'd once glimpsed from the train on the way to Fontainebleau. But Clotilde didn't like the countryside; she went there as little as possible, in fact only during the holidays of her son, Gustave, who was finishing his studies at the Lycée Bonaparte.

'Caroline is quite right not to want to have any children' she declared, turning to Madame Hédouin, who was sitting two chairs away from her. 'They do so interfere with all one's habits.'

Madame Hédouin said that she liked children very much. But she was far too busy for babies; her husband was always travelling about, here, there, and everywhere; and she had the entire business to look after.

As he stood behind her chair, Octave, glancing sideways, focused on the little black curls at the nape of her neck and the snowy whiteness of her bosom, disappearing from view in a wave of delicate lace. She succeeded in disconcerting him as she sat there so calmly, saying little, and with her beautiful smile. He had never met anyone so attractive, not even in Marseilles. She was certainly worth aiming for, even though it would be slow work.

'Having children spoils a woman's good looks,' he whispered in her ear, anxious to say at least something to her.

She slowly raised her large eyes, and said simply, just as if she were giving him an order at the shop: 'Oh, no! Monsieur

Octave, I'm not bothered by that ... It's just that to have children, you need a lot of time.'

Madame Duveyrier didn't let them finish. She had merely greeted the young man with a slight movement of the head when Campardon had introduced him to her. Now she watched him, and listened to his conversation with a new, undisguised interest. As she heard him talking to her friend, she couldn't resist enquiring: 'Please excuse my interrupting you, but ... what is your voice?'

At first he had no idea what she meant, but then said that he was a tenor. Clotilde was beside herself. A tenor indeed! What luck! Tenors were so difficult to find! Now, for the 'Consecration of the Swords',* which they were going to sing in a moment, she had never been able to find more than three tenors, though at least five were needed. And, as her eyes suddenly sparkled with excitement, she could hardly refrain from going over to the piano to audition him. He had to promise to come in one evening and let her try him out. Trublot kept nudging him from behind, apparently uninvolved but enjoying himself hugely.

'Ah! Now you're for it!' he murmured, when his hostess had moved on. 'My dear fellow, at first she thought I was a baritone. When that didn't work, she tried me as a tenor, which was worse still. So tonight she's decided to make use of me as a bass. My voice is supposed to be that of a monk.'

At that very moment, Madame Duveyrier called him over, so he had no choice but to leave Octave. They were going to sing the chorus from the *Huguenots*, the main event of the evening. There was a great bustle, and fifteen or so men, all amateurs recruited from the ranks of the guests, made their way with some difficulty through the ladies to reach their assembly-point near the piano. They kept on finding themselves blocked, mumbling their apologies as they made their way to the front, their voices drowned by the buzz of conversation, while fans moved more rapidly in the increasing heat. Madame Duveyrier counted them; they were all there; and she began to distribute the parts which she herself had copied out: Campardon took the role of Saint-Bris; a junior official at the Conseil d'État took over Nevers's few bars; and there were eight nobles, four aldermen and three monks, represented by barristers, clerks and simple landlords. Madame Duveyrier was to provide the accompaniment, having also reserved the part of Valentina for herself, shrieking passionately as she crashed out the chords on the piano. She was determined to have no ladies, directing her resigned troop of gentlemen with all the unrelenting vigour of a conductor.

Meanwhile, the talking went on, the noise in the parlour becoming positively intolerable, where obviously the political discussion had grown more animated. So, taking a key from her pocket, Clotilde gently tapped on the piano with it. There was a murmur in the room, a hush of voices, the black frock-coats again surging towards the doors. Above the rows of heads you could just see Duveyrier's blotchy face, which wore a look of anguish. Octave remained standing behind Madame Hédouin, looking down at the shadowy bosom swathed in filmy lace. But the silence was suddenly broken by a burst of laughter, and he looked up. It was Berthe, amused by some joke of Auguste's. She had heated up his anaemic blood to such a pitch that he was becoming quite rakish. Everyone present stared at them; mothers suddenly looked serious, and relatives exchanged eloquent glances.

'She's so full of fun!' murmured Madame Josserand, fondly, yet loud enough to be heard.

Doing her duty, Hortense stood by helping her sister, echoing her laughter and pushing her up against the young man, while a breeze from the window behind them lightly stirred the large red silk curtains.

Then the sound of a cavernous voice was heard, and all eyes were turned towards the piano. With mouth wide open and beard waving in a gust of lyrical fervour, Campardon declaimed the opening line.

'*Aye, by the Queen's command we gather here.*'

Clotilde trilled up and down the scale, then with her eyes fixed on the ceiling, and a look of terror in her face, she sang at the top of her voice.

'*Ah, me! I tremble!*'

And then the whole thing took off, as the eight lawyers, landlords, and clerks, with noses glued to the score, and looking like schoolboys mumbling over a page of Greek, swore one and all that they were ready to liberate France. This opening caused some bewilderment, as the voices were so deadened by the low ceiling that one could only hear a loud humming, like carts full of paving-stones, rattling the window-panes. But when Saint-Bris's melodious phrase, 'For this cause so holy . . .' introduced the principal theme, some of the ladies, recognising it, nodded to show how clever they were.

The room grew hotter, and the nobles roared together: '*We swear it! We will follow thee!*'

Every time it was like an explosion, a blow that struck each guest full in the face.

'They're singing too loudly,' murmured Octave, in Madame Hédouin's ear.

But she didn't react. Then unable to listen to Nevers and Valentina any longer, not least because the junior official from the Conseil d'État wasn't a baritone at all, Octave made a sign to Trublot, who was waiting to make his monk's entrance, and winked in the direction of the window recess, where Berthe still had Auguste imprisoned. The two were now by themselves, breathing in the cool outdoor air, while Hortense played sentry, leaning against the curtain and mechanically twisting the loop. No one was looking at them now; even Madame Josserand and Madame Dambreville had given up watching them, after exchanging glances.

Meanwhile, unable to take her fingers off the keys, Clotilde could only stretch out her neck, addressing to the music-stand the following vow, intended for Nevers: '*Ah, from this day forth my blood shall all be yours!*'

The aldermen had now joined in, as well as an assistant public prosecutor, two solicitors and a notary. The quartet electrified everyone with the phrase, 'For this cause so holy', itself repeated and gradually amplified as it was taken up by half the chorus. Campardon, his mouth growing wider all the time, gave the orders for battle with a tremendous volley of syllables. Then suddenly, the monks' chant began. Trublot seemed to draw up the words of the psalm from deep in his stomach, so as to get the low notes.

Octave, who had been curious enough to watch him singing, was taken aback when his gaze returned to the curtained window. As if inspired by the music, whether intentionally or not, Hortense had unhooked the loop; and the curtain, as it fell, had completely hidden Auguste and Berthe. They were there behind it, leaning against the window railing, though not a single movement betrayed their presence. Octave lost interest in

Trublot, who just then was blessing the swords: '*Ye holy swords, now by us be blessed.*'

What could they be doing behind the curtain? The fugal passages were beginning as, to the monks' deep tones, the chorus replied, 'Death! Death! Death!' yet the couple behind the curtain never moved. Perhaps, overcome by the heat, they were just leaning out to watch the passing cabs. Then, once again, it was Saint-Bris's melodious phrase; all the singers gradually took it up at the top of their voices, in a swelling finale of awesome force. It was like a sudden gust of wind sweeping through the narrow room, making the candles flare, as the guests grew pale, and there was a rush of blood to their ears. Clotilde furiously thumped the piano, galvanising the chorus with her eyes; then the voices sank to a whisper: '*At midnight, not a sound!*'

Then she played on by herself, using the soft pedal in time to the regular footfall of the patrol as it dies away in the distance.

But then, as the music swooningly expired, in the lull that had followed the storm, a voice was suddenly heard: 'Stop that! You're hurting me!'

Everyone looked round towards the window. Madame Dambreville, anxious to make herself useful, was kind enough to pull the curtain aside. And the whole room was treated to the sight of Auguste and Berthe leaning against the window railing, he looking embarrassed and she very flushed.

'What is it, my precious?' asked Madame Josserand with concern.

'Nothing, Mamma . . . Monsieur Auguste knocked my arm in opening the window . . . I was so hot.'

And she blushed deeper still. There was some tittering and a few raised eyebrows in the audience. Madame Duveyrier, who had been trying to keep her brother out of Berthe's way for the last month, turned quite pale, especially as the incident had completely spoiled the effort of her chorus. However, after the first momentary surprise, there was a burst of applause. Congratulations were showered on her, as well as compliments for the singers. How well they had sung! What pains she must have taken to blend the different voices! It was as good as at any theatre! But all this praise didn't prevent her from hearing the tittle-tattle. The girl had certainly been compromised; an engagement was inevitable.

'Well, so he's hooked!' said Trublot, on rejoining Octave.

'Of course he was going to give her a good squeeze while we were all bellowing away! I thought he was making the most of the opportunity. You know, when there's singing at these occasions, you can give a lady a little pinch, and if she cries out it doesn't matter, as nobody can hear her!'

Berthe, who had now completely regained her composure, was laughing again, while Hortense surveyed Auguste with the sullen air of a girl who has got her diploma. In their triumph, one could detect the mother's tuition based on her undisguised contempt for men. All the male guests now invaded the drawing-room, mixing with the ladies, and talking loudly. Upset by the scene in which Berthe had figured, Monsieur Josserand drew nearer to his wife. It irked him to hear her thanking Madame Dambreville for all her lavish attentions to Léon, in whom she'd certainly wrought a most beneficial change. But it was even worse when she started talking about her daughter again. She pretended to be confiding in Madame Juzeur, while ensuring that Valérie and Clotilde, standing next to her, could overhear her.

'Yes, you know, her uncle wrote to confirm it today: Berthe is to have fifty thousand francs. That's not much, certainly; but still, it's a lump sum, in hard cash, you know!'

This lie disgusted her husband. He couldn't help lightly touching her on the shoulder. She looked up at him with so resolute an expression on her face that he was forced to lower his eyes. Then, as Madame Duveyrier turned round, she smiled a gracious smile, and asked with a air of concern about her dear father.

'Oh! Papa must have gone off to bed,' replied Clotilde, now completely won over. 'You know, he does work so hard!'

Monsieur Josserand added that yes, that was right, her father had indeed retired for the night, so he'd be on top form in the morning. And he stammered out a few remarks about 'a most remarkable intellect, extraordinary faculties', wondering at the same time where on earth the dowry was coming from, and how he'd cope on the day fixed for signing the marriage-contract.

There was a great noise in the drawing-room as the chairs were pushed back, and the ladies trooped into the dining-room, where tea was being served. This included Madame Josserand, savouring her victory and surrounded by her daughters and the

Vabre family. Only the group of those engaged in serious discussion remained in the midst of the chairs no longer neatly aligned. Campardon had got hold of the Abbé Mauduit. The Calvary of Saint-Roch, it transpired, needed certain repairs. The architect declared that he was perfectly ready to undertake these, his work for the Evreux diocese wasn't too much of a burden: a pulpit, some heating and new ovens in His Grace's kitchen; besides, these were things that his surveyor could attend to. The abbé accordingly promised to submit the matter for consideration at the next meeting of the directors. They then both joined the others, who were complimenting Duveyrier on a parliamentary bill which, as he admitted, he himself had drafted. The President of the Court, who was his friend, put certain undemanding but high-profile tasks his way, which would allow him to shine.

'Have you read this new novel?' asked Léon, as he turned over the pages of a copy of the *Revue des Deux Mondes** lying on the table.

'It's well written, but it's yet another story of adultery; they really are getting quite tedious!'

Then they began to talk about morality. Some women, said Campardon, were perfectly blameless. Everybody agreed with him. Moreover, the architect observed, married life was easy enough if one knew how to give and take. Théophile Vabre remarked that that depended on the wife, without explaining himself further. They were anxious to have Doctor Juillerat's views on the matter, but he simply smiled. He thought that virtue lay in good health. Duveyrier, meanwhile, remained pensive.

'Why, dear me!' he murmured at last. 'Those novelists exaggerate; adultery is very rare among the well-educated classes . . . A woman, if she comes from a good family, has a flower in her soul . . .'

He took the high moral ground, and talked of ideals with such emotional fervour that his eyes misted over. And he supported the Abbé Mauduit when the latter spoke of the necessity of religious beliefs for the wife and mother. The conversation was thus brought back to religion and politics, exactly where these gentlemen had left it. The Church would never disappear, because it formed the basis of family life as well as the natural pillar of any government.

'In its policing capacity, granted,' muttered the doctor.

Duveyrier was not at all happy to have politics discussed in his home, and contented himself by remarking, as he glanced across the dining-room where Berthe and Hortense were stuffing Auguste with sandwiches: 'Gentlemen, let me just say this: we all know that religion makes marriage moral.'

At the same moment, Trublot, on the sofa, was leaning over and whispering to Octave.

'By the way,' he asked, 'would you like me to get you an invitation from a lady at whose house one can really enjoy oneself?'

And, as his companion wished to know what kind of lady, he added, as he pointed at Duveyrier: 'His mistress.'

'Never!' exclaimed Octave, in amazement.

Trublot slowly opened and shut his eyes. That was a fact. When one had married a wife who was less than obliging, disgusted at the idea of having babies, and who thrashed the piano with enough passion to lay low every dog in the neighbourhood, why, one went elsewhere about town to find consolation.

'Let us make marriage moral, gentlemen; let us make it moral,' repeated Duveyrier, stiltedly, and with the broken blood vessels in his face testifying, as Octave now noted, to a secret life.

The group was called to the dining-room, and the Abbé Mauduit, alone for a moment in the empty drawing-room, watched the crush of guests from afar. His fleshy, knowing face wore a sad expression. As confessor to these ladies and their daughters, he knew them from head to toe as intimately as Doctor Juillerat. Outward appearances only had become his concern, as a sort of master of ceremonies cloaking this corrupt bourgeoisie with religion, fearful at the certain prospect of a final collapse the day its rottenness should be unmasked. Sometimes he found it difficult to reconcile this attitude with his sincere faith. But his smile returned as he accepted the cup of tea brought to him by Berthe, and he chatted to her for a moment, so as to give priestly absolution to the scandal of the window incident. He was once again a man of the world, content merely to exact decorous behaviour from his penitent flock, the members of which had strayed far from the fold, and who would have compromised the Deity himself.

'Well, that's a nice state of affairs!' said Octave to himself, whose respect for the house had received another shock.

Then, seeing that Madame Hédouin was going to find her coat, and wishing to get there before her, he followed Trublot, who was also about to leave. Octave's plan was to see her safely home. She declined his escort, as it was barely midnight and she lived so close by. Then, as a rose fell from the bouquet at her bosom, he picked it up with a wounded look and made a show of keeping it as a souvenir.

For a moment her handsome brows contracted. Then she said, in her calm, self-possessed way: 'Kindly open the door for me, Monsieur Octave . . . thank you.'

When she had gone downstairs, Octave, at a loss what to do, looked around for Trublot. But, as before at the Josserands' Trublot had simply disappeared. He must have slipped away once again by the servants' staircase.

So, somewhat out of humour, Octave went up to bed with the rose in his hand.

At the top landing, leaning over the banisters, he saw Marie, just where he'd left her. She was waiting for his step, and had run to see him coming up. She invited him in, saying: 'Jules hasn't come home yet . . . Did you enjoy yourself? Was everyone beautifully dressed?'

But she didn't wait for an answer. She had just noticed the rose, and with childish delight, exclaimed: 'Ah! that's for me, that flower, is it? You were thinking of me, then . . . How kind of you; how kind of you!'

Her eyes filled with tears, and she blushed deeply, overcome by emotion. Moved by a sudden impulse, Octave kissed her tenderly.

About one o'clock the Josserands, in their turn, went home. On a chair in the hall, Adèle had left a candlestick and matches. None of them spoke as they came upstairs, but on reaching the dining-room, from which they'd set out in such despair, they let themselves go, in a sudden burst of mad merriment, wildly seizing each other's hands as they danced a sort of primitive dance round the table. Not even the father remained immune to it, as his wife threw her legs up in the air and his daughters uttered little inarticulate cries, while the candle on the table flung their huge dancing shadows along the wall.

'Well, at last that's settled!' sighed Madame Josserand, as she sank breathlessly into a chair.

But in a sudden paroxysm of maternal tenderness, she immediately got up again, and ran to kiss Berthe effusively on both cheeks.

'I'm so pleased, so pleased with you, my darling. All my efforts have finally been rewarded. My poor child! My poor child! So this time it's really going to happen.'

Her voice choked with sudden and heartfelt emotion, faltering there in her flame-coloured gown at the very moment of victory, prostrated by the terrible toll that three winters of campaigning had cost her.

Berthe protested that she was fine; but her mother thought that she was looking pale, fussing over her and even insisting on making her a cup of mint tea. When Berthe had gone to bed, her mother, barefoot, went softly to her bedside, as in the far-off days of her childhood.

Meanwhile, with his head on the pillow, Monsieur Josserand awaited his wife's return. She blew out the light, and climbed across him to her side, nearest the wall. He lay there thinking, feeling profoundly uneasy about the promised dowry of fifty thousand francs. Why make such promises when it was far from sure one could keep one's word? It was simply not honourable.

'Not honourable, indeed!' cried Madame Josserand, out of the darkness, as her voice assumed its usual ferocity of tone. 'I'll tell you what's not honourable, and that's to let your daughters turn into old maids; yes, old maids, which was probably what you had in mind. Anyway, we've lots of time, we can discuss it, we can get her uncle to make up his mind. Moreover, *my* family, I would have you know, have always acted honourably.'

The next morning, which was Sunday, Octave remained snugly in bed for an extra hour, but wide awake and in a mood of clear-sighted contentment. What was the hurry? He was quite happy at 'Au Bonheur des Dames'; he was shaking off his provincial airs, and he felt absolutely certain that one day Madame Hédouin would be his, and make his fortune. The matter, however, required patience, a long-drawn-out plan of seduction, which appealed to the sense of pleasure and voluptuousness with which he approached women. As he dropped off to sleep again, turning over tactics in his mind and giving himself six months in which to succeed, the vision of Marie Pichon served to soothe his impatience. A woman of that sort was very handy; he had only to stretch out an arm if he wanted her and she didn't cost him a penny. While waiting for the other one, this was surely an excellent arrangement. As he drowsily reflected on how useful and inexpensive she was, he became quite tender-hearted towards her: she was so good about it all; he resolved to treat her more kindly from now on.

'Goodness me! Nine o'clock!' he said, as the striking clock brought him round. 'I suppose I should get up.'

A fine rain was falling, so he decided he would stay in all day. He would accept an invitation to dine with the Pichons, an invitation he'd always turned down in his dread of the Vuillaumes. That would please Marie; and he would find some opportunity of kissing her behind the door. As she liked books, he even thought of taking her a whole parcelful as a surprise, some that he'd left in one of his trunks in the loft. When he had dressed, he went downstairs to Monsieur Gourd to get the key to the attic, used by all the different tenants for storing things they didn't need or couldn't use.

On this damp morning it was stifling downstairs, with the humidity in the heated hallway visible on the fake marble walls, long mirrors and mahogany doors. At the entrance, mère Péron, a badly dressed woman paid two pence an hour by the Gourds for any heavy housework that needed doing around the place, was scrubbing the front step in the icy blast from the courtyard.

'Now then, old girl, just you scrub that properly, and don't let me find a single stain!' cried a warmly clad Monsieur Gourd from the door of his lodge.

And as Octave arrived, he spoke to him about mère Péron in the brutally domineering way that ex-servants have when they finally get their revenge and are waited upon themselves.

'Lazy old thing! I can do nothing with her! What I would give to see her at my lord duke's! They'd have made her sit up. She won't be working here much longer if I don't get my money's worth . . . But, do forgive me, what was it you wanted, Monsieur Mouret?'

Octave asked for the key. Then the concierge, without hurrying himself, explained that he and Madame Gourd could have lived, of course, in their own house at Mort-la-Ville, only Madame Gourd adored Paris, in spite of swollen legs which prevented her from venturing as far as the pavement. They were just waiting until they had a slightly larger income from their savings, longing for retirement and yet just a bit cautious every time they were tempted finally to live off the little fortune that they'd amassed.

'I don't have to do everybody's bidding, you know,' he said, as he drew up his majestic figure to its full height. 'I've no longer any need to work for my daily bread. The key to the attic, I think you said, Monsieur Mouret? I say, my dear, where did we put the key to the attic?'

Cosily ensconced in an easy-chair, his wife was drinking her coffee out of a silver cup in front of the blazing wood fire which cheered up the whole room. She didn't know where the key was; at the back of the chest of drawers, perhaps. And, while dipping pieces of toast in her coffee, she kept her eyes fixed on the door of the servants' staircase at the other end of the courtyard, which looked bleaker and more gloomy than ever on this rainy morning.

'Ah! Look! There she is!' grunted Madame Gourd, as a woman came through the door in question.

Monsieur Gourd immediately went to stand in front of his lodge to block the woman's way. She slowed, looking uneasy as she came towards them.

'We've been watching her all morning, Monsieur Mouret,' said Gourd, under his breath. 'We saw her go by yesterday evening. She's come from the carpenter upstairs, the only working man we've got in the building, thank God! And if the landlord would only listen to me, he'd keep the room empty. It's only a servant's room under the eaves, and for the sake of a hundred and thirty francs a year, it's really not worth while having filthy goings-on in your house.'

Interrupting himself, he roughly asked the woman: 'Where have you come from?'

'Why, from upstairs, of course,' she replied, as she went on without stopping.

Then he burst out: 'We're not going to have any women here; do you understand? The man who brings you here has been told as much already. If you come back here tonight, I'll call a policeman, and then we'll see if you think you can carry on like that in a decent house.'

'Oh, leave me alone!' said the woman. 'It's my home, and I shall come back to it when I like.'

And she went off, pursued by the righteous wrath of Monsieur Gourd, who talked of going upstairs to fetch the landlord. Did you ever hear of such a thing? That sort of woman in a house full of respectable people where not a hint of immorality was tolerated! It was clear that the carpenter's garret was the cesspool of the house, a den of vile iniquity which offended the concierge's sensibilities and kept him awake at night.

'And the key?' Octave tried to repeat.

But Monsieur Gourd, furious that one of his tenants should have seen his authority flouted, seized on poor mère Péron again, to show that his orders were obeyed. She had just splashed his door again with her broom. If he paid her out of his own pocket, it was because he didn't want to soil his hands, and yet he always had to clean up after her! He'd see her damned before he'd give her another job just for charity's sake. She could starve to death first.

Worn out by such work, which was too hard for her, the old woman, without answering, went on scrubbing with her skinny arms, holding back the tears in awe of this alarming person in smoking-cap and slippers.

'Now I do remember, my dear,' called Madame Gourd from the armchair in which she spent the whole day warming her fat body.

'I hid the key under some shirts, so that the maids wouldn't be able to go and mess about in the attic. Go ahead and give it to Monsieur Mouret.'

'And they're a nice lot, too, those maids!' muttered Monsieur Gourd, whose long life in domestic service had led him to loathe all servants. 'Here's the key, sir, but please do let me have it back again, because if anywhere is left open the maids use it to get up to no good.'

Not wishing to cross the wet courtyard, Octave went up the front staircase as far as the fourth floor, and then went through to the back stairs via the door close to his own room. At the top was a long passageway, with two turnings at right angles painted in light yellow, with a darker dado; and, like in hospital corridors, the doors of the servants' rooms, also yellow, were spaced along it at regular intervals. It was freezing cold under the zinc roofing, bare and scrubbed, with the stale smell of poverty.

The attic looked out on to the courtyard at the extreme end of the right-hand wing of the building. But Octave, who had never been up there, went along to the left where suddenly, through one of the half-open doors, he was confronted by a spectacle that stopped him in his tracks. A man in his shirt sleeves was standing in front of a small looking-glass, tying his white tie.

'What are you doing here?' he exclaimed.

It was Trublot. To start with, he too was frozen in amazement. No one ever came up there at that hour.

Octave, who had gone in, looked first at him and then at the room, with its narrow iron bedstead and washstand, where a little ball of women's hair was floating on the dirty water in the basin. Seeing a black dress-coat still hanging up beside the aprons, he blurted out: 'So you're sleeping with the cook?'

'No, certainly not,' answered Trublot, in a panic. Then, aware of how stupid he looked, he laughed off his lie. 'Well, she's quite a one, my dear fellow; really rather special, I assure you.'

Whenever he dined out, he used to slip out of the drawing-room and go and squeeze the cooks busy at their ovens, and when one of them let him have her key, he managed to get away before midnight, and would go and wait patiently for her in her room, sitting on her trunk in his evening clothes and white cravat. The next morning, about ten o'clock, he would leave by the front stairs, giving the concierge the impression that he had been calling on one of the tenants at an early hour. As long as he was more or less on time for work, his father was satisfied. Besides, he had to be at the Bourse now every day from twelve to three. On Sundays he sometimes happily spent the whole day in some servant's bed, with his nose buried under her pillow.

'But you're the one with ambitions to be rich!' said Octave, with a look of disgust.

Then Trublot pretentiously remarked: 'My dear boy, you don't know anything about such things, so don't start pronouncing.'

And he spoke up for Julie, a tall Burgundian woman of forty, her wide face all pock-marked, but whose body was superbly built. One might strip all the other woman of the house; they were all sticks; not one of them would measure up to her. What's more, she was rather classy; and, to prove it, he opened drawers, pointing to a bonnet, some jewellery, and some lace-trimmed skirts, all of which had doubtless been stolen from Madame Duveyrier. Octave, in fact, now noticed a certain coquettishness about the room, some gilt cardboard boxes on the chest of drawers, a chintz curtain hanging over the petticoats, and other things that testified to the cook trying to play the fine lady.

'In the case of this girl,' repeated Trublot, 'I don't mind admitting it. If only all the others were like her!'

Just then there was a noise on the back stairs; it was Adèle coming up to wash her ears, as a furious Madame Josserand had forbidden her to touch the meat until she had washed them thoroughly with soap and water. Trublot, peeping out, recognised her.

'Shut the door, quick!' he cried, anxiously. 'Hush! Not a word!'

Listening attentively, he heard Adèle's heavy footsteps along the passage.

'So you're sleeping with her too, then?' asked Octave, astonished to see him turn so pale, and guessing he was afraid of a scene.

This time, however, Trublot didn't have the courage to be honest. 'With that filth! My good fellow, what do you take me for?'

He sat down on the edge of the bed, waiting to finish dressing himself, begging Octave not to move. So they both remained perfectly quiet, while Adèle was scrubbing her ears, an operation that lasted a good ten minutes. They heard the whirlpool in the basin.

'There is a room, though, between this one and hers,' Trublot explained, in a whisper. 'It's let to a carpenter, who stinks the whole place out with his onion soup. This morning, yet again, it almost made me retch. And, you know, the partitions in the servants' quarters are nowadays paper-thin. I can't think what the landlords are about, but it's simply not decent. Why, you can hardly turn over in bed. Most inconvenient, I assure you!'

When Adèle had gone down again, his boldness returned as he finished dressing with the help of Julie's combs and ointments. When Octave mentioned the attic, he insisted on showing him where it was, as he knew every hole and corner on the top floor. And, as they passed the doors, he familiarly referred to each of the servants by name. At this end of the passage, next to Adèle, there was Lisa, the Campardons' maid, a wench who got what she wanted outside; then there was Victoire, their cook, an old whale of seventy, but the only one for whom he had any respect. Then came Françoise, who had started working for Madame Valérie only yesterday and whose trunk wasn't likely to remain more than twenty-four hours behind that narrow bed, in which so many maids had slept that one was never quite sure who was going to turn up as you lay there waiting in the warm sheets. Then there was a quiet couple who worked for the people on the second floor; then their coachman, a strapping fellow, of whom he spoke jealously, as one handsome man might speak of another, suspecting him of quietly enjoying himself as he proceeded from door to door. At the other end of the passage, there was Clémence, the Duveyriers' maid, who had a conjugal visit from her neighbour, Hippolyte the footman, every night. Last of all, there was little Louise, the orphan engaged by Madame Juzeur for a trial period, a hussy of fifteen, who must hear some queer things at night, if she were a light sleeper.

'Don't lock the door again, there's a good fellow,' said Trublot, when he had helped Octave to get the books out of his trunk. 'You see, when the attic's open, one can hide in there and wait.'

Having consented to deceive Monsieur Gourd, Octave returned with Trublot to Julie's room, as he had left his overcoat

there. Then he couldn't find his gloves, shaking out the petticoats and turning the bedclothes inside out, releasing so much
dust and such a fusty smell of dirty linen that Octave, half
choked, opened the window. It looked on to the narrow inner
courtyard, from which all the kitchens in the house got whatever
light they had. And, leaning out, he looked down into this damp
well, from which there rose the fetid odours of dirty sinks, when
a sound of voices made him hastily pull his head back in.

'That's their little morning gossip,' said Trublot, still looking
under the bed on all fours. 'Just listen to it.'

It was Lisa, who from the Campardons' kitchen was leaning
out to talk to Julie, two floors below her.

'So it's come off this time, has it?'

'Seems so,' replied Julie, looking up. 'You know, she all but
pulled his trousers down. Hippolyte came back from the drawing-room so disgusted that he was nearly sick.'

'If we were only to do a quarter as much!' said Lisa.

For a moment she disappeared to drink some broth that
Victoire had brought her. They got on wonderfully together,
pandering to each other's vices, the maid hiding the cook's
drunkenness, and the cook helping the maid to have those
outings from which she came back dead-beat with her back
aching and her eyelids blue.

'Ah, my children,' said Victoire, who in her turn leaned out,
with her elbows next to Lisa's, 'you're young! Wait till you see
what I've seen! At old Campardon's there was his niece, a girl
who had been well brought up, and she used to look at men
through the keyhole.'

'That's a fine thing!' muttered Julie, putting in airs. 'If I'd
been the young lady on the fourth floor, I'd have given Monsieur Auguste such a slap if he had touched me in the drawing-
room. A nice fellow, indeed!'

At these words, shrill laughter came from Madame Juzeur's
kitchen. Lisa, who was opposite, spotted Louise, precociously
enjoying the other maids chatter.

'That brat keeps spying on us from morning to night,' she
said. 'What a nuisance it is to have a child like that hanging
about! We soon shan't be able to talk at all!'

She didn't finish, for the noise of a window opening suddenly
made them all vanish. There was utter silence; then they gingerly
poked their heads out again. What could it be? They thought it

was Madame Valérie or Madame Josserand, who was going to catch them gossiping.

'It's all right,' said Lisa. 'They've all got their heads in the basin by now. Far too busy with their complexions to think about bothering us! It's the only minute in the day when one can breathe!'

'So nothing new with your lot, then?' enquired Julie, as she peeled a carrot.

'Same old story. Nothing doing, she's as tight as a cork in a bottle.'

'Well, what does your big idiot of an architect do, then?'

'Why, he uncorks her cousin, of course!'

They laughed louder still, until Françoise, Madame Valérie's new maid, looked out. It was her opening the window that had startled them. First of all they engaged in polite conversation.

'Oh, it's you, mademoiselle!'

'Yes, indeed, mademoiselle! I'm trying to get things straight in this kitchen, but, my word, it's in such a disgusting state.'

Then came the nauseating details.

'Ah! You'll be a marvel of patience if you stay working for them for long. The last one had her arms all scratched by the child, and Madame made her slave so much that we could hear her crying from here.'

'Ah, well, in that case I won't last!' said Françoise. 'Thanks, all the same, for telling me.'

'Where's she gone – your missus?' asked Victoire, inquisitively.

'She's just gone out to a lunch appointment with a lady.'

Leaning out, Lisa and Julie exchanged glances. Oh! Yes, they knew her well, that lady. And some lunch, too, with her head down and her legs in the air! How people dared tell such shocking lies! They didn't pity the husband, who deserved more than that; but, all the same, it was a disgrace to humanity when a woman carried on in that sort of way.

'There's Dish-Cloth!' cried Lisa, as she caught sight of the Josserands' maid above her.

Then a volley of gross abuse surfaced from this hole, as dark and stinking as a sewer. All of them looking up at Adèle, yelled violently at their scapegoat – the filthy, clumsy creature on whom all the servants vented their spite.

'Oh, look! She's washed herself, you can see that!'

'Just you throw your offal into the yard again, and I'll come and rub your face in it!'

'Go and stuff your face at communion, you priest-licking slut! Do you know, she doesn't brush her teeth so she can feed off it for the rest of the week.'

Adèle, bewildered, looked down at them, leaning half out of the window. At last she said: 'Leave me alone, can't you, or I'll piss on you.'

But the cries and laughter increased.

'You got your young mistress married last night, did you? Perhaps it's you who taught her how to get a man!'

'Ah, what a wretch! She carries on working where they don't give you enough to eat! That's what gets me about her! What a big fool you must be! Why don't you send them all packing?'

Adèle had tears in her eyes.

'You don't know anything about it,' she blurted out. 'It's not my fault if I don't get enough to eat.'

And the voices grew louder. Lisa started to berate the new-comer, Françoise, who was taking Adèle's side; but the the latter, forgetting the insults and yielding to an instinctive solidarity, cried: 'Watch out! here comes madame!'

Instantly there was a deathly hush. All of them rushed back into their kitchens; and from the dark, narrow hole of the courtyard there was just the stench of blocked drains, like the fumes of the filth left there by the inhabitants, out of sight but stirred up by the servants in their rancour. Here was the sewer of the house, the very dunghill of its shames; while the gentry still lounged about in slippers, and the front stairwell lay revealed in all its majesty amid the stuffy silence of the hot-air stove. Octave remembered the sudden explosion of noise that had greeted him from this inner courtyard, when he had gone into the Campardons' kitchen, the day of his arrival.

'How charming they are,' he said, simply.

And, leaning out in his turn, he looked at the walls almost as if vexed that he had not been able to see through the whole sham right from the start, covered up as it was by imitation marble and gilt stucco.

'Where the devil has she put them?' said Trublot yet again, even looking in the chamberpot cupboard for his white gloves.

At last he discovered them at the bottom of the bed; they were flattened out and quite warm. He glanced once more at the mirror, and went and hid the bedroom key, as agreed, at the end of the passage, under an old sideboard which had been left behind by some tenant. Then he led the way downstairs, accompanied by Octave. In the main staircase, once he'd got past the Josserands' door, all his self-assurance returned as he buttoned his overcoat up to his neck to hide his evening clothes and white tie.

'Good-bye, my friend,' he said, raising his voice. 'I was rather worried, so I just called to see how the ladies were. They have had a very good night, it seems. See you soon.'

Octave, smiling, watched him as he went downstairs. Then, as it was almost noon, he decided he would return the attic key later on.

At lunch-time, at the Campardons', he watched Lisa with particular interest, as she waited at table. She looked pleasant and neat, as usual, though her vile words still echoed in his brain. His instinct for women had not deceived him as far as this flat-bosomed wench was concerned. Madame Campardon might well be delighted with her, still surprised that she didn't steal anything. But there she was right, for her vice was another kind. Moreover, the girl appeared to be very kind to Angèle, and the mother's confidence in her seemed entirely justified.

That very morning, as it happened, Angèle disappeared at dessert, and they heard her laughing in the kitchen.

Octave ventured to remark: 'Perhaps it's a little unwise to let her be so familiar with the servants.'

'Oh, there's no great harm in that!' replied Madame Campardon, in her languid way. 'Victoire worked for our family when my husband was born, and Lisa gives me not the slightest cause for concern. Then you know, that child makes my head ache. I should go mad if she were always dancing about me all day long.'

The architect sat gravely chewing the end of his cigar.

'It's my idea,' he said, 'that Angèle should spend two hours in the kitchen every afternoon. I want her to learn housekeeping, and that's the best way to teach her. She never goes out, my dear boy; she's always under our wing. You'll see what a jewel we shall make of her!'

Octave let the matter rest. Some days Campardon seemed to him absolutely stupid; and when the architect urged him to come to Saint-Roch to hear a famous preacher, he refused, obstinately persisting in remaining at home. Having told Madame Campardon that he would not dine there that evening, he was on his way to his room, when he felt the attic key in his pocket. He thought it better to return it at once.

On the landing an unexpected sight caught his eye. The door of the room let to the distinguished gentleman, whose name nobody knew, was open. This was quite an event, for it was normally shut, barricaded as by the silence of the dead. He was even more surprised when, on looking for the gentleman's wrtiting-table, he saw in its place the corner of a large bedstead, and perceived a graceful woman coming out of the room. She was dressed in black, and wore a thick veil which concealed her features. The door closed noiselessly behind her.

His curiosity roused, he followed the lady downstairs to see if she was pretty. But, looking slightly anxious, she tripped along at such a rate, with her dainty little boots barely touching the stair carpet, that she left behind her merely a faint trace of perfume. As he got to the hall, she disappeared, and he could only see Monsieur Gourd standing in the doorway, making her a low bow with cap in hand.

As Octave returned the key, he tried to draw out the concierge.

'She looks very respectable,' he said. 'Who is she?'

'A lady,' replied Monsieur Gourd.

And that was all he was prepared to say. But he was less discreet about the gentleman on the third floor.

Of the highest social standing, you know, who had rented the room just to be able to work quietly there one night a week.

'Oh, he works does he? I wonder what at?' asked Octave.

'He was good enough to ask me to look after his room,' continued Monsieur Gourd, pretending not to have heard, 'and, you know, he pays on the nail. Ah! when you're somebody's housekeeper you soon find out if they're all right or not. He's a thorough gentleman, he is; you can tell that from his linen.'

He was obliged to stand to one side, and even Octave had to step back for a moment in the lodge, so as to let the carriage of the people on the second floor come out on its way to the Bois de Boulogne. The horses, reined in by the coachman, pawed the ground; and, as the large closed landau rolled through under the arch, two handsome children could be seen behind the glass, their smiling faces almost hiding the indistinct profiles of their father and mother. Monsieur Gourd stood at attention, polite but cold.

'Those people don't make much noise in the house,' said Octave.

'Nobody makes any noise,' replied the concierge dryly. 'Every one lives as they see fit, that's all. Some people know how to live, and some don't.'

The people on the second floor provoked criticism, because they associated with no one. They appeared to be rich, however. The husband wrote books, but Monsieur Gourd's curling lip showed that he put little faith in that sort of thing, especially as nobody knew what went on in that household, apparently self-sufficient and always perfectly happy. It didn't seem at all normal, at least to him.

Octave was opening the hall door when Valérie came in. He politely stood aside to let her pass.

'Are you quite well, madame?'

'Yes, thank, you monsieur.'

She was out of breath, and as she went upstairs he looked at her muddy boots, and thought about that lunch flat on her back that the maids had been talking about. No doubt she had walked home, not having been able to get a cab. A warm, stale smell came from her damp petticoats.

Exhaustion and physical languor made her catch hold of the banisters every now and then.

'What an awful day, madame, isn't it?'

'Awful, and so close, too!'

She had reached the first floor, where they politely parted company. At a glance he saw how haggard her face was, how heavy her eyelids were with sleep, and noted her uncombed hair beneath the hastily tied bonnet. And, as he continued on his way upstairs, he got angry. Why, then, would she not do that with him?

He wasn't more stupid or uglier than anybody else.

On passing Madame Juzeur's on the third floor, he remembered his promise to her of the previous evening. That discreet little woman with bright blue eyes pricked his curiosity. He rang the bell, and it was Madame Juzeur herself who answered the door.

'Oh, how good of you to call, Monsieur Octave. Do come in!'

There was a certain stuffiness about the apartment. Carpets and curtains everywhere; chairs as soft as eiderdown, and the atmosphere as warm and heavy as that of a chest lined with old dyed silk satin. In the drawing-room, which with its double curtains had the solemn stillness of a vestry, Octave was invited to take a seat on a broad, very low sofa.

'This is the lace,' said Madame Juzeur, as she came back with a sandalwood box full of pieces of cloth. 'I want to make a present of it to somebody, and I'm curious to know its value.'

It was a piece of very fine old lace. Octave examined it with his professional eye, and declared that it was worth three hundred francs. Then, without more ado, as they were both handling the lace, he leaned forward and kissed her fingers, which were as tiny as those of a little girl.

'Oh, Monsieur Octave, at my age! You must be forgetting yourself!' exclaimed Madame Juzeur, with a pretty air of surprise, though not at all annoyed.

She was thirty-two, and made out she was quite an old woman. As usual, she spoke of her troubles. Gracious goodness! After ten days of married life, the cruel man had gone and left her one morning, never to return and nobody ever knew why.

'You can well understand,' she said, looking up to the ceiling, 'that after such a shock, it's all over for any woman.'

Octave had kept hold of her warm little hand, which seemed to melt into his own, and he kept lightly kissing it on the fingertips. She looked down at him vaguely, tenderly, and then, in a maternal way, she exclaimed: 'Oh, you dear child!'

Believing himself to be encouraged, he tried to put his arm round her waist and pull her on to the sofa, but she gently slipped away from him, laughing as if she thought he was just playing a game.

'No, leave me alone, and don't touch me if you wish us to remain good friends.'

'Then you don't want to?' he asked, in a low voice.

'Want to do what? I don't know what you mean. Oh! You may have my hand as much as you like.'

He caught hold of her hand again. But this time he opened it, kissing the palm. With half-shut eyes, she treated the process as a joke, opening her fingers as a cat puts out its claws to have its paw tickled. She would not let him go beyond the wrist. That first day a sacred line was drawn there, marking the point where innocence would be transgressed.

'Monsieur le Curé is coming upstairs,' announced Louise, abruptly, as she returned from an errand. With her yellowish complexion and crushed features, the orphan looked every bit a foundling. She giggled idiotically when she caught sight of the gentleman nibbling at madame's hand. But Madame Juzeur gave her such a look that she fled.

'I fear I shall not be able to make anything of her,' she said. 'Nevertheless, one has to try and put one of these poor creatures on the right road. Monsieur Mouret, would you like to come through here?'

She took him to the dining-room, so that the other room might be left for the priest, whom Louise showed in. And, as she said good-bye, she expressed a hope that Octave would come again and have a chat. It would be a little company for her; she was always so lonely and depressed. But, happily, in religion she had her consolation.

About five o'clock that evening Octave felt it a positive relief to make himself at home at the Pichons, while waiting for dinner. The house and its inmates bewildered him somewhat. Having initially been taken in, in all his provincial naïvety, by the solemn splendour of its staircase, he was gradually becoming filled with excessive contempt for everything he imagined took place behind those big mahogany doors. He didn't know what to think; these middle-class women whose icy virtue had at first discouraged him, seemed now as if they ought to grant him their favours even without being asked, and, if one of them resisted, it filled him with surprise and bitterness.

When she saw him put down the parcel of books which he had fetched for her that morning, Marie grew crimson with pleasure.

'How good of you, Monsieur Octave!' she kept repeating. 'Thank you so much. How nice of you to come so early. Will you have a glass of sugar and water, with some cognac in it? That will give you an appetite.'

Just to please her, he accepted. It was all very agreeable; even Pichon and the Vuilaumes, who gossiped on in their doddering Sunday fashion. Every now and then Marie ran to the kitchen, where she was cooking a shoulder of mutton, and Octave mischievously followed her out, and catching her round the waist, in front of the oven, kissed the back of her neck. Without a cry, without a start, she turned round and kissed him on the mouth with her bloodless lips. To the young man their coldness seemed delicious.

'Well, what about your new minister then?' he said to Pichon, on coming back into the room.

The clerk was startled. What! There was going to be a new Minister of Education. He'd heard nothing about it; in his office they never took any interest in that sort of thing.

'It's such a horrid weather,' he said in the same breath. 'It's quite impossible to keep one's trousers clean!'

Madame Vuillaume was talking about a girl in the Batignolles district who had strayed from the straight and narrow.

'You would hardly believe it, monsieur,' she said. 'The girl had been extremely well brought up, but she was so bored at having to live with her parents that she twice tried to jump out of the window. It's totally incredible!'

'They should put bars over the windows,' remarked Monsieur Vuillaume, simply.

The dinner proved delightful. Talk of this sort went on all evening, as they sat around the unpretentious table, lit by one small lamp. Pichon and Monsieur Vuillaume, having got on to the subject of government officials, went on and on about directors and sub-directors. The father-in-law insisted on talking about those of his day, and then remembered that they were dead, while Pichon, for his part, was still referring to the new ones, amid an endless muddle of names. On one point, however, the two men, as well as Madame Vuillaume, were agreed: that big slob, Chavignat, whose wife was so plain, had had far too many children. On his income, it was simply absurd. Octave, feeling happy and relaxed, smiled. It had been a long time since he'd spent such a pleasant evening; he even ended up as one of Chavignat's most uncompromising critics. Marie seemed to soothe him with her clear, innocent gaze, untroubled by the fact he was sitting next to her husband, and helping them both to what they liked best in her languidly obedient way.

At ten o'clock exactly, the Vuillaumes rose to go. Pichon put on his hat. Every Sunday he went with them as far as their omnibus. It was a habit which, out of deference, he had observed ever since his marriage, and the Vuillaumes would have been very hurt if he had now tried to discontinue it. All three of them set out for the Rue de Richelieu, and walked slowly up it, scrutinising the Batignolles omnibuses, which were always full. Pichon was thus often obliged to go as far as Montmartre, for it would never have done for him to leave the Vuillaumes before making sure they were safely on their way home. As they walked very slowly, it took him nearly two hours to go there and back.

There was much friendly shaking of hands on the landing. As Octave went back inside with Marie, he said: 'It's raining. Jules won't get back before midnight.'

As Lilitte had been put to bed early, he immediately made Marie sit on his knee, drinking the remainder of his coffee with her out of the same cup, like a husband glad that his guests have gone, finally having his home to himself, fired up by the little family gathering just ended, and able to kiss his wife behind closed doors. A drowsy warmth pervaded the poky little room, as well as a faint odour of vanilla from a dish of *oeufs à la neige*. As he was lightly kissing the young woman under the chin, someone knocked at the door. Marie didn't even jump up in fear. It was young Josserand, the half-witted lad. Whenever he could escape from the apartment opposite, he used to come across and chat to her, as her gentleness had an attraction for him; and they both got on very well together as they exchanged non-sequiturs at ten-minute intervals.

Octave, greatly annoyed, remained silent.

'They've got some people there tonight,' stammered Saturnin. 'I don't care if they won't have me at table. I've taken the lock off and got away. That will worry them.'

'But they'll wonder what's happened to you. You ought to go back,' said Marie, aware of Octave's impatience.

Then the idiot grinned with delight as, in his faltering way, he reported what was going on at home. Each of his visits to Marie seemed to be in order to clear his memory.

'Papa has been working all night again, and Mamma slapped Berthe. By the way, when one gets married, does it hurt?'

Then, as Marie didn't answer, he went on excitedly: 'I don't want to go away to the country! If they lay a hand on her, I'll strangle them all; that'll be easy enough, at night, while they're asleep. The palm of her hand is as smooth as notepaper; but the other is a beast of a girl.'

Then he started all over again, getting increasingly muddled, unable to express what he had come to say. Marie at last persuaded him to go back to his parents without his even having noticed her companion.

Fearing another interruption, Octave wanted to take the young woman across to his own room; but, blushing violently, she refused. Not understanding her qualms, he kept on assuring her that they would be certain to hear Jules coming upstairs, and there would be plenty of time for her to get back to her room. Then, as he was pulling her along, she became quite angry, as indignant as a woman being assaulted.

'No, not in your room; never! It would be too dreadful. Let's stay here.' And she rushed away to the back of her apartment.

Octave was still on the landing, amazed at such unexpected resistance, when he heard a loud wrangling in the courtyard below. Clearly everything was going wrong today; it would have been better if he had gone to bed. A noise of this sort was so unusual at this hour, that at last he opened a window to listen.

Monsieur Gourd was shouting out: 'I'm telling you you're not going past his door! The landlord has been sent for. He will come down and kick you out himself!'

'Kick me out? What for?' said a gruff voice. 'Don't I pay my rent? Go on Amélie, and if the man touches you, he'll know about it!'

It was the carpenter from upstairs, who was returning with the woman they had sent packing that morning. Octave leaned out to look; but in the black courtyard he only saw great moving shadows thrown by the dim gaslight in the hall.

'Monsieur Vabre! Monsieur Vabre!' cried the concierge, as the carpenter pushed him aside. 'Quick, quick! She's coming in!'

Despite her bad legs, Madame Gourd had gone to fetch the landlord, busy at that very moment on his great work. He was coming down.

Octave heard him furiously repeating: 'It's scandalous, disgraceful! I won't allow such a thing in my house!'

Then, addressing the workman, who at first seemed somewhat abashed: 'Send that woman away at once! At once, do you hear? We don't want any women brought in here.'

'But she's my wife!' replied the carpenter, looking terrified. 'She's in domestic service, and only comes once a month, when her people let her have a day off. That's the plain truth of it. It's not your place to prevent me from sleeping with my wife, if you don't mind me saying so!'

Then both concierge and landlord lost their heads.

'I give you notice to quit,' stuttered old Vabre, 'and, meanwhile, I forbid you to turn my premises into a brothel! Gourd, throw that person out on to the street. No, sir, none of your nonsense with me. If a man's married, he ought to say so. Hold your tongue, and let me have no more of your insolence!'

The carpenter, good-natured fellow that he was, and who, no doubt, had had a little too much wine, burst out laughing.

'It's a damned funny thing, all the same. Well, Amélie, as the gentleman objects, you had better go back to your employer's. We'll make our baby some other time. We wanted to make a baby, that's all we wanted. I'll take your notice with pleasure! Don't think I want to stay any longer in your hovel. Nice goings-on there are, too. He won't have women brought into the house – oh, no! But on every floor he lets well-dressed whores carry on behind closed doors. Oh, you bloody fools!'

Amélie had left, so as not to get her husband into any more trouble, while he continued his good-humoured banter. Meantime, Gourd covered Monsieur Vabre's retreat, while voicing his own reflections on the matter. What a filthy lot the lower orders were! One workman in the house was quite enough to infect it.

Octave shut the window. Then, just as he was returning to Marie, someone lightly brushed past him in the passage.

'Hello! You again!' he said, recognising Trublot.

For a moment the latter was speechless; then he tried to explain. 'Yes; I've been dining with the Josserands, and I was going up to—'

'To that slut, Adèle, I suppose? And you swore you didn't!'

Then brazening it out in his usual way, Trublot said, with enthusiasm: 'I assure you, my dear fellow, it's worth it! She's got absolutely wonderful skin, you've no idea!' Then he cursed the workman, whose damned nonsense about women had been responsible for his nearly being caught coming up the back stairs. He had been obliged to come round by the front staircase. Then, as he hurried away, he added: 'Remember, it's next Thursday that I'm taking you to Duveyrier's mistress. We'll dine together first.'

With its tranquillity restored, the house was pervaded by a holy calm coming from each of its chaste recesses.

Octave had rejoined Marie in her bedroom, sitting beside her on the conjugal bed while she was arranging the pillows.

Upstairs, meanwhile, in Adèle's room, the only chair had a basin on it and an old pair of slippers, so Trublot sat down on her narrow bed and waited for her there in evening dress. When he recognised Julie's step as she came up to bed, he held his breath, terrified of women's quarrels.

At last Adèle appeared. She was angry, and, seizing his arm, said: 'Why do you treat me like that when I'm waiting at table?'

'What do you mean?'

'Well, you never so much as look at me, and you never say please when you want some bread. This evening, as I was handing the veal round, you looked as if you had never had anything to do with me. I've just had about enough of it. Everybody in the building is wearing me down with insults and there's no need for you to side with them too!'

She undressed in a fury and, flinging herself down on the creaking old bed, turned her back on him. He had to beg for mercy. Meanwhile, in the next room, the carpenter, still full of wine, was talking to himself at the top of his voice, so that the whole corridor could hear him.

'Well, that's a funny thing, ain't it; when they won't let you sleep with your own lawful wife? You won't have any women in the house, won't you, you silly old bugger! Go and sniff around under all the bedclothes at this very moment, and you'll soon see what's what!'

In order to induce Uncle Bachelard to give Berthe a dowry, for the past fornight the Josserands had asked him to dinner almost every evening, in spite of his revolting habits.

When they told him about the marriage, all he did was pat his niece on the cheek and say: 'What! So you're going to get married? That's nice, isn't it, my girlie?'

To every hint he turned a deaf ear, exaggerating his role as a bibulous old rake, becoming suddenly drunk whenever the subject of money was raised.

Madame Josserand then had the idea of inviting him to meet Auguste, the bridegroom-elect, feeling sure that his actually seeing the young man would be decisive. This was pretty heroic, for the family generally took care to keep their uncle out of sight, fearing their reputation would suffer. However, he behaved fairly well; there was only one large syrup stain on his waistcoat, the result no doubt of a visit to some café. Yet when his sister, after Auguste's departure, asked what he thought of the bridegroom, without committing himself, he merely said: 'He's charming, quite charming.'

But the matter had to be settled somehow, for time was short. So Madame Josserand decided to take the bull by the horns.

'As we're now alone,' she continued, 'let's make the most of this family occasion. You must run along, dears, as we have to talk to your uncle. Berthe, go and look after Saturnin, and see he doesn't take the lock off the door again.'

Ever since they had been busy planning his sister's marriage, keeping it a secret from him, Saturnin wandered about the house, with wild eyes, suspicious that something was going on; he dreamed up such diabolical schemes that the family was deeply uneasy.

'I have made all my enquiries,' said the mother, when she had shut herself in with the father and the uncle. 'This is the Vabres' financial situation.'

Then, and at length, she went into the details. Old Vabre had brought half a million with him from Versailles. If the house had cost him three hundred thousand francs, he would have two hundred thousand left, which in the last twelve years had been producing interest. Besides, every year his rents brought him in twenty-two thousand francs; and, as he lived with the Duveyriers and hardly spent anything at all, he must therefore be worth five or six hundred thousand francs, not counting the house. So, on that side, there were handsome expectations.

'He has no vices, then?' asked Bachelard. 'I thought he speculated on the Bourse.'

At this Madame Josserand loudly protested. Such a quiet old man, absorbed in such important work! He, at least, had shown that he could amass a fortune! She smiled bitterly as she glanced at her husband, who lowered his head.

As for Vabre's three chldren, Auguste, Clotilde and Théophile, they had each had a hundred thousand francs at their mother's death. Théophile, after losing a lot of money, was living as best he could on the remains of his inheritance. Clotilde, whose only passion was her piano, had probably invested her share. With his hundred thousand francs, long kept in reserve, Auguste had bought those ground-floor premises to launch himself in the silk trade.

'Of course, the old fellow won't give his children anything when they marry,' remarked Bachelard.

Well, no, he didn't seem keen on giving away his money; that was only too plain. When Clotilde had got married, he had undertaken to give her a dowry of eighty thousand francs; but Duveyrier had never received more than ten thousand. Far from asking for the balance, he even gave his father-in-law free board and lodging, indulging his avarice, no doubt in the hope of one day acquiring his whole fortune. In the same way, after promising Théophile fifty thousand francs when he married Valérie, he at first merely paid the interest on such a sum, and since then had not parted with a single penny, even going so far as to demand rent from the young couple, which they paid for fear of being struck out of his will. So, all things considered, it would be a mistake to rely too much on the fifty thousand francs that Auguste was to receive when the marriage-contract was signed. He'd be lucky if his father let him have the ground-floor premises rent-free for a few years.

'Well,' declared Bachelard, 'it's difficult for the parents, you know . . . dowries are never really paid.'

'Let's go back to Auguste,' continued Madame Josserand.

'I've told you about what he might get in due course; the only
danger there is the Duveyriers, and Berthe, when she becomes
one of the family, should keep a close watch on them . . . The
present position is that Auguste, after buying the business for
sixty thousand francs, has set himself up with the other forty
thousand. Only that's not proving enough; then, again, he's
single and wants a wife, so he means to marry . . . Berthe is
pretty, and he can already imagine her working for him behind
the counter; and, as for her dowry, well, fifty thousand francs is
a tidy enough sum to have made up his mind.'

Uncle Bachelard never moved an eyelash. At last, affecting
deep concern, he said that he had really hoped for something
much better. And he began to criticise the bridegroom-elect. A
charming fellow, certainly, but too old, much too old; why, he
was over thirty-three. What's more, he was always in poor
health, racked by neuralgia; doleful-looking too, not half
sprightly enough to succeed in business.

'Have you got anybody else in mind?' asked Madame Josser-
and, whose patience was well-nigh exhausted. 'I hunted all over
Paris before I could find even him.'

She herself had no illusions about Auguste and proceeded to
pick him to pieces.

'Oh, he's not a paragon, I grant you; in fact, I think he's
rather a fool. But then I always mistrust men who've never had
their fling when young, and who have to reflect for years before
risking a step in life. When he left college, as headaches put a
stop to his studies, he remained a mere clerk for fifteen years
before daring to touch his hundred thousand francs; while his
father, so it seems, cheated him out of the interest on it. No,
he's not a wonderful catch, I admit.'

Up to now Monsieur Josserand had said nothing. He now
ventured to remark: 'But, my dear, why insist on this marriage,
if the young man is in such poor health . . .'

'Oh!' said Bachelard. 'Poor health needn't be an obstacle.
Berthe would find it easy enough to marry again.'

'But suppose he's impotent,' suggested the father. 'Suppose he
should make our child unhappy?'

'Unhappy, indeed!' cried Madame Josserand. 'Why don't
you just come out and say that I've thrown my girl at the first
man to turn up. Between ourselves, surely, we can discuss him,
and say he's this, or that, not young, not good-looking, not

clever ... We can talk about it, and that's perfectly normal. However, he'll do. We're never going to find anybody better; and, let's face it, it's an uphoped-for match for Berthe. I was going to give it all up as a bad job, that's for sure.'

She rose; and Monsieur Josserand, reduced to silence, pushed back his chair.

'I'm only afraid of one thing,' she continued, as she resolutely planted herself in front of her brother, 'and that's that he may break it off if the dowry is not forthcoming on the day the contract is to be signed. That's understandable; he needs money, you know.'

Just then she heard the sound of laboured breathing close behind her, and she turned round. It was Saturnin, who had thrust his head round the door, glaring at her with wolfish eyes. They were all panic-stricken, for he had stolen a spit from the kitchen, to roast the geese, so he said. Uncle Bachelard, who had felt very uncomfortable at the turn their conversation was taking, took advantage of the crisis.

'Don't disturb yourselves,' he called out from the ante-room. 'I'm off; I've got a midnight appointment with one of my clients, who has come over specially from Brazil.'

When they had succeeded in putting Saturnin to bed, Madame Josserand, in her exasperation, declared that it was impossible to keep him at home any longer. He would end up doing them some injury if he were not shut up in an asylum. It was simply insufferable always having to keep him hidden away. His sisters would never get married as long as he was there to disgust and terrify everybody.

'Let us wait a while longer,' muttered Monsieur Josserand, whose heart bled at the thought of this separation.

'No, no,' declared his wife. 'I don't want him to finish up by putting me on a spit. I had just got my brother into a corner, and was going to make him do something. Never mind. We'll go with Berthe tomorrow, and have it out with him at his own place, and then we'll see if he has the cheek to keep on getting out of his promises. Besides, Berthe ought to pay her godfather a visit. It's only right and proper.'

Next day all three of them, mother, father and daughter, paid an official visit to the uncle's premises, on the ground floor and the basement of an enormous house in the Rue d'Enghien.* The entrance was blocked by large vans. In the covered courtyard

numerous packers were nailing up cases, and through open
doorways one caught sight of piles of goods, dried vegetables,
and remnants of silk, stationery and tallow, representing the
thousands of orders on which Bachelard received a commission,
or his stockpiling when prices were low. He was there, with his
big red nose, his eyes still inflamed by last night's debauch, but
with his intellect clear, as his business acumen and enterprise
came back to him the moment he pored over his account-books.

'Hello! Is that you?' he said, utterly weary at the sight of
them. He took them into a little office, from which he could
supervise his men through the window.

'I have brought Berthe to see you,' explained Madame Josserand. 'She knows how much she is indebted to you.'

Then, when the girl had kissed her uncle and taken her
mother's hint to go off and look at the goods in the courtyard,
Madame Josserand resolutely broached the subject.   ·

'Look here, Narcisse, this is the situation. Relying on your
kindheartedness and your promises, I'm committed to give
Berthe a dowry of fifty thousand francs. If I don't, the engagement will be broken off, and now that things have gone so far,
this would be a disgrace. You cannot possibly leave us in such
an awkward position.

A film came over Bachelard's eyes, and he stammered out, as
if quite drunk: 'Eh? What's that? You've made a promise . . .
You should never promise; bad thing to promise . . .'

Then he pleaded poverty. For instance, he had bought a
whole lot of horse-hair, thinking that the price of it would go
up. Not a bit of it; the price had fallen lower still, and he'd been
obliged to get rid of it at a loss. Rushing to his books, he opened
his ledger, and insisted on showing them the invoices. He was
ruined.

'Rubbish!' exclaimed Monsieur Josserand, at the end of his
patience. 'I know all about your business, and you're doing very
well indeed. You would be rolling in money if you didn't
squander it as you do. Mind, I'm not asking you for anything.
It was Eléonore's idea. But allow me to tell you, Bachelard, that
you've been leading us a merry dance. For fifteen years every
Saturday, when I went through your books for you, you always
promised that—'

The uncle interrupted him, violently beating his chest. 'I
promised? Nothing of the sort. No, no! Leave me alone and

then you'll see. I don't like to be asked; it annoys and upsets me. One day you'll see what I shall do.'

Even Madame Josserand herself could wring nothing further from him. Shaking them by the hand, he brushed away a casual tear, spoke of his true feelings, of his affection for the family, and begged them to torment him no further, as, by God! they would never have cause to repent it. He knew his duty, and would do it to the letter. Later on Berthe would find out how much her uncle loved her.

'And what about the insurance you took out to provide a dowry?' he asked, resuming his matter-of-fact tone. 'Those fifty thousand francs for which you had insured the girl's life?'

Madame Josserand shrugged her shoulders.

'That all went by the board fourteen years ago. We've told you twenty times that when the fourth premium became due we were unable to pay the two thousand francs.'

'That doesn't matter,' he muttered, with a wink. 'You must talk about this insurance to the Vabres, and take your time about paying the dowry money. One never pays a dowry.'

Monsieur Josserand rose in disgust.

'So that's all you have to say to us, is it?'

Pretending not to understand, the uncle insisted that that was quite normal.

'One never pays, I tell you. You pay something on account, and then the interest. Why, look at Monsieur Vabre himself! Did my father ever pay you Eléonore's dowry? Of course not. People hang on to their money.'

'In short, you advise me to do something entirely dishonest!' cried Monsieur Josserand. 'It would be a lie! I should be committing forgery if I produced that insurance policy—'

Madame Josserand cut him short. At this suggestion of her brother's she became grave. It was surprising that she had never thought of this before.

'Good gracious me! How touchy you are, my dear! Narcisse never told you to commit forgery!'

'Of course I didn't,' muttered Bachelard. 'There's no need to show any papers.'

'The point is to gain time,' she continued. 'Promise the dowry now, and later on we'll give it.'

But the worthy man's conscience was having none of it. No, absolutely not, never again was he going to go down that slippery slope. They were always taking advantage of his easy-going nature, getting him to agree to things he later bitterly regretted. Since he had no dowry to give, he couldn't possibly promise one. Bachelard whistled and drummed on the window-pane, as if to show his utter contempt for such scruples. Madame Josserand listened, her face livid with a pent-up fury which suddenly exploded.

'Well, the marriage is going to take place anyway. It's my daughter's last chance. I would rather cut off my right hand than let it slip. I don't care about anybody else. When you're driven to it, you're capable of anything.'

'Then I presume you would commit murder in order to get your daughter married?'

She drew herself up to her full height.

'Yes I would!' she retorted, angrily.

Then she smiled. Bachelard was obliged to quell the tempest. What was the use of getting angry? It was far better to come to some amicable arrangement. Thus, worn out and trembling from the effects of the quarrel, Monsieur Josserand agreed to talk matters over with Duveyrier, on whom, according to Madame Josserand, everything depended. In order to get hold of the counsellor when he was in a good mood, Bachelard proposed to set up a meeting with his brother-in-law somewhere Duveyrier could refuse nothing.

'It's merely to be a preliminary meeting,' said Josserand, still protesting. 'I'm not going to enter into any commitment, that I swear.'

'Of course not, of course not,' said Bachelard. 'Eléonore doesn't want you to do anything dishonourable.'

The Berthe came back. She had spotted some boxes of dried fruit, and with much kissing and coaxing tried to get her uncle to give her one. But at this point his stammer returned. He couldn't possibly do so; they were all counted, and had to be sent off to St Petersburg that very evening. He gradually got them out towards the street, while his sister, at the sight of these huge warehouses packed to the roof with every conceivable merchandise lingered behind, mortified to think that such a fortune should have been made by a man totally devoid of principle, and comparing it bitterly with her husband's impotent honesty.

'Till tomorrow night then about nine o'clock, at the Café de

Mulhouse,' said Bachelard, as he shook Monsieur Josserand's hand when they got into the street.

It so happened that the next day, Octave and Trublot, who had dined together before going to see Clarisse, Duveyrier's mistress, went into the Café de Mulhouse so as not to arrive too early, though she lived a good way off, in the Rue de la Cerisaie.* It was hardly eight o'clock. On entering, they heard violent quarrelling at the far end of the room. There they saw Bachelard, drunk already, with flaming cheeks and looking enormous, who was having a row with a little pale-faced, testy gentleman.

'You've been spitting in my beer again,' he roared. 'I won't stand it, sir!'

'Hold your tongue or I'll give you a beating!' said the little man, standing on tiptoe.

Then Bachelard raised his voice, without budging an inch. 'Just you dare, sir! Just you dare!'

And when the other man knocked his hat off, which he always wore cocked on one side of his head, he repeated even more forcefully: 'Just you dare, sir! Just you dare!'

Then, picking up his hat, he sat down majestically, and called to the waiter: 'Alfred, change this beer!'

Octave and Trublot had noticed Gueulin sitting beside Bachelard, with his back to the wall, smoking away with utter indifference. Astonished by what they'd witnessed, they asked him what was going on.

'Don't know,' he replied, watching his cigar smoke curling upwards. 'There's always some row or other. He's a right one for getting his head punched! He never gives in!'

Bachelard shook hands with the newcomers. He loved being with the young fellows. He was delighted to hear that they were going to see Clarisse. So was he; Gueulin was coming too; only he'd arranged to meet Josserand, his brother-in-law, here first. And the little room resounded with his strident voice as he wildly ordered every imaginable sort of drink for his young friends, with the prodigality of someone out for a spree and oblivious of the cost. Uncouth, with glittering false teeth, bulbous red nose and snowy, close-cropped hair, he hobnobbed with the waiters and ran them off their legs, while becoming so unbearable to his neighbours that the proprietor twice asked

him to leave if he couldn't behave. The night before, he had
been turned out of the Café de Madrid.

Just then a prostitute came in, and went out again after
walking round the room with a tired look in her eyes. This led
Octave to talk about women. Bachelard, spitting sideways, hit
Trublot, without even apologising. Women had cost him far too
much; he flattered himself he had had the best available in Paris.
In his line of business there was no point in being a cheapskate:
you had to show the price was of secondary importance. But
he'd finished with all that sort of thing now; he wanted to be
loved for his own sake. And as Octave watched this swaggerer
flinging bank-notes to the wind, he thought with surprise of the
uncle who put on a drunk stutter to get out of the machinations
of his relatives.

'Don't brag, my dear uncle,' said Gueulin. 'One can always
have more women than one wants.'

'Then, you silly idiot,' retorted Bachelard, 'why don't you
ever have any?'

Gueulin shrugged his shoulders with a look of profound
disdain.

'Why not . . . Well, only yesterday I dined with a friend and
his mistress. It wasn't long before she was playing with my foot
under the table. There was a chance, wasn't there? But when
she asked me to see her home, I bolted and haven't been near
her since . . . Oh! I'm not saying that it wouldn't have been very
pleasant. But afterwards, uncle, afterwards! She might have
turned out to be one of those women who stick to you like glue!
No, I'm not that stupid!'

Trublot nodded approvingly, for he too had given up society
women, terrified of the morning after. Then, Gueulin, getting
going, proceeded to cite examples. One day, in the train, a
splendid brunette, whom he didn't know, had gone to sleep on
his shoulder; what would he have done with her when he got to
the station? Another time, after a wedding, he found a neighbour's wife in his bed. A bit much, wasn't it? And he would
certainly have done something foolish, had he not been haunted
by the idea that afterwards she would ask him to buy her some
boots.

'Talk about opportunities, uncle,' he concluded. 'Why,
nobody has had as many as I have! But I hold back, like
everyone else afraid of the consequences. If it weren't for the

consequences, why, that would be all right. Hello, good-bye, if that was all there was to it, you'd see nothing else but that going on in the streets!'

But Bachelard, daydreaming, was no longer listening to him. His noisy mood had vanished, and his eyes were misted over.

'If you're very good,' he said suddenly, 'I'll show you something.'

And, after paying, he led them out.

Octave reminded him of his appointment with Monsieur Josserand. That didn't matter; they would come back for him. Before leaving the café, Bachelard looked round furtively and then stole the lumps of sugar left by a customer at an adjoining table.

'Follow me,' he said when they were out on the street. 'It's close by.'

He walked along, meditating, without a word, and stopped in front of a door in the Rue Saint-Marc. The three young men were about to follow him, when suddenly he seemed to hesitate.

'No, let's go back, I don't think I will.'

But they protested. What did he think he was doing?

'Well, Gueulin can't come up, nor you, Monsieur Trublot. The two of you would only laugh and jeer. Come on, Monsieur Octave, you're a serious young man.'

He made Octave go up the stairs in front of him, while the other two laughed, and from the pavement begged to be kindly remembered to the ladies. On reaching the fourth floor he knocked, and an old woman opened the door.

'Oh! It's you is it, Monsieur Narcisse? Fifi didn't expect you this evening.'

She was fat and smiling with a face as white and calm as that of a sister of mercy. In the narrow dining-room which she ushered them into, a tall, fair girl, pretty and simple-looking, was embroidering an altar-cloth.

'Good-day, uncle,' she said, rising and offering her forehead to Bachelard's thick, tremulous lips.

When the latter introduced Monsieur Octave Mouret, a distinguished young friend of his, the two women dropped him an old-fashioned curtsey, and they all sat down at the table; lit by an oil lamp. It was like some calm provincial interior; two ordered lives hidden from the outside world, surviving off next to nothing. As the room looked on to an inner courtyard, even the sound of traffic was inaudible.

While Bachelard, with paternal solicitude, questioned the girl as to what she'd done and how she'd been feeling since the previous evening, her aunt, Mademoiselle Menu, confided their whole history to Octave, with the frankness of an honest woman who has nothing to conceal.

'Yes, sir, I come from Villeneuve, near Lille. I'm well known at the Mardienne Brothers, in the Rue Saint-Sulpice, where I worked as an embroideress for thirty years. Then, when a cousin of mine left me a house in the country, I was lucky enough to let it for life, at a thousand francs a year, to some people who hoped that they would bury me the next day, but who have been nicely punished for their evil presumption, for I'm still going strong, in spite of my seventy-five years.'

She laughed, showing teeth as white as those of a young girl.

'I could no longer work,' she went on, 'for my eyesight was gone, when my niece Fanny needed looking after. Her father, Captain Menu, died without leaving a farthing, and not a single relative to help her, sir. So I had to take the girl away from school, and I've taught her embroidery, not much of a trade, it's true, but either that or nothing; it's always the women who starve to death. Luckily, she met Monsieur Narcisse, so now I can die happy.'

And with hands across her stomach, like some old seamstress who has sworn never to touch a needle again, she enveloped Bachelard and Fifi with silent tenderness.

Just then the old man was saying to the girl: 'Now, did you really think about me? And what have you been thinking then?'

Fifi raised her clear eyes, while her fingers pulled through her golden thread.

'Why, that you were a good friend, and that I loved you very much.'

She hardly glanced at Octave, as if indifferent to his youthful good looks. However, he smiled at her, struck by her grace, and not knowing quite what to think; while the spinster aunt, staled by a chastity that had cost her nothing, continued in an undertone: 'I could have married her to somebody, eh? A workman would beat her; a clerk would only make her bear him endless children. It's much better that she should be nice to Monsieur Narcisse, who seems such a good, kind gentleman.'

Then raising her voice: 'Well, Monsieur Narcisse, it's not my fault if you're not satisfied with her. I always tell her, "Make yourself pleasant, show him how grateful you are." It's only natural that I should be glad to know that she's well looked after. When one has no relatives, it's not easy to give a young girl a start in life.'

Then Octave relaxed into the uncomplicated charm of his surroundings. The heavy air of the apartment was charged with an odour of ripe fruit. Only Fifi's needle, as it pricked the silk, made a slight noise at regular intervals, like the ticking of a cuckoo-clock domesticating Bachelard's romantic idyll. The old spinster, however, was probity personified; she lived on her income of a thousand francs, and never touched a farthing of Fifi's money, who spent it just as she pleased. The only things she ever allowed her to pay for occasionally were roast chestnuts and white wine, when she emptied the money-box full of coins given her as good-conduct medals by her kind friend.

'My little duck,' said Bachelard, as he rose to go, 'we've got some business to attend to. I shall look in tomorrow. Be a good girl.'

He kissed her on the forehead. Then, looking affectionately at her, he said to Octave: 'You may give her a kiss, too. She's only a child.'

The young man's lips touched her cool skin. She smiled; she was so modest. It seemed as if he were one of the family; he'd never met worthier folk. Bachelard was on his way out when he suddenly came back.

'Oh, I forgot! Here's a little present for you!'

And, emptying his pocket, he gave Fifi the sugar that he had just stolen at the café. She thanked him profusely, and blushed with pleasure as she crunched one of the lumps. Then, growing bolder, she said: 'You haven't got any four-sou pieces, have you?'

Bachelard searched his pockets, but in vain. Octave happened to have one, which the girl accepted as a souvenir. She didn't go to the door with them, no doubt for propriety's sake; and they could hear the click of her needle as she got immediately back to work on her altar-cloth, while Mademoiselle Menu showed them out in her good-natured, old-fashioned way.

'Well, that's worth seeing, eh?' said Bachelard pausing on the stairs. 'You know, that doesn't cost me five louis a month. I've

had about enough of money-grabbing little bitches. I wanted
something with a heart.'

Then, as Octave laughed, his misgivings returned.

'You're a decent chap, now; you won't take advantage of my
good-nature. Not a word, mind, to Gueulin; swear it, on your
honour! I'm not going to let him see that angel until he's worthy
of the privilege. Say what you like, virtue is a good thing; it's
rejuvenating. I myself have always been an idealist.'

His old drunkard's voice trembled; tears filled his flabby
eyelids. Down below, Trublot began teasing him, pretending he
was taking down the number of the house, while Gueulin
shrugged his shoulders and asked Octave, to his astonishment,
what he thought of the young thing. When he became sentimental after a night on the town, Bachelard could never resist taking
people to see those ladies, torn between the vanity of displaying
his treasure and the fear that someone might steal it. Then, next
day, he'd forget he'd revealed his secret, and go back to the Rue
Saint-Marc with his air of mystery.

'Everybody knows Fifi,' said Gueulin, quietly.

Bachelard, meanwhile, was looking for a cab, when Octave
exclaimed: 'What about Monsieur Josserand, who is waiting for
you at the café?'

The other two had forgotten all about him. Extremely
annoyed at wasting his evening, Monsieur Josserand stood
fidgeting at the door, as he never went inside cafés. At last they
set off for the Rue de la Cerisaie. But they had to take two cabs,
Bachelard and Josserand going in one, and the three young men
in another.

Gueulin, his voice virtually drowned by the rattling of the old
vehicle, began talking about the insurance company where he
was employed. In Trublot's view, insurance companies were as
boring as stocks and shares. Then the conversation turned to
Duveyrier. Wasn't it sad that a man that rich, and a magistrate
to boot, should let himself be led by the nose by women in the
way he did! He couldn't do without them, finding them all over
the place, in the furthest reaches of the city, where the omnibuses turned round: little so-called widows living in a room of
their own; nondescript milliners or laundresses who kept shops
devoid of customers; wenches picked out of the gutter, cleaned
up and cosily installed, visited regularly once a week, like a
clerk going to the office. But Trublot took his side: in the first

place, his temperament was responsible and then, again, it wasn't everybody that had got his kind of wife. People said that ever since their wedding-night she'd been repulsed by him, his red blotches filling her with disgust. And she didn't mind his having mistresses, who were in point of fact doing her a favour; although occasionally she did put up with it herself, playing the virtuous wife resigned to every duty.

'And she is virtuous, is she?' asked Octave, becoming interested.

'Oh, yes, my friend! Virtuous in every way: attractive, serious, well-bred, educated, lots of taste, pure, and insufferable!'

At the bottom end of the Rue Montmartre, a block in the traffic stopped the cab. The young men, having lowered the windows, could hear Bachelard abusing the drivers in a furious voice. Then, as they moved on again, Gueulin filled in his listeners with certain details about Clarisse. Her name was Clarisse Bocquet, the daughter of a man who once kept a small toy shop, but now went about to fairs with his wife and a troop of unwashed brats. One winter's evening, as a thaw was setting in, Duveyrier had come across her just after she'd been kicked out on to the street by one of her lovers. Probably this buxom wench corresponded to some long-sought ideal, for the very next day he was hooked, weeping as he kissed her eyelids, overcome by his yearning to cultivate just one little blue flower of romance in the midst of his baser appetites. Clarisse had consented to live in the Rue de la Cerisaie, so as not to make it public that they were a couple; but she led him a rare dance, had made him buy her twenty-five thousand francs' worth of furniture, and was eating her way through his fortune with the help of some artistes from the Théâtre de Montmartre.

'I don't care a damn,' said Trublot, 'as long as she gives us a good time. At least, she doesn't make you sing or spend her life playing the piano, like that other woman. Oh, that piano! Well I'll say this: if one is deafened at home, and unlucky enough to have as a wife a pianola nobody can stand, it seems to me that a man would be a precious fool not to fix himself up with some snug little corner where he could receive his friends in his slippers.'

'Last Sunday,' said Gueulin, 'Clarisse wanted me to lunch with her alone. I declined. After lunches of that kind one is apt to do something foolish, and I was afraid she might come and plant herself on me when she left Duveyrier. She detests him, you know. She's so disgusted by him that it almost makes her ill. She doesn't like his pimples much either, it seems! But she can't send him elsewhere, as his wife does; if she could pass him on to her maid, she'd be delighted to get rid of him.'

The cab stopped. They alighted in front of a dark, silent house in the Rue de la Cerisaie. But they had to wait a good ten minutes for the other cab, Bachelard having taken his driver to have some grog, after their quarrel in the Rue Montmartre. Going up the austerely bourgeois staircase, Bachelard responded to yet another of Josserand's questions about this friend of Duveyrier's.

'A proper lady, and a very nice one too. She won't eat you.'

The door was opened by a little rosy-faced maid. With a warm and friendly smile, she helped the gentlemen off with their coats. Trublot remained in the ante-room with her for a moment, whispering something in her ear which set her giggling as if she were being tickled. Bachelard had already pushed open the drawing-room door and immediately introduced Monsieur Josserand. The latter felt momentarily ill at ease; Clarisse seemed quite plain; he couldn't imagine why Duveyrier, instead of his own wife, one of the most beautiful women in society, preferred this boyish creature, very dark and thin, and with a fluffy head like a poodle's. However, Clarisse had charm. She still retained that Parisian gift of the gab, an outwardly assured sparkle, and had an infectious sense of humour, picked up from having often been in male company; though, if need be, she could put on her fine-lady airs when it suited her.

'Monsieur, I'm delighted . . . All Alphonse's friends are mine. Do make yourself at home.'

Duveyrier also received Monsieur Josserand most cordially, forewarned by a letter from Bachelard. Octave was surprised at his youthful appearance. He was no longer the severe-looking, restless individual of the Rue de Choiseul, who never looked as if he were at home in his own drawing-room. The unsightly blotches on his face were now just pink; his wizened eyes sparkled with childish glee as Clarisse was telling a group of guests that he sometimes paid her a flying visit during a brief adjournment of the court, having only just time to jump into a cab, kiss her and drive back again. Then he complained of being overworked, what with four sittings a week, from eleven to five;

always the same tangled skein of roguery to be unravelled; it positively shrivelled up all feeling.

'In the midst of that lot,' he said, laughing, 'one really needs a few roses. I feel the better for it afterwards.'

He was not wearing his red ribbon, however, which he always took off when visiting his mistress. This was a last scruple, a certain delicate distinction which, from a sense of decency, he obstinately observed. Though she didn't mention it, this greatly offended Clarisse.

Octave, who had shaken her by the hand like an old friend, listened and looked around him. The room, with its flowered carpet, red satin furniture and hangings, was very much like the drawing-room in the Rue de Choiseul, and, as if to complete this resemblance, several of the counsellor's friends whom Octave had seen on the night of the concert were here too, forming the same groups. But people smoked and talked loudly; everybody seemed bright and merry in the brilliant candlelight. Two gentlemen, with outstretched legs, took up the whole of a divan; another, seated cross-wise on a chair, was warming his back by the fire. It was all agreeably relaxed, though that freedom had limits. Clarisse never invited any women, for propriety's sake, as she said. When her guests remarked on the lack of ladies, she would laughingly respond: 'Well, and what about me? Don't you think I'm enough?'

Thoroughly middle-class deep-down, she had made a comfortable little home for Alphonse consistent with her passion for respectability. When she had company she insisted on being addressed in a formal manner; but when her guests had gone, and the doors were closed, everybody enjoyed her favours, whether they were Alphonse's friends or those of her own, clean-shaven actors and painters with bushy beards. It was an ingrained habit, this need to enjoy herself a bit behind her keeper's back. Only two of her circle had turned her down: Gueulin with his fear of consequences, and Trublot, whose heart lay elsewhere.

The little maid was just then handing round some glasses of punch in her engaging way. Octave took one, and whispered in Trublot's ear: 'The maid is better looking than the mistress.'

'Of course; that's always the case,' replied Trublot, shrugging his shoulders with an air of disdainful conviction.

Clarisse came up and talked to them for a moment. She was

everywhere, moving from one group to another, joking, laughing, gesticulating. As each newcomer lit his cigar, the room soon filled with smoke.

'Oh, you horrid men!' she archly exclaimed, as she went to open a window.

Bachelard, in a flash, steered Monsieur Josserand towards it so that, as he said, they might get a breath of air. Then, by a masterly manoeuvre, he got Duveyrier to the same window-seat and without more ado put his plan into action. So the two families were about to be united by a close tie; he felt extremely honoured. Then he enquired what day had been fixed for signing the contract, and this gave him the chance to broach the subject.

'We had meant to call on you tomorrow, Josserand and I, to settle everything, being well aware that Monsieur Auguste can do nothing without you. We did want to come round and talk about a dowry, but as we're all so comfortable here . . .'

Seized by fresh qualms of conscience, Monsieur Josserand looked down on the gloomy depths of the Rue de la Cerisaie, with its deserted streets and sombre façades. He was sorry he had come. They were again going to take advantage of his weakness to involve him in something he would live to regret. In a sudden gesture of revolt, he interrupted Bachelard.

'Some other time; this is hardly the place.'

'Why not?' exclaimed Duveyrier, very graciously. 'We're more comfortable here than anywhere else. You were saying, sir, that . . .'

'We are going to give Berthe fifty thousand francs. Only, these fifty thousand francs represent the maturity value of a twenty-year insurance policy, which Josserand took out for his daughter when she was four years old, precisely in order to provide her with a dowry. It will be three years, therefore, before she can draw the money.'

'Can I just say . . .?' interrupted Josserand, beside himself.

'No, just let me finish; Monsieur Duveyrier understands perfectly . . . We don't want the young couple to wait three years for money which they may need now and so we'd promise to pay the dowry in instalments of ten thousand francs every six months, on condition that we repay ourselves later with the insurance money.'

There was a silence. Monsieur Josserand, chilled and unable

to speak, looked out again into the dark street. The counsellor appeared to be thinking the matter over for a moment. Perhaps he smelled something fishy, savouring the thought that those who would lose out would be the Vabres, whom he detested in the person of his wife.

'It all seems to me a most reasonable arrangement. We're the ones who ought to thank you. A dowry is seldom paid in full.'

'Indeed not,' agreed Bachelard energetically. 'Never, in fact.'

And the three shook hands, after making an appointment to meet at the notary's on the following Thursday.

When Monsieur Josserand came back into the light, he looked so pale that they asked him if he felt unwell. No, he wasn't actually feeling very well, and he left, not caring to wait for Bachelard who had just gone into the dining-room, where the traditional tea had been replaced by champagne.

Meanwhile, Gueulin, sprawling on a sofa near the window, muttered: 'Oh, that old wretch of an uncle!'

He had overheard something about the insurance money, and chuckled as he told Octave and Trublot the truth of the matter. The policy had been taken out at his office: there was not a penny coming to them: the Vabres were being utterly tricked. Then as the other two, holding their sides, roared at their splendid joke, he added with absurd vehemence: 'I need a hundred francs . . . If Uncle Bachelard doesn't give me a hundred francs, I'll spill the beans.'

The buzz of voices grew louder as the champagne gradually upset the decorum on which Clarisse insisted. Her parties always became rather rowdy towards the end. Even she herself had occasional lapses. Trublot drew Octave's attention to her. She was standing behind a door with her arms round the neck of a strapping young fellow with the build of a peasant, a stone-cutter from the South, whose transformation into an artist was being supported by his home town. However, when Duveyrier came through the door, she quickly removed her arms and introduced him to the young man – Monsieur Payan, a sculptor of wonderful talent. Duveyrier, very pleased to meet him, to be sure, promised to get him some work.

'Work, indeed!' muttered Gueulin, under his breath. 'He's got as much work as he wants here, you silly idiot!'

About two o'clock, when the young men left the Rue de la Cerisaie with Bachelard, he was completely drunk. They wanted to shove him into a hansom, but the whole neighbourhood was wrapped in solemn silence, not the sound of a wheel, nor even of some belated footstep; so they decided to hold him up. The moon had risen clear and bright, whitening the pavements. In the deserted streets their voices assumed a grave sonority.

'For God's sake don't fall over, uncle! You're enough to break our arms!'

Overcome by sentimentality, he was now in his tenderest, most moralising mood.

'Go away, Gueulin! Go away!' he spluttered. 'I don't want you to see your uncle in this state! No, my lad, it's not proper you should. Go away!'

And when his nephew called him an old swindler, he said: 'Swindler? I don't know what you're talking about. The only thing you need is respect. For my part I value women – virtuous women that is; you're making your uncle blush. I don't need anyone other than these two.'

'Very well, then,' said Gueulin. 'I need a hundred francs from you. It's for my rent, or I'll be kicked out.'

At this unexpected demand Bachelard's drunkenness increased to such an extent that he had to be propped up against the shutters of a shop.

'Eh? What? A hundred francs? Don't bother to search my pockets, I've only got a few pence. So that you can go and squander the money in some brothel? No, it's not for me to support you in life of vice. I remember my promise to your mother on her death-bed, when she confided you to my care! Now, if you grab my pockets, I'm going to call out for help!'

And he meandered on, inveighing against the dissolute ways of youth, and coming back to the importance of virtue.

'Well, anyhow,' cried Gueulin, 'I haven't yet swindled whole families! Ah, you know what I mean! If I were not to keep my mouth shut you would jolly soon give me my hundred francs!'

His uncle instantly became stone deaf, as he went stumbling and grunting along. In the narrow street where they found themselves, behind the church of Saint Gervais, only one white lamp burned feebly as a night-light, showing a huge number painted on the grained glass. A sort of muffled noise inside the house could be heard; a few thin rays of light came through the close shutters.

'I've had about enough of this!' exclaimed Gueulin, abruptly. 'Excuse me, uncle; I left my umbrella upstairs.'

So saying, he went into the house. Bachelard, indignant and full of disgust, declared that one ought at least to have a little respect for women. Immorality of that sort would be the ruin of France. Finally, at the Place de l'Hôtel-de-Ville, Octave and Trublot found a cab, into which they thrust him as if he were a package.

'Rue d'Enghien,' they told the driver. 'Take the fare out of his pockets.'

On the Thursday, the marriage-contract was signed in the presence of the notary Maître Renaudin, Rue de Grammont. Just as they were starting out, there had been another furious row at the Josserands', as the father, in a supreme moment of revolt, had told his wife that she was the one responsible for the lie he was going to have to tell. And once again they flung their families in each other's teeth. Where did they suppose he was going to get ten thousand francs every six months? Such an agreement was monstrous. Uncle Bachelard, who was there, kept raising his hand vigorously to his heart as he bubbled over with fresh promises, now that he had arranged things in such a way that he wouldn't have to part with a penny, tenderly declaring that he would never leave his dear little Berthe in a fix. But the father, exasperated, merely shrugged his shoulders, asking him if he really took him for quite such a fool.

However, at the notary's, the reading of the contract, drawn up from notes furnished by Duveyrier, somewhat soothed Monsieur Josserand. There was no mention of an insurance policy; moreover, the first instalment of ten thousand francs was only to fall due six months after the marriage. This, at any rate, left them a bit of breathing-space. Auguste, who listened most attentively, didn't seem entirely happy with the details. He looked at Berthe's smiling face, at the Josserands, at Duveyrier, and at last dared to refer to the insurance policy, a guarantee which he thought it only reasonable should be mentioned. They all appeared astonished. What was the good of that? It went without saying; and they quickly signed the paper, while Maître Renaudin, a most obliging young man, said not a word as he handed the ladies a pen. It was not till they had got outside that Madame Duveyrier ventured to express her surprise. What was all this about an insurance policy? But Madame Josserand disingenuously remarked that her brother's name had never even been mentioned by her in connection with so paltry a sum. It was the whole of his fortune that he would eventually leave to Berthe.

That same evening a cab came to take away Saturnin. His mother had declared that it was too dangerous to let him be present at the ceremony. It would never do, at a wedding, to let loose among the guests a lunatic who talked of putting people on a spit; and Monsieur Josserand, broken-hearted, had to get the poor lad into Doctor Chassagne's asylum at Les Mouli-neaux.* The cab was brought up to the front gates at dusk. Saturnin came down holding Berthe's hand, thinking he was going to the country with her. But, once in the cab, he struggled furiously, breaking the windows and shaking his bloodstained fists. Monsieur Josserand went upstairs in tears, his ears still ringing with the wretched boy's shrieks, the crack of the whip and the sound of hooves disappearing into the falling darkness.

During dinner, as tears again rose to his eyes at the sight of Saturnin's empty place, his exasperated wife didn't understand: 'Come, that's enough of that! Are you going to your daughter's wedding with that gloomy face? Listen! I swear on my father's grave that her uncle will pay the first ten thousand francs. He swore solemnly to me that he would, as we were leaving the notary's!'

Monsieur Josserand didn't even answer. He spent the night addressing wrappers. By daybreak, on that chilly morning, he'd finished his second thousand, and had earned six francs. Several times he raised his head, listening for Saturnin moving about in his room. Then, at the thought of Berthe, he worked with renewed fervour. Poor child! She would have liked a shimmering white wedding-dress. Never mind; six francs would mean she could have more flowers in her bridal bouquet.

CHAPTER 8

The civil marriage had taken place the previous Thursday. On the Saturday morning, some of the lady guests had been in the Josserands' drawing-room since quarter past ten, waiting for the religious ceremony at Saint-Roch fixed for half past eleven. Madame Juzeur was there, in black silk as usual; Madame Dambreville was squeezed into a gown the colour of faded leaves; Madame Duveyrier was very simply dressed in pale blue. All three of them were talking in hushed tones among the rows of empty chairs, while Madame Josserand, in the next room, was putting the finishing touches to Berthe's dress assisted by her maid and the two bridemaids, Hortense and Angèle Campardon.

'Oh that's not what I'm bothered about!' murmured Madame Duveyrier. 'The family's quite respectable . . . But I do confess that I'm rather afraid, on Auguste's account, of the mother's domineering character . . . One cannot be too careful, you know!'

'No, indeed!' said Madame Juzeur. 'One often marries the mother as well as the daughter; and it is so very disagreeable if she interferes.'

At that moment the door of the bedroom opened, and Angèle ran out, exclaiming: 'A hook, at the back of the left-hand drawer. Wait a moment!'

She rushed across the drawing-room, and then back again, her white frock, tied at the waist by a broad blue sash, floating in her wake like foam.

'You're mistaken, I think,' resumed Madame Dambreville. 'The mother is only too glad to get rid of the girl. The only thing she cares about is her Tuesdays. After all she's still got another victim.'

Valérie then came in, wearing a red dress you would hardly fail to notice. She'd virtually run up the stairs, afraid she might be late.

'Théophile will never be ready,' she said to her sister-in-law. I had to get rid of Françoise this morning, and now he's looking everywhere for his tie ... I left him in the middle of such a mess!'

'You've also got to take health into account,' continued Madame Dambreville.

'Yes, indeed,' replied Madame Duveyrier. 'We made discreet enquiries with Doctor Juillerat. It seems that the girl has an excellent constitution. The mother's, as you know, is astonishing; and in a sense, that was the deciding factor, for nothing's worse than sickly relatives to look after. It's always best to have sound, healthy relatives.'

'Especially if they have nothing to leave,' said Madame Juzeur, in her dulcet voice.

Valérie had taken a seat, but not being party to the conversation and still out of breath, she asked: 'What? who are you talking about?'

Once again the door was thrown open and the sound of quarrelling could be heard in the other room.

'I'm telling you that the box is on the table.'

'It's not true; I saw it over there a moment ago.'

'Oh, you obstinate thing! Go and see for yourself.'

Hortense, also in white and with a large blue sash, passed through the drawing-room. The snowy folds of the muslin made her look older, giving a hardness to her features and a yellowness to her complexion. She returned, furious, with a bridal bouquet for which they had been hunting for the last five minutes all over the apartment.

'Well, you see,' said Madame Dambreville, by way of conclusion, 'before a marriage, there are many aspects of it that leave a lot to be desired ... The only sensible thing is to come to the best possible arrangement afterwards.'

Angèle and Hortense now opened the folding doors so that the bride's veil wouldn't catch on anything, and Berthe appeared, dressed in white silk, with white flowers on a white background, a white wreath, a white bouquet, and a spray of white flowers across her skirt, which vanished near the train in a shower of little white buds. In this white array she looked enchanting, with her fresh complexion, golden hair, laughing eyes and pretty knowing mouth.

'How sweet she looks!' cried all the ladies.

They all embraced her ecstatically. The Josserands had been at their wits' end to find the couple of thousand francs to pay for the wedding – five hundred francs for the dress, and another fifteen hundred for their share of the dinner and ball. So they had to send Berthe to Doctor Chassagne's asylum to see Saturnin who'd just been left three thousand francs by an aunt. Then Berthe, having obtained permission to take her brother out for a drive, coaxed and petted him in the carriage before taking him, still smothered in kisses, to the notary, who, ignorant of the poor lad's witless condition, had everything ready for him to sign. The silk dress and the profusion of flowers came as a surprise to all these ladies, costing them with a glance while exclaiming: 'Exquisite! What perfect taste!'

Madame Josserand came in, resplendent in a mauve gown with hard edge to the colour, which made her look rounder and taller than ever like a majestic tower. She cursed Monsieur Josserand, told Hortense to fetch her shawl, and energetically forbade Berthe to sit down.

'Watch out, you'll crush your flowers!'

'Don't get yourself into a state,' said Clotilde, in her calm voice. 'We have plenty of time. Auguste has to come up and fetch us.'

As they were all waiting in the drawing-room, Théophile suddenly burst in, without a hat, his coat awry, and his white tie tied so tightly that it looked like a piece of cord. His face, with its wispy moustache and discoloured teeth, was livid; he was trembling with rage, like a feverish child.

'What is the matter with you?' asked his sister, in astonishment.

'The matter is . . . the matter is —'

A fit of coughing cut him short, and he stood there for a minute, choking and spitting into his handkerchief, furious at being unable to give vent to anger. Valérie, disconcerted, watched him, as if some instinct told her the cause for this outburst. Finally, he shook his fist at her, ignoring the presence of the bride and the ladies gathered around her.

'Yes, as I was hunting everywhere for my tie, I found a letter in front of the wardrobe . . .'

He nervously crumpled a piece of paper between his fingers. His wife turned pale. She saw the situation at a glance and, to avoid a public scandal, went out into the room that Berthe had just left.

'Oh! Well,' she said quietly, 'I would rather not stay, if he's going to behave like a madman.'

'Leave me alone!' shouted Théophile, as Madame Duveyrier tried to pacify him. 'I want to confront her with it. This time I've got proof, and it's as certain as certain can be. Refusing to listen isn't going to be the end of it, for I know the fellow . . .'

His sister, seizing his arm, shook it with a gesture of authority.

'Be quiet! Don't you realise where you are? This is hardly the right time . . .'

'Yes, it *is* the right time! I don't give a damn about the others. Too bad that it's happened today. It will be a lesson for everybody.'

He lowered his voice, however, and sank exhausted into a chair, almost bursting into tears. Everyone in the drawing-room felt thoroughly uncomfortable. Madame Dambreville and Madame Juzeur politely moved away, pretending not to understand. Madame Josserand, greatly annoyed that a scandal of this sort should throw a gloom over the wedding, went into the adjoining room to cheer up Valérie. As for Berthe, she kept looking at her garland in the mirror, so as not to hear, while quickly quizzing Hortense. They carried on whispering while the elder sister pointed to Théophile and explained what was going on, at the same time as apparently busying herself straightening out the folds of the veil.

'Oh, that's it!' said the bride, with a chaste air of amusement, as she gazed at Théophile, perfectly self-possessed beneath her halo of snow-white flowers.

Clotilde, under her breath, was grilling her brother. Madame Josserand came back, spoke to her for a moment, and then returned to the next room. It was like a flurry of diplomatic formalities in a crisis. The husband was accusing Octave, whose head he would punch at the church, if he dared come. Only the day before, he would swear that he'd seen him on the steps of Saint-Roch's with his wife. At first he'd had his doubts, but now he was perfectly certain; everything tallied, his height, his walk. Oh, yes, madame invented stories about luncheons with her lady friends, or else went into Saint-Roch's with Camille, by the main entrance, to pray. Then she left the child with the person who rented out chairs and she and monsieur went off together out the back through a dirty passageway, where nobody would have thought of looking for her. However, when Octave's name was mentioned, Valérie smiled. It certainly wasn't him, she swore to Madame Josserand. It wasn't anybody at all, for that matter, she added, but least of all him. Feeling strong in the knowledge that truth was on her side, she, in turn, talked of challenging her husband with the proof that the letter was not in Octave's handwriting, any more than he was the mysterious gentleman at Saint-Roch's. Madame Josserand, listening, watched her knowingly, merely anxious to discover some way for Valérie to deceive her husband. And she plied her with good advice.

'Let me manage things; don't you interfere. As he insists that it's Monsieur Mouret, very well, then, let it be Monsieur Mouret. There's no harm, is there, in being seen on the steps of a church with Monsieur Mouret? Only that letter is compromising. It will be a triumph for you when our young friend shows him a couple of lines of his own handwriting. Above all, mind you say exactly what I do. I can't allow him, you know, to go and spoil our day.'

When she brought back Valérie, who seemed greatly upset, Théophile was saying to his sister, in a choking voice: 'For your sake, then, I promise not to make a scene here, for it wouldn't be right because of the wedding. But, at the church, I can't answer for my actions. If that scoundrel dares to confront me there, in the presence of my whole family, I will do for both of them.'

Auguste, carefully got up in a black frock-coat, with his left eye half closed by the neuralgia that for the past three days he'd been dreading, arrived at that moment to pick up his bride. He was accompanied by his father and his brother-in-law, both looking very solemn. There was a bit of a to-do, as they were all rather behind time. Two of the ladies, Madame Duveyrier and Madame Dambreville, had to help Madame Josserand put on her shawl. It was like a huge yellow tapestry, and she always brought it out on state occasions, although it was completely out of fashion. It enveloped her in folds so ample and so striking that passers-by were always transfixed. They still had to wait for Monsieur Josserand, who was searching under the furniture for a cuff-link which had been swept up with the rubbish from the night before. At last he made his appearance, stammering out excuses, looking forlorn, yet happy, as he led the way downstairs, with his arm tightly holding Berthe's own. Then came Auguste and Madame Josserand, followed by the others in no particular order, their chatter disturbing the dignified silence of the hallway. Théophile had got hold of Duveyrier, who was rather put out to have to listen to the former's story. Pouring his woes into his ear, he begged for advice, while Valérie, who had recovered her self-possession, walked modestly in front, Madame Juzeur comforting her tenderly. She appeared not to notice that her husband was looking daggers at her.

'Oh, your prayer-book!' cried Madame Josserand, suddenly, in a tone of despair.

They had already got into the carriage. Angèle was obliged to go back up and fetch the prayer-book bound in white velvet. At last they set off. The whole household was there to see them, the maids and the concierges. Marie Pichon had come down with Lilette, dressed as if about to go for a walk. The sight of the bride, looking so pretty and smart, moved her to tears. Monsieur Gourd remarked that the second-floor people were the only ones who hadn't budged, a queer set of tenants always behaving differently from anyone else!

At the church of Saint-Roch both the main doors had been thrown open, and a red carpet exended as far as the pavement. It was raining, and the air was very chilly for a May morning.

'Thirteen steps,' whispered Madame Juzeur to Valérie, as they went in. 'That's a bad omen.'

As soon as the procession moved up the aisle between rows of seats towards the altar, on which the candles burned like stars, the organ overhead burst into a paean of joy. It was a snug, pleasant-looking church, with its large white windows edged with yellow and pale blue, its dado-rails of red marble on the walls and the pillars, its gilded pulpit supported by the four Evangelists, and its side chapels glittering with metal ornaments. Scenes from the Opéra brightened the ceiling; crystal chandeliers hung from it, suspended by long cords. As the ladies passed over the broad gratings of the heating a warm breath penetrated their skirts.

'Are you sure you've got the ring?' asked Madame Josserand of Auguste, who with Berthe had taken his seat by the altar.

He panicked, fearing that he might have forgotten it, but then discovered it in his waistcoat pocket. But she hadn't waited for his reply in any case. Ever since she had made her entrance, she'd drawn herself up to her full height in order to inspect everybody: Trublot and Gueulin, the ushers; Uncle Bachelard and Campardon, the bride's witnesses; Duveyrier and Doctor Juillerat, witnesses for the bridegroom, and the host of acquaintances of whom she felt so proud. She had just caught sight of Octave, who was doing his utmost to make room for Madame Hédouin to get by. She drew him aside, behind a pillar, and hastily whispered something to him. The young man seemed totally bemused. He bowed, however, with an air of polite compliance.

'I've arranged it,' whispered Madame Josserand in Valérie's ear, as she returned and took a seat behind Berthe and Auguste in one of the places reserved for the family. Monsieur Josserand, the Vabres and the Duveyriers were there too. The organ heaved out a succession of crystal notes, pausing between each sequence as if to draw breath. The crush grew greater, with all the seats in the chancel now filled and men standing in the aisles. Abbé Mauduit had reserved for himself the joy of pronouncing a blessing on the nuptials of one of his cherished flock. When he appeared, arrayed in his surplice, he exchanged a friendly smile with the congregation, whose every face he knew.

The choir began the *Veni Creator* as the organist struck up the triumphant bars, and it was just at this moment that Théophile spied Octave, to the left of the chancel, standing in front of the Saint Joseph side chapel. His sister, Clotilde, tried to restrain him.

'I can't,' he stuttered. 'It's absolutely intolerable!' and he made Duveyrier follow him, as the family's representative. The *Veni Creator* went on. A few people looked round.

Théophile, who had talked about head-punching, became so agitated on going up to Octave, that at first he couldn't say a word, conscious of his lack of height, and standing on the tips of his toes.

'Sir,' he said at last, 'I saw you yesterday with my wife.'

The *Veni Creator* was now over, and the sound of his own voice alarmed him. Annoyed by the incident, Duveyrier was trying to persuade him that he couldn't have chosen a worse time or place. The ceremony had now begun up at the altar. After a touching address to the happy couple, the priest proceeded to bless the ring.

'*Benedic, Domine Deus noster, annulum nuptialem hunc, quem nos in tuo nomine benedicimus.*'

This allowed Théophile to repeat in a low voice: 'Sir, you were in this church yesterday with my wife.'

Octave, still bewildered by Madame Josserand's imperfectly understood injunctions, nevertheless, casually went through his tale.

'Yes, that's quite true. I met Madame Vabre, and together we went and looked at the repairs to the Calvary, which my friend Campardon is supervising.'

'So you admit it!' stammered Théophile, in a fresh outburst. 'You admit it.'

Duveyrier had to tap him on the shoulder to calm him down. A boy's voice now rang out a piercing *Amen*.

'And doubtless, you'll recognise this letter!' continued Théophile, offering Octave a piece of paper.

'Oh! Not here, of all places,' groaned Duveyrier in a whisper. 'You must be off your head.'

Octave looked at the piece of paper.

In the congregation there were now whispers, a lot of elbow-nudging and furtive glances over the tops of prayer-books. No one was paying the least attention to the ceremony. Only the bridal couple facing the priest remained grave and stiff. But even Berthe herself finally looked round, and saw Théophile, livid with anger, as he talked to Octave. From that moment on, she couldn't concentrate as her shining eyes continually returned to the Chapel of Saint Joseph.

Meanwhile Octave, in an undertone, read as follows: 'My darling, what bliss yesterday. Until Tuesday next, at the Chapel of the Holy Angels, in the confessional.'

Having obtained a 'yes' from the bridegroom, the assent of a serious man who signs nothing until he has seen the small print, the priest had just turned towards the bride.

'Will you promise and swear to be faithful to Monsieur Auguste Vabre in all things, as behoves a dutiful wife, and in accordance with God's holy commandment?'

But Berthe, who had earlier seen the letter, was so looking forward to the exchange of blows that she was no longer listening and kept looking sideways at the two men from under her veil. There was an embarrassing silence. At last, suddenly aware that they were waiting for her response, she hastily replied, 'Yes, yes!' as if she couldn't care less.

The abbé, surprised, followed her gaze, guessing that something unusual was taking place in one of the side aisles, and he in turn became absent-minded. The story by this time had gone the rounds; everybody knew it. The ladies, pale and grave, could no longer take their eyes off Octave. The men smiled in a discreetly rakish way. And while Madame Josserand, with a slight shrug of the shoulders, sought to reassure Madame Duveyrier, Valérie alone seemed to take any interest in the ceremony, apparently oblivious to anything else, as if overwhelmed by emotion.

'My darling, what bliss yesterday.' Octave read it over again, pretending to be astonished.

Then, returning the letter to Théophile, he said: 'I don't know what you mean, sir. That's not my handwriting. You can see for yourself.'

And taking from his pocket a notebook, in which he always carefully put down his expenses, he showed it to Théophile.

'What? Not your handwriting?' stammered the latter. 'Are you having me on? It must be your handwriting.'

The priest was about to make the sign of the cross on Berthe's left hand. As his eyes were elsewhere, he made it on her right one, by mistake.

'*In nomine Patris, et Filii, et Spiritus Sancti.*'

'*Amen*!' responded the choirboy, also on tiptoes to get a better view.

At any rate, a scandal had been avoided. Duveyrier had proved to Théophile, now totally confused, that the letter could not have been written by Monsieur Mouret. For the congregation this was almost a disappointment. There were deep sighs and a few quiet words. Then everyone, still palpitating with excitement, turned back towards the altar to find that Auguste and Berthe had become man and wife, she apparently unaware of what had taken place, while he hadn't missed a single word uttered by the priest, his concentration only disturbed by his headache which had succeeded in closing his left eye.

'Ah! The dear children!' whispered Monsieur Josserand, in a trembling voice to Monsieur Vabre, who ever since the beginning of the ceremony had been counting the lighted candles, continually getting it wrong and starting all over again.

The organ again resounded from the nave; Abbé Mauduit reappeared in his chasuble; the choir had begun the Mass, a choral one of the most grandiose kind. Uncle Bachelard was wandering round from chapel to chapel, reading the Latin epitaphs, which he didn't understand. He showed a particular interest in the Duc de Créquy's.

Trublot and Gueulin, eager to have the details of the incident, joined Octave, and the three of them were chuckling behind the pulpit. There were sudden bursts of song, like gusts of wind in a storm; choirboys swung their censers; and then, as a bell tinkled, there were periods of silence, when the priest could be heard mumbling at the altar.

Théophile couldn't stand still; he kept following Duveyrier around, ranting on incoherently, at a loss to understand how the gentleman of the assignation was not the gentleman of the letter. The whole congregation continued to observe his every gesture; the entire church, with its procession of priests, its Latin, its music, its incense, excitedly discussed the incident. When, after the *Pater*, the abbé came down to give the newly married pair his final benediction, he looked askance at this commotion among his faithful flock, noticing the women's excited expressions and the sly merriment of the men, in the bright light that streamed down upon them from the windows above the richly decorated side chapels and nave.

'Don't admit anything,' whispered Madame Josserand to Valérie, as they moved towards the vestry after Mass.

In the vestry the newly married pair and their witnesses had, first of all, to sign the register. However, they were kept waiting some time by Campardon, who had taken several ladies to see the newly restored Calvary at the end of the choir, behind a wooden hoarding. At last he arrived, full of apologies, and signed his name on the register with an enormous flourish. The Abbé Mauduit wished to pay both families a compliment by handing round the pen himself, pointing with his finger to where each had to sign; and he smiled with his air of good-humoured urbanity as he stood in the centre of the solemn room with its panelling impregnated with the odour of incense.

'Well, mademoiselle,' said Campardon to Hortense, 'don't you feel tempted to do likewise?'

Then he regretted his lack of tact. Hortense was the elder sister; she bit her lip. That evening, at the ball, she was expecting to have a definite answer from Verdier who she was urging to choose between herself and that creature of his. So she replied icily: 'There's plenty of time . . . when it suits me.'

And, turning her back on the architect, she flew at her brother Léon who, late as usual, had only just arrived.

'Well, that's nice of you. You've done your parents proud. You couldn't even be here in time see one of your sisters get married! At least, we thought you would have come with Madame Dambreville.'

'Madame Dambreville does what she likes; I do what I can,' said Léon drily.

They had fallen out. Léon considered that she was keeping him overlong for her own use, and was tired of an affair he'd only put up with in the hope that it might lead to some desirable match; and for the last fortnight he'd been pestering her to keep her promises. Madame Dambreville, passionately in love, had even complained to Madame Josserand about what she called her son's whims. So his mother was more than ready to berate Léon, reproaching him for his lack of love and respect for his family, judging by his failure to attend so solemn a ceremony. In his supercilious voice, the young democrat offered a variety of explanations, unexpected work which had to be done for the deputy whose secretary he was, a lecture he had to prepare, and a number of other things including vitally important matters he had had to deal with.

'A marriage, though, doesn't take much time!' observed Madame Dambreville, without thinking what she was saying, as she looked at him with pleading eyes to soften him.

'That's not always the case,' he coldly replied.

Then he went up to kiss Berthe and shake hands with his new brother-in-law, while Madame Dambreville, turning pale in her torment, remained upright in her dead-leaf-coloured dress, smiling vaguely at everybody coming in.

A long procession of friends, mere acquaintances and guests who had thronged the church, were now filing into the vestry. The newly married pair stood shaking hands continually, both looking delighted yet embarrassed. The Josserands and the Duveyriers found it impossible to introduce everyone. Now and again they exchanged glances of surprise, for Bachelard had brought along people nobody knew, and who talked much too loudly.

'Oh look!' whispered Gueulin. 'He's kissing the bride! How nice for her if she doesn't mind the smell!'

At last the crowd gradually dispersed. Only the family and a few intimate friends remained. News of the much-wronged Théophile had continued to do the rounds during all the hand-shaking and congratulations; in fact, nobody talked of anything else while engaging in the usual small talk. Madame Hédouin, who had just heard the story, looked at Valérie with the amazement of a woman for whom virtue and well-being are synonymous. Doubtless the Abbé Mauduit must also have been apprised of the facts, for his curiosity seemed appeased, and his manner became more than usually unctuous amid all the secret sorrows of his flock. Here was another gaping sore which had suddenly begun to bleed, and which he had to cover with the mantle of religion! And he went to have a quiet word with Théophile, discreetly dwelling on the need for forgiveness, allud-ing to God's mysterious, unfathomable designs; while seeking, above all, to quash the scandal, embracing all his hearers in one broad gesture of pity and despair, as if to hide their shame from the very eye of heaven itself.

'He's a good man, that priest,' murmured Théophile as he listened to the homily, his bewilderment now complete. 'He can have no idea what it's all about.'

Valérie, clinging to Madame Juzeur to keep her composure, listened with emotion to the conciliatory words which the Abbé Mauduit deemed it his duty to address to her too. Then, as everybody was leaving the church, she stopped in front of the two fathers, to let Berthe go by on her husband's arm.

'You must feel very satisfied,' she said to Monsieur Josserand, anxious to show that her conscience was clear. 'Allow me to congratulate you.'

'Yes, yes,' said Monsieur Vabre, in his guttural voice, 'it's another great responsibility off our minds.'

And while Trublot and Gueulin busied themselves putting all the ladies into their carriages, Madame Josserand, whose shawl got in everybody's way, obstinately remained on the pavement to the last, as if to assert publicly her triumph as a mother.

That evening the dinner which took place at the Hôtel du Louvre* was also marred by Théophile's unfortunate little problem. It was like an obsession; people had talked about it the whole afternoon, during their drive in the Bois de Boulogne;

all the ladies were of the opinion that the husband ought certainly to have waited until the following day before finding the letter. At the dinner, however, only intimate friends of the two families were present. The one merry episode was a toast proposed by Uncle Bachelard whom, despite their worst fears, the Josserands could not help inviting. By the time they got to the main course, indeed, he was intoxicated, and raising his glass, he embarked upon a speech beginning with the phrase, 'It gives me great pleasure.' This he repeated over and over again, without ever getting any further, while his hearers were good enough to smile indulgently. Auguste and Berthe, both of them utterly worn out, exchanged occasional glances, surprised to find themselves sitting opposite each other. Then, remembering the reason for this, they looked down in embarrassment at their plates.

For the wedding ball, nearly two hundred invitations had been sent out. About half past nine, people began to arrive. The large red drawing-room was lit by three chandeliers and the chairs had been pushed back along the walls, leaving a space at one end, in front of the fire place, for the small orchestra. There was also a buffet in an adjoining room with another having been reserved for the two families, to which they could retire.

Just as Madame Duveyrier and Madame Josserand were receiving the first arrivals, that wretched Théophile, whom they had been keeping an eye on ever since the morning, did something outrageous. Campardon had asked Valérie for the pleasure of the first waltz. She was laughing, and her husband considered that this levity was tantamount to a provocation.

'Yes, go on, laugh!' he stuttered. 'But tell me who sent that letter? It must have come from somebody!'

It had taken him the whole afternoon to disengage that one idea from the perplexity with which Octave's reply had filled him. Now, he was quite sure about one thing: if it wasn't from Monsieur Mouret, it was from somebody else. And he had to get hold of the name of that somebody. As Valérie, without answering, was moving away, he caught hold of her arm and twisted it viciously, like an infuriated child, saying: 'I'll break it, if you don't tell me who sent that letter.'

Valérie, terrified and barely suppressing a cry of pain, turned quite white. Campardon felt her sink on to his shoulder in one of those nervous seizures which occasionally lasted for hours.

He had only just time to take her into the room set aside for the two families, where he laid her on the sofa. Madame Juzeur and Madame Dambreville, who had followed him out, proceeded to unlace her, while he discreetly withdrew.

Meanwhile, in the ballroom, only three or four people had noticed the violent little drama. Madame Duveyrier and Madame Josserand continued to receive the guests who gradually filled the vast room as they streamed in in their bright dresses and black frock-coats. There was a hum of compliments as smiling faces revolved round the bride: the thickening faces of fathers and mothers, the angular profiles of their daughters, and the delicate, sympathetic countenances of young married women. At the far end of the room a violinist was tuning his instrument which gave out little plaintive cries.

'Sir, I have to ask your pardon,' said Théophile, accosting Octave, whose eyes had met his when he was twisting Valérie's arm. 'Anyone in my place would have suspected you, would he not? But I'm anxious to shake your hand to acknowledge my mistake.'

So doing, he took him aside, desperate to confide his woes to somebody to whom he could unburden himself.

'Ah! Sir, if I were to tell you . . .'

And he began to talk at length about his wife. As a girl she was delicate, and people joked that marriage would set her right. There was no fresh air in her parents' shop, where he'd seen her every evening for three months, when she seemed so nice, so obedient, somewhat melancholy perhaps, but quite charming.

'Well, marriage did *not* set her right; far from it . . . After a few weeks she was simply awful; we could never agree about anything. Quarrels about nothing at all; changes of mood every minute, laughing and then weeping for no apparent reason. Absurd opinions; ideas that took your breath away; a constant need to infuriate other people . . . In short, my dear sir, my home has become a living hell!'

'How very odd,' murmured Octave, who felt obliged to say something.

Then the husband, white with fury and straightening his stumpy legs to avoid looking ridiculous, approached the subject of what he termed his wretched wife's misconduct. Twice before he'd had his suspicions; but he wasn't the sort of person to harbour such unworthy thoughts. On this occasion, however, he couldn't get away from the evidence. There was absolutely no doubt about it whatever, was there? And with his trembling fingers he felt about in his waistcoat pocket for the letter.

'If she did it for money, I could understand,' he added, 'but they don't give her any, of that I'm sure, or I would know about it. So what's got into her? I'm always very nice to her, she's got everything she wants at home. I can't make it out . . . If you can understand it, please enlighten me.'

'How very odd, very odd indeed,' repeated Octave, finding all these confidences embarrassing, and wondering how he could extricate himself from the situation.

But the husband wouldn't let him go, in his feverish anxiety to get at the whole truth. At this moment Madame Juzeur came back and whispered to Madame Josserand, just then making a welcoming curtsey to a wealthy jeweller from the Palais-Royal, who swung right round and hastily followed her out.

'Your wife is having a very bad attack,' said Octave to Théophile.

'Never mind about her!' he exclaimed, exasperated at not being taken ill himself, so that he could be looked after as well. 'She's only too glad to have hysterics; it always makes everybody sympathise with her. My health is no better than hers, but I've never been unfaithful.'

Madame Josserand did not return. Among those in the know, it was rumoured that Valérie was having the most frightful convulsions. Only men would have been strong enough to hold her down; but as they had to undress her partially, the proffered services of Trublot and Gueulin had been declined. Meanwhile the orchestra was playing a quadrille; Berthe was about to open the ball with Duveyrier, who danced ceremoniously, as her partner, while Auguste, not being able to find Madame Josserand, partnered Hortense to make up the eight. The news of Valérie's attack was kept secret from the bridal pair, as it might be dangerously upsetting. The dancing got going and there was a sound of silvery laughter under the gleaming chandeliers. The violins stepped up the tempo to a lively polka which set all the couples and their floating trains whirling round the room.

'Doctor Juillerat! Where's Doctor Juillerat?' cried Madame Josserand, rushing back in.

The doctor had been invited, but no one had seen him yet.

Then she could no longer contain the rage seething within her since the morning. In front of Octave and Campardon, she came out with what she really wanted to say.

'I've just about had enough. Not very nice for my daughter, is it, all this talk of adultery.'

She looked around for Hortense and finally caught sight of her talking to a man she could only see from behind, but who she recognised by his broad shoulders. It was Verdier. This served to increase her ill-humour. She coldly summoned her daughter, and whispered to her that it would be better if she remained at her mother's beck and call on an occasion such as this. Hortense ignored the rebuke. She was triumphant, for Verdier had just fixed their marriage for June, in two months' time.

'Don't give me that nonsense,' said her mother.

'I assure you he has, Mamma. He already sleeps elsewhere three nights a week, to get that other woman used to it, and in a fortnight he's going to stop coming back in the evenings altogether. It will be all over then, and he'll be mine.'

'I said that I don't want to hear any more about it; I've had it up to here with your romance! Be good enough, please, to wait by the door until Doctor Juillerat arrives, and send him to me as soon as he does. And not a word about this to your sister!'

Then she went back into the adjoining room, leaving Hortense muttering to herself that she didn't need their approval, thank you very much, and that they'd soon come round once it was discovered that she'd made a better match than any of them. But she did go off and wait for the doctor's arrival.

The orchestra was now playing a waltz. Berthe was dancing with her husband's cousin, so as to get through each of her relations in turn. Madame Duveyrier hadn't been able to decline Uncle Bachelard, who made her feel most uncomfortable by puffing into her face. The heat was increasing and the buffet was already crowded with gentlemen mopping their brows. Two little girls hopped about in a corner, while mothers, sitting together away from the fray, mused dreamily about the weddings of their own daughters which had somehow never taken place. Congratulations were showered on the two fathers, Monsieur Vabre and Monsieur Josserand, who sat side by side the whole evening, without exchanging a word. Everyone appeared to be enjoying themselves, coming up to the two of them to declare that it was a most delightful wedding ball. The joy of the occasion had been of exactly the right level so Campardon sententiously observed.

Though the architect gallantly professed great concern at Valérie's condition, he managed not to miss a single dance. He had the brilliant idea of sending his daughter Angèle to ask for news on his behalf. The fourteen-year-old, precociously excited by the lady on everybody's lips, was more than happy to be able to peek into the adjoining room; but, as she didn't return, Campardon took the liberty of putting his head round the door, and saw his daughter standing by the sofa intently watching Valérie, whose breasts had fallen free of her unloosened stays with each spasm. There were loud feminine cries of protest that he wasn't to come in; so he withdrew, declaring that he only wanted to know how she was getting on.

'No better, I fear; no better!' he said, mournfully, to enquirers at the door. 'There are four of them holding her down. What a frame the woman must have, to fling herself about without hurting herself!'

There was now quite a group of commentators. The slightest phases of the attack were discussed in an undertone. Ladies, hearing what had happened, rushed over sympathetically between dances, entered the little drawing-room, returned with details for the men and then went back to the ball. It became a sort of mysterious corner for the exchange of whispers and glances in the midst of the ever-increasing din.

Théophile, meanwhile, forsaken and alone, walked up and down in front of the door, tortured by this one idea that he was being made a fool of, and that he ought not to tolerate it.

But then Doctor Juillerat swiftly crossed the ballroom, accompanied by Hortense, who was explaining the situation. They were followed by Madame Duveyrier. There was some surprise and the air was rife with fresh rumours. No sooner had the doctor gone in than Madame Josserand came out of the room with Madame Dambreville. Her fury was mounting; she had just emptied two jugs of water over Valérie's head; never before had she seen such uncontrollable hysteria. So she decided to go round the ballroom putting a stop to all the silly gossip simply by showing her face. However she sailed past with so acid a smile that everyone in her wake didn't need to guess what was afoot.

Madame Dambreville never left her side. Ever since the morning she had been complaining to her about Léon generally, trying to persuade her to intercede on her behalf, and to patch up their relationship. She pointed to him as he was escorting a gaunt girl to her seat and pretending to be very attentive.

'Look how he's avoiding us,' she tried to laugh, while holding back her tears. 'You really should tell him off for not even looking at us.'

'Léon!' called Madame Josserand. And, as he approached, she said bluntly, being in no mood for subtlety: 'Why are you angry with Madame Dambreville? She bears you no ill-will. Go and make it up with her. Sulking won't do any good.'

And she left them together, both disconcerted. Madame Dambreville took Léon by the arm to a window seat, where they talked, and then left the ballroom together in an affectionate manner. She had faithfully promised to arrange a marriage for him in the autumn.

Meanwhile, Madame Josserand went along distributing smiles all round, and as she came to Berthe, all breathless from dancing, and looking flushed in her rumpled white dress, she was suddenly overcome with emotion. She clasped her daughter in her arms, appalled perhaps by a vague association of ideas, as she remembered Valérie lying there with her face convulsed and distorted.

'My poor darling, my poor darling!' she murmured, as she gave her two resounding kisses.

'Well, how is she?' asked Berthe, coolly.

Instantly Madame Josserand's severe look returned. What? Berthe knew about it, then? Why, of course she did; everybody knew about it. It was only her husband over there, leading an old lady towards the buffet, who was still ignorant of what had happened. She had even intended to ask someone to tell him, for it made him look so stupid, blithely being the last to get to know anything.

'And to think that all this time I've been doing my damnedest to keep it quiet,' cried Madame Josserand, beside herself. 'Well, I shan't bother with that any more; but what I won't tolerate is you looking ridiculous as a result of it.'

As a matter of fact, everybody did know, though they weren't going to ruin the evening by talking about it. The first expressions of sympathy had been drowned by the orchestra, and as the dancers became less restrained, they found it rather amusing. It was growing late, and the heat was becoming intense. Servants handed round refreshments. On a sofa, overcome by fatigue, two little girls had fallen asleep in each other arms, cheek to cheek. Near the orchestra, and struggling to be heard above the sonorous grunting of a cello, Monsieur Vabre had decided to raise with Monsieur Josserand a problem that had plagued him for the last fortnight in respect of his monumental work, notably that of which canvasses had been done by two painters of the same name. Close by, Duveyrier, in the centre of the group, was bitterly censuring the Emperor for having permitted the production, at the Comédie Française, of a play that attacked modern society.* But whenever the band struck up a waltz or a polka, the men had to move, as couple after couple swelled the dance, while skirts swept the polished floor, filling the heated air with invisible dust and a vague odour of musk.

'She's feeling better,' said Campardon, running up, after another peep round the door. 'One can go in now.'

Some of the men thought they might do just that. Valérie was still lying full length on the sofa but the hysteria had subsided; and, for decency's sake, her breasts had been covered by a napkin found lying on the sideboard. At the window, Madame Juzeur and Madame Duveyrier stood listening to Doctor Juillerat, who was explaining that attacks of this kind were sometimes relieved by the application of hot-water compresses to the neck. Then, as the patient noticed Octave coming in with Campardon, she beckoned to him, addressing him incoherently, as if in a dream. He had to sit down beside her, at the doctor's instruction, anxious to avoid annoying her. And so the young man listened to her just as, earlier in the evening, he had been confided in by her husband. Trembling with fright, she took him for her lover and begged him to take her into hiding. But then she recognised him and burst into tears, thanking him for his lie in church that morning. With the greed of a schoolboy, Octave thought of that other fit of hysterics which he had turned to his advantage. He was now her friend, she would tell him everything, and perhaps better things might come of it.

At this moment Théophile, who had been pacing up and down outside the door, tried to come in. Other men had gone in, so why shouldn't he? This, however, created quite a panic.

At the mere sound of his voice, Valérie's trembling fits started again. Everybody feared that she would have another seizure. As he was pushed back by the ladies, her husband kept doggedly repeating: 'I only want to ask her for the name. She has to tell me the name.'

Then Madame Josserand, who had just returned, exploded. Pulling Théophile into the little room, to avoid a scene, she shouted angrily: 'Look here, are you going to hold your tongue, sir, or are you not? All day long you've been boring us to death with your nonsensical rubbish. You've no tact, sir, no tact whatever. This kind of thing is hardly appropriate for a wedding-day.'

'Excuse me, madam,' he murmured, 'but this is my business and it's certainly none of yours.'

'What do you mean, none of my business? I'm a member of your family now, sir, and do you suppose my feelings for my daughter allow me to be amused by your little story? A nice wedding she's had, thanks to you! Not another word, sir; you have no tact at all!'

He looked around him, bewildered, as if searching for someone to take his side. But the ladies' frigid demeanour showed that they judged him equally severely. He had no tact, that was indeed the word for it, for really there were times when one ought to be able to control one's temper. Even his own sister sided against him. When he again tried to protest, there was a general revolt. No, no, he needn't bother to respond; conduct such as his was simply monstrous.

This silenced him. He looked so scared and puny, with his slender limbs and his face like a stale spinster's, that the women tittered contemptuously. When one had not the wherewithal to give a woman pleasure, one ought not to marry. Hortense summed him up in a single disdainful glance, and little Angèle, whom they had forgotten kept hovering around him with her shifting look as if she were searching for something; and he retreated in blushing embarrassment before these fleshy women surrounding him with their opulent hips. They felt, however, that the matter must be sorted out some way or other. Valérie had begun to sob again, while the doctor kept bathing her temples. At a glance, the ladies were drawn together by a solidarity committed to protecting each other. They cudgelled their brains to try and see how to explain the letter to Théophile.

'Bah!' muttered Trublot, who had just joined Octave. 'That's easy enough, just say that it belongs to the maid.'

Madame Josserand overheard his suggestion. She looked round at him, her eyes sparkling with admiration. Then she addressed Théophile.

'Do you suppose, sir, that an innocent woman would lower herself to offer any explanation when accused in such a brutal fashion? But I myself can tell you that the letter was dropped by Françoise, the maid your wife had to dismiss for misconduct. There, will that satisfy you? Aren't you ashamed to look us in the face?'

At first Théophile shrugged his shoulders incredulously. But all the ladies looked so serious, and met his objections with irresistible logic. To complete his discomfiture, Madame Duveyrier angrily denounced his conduct as abominable, and declared that she would have nothing more to do with him. Then, vanquished and yearning for someone to embrace him, he threw his arms round Valérie's neck, begging her to forgive him. It was touching. Even Madame Josserand seemed much moved.

'It's always best to come to some understanding,' she observed, with relief. 'The day won't end so badly, after all.'

When they had dressed Valérie, and she appeared in the ballroom on Théophile's arm, the gaiety of the guests became complete. By this time it was nearly three o'clock in the morning and people had began to leave; still the orchestra played on, however, quadrille after quadrille, with a final feverish energy. Men smiled at one another behind the backs of the reconciled pair. Some medical remark of Campardon's about poor Théophile sent Madame Juzeur into ecstasies. Young women crowded to look at Valérie, and then reassumed their sheepish airs as their scandalised mothers glared at them. Berthe, who at last was dancing with her husband, must have whispered something in his ear, for he turned his head and, without getting out of step, looked at his brother Théophile with astonishment and the superiority of a man to whom things of that sort could never happen. There was one final gallop in which everybody lost all restraint. The stifling heat and the lurid light of the flickering candles made them lose their heads momentarily.

'You're on the most intimate terms with her, then?' asked Madame Hédouin, as she whirled around on Octave's arm, having accepted his invitation to dance.

The young man almost fancied that he felt a slight shiver pass through her straight, calm figure.

'Nothing of the sort,' he replied. 'They involved me in the story, to my great annoyance. The poor devil swallowed it hook, line and sinker.'

'That's very malicious,' she said, in her grave way.

Octave must surely have been mistaken, for, as he withdrew his arm from her waist, Madame Hédouin was not even out of breath; her eyes were untroubled, her hair as smooth as ever. But before the ball ended there was another disgraceful incident. Uncle Bachelard, who had spent most of the evening at the buffet, had thought it was time for a little jollity. He was suddenly seen dancing a grossly indecent dance in front of Gueulin. Inside his buttoned up jacket, rolled-up napkins endowed him with a bosom a wet-nurse would have been proud of; and two huge oranges, as red a grazed skin, bulged out from his lapels. This time there was a general protest. It was all very well to earn a lot of money, but really there were limits which no respectable man should ever overstep, especially when young people were present. In shame and despair, Monsieur Josserand got his brother-in-law to leave, while Duveyrier did not conceal his intense disgust.

At four o'clock the bride and groom returned to the Rue de Choiseul. They brought Théophile and Valérie back in their carriage. As they went up to the second floor, where an apartment had been furnished for them, they met Octave, who was also going upstairs to bed. The young man politely stood to one side to let them by, but Berthe did likewise and they bumped into each other.

'Oh, I do beg your pardon, mademoiselle!' he said.

At the word 'mademoiselle' they were much amused. She looked at him, and he remembered the first time their eyes had met on this very staircase, that same merry, bold glance, so charmingly inviting. Perhaps they understood each other. She blushed; and he went upstairs to his room, alone, in the death-like silence of the upper floors.

Auguste, with his left eye closed, and now totally in the grip of the headache that had persecuted him all day, had already reached the apartment, where other members of the family were assembling. Then, just as she was saying goodbye to Berthe,

Valérie, in a sudden fit of emotion, impulsively embraced her, thus crumpling her white dress once and for all; and as she kissed her, she said in a low voice: 'Ah, my dear, I do hope you'll be luckier than I was!'

CHAPTER 9

Two days later, at about seven o'clock, as Octave got to the Campardon's in time for dinner, he found Rose by herself, dressed in a cream-coloured silk gown trimmed with white lace.

'Are you expecting somebody?' he asked.

'Oh, no!' she said, looking somewhat confused. 'We'll have dinner as soon as Achille gets here.'

Latterly the architect was always out and about, never came back to meals at the proper time, and when he did appear, he was flushed and out of sorts, cursing his business problems. Then every night he went off somewhere, running through every pretext in the book, appointments in cafés, meetings on the other side of town, and the like. Thus Octave often kept Rose company until eleven o'clock, for he'd realised that Campardon, in offering him board and lodging, only wanted him as a companion for his wife. Plaintively, but without bitterness, she used to express her fears. Oh, yes, she let Achille do just as he pleased, only she always felt anxious if he wasn't home by midnight!

'Don't you think he looks rather sad lately?' she ventured with concern in her voice.

No, such a thought hadn't struck Octave. 'I rather think he's got a lot on his mind. The restorations at Saint-Roch are probably causing him a lot of worry.'

She shook her head, but let the matter drop. Then, affectionately, like a mother or a sister, she asked Octave, as usual, how he had spent his day. During the almost nine months that he'd been with them, she treated him as if he were one of the family.

At last Campardon appeared.

'Good evening, my pet! Good evening, my treasure!' he said, fondly kissing her like a model husband. 'Yet another idiot who buttonholed me for a whole hour in the street!'

Octave, moving away, heard them exchange a few words under their breath.

'Is she coming?'

'No; there's no point anyway; but don't get yourself in a state about it.'

'You swore that she would come.'

'Well yes, all right, she *is* coming. Are you happy now? I only did it for you.'

Then they sat down to eat. During the whole dinner they talked about the English language, which little Angèle had started learning a fortnight ago. Campardon had suddenly insisted that a young lady had to know English, and, as Lisa's last employer was an actress who had just returned from London, every meal was devoted to discussing the English names for dishes that the maid brought in. On that evening, after long and ineffectual attempts to pronounce the word 'rump-steak', they had to send the roast back, for Victoire had left it cooking too long, and it was as tough as boot leather.

During dessert, a ring at the bell made Madame Campardon start.

'It is madame's cousin,' said Lisa, on returning, in the wounded tone of a servant left out of some family secret.

And it was, indeed, Gasparine. She wore a plain black woollen dress and came in with her thin face and jaded shop-girl air. Rose, snug in her cream-coloured silk dressing-gown, looking plump and fresh, got up to greet her, with tears in her eyes.

'Oh, my dear,' she murmured, 'this is so nice of you . . . We'll let bygones be bygones, won't we?'

Then, putting her arms around her, she kissed her effusively on both cheeks. Octave was about to withdraw discreetly, but they insisted on his remaining; he was one of the family. So he amused himself by watching the whole scene. Campardon, at first greatly disconcerted, avoided looking at the women, but fussed about in search of a cigar; while Lisa, as she noisily cleared the table, exchanged glances with the astonished Angèle.

Finally the architect turned to his daughter: 'This is your cousin. You've heard us talk about her often. Go and give her a kiss.'

Angèle kissed her in her sulky way, feeling uncomfortable beneath the scrutiny of Gasparine's governess eyes, after she'd been asked how old she was and what she was learning. Then, as they retired to the drawing-room, she slunk behind Lisa, who, banging the door, remarked, indifferent as to whether she was overheard or not: 'Things are certainly hotting up here!'

In the drawing-room, Campardon uneasily began to make excuses.

'I can assure you, it was Rose's idea, not mine. She wanted to make it up. Every day, for the last week, she's been saying to me, "Do get her to come . . ." And here she is.'

Then, as if he felt that that ought to convince Octave, he led him aside to the window.

'Ah, well, women are women, you know. I wasn't keen, because I dread scenes myself. Keeping them apart, with one on the right, and the other on the left, meant there couldn't be a collision. However, I had to give in. Rose is sure that we shall all be far happier. Well, we'll give it a try. It's now up to those two whether my life is an agreeable one or the reverse.'

Meanwhile, Rose and Gasparine sat on the sofa side by side. They talked of old times, of days spent with good old papa Domergue in Plassans. Rose, at that time, had a complexion the colour of lead, and the frail limbs of a child ailing since birth; while Gasparine, at fifteen already a woman, was tall and attractive with beautiful eyes. Now they hardly recognised each other, the one cool and plump in her enforced chastity, and the other dried up, consumed by a life of nervous passion. For a moment Gasparine felt mortified, as her sallow face and shabby gown formed such a contrast to Rose, arrayed in silk, whose soft, white neck was swathed in filmy lace. But she mastered this touch of jealousy, accepting her position of poor relation grovelling before her cousin's grace and elegance.

'Well, how are you feeling?' she enquired quietly. 'Achille told me about your poor health. Is there no improvement at all?'

'No, no improvement,' replied Rose, mournfully. 'I can't eat, you see, and I look perfectly well. But it doesn't get any better; and it never will get any better.'

As she began to cry, it was now Gasparine's turn to embrace her, pressing her close to her flat, burning bosom, while Campardon rushed over to try and console them.

'Why are you crying?' she asked, with motherly tenderness. 'The main thing is that you're not in pain. What does it matter, if you always have people around you who love you?'

Rose, growing calmer, smiled through her tears.

Then, carried away by his feelings, Campardon clasped them in one embrace, kissing them both as he murmured: 'Yes, yes, we'll all love one another; and love you, too, my poor darling.

You'll see how well everything turns out now that we're together.'

Then, turning to Octave: 'Say what you like, my dear boy, there's nothing like family life, after all.'

The evening ended delightfully. Campardon who, when he was at home, usually went to sleep directly after dinner, rediscovered some of the gaiety of his artist days as he rehearsed the old jokes and the ribald songs of the École des Beaux-Arts.*

When Gasparine was leaving, at about eleven o'clock, Rose insisted on seeing her out in spite of the difficulty she was having in walking that day. Leaning over the banisters, in the solemn silence of the staircase, she called after her cousin: 'Come and see us often!'

Next day, feeling curious, Octave tried to sound out Gasparine at the shop, as they were sorting a consignment of linen goods. But she was curt and he felt she was hostile, irritated that he'd been a witness of the previous evening's reconciliation. Moreover, she didn't like him; even in their working relationship she showed towards him a kind of spite. For a long time she'd seen through the game he was playing in respect of Madame Hédouin, and for his assiduous courtship she had only black looks and a contemptuous curl of the lip which made him uneasy. As long as this lanky wretch of a woman kept her bony fingers between them, he had the impression, at once firm and unpleasant, that Madame Hédouin would never become his.

Octave, however, had given himself six months. Barely four had passed, and he was growing more impatient. Every morning he asked himself whether he shouldn't hasten matters somewhat, since he seemed to be making so little progress in gaining the affections of this woman, always so icy and so gentle. But she showed real respect for his ideas, taken by his grand schemes, by his dreams of huge modern warehouses, unloading millions of bales of merchandise on to the streets of Paris. Often, when her husband wasn't there, as she and the young man opened the morning mail, she detained him and consulted him, glad of his advice. Thus a sort of commercial intimacy was established between the two. Their hands met amid piles of invoices; as they counted rows of figures, each felt the other's warm breath as they pored excitedly over the cash-desk after unusually good takings. He even thought of taking advantage of such a moment, his plan now being to touch her tradeswoman's instincts and to conquer her on some day of weakness when she was under the influence of an unlooked-for sale. So he kept waiting for a stroke of luck that would prompt her to surrender. But, whenever he stopped talking business, she immediately resumed her quiet tone of authority, politely ordering him to do this or that, just as she would the other assistants. Her control extended to the whole establishment which she supervised with her man's cravat around her statuesque neck, and a demure, tightly fitting black bodice, with not a hint of colour.

About this time, as Monsieur Hédouin became ill, he went to take the waters at Vichy,* much to Octave's undisguised delight. Though as cold as marble, Madame Hédouin, during this vulnerable period of widowhood, would surely relent. But not once did he spot a single languorous symptom of desire. Never had she seemed so active, her head so clear, her eyes so bright.

Rising at daybreak, she herself received the consignments of goods in the basement, looking as busy as a clerk with her pen behind her ear. She was everywhere; upstairs, downstairs, in the linen department, at the silk counter, superintending the window-dressers and the saleswomen, moving noiselessly among the piles of cloth without picking up so much as one speck of dust in this shop bursting to the seams. When meeting her in some of these narrow gangways between walls of material and napkins, Octave would stand awkwardly to one side, on purpose, so that for a second she might be crushed close against his breast. But she moved through the gap so busily that he hardly felt her dress brush past him. Moreover, he was much embarrassed by Mademoiselle Gasparine's cold eyes, unfailingly fixed upon them at such moments as these.

However, the young man did not despair. At times he thought he was almost there, mapping out his life for the day, so close at hand, when he would be Madame Hédouin's lover. He had kept Marie as his mistress merely to pass the time while he was waiting; nevertheless, though obliging and cheap, she might eventually prove troublesome with her dog-like devotion. And while still returning to her on nights when he had nothing else to do, he was already thinking of how he could drop her. To do this abruptly seemed clumsy. One morning when he didn't have to go to work, as he was heading for the bed of his neighbour's wife, while Monsieur Pichon was taking an early constitutional, he had the idea of giving Marie back to Jules, letting them fall into one another's arms so lovingly that, with conscience clear, he could retire. It would be so generous of him and the idea was so touching, indeed, that he was left with no remorse. Nevertheless, he waited, not wishing to be without female consolation of some kind.

At the Campardons' there was another complication. Octave felt that the moment was coming for him to get his meals elsewhere. For three weeks Gasparine had been making herself thoroughly at home there with her authority growing by the day. First she began by coming every evening, then she made an appearance at lunch, and, in spite of her work at the shop, she began to take charge of everything, whether it was Angèle's education or provisions for the house. Rose kept on saying: 'Ah, if only Gasparine lived with us!' Yet every time Campardon blushed shamefacedly as his scruples got the better of him.

'No, no; that would never do! Besides, where would she sleep?' And the architect explained that he would have to give up his study to Gasparine as a bedroom, and move his table and plans into the drawing-room. Certainly, it wouldn't inconvenience him at all, and one day, perhaps he would agree to the alteration, for while he didn't need a whole drawing-room, his study was too small for all the work that he now had in hand. Yet, Gasparine, after all, had better stay where she was. It was no good living on top of one another.

About that time he had to go to Evreux for a couple of days. The work for the archbishop was causing him concern. He had given in to the wishes of His Grace, though no credit had been opened for the purpose, to provide new kitchens and heating; the expenses for this seemed likely to be far too heavy to include in the cost of the repairs. Besides this, the pulpit, for which there was a grant of three thousand francs, would cost ten, at the very least. He wanted to come to some arrangement with the archbishop, so that there wouldn't be problems later on.

Rose did not expect him home before Sunday night; but he arrived in the middle of lunch, and his sudden appearance caused something of a panic. Gasparine was at the table, sitting between Octave and Angèle. They pretended to be perfectly at ease, but there was evidently something mysterious in the air. Lisa had just shut the drawing-room door, at a despairing sign from her mistress, while Gasparine kicked out of sight various bits of paper that were lying about. When he talked of going to change his things, they stopped him.

'Oh! there's no hurry. Have some coffee, as you lunched at Evreux.'

Then, as he noticed how embarrassed Rose was, she flung her arms round his neck.

'Please don't be cross with me, dear. If you hadn't come home until this evening you would have found everything straight.'

Trembling, she opened the folding doors, and took him into the drawing-room and the study. A mahogany bedstead, delivered that morning by a furniture dealer, had replaced his drawing-table, which had been moved into the middle of the next room. But nothing had been put straight yet; portfolios were jumbled up with some of Gasparine's clothes, while the Virgin of the Bleeding Heart was leaning against the wall, propped up by a new washstand.

'It was going to be a surprise!' murmured Madame Campardon, close to tears and hiding her face in the folds of her spouse's waistcoat.

Much moved, he looked at her in silence, while avoiding meeting Octave's gaze.

Then Gasparine, in her dry voice, asked: 'Will it put you out, cousin? Rose pestered me to have it done. But if you think I shall be in your way, of course, I can go.'

'No, cousin!' cried the architect at last; 'whatever Rose does is right.'

Then, as his wife burst out sobbing on his breast, he said: 'There, there, darling; it's silly to cry. I'm very pleased. You want to have your cousin with you; very well, so you shall. It won't disturb me in the least. Now, don't cry any more! See, I'll kiss you because I love you, oh, so much!'

And he devoured her with kisses. Then Rose, who could dissolve in tears and then be smiling again a moment later, kissed him on his beard, saying gently: 'You were rather hard on her. Give her a kiss, too.'

Campardon embraced Gasparine. Angèle was called from the dining-room from where she'd been watching with mouth agape; she, too, had to kiss the cousin. Octave had moved to one side, having come to the conclusion that in this family they were really getting rather too affectionate. He had noticed with surprise Lisa's respectful manner and smiling attentiveness towards Gasparine. A sharp girl, evidently, that strumpet with the blue circles around her eyes!

Meanwhile the architect had taken off his coat, whistling and singing like a merry schoolboy, and spent the whole afternoon arranging the cousin's room. She helped him push the furniture into place, unpack the bed-linen and shake out the clothes, while Rose, sitting down so as not to tire herself, made various suggestions for putting the washstand here or the bed there, so that it would be convenient for everyone. It was then that Octave became aware that he was a dampener on this collective enthusiasm; he felt out of place in this closely knit household. So he told them that he was going to dine out that evening, having decided that, the next day, he would express his thanks to Madame Campardon for her hospitality, and invent some tale or other for not trespassing on it further.

About five o'clock, as he was regretting that he didn't know where to find Trublot, he suddenly thought he would invite himself to dinner at the Pichons', so as not to spend the evening by himself. No sooner had he got to their apartment, however, than he found himself in the midst of a great family row. The Vuillaumes were there, indignant and enraged.

'It's disgraceful,' said the mother, standing erect as she lectured her son-in-law, cowering in a chair. 'You gave me your word of honour.'

'And you,' added the father, making his trembling daughter retreat in terror to the sideboard, 'don't make any excuses; you're just as much to blame. I suppose you both want to starve, eh?'

Madame Vuillaume had put on her bonnet and shawl again, declaring solemnly: 'Good-bye! This kind of socialising obviously encourges your lack of self-control. Since you no longer pay the least attention to our wishes, we have nothing more to do here. Good-bye!'

And as Jules, from force of habit, rose to accompany them, she added: 'No, don't bother; we're quite capable of getting an omnibus without you. Come on, Monsieur Vuillaume. Let them eat dinner, and much good may it do them, for they won't always have one!'

Octave, astonished, stood aside to let them pass. When they had gone, he looked at Jules, prostrate in his chair, and Marie standing by the sideboard, deathly pale. Both were speechless.

'What's the matter?' he asked.

But without answering him, the young woman dolefully began to scold her husband.

'I told you. You should have waited until you could break it to them gently. There was no hurry about it; nothing shows yet.'

'Why, what is it?' asked Octave, again.

Then, not even looking away, she blurted out, 'I'm pregnant.'

'Oh! They're a damned nuisance!' cried Jules, indignantly, as he rose from his chair. 'I thought it right to tell them straight away. Do they think it amuses me? Not a bit of it. It's far worse for me, especially as it's through no fault of mine. We can't imagine where this one's come from, can we, Marie?'

'No, indeed!' said the young woman.

Octave made a calculation. She was five months gone, from the end of December to the end of May. His calculation was correct: he was overcome with emotion. Then he preferred to have his doubts; but, still in his mawkish state, he felt a longing to do the Pichons a kindness of some sort. Jules went on grumbling. They would look after the child, of course they would; but, all the same, it would have been better if it hadn't happened. Marie, usually so quiet, got into a temper, too, siding with her mother, who never forgave disobedience. A quarrel seemed imminent, each blaming the other for the baby, when Octave gaily butted in.

'Come, come, it's no use quarrelling now that it's on the way. I vote we don't dine here, it would be too depressing. I'll take you both out to a restaurant. Would you like that?'

Marie blushed. There was nothing she liked better than eating in a restaurant. But she mentioned her little girl, who always prevented her from getting out to enjoy herself. However, they settled that this time Lilitte should come too. And they had a lovely evening. Octave took them to the Boeuf à la Mode, where they had a private room, as they would be more relaxed. Here he lavishly plied them with all sorts of food. When dessert came, and they had laid little Lilitte down between two cushions on the sofa, he even ordered champagne, and they sat dreaming there, with their elbows on the table and eyes moist with emotion, the three of them sentimentally drowsy in the suffocating atmosphere of the room. Finally, at eleven o'clock, they talked of going home; but the cool night air, as it touched their flushed cheeks, seemed intoxicating. Then, as Lilitte, utterly exhausted, refused to walk, Octave, anxious to do the whole thing handsomely, insisted on having a cab, even though the Rue de Choiseul was close by. In the cab he scrupulously avoided squeezing Marie's legs between his own. Only once upstairs, while Jules was tucking Lilitte up, did he kiss the young woman's forehead, the parting kiss of a father surrending his daughter to her husband. Then, as he saw them looking amorously at each other, he sent them to bed, wishing them through the door a very good-night and lots of sweet dreams.

Well, he thought, as he slipped between the sheets, it's cost me fifty francs, but I owed them at least that. After all, the only thing I want is for that husband of hers to make the poor little woman happy!

And quite overcome by his own kindheartness, he resolved, before going to bed, to make his planned conquest the very next evening.

Every Monday, after dinner, Octave helped Madame Hédouin to check the orders for the week. For this purpose they both withdrew to a little parlour at the back, a narrow room which only contained a safe, a bureau, two chairs, and a sofa. It so happened that on this particular Monday, the Duveyriers were going to take Madame Hédouin to the Opéra-Comique. So she sent for the young man early, at about three o'clock. In spite of the bright sunshine, they had to light the gas lamp, as the room was only dimly lit by windows overlooking the inner courtyard. He bolted the door, and, noticing her surprised look, he said softly: 'Now nobody can come and disturb us.'

She nodded and they started work. The summer fashions were going splendidly; business was always increasing. That week, in particular, the sale of little woollen goods had looked so promising that she heaved a sigh.

'Ah, if we only had enough room!'

'But you know,' he said, launching his attack, 'that's entirely up to you. For some time I've had an idea I'd like to talk to you about.'

It was the bold initiative he had been dreaming of. It involved buying the adjoining house, in the Rue Neuve-Saint-Augustin, giving the umbrella merchant and the toy-maker their notice to quit, and then enlarging their own shop to which several extensive departments could be added. And he was fired up, full of disdain for the old way of doing business at the back of damp, dark shops, with no display in their window-fronts. He conjured up, instead, a new kind of establishment providing every sort of luxury for women in huge palaces, amassing millions in the crystal light of day and the artificial brilliance of the night, a celebration of majestic proportions.

'You'll kill off all the shops in the Saint-Roch neighbourhood,' he said, 'while taking over their trade. For instance, Monsieur Vabre's silk firm is in competition with you at present; but if you enlarge your shop-front and open a special silk department, you'll make him bankrupt in less than five years. Then again, there's talk of driving a Rue du Dix-Décembre from the new Opera House to the Bourse. My friend Campardon has sometimes mentioned it. That would have the effect of increasing business around here tenfold.'

With her elbow on the ledger, Madame Hédouin listened, resting her beautiful grave face on her hand. She had been born at 'Au Bonheur des Dames', founded by her father and her uncle. She loved the house, imagined it expanding, engulfing the adjoining buildings, and displaying a broad, magnificent frontage. The dream suited her keen, active intelligence, her determination and her woman's intuition of the Paris of the future.

'Uncle Deleuze would never consent to it and, in any case, my husband isn't well enough.'

But, noticing that she herself was excited by the idea, Octave assumed his most seductive voice, that of an actor, both gentle and lulling. Simultaneously, he fixed her with a melting gaze, his eyes the colour of old gold, and which some women found irresistible. But though the jet of the gas lamp was close to the back of her neck, she felt not even a trace of sensual warmth flickering across her skin, relapsing into a reverie, half dazed by the young man's eloquence. He had got as far as figures counting up the probably cost with all the ardour of a page finally making a romantic declaration of undying love. Roused from her daydreams, she suddenly found herself in his arms. He pushed her on to the sofa, believing that now at last she would surrender.

'Good Lord! So that's what it was all about,' she said sadly, as she shook him off as if he were some tiresome child.

'Yes, indeed, for I'm in love with you!' he exclaimed. 'Don't turn me down. With you at my side I could do such great things . . .'

And he went on to the end of his great prepared speech, which somehow rang false. She didn't interrupt him, but stood turning over the leaves of the ledger.

Then when he'd said his piece, she replied: 'I know all that; I've heard it all before. But I thought that you, Monsieur Octave, had more sense than the others. I really am very sorry, for I'd been counting on you. Ah, well, all young men are unreasonable. A firm like this needs a great deal of stability, and all you can think of are things that would unsettle us from morning to night. I'm not a woman here; there's far too much for me to do. Come, now, how can somebody as intelligent as you not see that that's the last thing I would do; first, because it's silly; second, because it's pointless, and third, because, luckily for me, it doesn't tempt me in the slightest!'

He would have preferred her wrath and indignation, over-flowing with high-minded ideas. Her calm voice, her quiet way of reasoning like a practical, self-possessed woman, disconcerted him. He felt that he was becoming ridiculous.

'Oh, have pity on me,' he stammered. 'You can see how miserable I am!'

'Nonsense! You're not miserable at all. Anyhow, you'll soon get over it. Listen! There's somebody knocking; you'd better go and open the door.'

So he had to draw back the bolt. It was Mademoiselle Gasparine, who wanted to know about some shirts with lace inserts. She had been surprised to find the door bolted. But she knew Madame Hédouin too well, and when she saw her gla-cially confronting Octave, who looked thoroughly ill at ease, there was something mocking in her smile. It exasperated him and he vaguely ascribed his failure to her.

'Madame,' he said, as soon as Gasparine had gone. 'I'm resigning as from this evening.'

Madame Hédouin looked at him in surprise.

'What for? I'm not dismissing you. Oh, that won't make any difference! I'm not afraid!'

This drove him frantic. He would leave now, unwilling to endure this martyrdom a moment longer.

'Very well, Monsieur Octave,' she continued, in her calm

way. 'I will settle up with you right away. All the same, the firm
will be sorry to lose you, for you were a good assistant.'

Once in the street, Octave saw that he had acted like a fool.
It was striking four, and the bright May sunshine lit up a whole
corner of the Place Gaillon. Furious with himself, he meandered
down the Rue Saint-Roch, internally debating how he ought to
have acted. First of all, why hadn't he touched up that Gasparine? Probably that was what she wanted, but, unlike Campardon, he didn't care for women as scraggy; anyway, that might
have been another bad move, for she looked like one of those
creatures who are strictly virtuous on Sunday when they're on
their backs from Monday to Saturday. Then again, what a
stupid idea to try and become Madame Hédouin's lover!
Couldn't he have just earned his money in the firm without
expecting at the same time both bread and bed? He felt so
downcast that he was on the point of returning to 'Au Bonheur
des Dames' and admitting his error. But the thought of Madame
Hédouin, so majestically calm, reawakened his wounded vanity,
and he carried on down the street towards Saint-Roch's. A
shame; but it was over and done with now. He would go and
see if Campardon was in the church, and take him to the café
for a glass of Madeira. It would take his mind off it. He went in
an entrance leading to the vestry. It was a dark and dirty
passage, like that of a brothel.

'Would you be looking for Monsieur Campardon?' said a
voice close behind him, as he stood hesitating, gazing intently
along the nave.

It was the Abbé Mauduit, who had just recognised him. As
the architect wasn't there, he insisted on showing Octave the
Calvary restorations himself, about which he was full of enthusiasm. He took him behind the choir, first showing him a side
chapel, that of the holy Virgin, with its walls of white marble
and its altar crowned by the manger scene, a rococo representation of Jesus between Joseph and Mary. Then, further back still,
he took him through the Chapel of Perpetual Adoration, with
its seven golden lamps, gold candelabra, and gold altar shining
in the dim light that came through gold-coloured windows.
There, to right and left, wooden hoardings fenced off the last
part of the apse; and amid the silence, above the black kneeling
shadows mumbling prayers, could be heard the blows of pick-
axes, the voices of workmen, all the din of a building site.

'Come in,' said the Abbé Mauduit, lifting up his cassock. 'I'll explain it to you.'

On the other side of the hoarding, plaster kept falling from a corner of the church open to the outside air; it was white with lime, and damp with water that had been spilt here and there. To the left, the Tenth Station could still be seen, with Jesus nailed to the cross, while, on the right, there was the Twelfth, showing the women grouped around Christ. But the Eleventh Station, the group with Jesus on the cross, had been removed and placed against a wall; it was here that the men were at work.

'Here it is,' continued the priest. 'It was my idea to light up the central group of the Calvary by means of an opening in the cupola. You see the effect I wanted to get?'

'Yes, yes,' murmured Octave, forgetting his troubles during his guided tour.

Talking at the top of his voice, the abbé seemed like a stage-designer, directing the artistic arrangement of some huge set.

'It's got to look absolutely bare; nothing but stone walls, not a touch of paint, not the least hint of gilding. We've got to imagine that we're in a crypt, in some desolate subterranean chamber. What will dominate it, of course, will be the figure of Christ on the cross, with the Virgin Mary and Mary Magdalene at His feet. I'm going to place the group on the summit of a rock, the white statues sharp against a grey background; while the light from the cupola, like some invisible ray, will illuminate them with such brilliance that they'll stand out as if palpitating with the breath of supernatural life! Ah, you'll see, you'll see!'

Then he turned around and called out to a workman: 'You'd better move the Virgin! You'll smash her thigh if you don't.'

The workman called over one of his mates. Between them they took the Virgin by the loins and carried her off, as if she were a tall white wench, stiff and prostrate as a reuslt of some nervous seizure.

'Be careful!' repeated the priest, who followed them through all the rubbish; 'her robe has already got a crack in it. Wait a minute!'

He gave them a hand, seizing the Virgin Mary around the waist, and emerged from his embrace all white with plaster. Then, turning to Octave, he said: 'Now, just imagine that the two bays of the nave there, in front of us, are open, and that you're standing in the Chapel of the Holy Virgin. Above the altar, through the Chapel of Perpetual Adoration, right at the back, you'll be able to see the Calvary. Imagine the impact of those three great figures and this dramatic simplicity in the dim tabernacle, visible beyond the mysterious twilight from stained-glass windows, amid candelabra and lamps of gold. Ah, I think it will be irresistible!'

He was waxing eloquent, happy and proud of his conception.

'The most sceptical of unbelievers will be touched,' said Octave, just to please him.

'So they will,' he exclaimed. 'I'm impatient to see it finished.'

Returning to the nave, still carried away, he boomed on like some successful set designer, praising Campardon to the skies, as a fellow who, in the Middle Ages, would have been the incarnation of the power of religion. He led Octave out through the small doorway at the back, keeping him for a moment longer in the courtyard of the presbytery, from which one could see the main body of the church almost submerged by surrounding buildings. This was where he lived, on the second floor of a lofty house with a crumbling façade. All the clergy of Saint-Roch lived there. A clerical mustiness and the hushed whisperings of the confessional seemed to come from the entrance, adorned by an image of the Holy Virgin and with its high windows veiled by thick curtains.

'I shall come and see Monsieur Campardon this evening,' said the Abbé Mauduit as they parted. 'Please ask him to wait for me. I'd like to discuss with him some further refinements.'

And he bowed with the easy grace of a man of the world. Octave was calmer; Saint-Roch, with its cool vaulted aisles, had soothed his nerves. He looked with curiosity at this entrance to a church through an ordinary house, at this porter's lodge, where at night the latch had to be lifted to let the Almighty pass, at this monastic corner hidden in the darkness of the seething neighbourhood. On reaching the pavement, he looked up once again at the bare frontage of the house with its barred, curtainless windows. The window sills on the fourth floor were bright with flowers, while below there were little shops which the clergy found handy, a cobbler's, a watch-maker's, an embroiderer's, and even a wine-merchant's where undertakers got together for a drink whenever there was a funeral. Octave, still smarting from his rejection, felt in a mood to renounce worldly things, and envied the peaceful existence which the priest's servants must lead up there in those rooms decked with verbena and sweet peas.

That evening, at half past six, as he went into the Campardons' apartment without ringing, he caught the architect and Gasparine kissing in the ante-room. She had only just got home from the shop, and had not even shut the door. They both looked startled. 'My wife – er – is combing her hair,' stammered the architect, just to say something. 'Do go and see her.'

Octave, feeling as uncomfortable as they did, hastily knocked at the door of Rose's bedroom to which, as a relative, he had access. He certainly couldn't carry on taking his meals there, now that he'd caught them kissing in secret.

'Come in!' cried Rose. 'Oh! It's you, Octave . . . well, that's fine . . . come in anyway.'

She had not put her dressing-gown back on, and her soft, milk-white shoulders and arms were bare. Carefully looking at herself in the mirror, she was twisting her golden hair into tiny curls. Every day she sat like this for hours, obsessed with the minutest of details of her appearance, thinking of nothing but the pores of her skin. Then, when she'd finished beautifying herself, she would recline at full length in an easy-chair, luxurious and lovely, like some sexless idol.

'You're making yourself look wonderful again tonight, I see,' said Octave, smiling.

'Well, it's all I've got,' she replied. 'It's something to do. I never did care about running the house, you know; and now that Gasparine's here . . . don't you think these little curls suit me? It's a sort of consolation to be nicely dressed, and to feel that I look pretty.'

As it wasn't time for dinner yet, he told her how he had left 'Au Bonheur des Dames'. He invented a story about some other opening which he had long been looking out for; thus preparing the ground for the moment when he would announce his intention of taking his meals elsewhere. She was surprised at his leaving a firm like that, where he had such good prospects. But she was far too busy at her looking-glass to listen properly.

'Do you see that red spot behind my ear? I wonder if it's a pimple?'

He was obliged to examine her neck, which she held out to

him with the beautiful repose of a woman whose chastity is
sacred, inviolate.

'It's nothing,' he said. 'I expect you rubbed yourself too hard
with the towel.'

Then, after he had helped her to put on her blue satin and
silver gown, they went into the dining-room. As soon as they
sat down to eat, the conversation turned to Octave leaving the
Hédouins. Campardon expressed great surprise, while Gasparine smiled her usual affected smile. Both seemed to be thoroughly at ease. Octave even felt touched by the tender attentions
that they lavished on Rose. Campardon poured out her wine,
while Gasparine carefully chose for her the nicest pieces of the
dish. Did she like the bread? If not, they would go to another
baker's. Would she like a cushion for her back? Rose, full of
gratitude, begged them not to go to so much trouble. She ate a
great deal, sitting majestically between them, with her soft,
white neck and stately gown, her husband, short of breath and
getting thinner every day, was on her right, while on her left sat
her stale, sallow cousin, with shrunken shoulders covered by a
black dress, and flesh dissolved by the fires of secret passion.

At dessert, Gasparine sharply scolded Lisa, who had answered
rudely when Madame Campardon enquired about a piece of
cheese that was missing. The maid became very meek and mild.
Gasparine had already taken the household in hand, and kept
the servants in their place; a word from her was enough to set
even Victoire shaking among her saucepans. Rose thanked her
with a glance that spoke volumes; they respected her, now that
Gasparine was there, and if her cousin too were to leave 'Au
Bonheur des Dames', she could take responsibility for Angèle's
education, and everything would be perfect.

'Come now,' she said, coaxingly, 'there's quite enough for
you to do here. Angèle, beg your cousin to leave; tell her how
pleased you would be.'

The child entreated her cousin to leave, while Lisa nodded
approvingly. Campardon and Gasparine, however, looked
grave. No, no; it was better to wait; one shouldn't take a leap
of that sort without having anything to hold on to.

Evenings in the drawing-room had become delightful. The
architect never went out now. That evening, as it happened, he
was going to hang up some engravings in Gasparine's bedroom.
They had just come back from the framers; they included one

of Mignon yearning for heaven, together with a view of the Fountain of Vaucluse.* Hale and hearty, with his yellow beard all over the place, and his cheeks flushed from eating too much, he was in the high spirits of a man whose every appetite is satisfied.

He called Gasparine to give him some light, and they heard him hammering in the nails as he stood on a chair.

Octave, finding himself alone with Rose, went on to explain that, at the end of the month, he would be obliged to take his meals elsewhere. She seemed surprised, but her head was full of other things, as she listened to the laughter of her husband and Gasparine in the other room.

'What a good time they're having hanging those pictures! Well, Achille never stays out now; he's not left me alone for a single evening during the last fortnight. No more appointments at cafés, no more business engagements! You remember how anxious I used to be if he was out after midnight. Oh! It's such a relief! At least he won't walk out on me!'

'Of course, of course,' muttered Octave.

Then she began to talk about how economical this new arrangement was. It was all much more efficient and there was laughter at home from morning till night.

'When I see Achille happy,' she continued, 'why, I'm happy, too.'

Then suddenly reverting to the young man's affairs, she added; 'So you're really going to leave us? You ought to stay, now that we're all going to be so happy.'

When he'd explained the situation once again, she understood at last, and looked down; the young man really was rather getting in the way of their domestic bliss. She herself was somewhat relieved that he was going, since she no longer needed him to keep her company in the evenings. He had to promise that he would often come and see her.

'There's your "Mignon" for you!' cried Campardon, gaily. 'Wait a minute, cousin, and I'll help you down.'

They heard him take her in his arms and deposit her somewhere. Then there was silence, followed by a suppressed laugh. But almost immediately the architect came back to the drawing-room, and held out his flushed cheek to his wife.

'It's done, my darling. Kiss your old thing for working so hard.'

Gasparine came in with some embroidery, and sat down near the lamp. Campardon, for fun, began cutting out a gilt cross of the Légion d'Honneur, which had come off some label. He blushed deeply when Rose tried to pin this paper decoration to his coat. He'd in fact been promised the real thing, but there was something mysterious about it. On the other side of the lamp, Angèle, learning her Scripture history, kept looking across with her puzzled air of a well-brought-up young person, taught to keep her thoughts to herself. It was a quiet evening at home enveloped in patriarchal harmony.

But suddenly, Campardon's sense of propriety was outraged. He'd just noticed that, instead of studying her Scripture history, the child was reading the *Gazette de France*, which lay on the table.

'Angèle!' he said sternly. 'What do you think you're doing? This morning I crossed out that article with a red pencil. You know very well that you are not to read what is crossed out.'

'I was reading the piece next to it, Papa,' said the girl.

But he still took the newspaper away, as he quickly complained to Octave about the utter demoralisation of the press. That very day there was another report of some abominable crime. If the *Gazette de France* could no longer be admitted into respectable family circles, what paper could they take? And as he was turning his eyes heavenwards, Lisa announced the Abbé Mauduit.

'Oh! Of course,' said Octave. 'He asked me to tell you he was coming.'

The abbé came in smiling. Campardon had forgotten to take off the paper cross, and the cleric's smile flustered him. The Abbé Mauduit, as it happened, was the very person about whom there was all this mystery, and whose name had to be kept secret. It was he who had undertaken to secure the nomination.

'The ladies did it, silly things!' murmured Campardon, as he started to take off the cross.

'No, no! Keep it on,' replied the priest, pleasantly. 'It's where it belongs and we'll find a more substantial susbtitute for it before long.'

He immediately enquired after Rose's health, and gave his stamp of approval to Gasparine having moved in with her relatives; young unmarried women living alone ran such risks in a city like Paris. He said all this unctuously, like a man of the Church, though he was perfectly aware how matters really stood. Then he spoke of the Saint-Roch restorations, and suggested an important alteration. It seemed as if he had come to bless the unity of this family, and thus redeem a somewhat delicate situation which might give rise to local gossip. The architect of the Saint-Roch Calvary merited the respect of the whole comunity.

When the abbé came in, Octave bade the Campardons good evening. As he made his way out through the dark ante-room, he heard Angèle's voice, for she, too, had managed to slip away.

'Was it about the butter that she was making all that fuss?' she asked.

'Yes, of course it was,' replied another voice, which was Lisa's. 'She's as spiteful as some mangy cat. You saw how she went on at me during dinner! Not that I care! One has to pretend to obey with a person of that sort, and it doesn't prevent our having our own little jokes, all the same.'

Then Angèle must have flung her arms around Lisa's neck, for her voice sounded muffled, as if by the maid's bosom.

'Oh yes, and that's what counts because it's you, you, I love!'

Octave was about to go upstairs to bed, when he felt a need for fresh air. It was barely ten o'clock; he would take a stroll as far as the Palais Royal. Now he was unattached again, with no woman whatever in tow. Neither Valérie nor Madame Hédouin had wanted anything to do with him, and he'd been in too great a hurry to give back Marie to Jules, his only conquest, and then with no effort on his part. He endeavoured to laugh at it all, but at heart he felt sad, bitterly recollecting his successes in Marseilles. In the repeated failure of all his attempts at seduction, he saw an evil omen, an obstacle to his dreams for the future. He felt cold inside, with no petticoats around him. Even Madame Campardon had let him go without a tear. What terrible revenge he would one day wreak. Was Paris going to deny him her favours, after all?

No sooner had he got into the street than he heard a woman's voice calling him. It was Berthe, standing at the door of the silk shop. A man was just putting up the shutters.

'Oh, Monsieur Mouret!' she asked. 'Is it true that you have left 'Au Bonheur des Dames'?'

He was surprised to find that the neighbourhood had already

heard the news. Berthe called her husband. He had meant to go
up and have a talk with Monsieur Mouret the next day; well,
he might just as well do it now. And, there and then, Auguste,
in his sulky way, offered the young man a job. Taken aback,
Octave hesitated, and was on the point of refusing, as he
reflected on what a small business it was. But when he saw
Berthe's pretty face, and welcoming smile, the same bright
glance that twice had met his, once on the day of his arrival,
and again on her wedding day, he said decisively: 'All right; I'll
take it.'

Octave now found himself brought into closer contact with the Duveyriers. Often, as Madame Duveyrier came through her brother's shop on her way home she would stop and talk to Berthe for a moment; and the first time she saw the young man behind one of the counters, she good-humouredly scolded him for not keeping his promise to come and see her one evening and try out his voice. She was going to put on the *Consecration of the Swords* at one of her first Saturday parties the following winter, with two more tenors this time – to make it a real performance.

'If it isn't inconvenient,' said Berthe one day to Octave, 'could you go upstairs after dinner to my sister-in-law's? She's expecting you.'

The attitude she maintained towards him was no more than that of a polite employer.

'Well, actually,' he said, 'I had thought of sorting out these shelves.'

'Never mind about them,' she replied; 'there are plenty of people to do that. You have the evening off.'

About nine o'clock Octave found Madame Duveyrier waiting for him in her large white and gold drawing-room. Everything was ready, the piano open, the candles lit. A lamp, placed on a small table near the instrument, partly lit the room, and the rest remained in darkness. Seeing that she was alone, Octave thought to ask how Monsieur Duveyrier was. He was very well, she said; his colleagues had assigned him the task of drafting a report on a most serious matter, and he had just gone out to obtain certain vital information.

'You know the Rue de Provence affair,' she said casually.

'Oh, he's dealing with that, is he?' exclaimed Octave. It was a scandal that had become the talk of Paris – a prostitution ring providing fourteen-year-olds for prominent figures.

'Yes, it gives him a great deal to do,' she added. 'For the past fortnight, every evening has been taken up with it.'

He looked at her, knowing from Trublot that Bachelard had invited Duveyrier to dinner and that they were going to spend the rest of the evening at Clarisse's. She seemed quite serious, however, and talked gravely about her husband, rehearsing, in her eminently respectable way, incredile explanations for his always being absent.

'He has a great deal of responsibility,' said Octave, feeling somewhat uneasy beneath her steady gaze.

He found her very attractive, sitting there alone in the empty room. Her reddish hair heightened the pallor of her somewhat long face, which expressed the quiet determination of a woman resigned to her lot. Dressed in grey silk, her waist and bosom tightly squeezed into a stiffened corset, she treated him with reserved politeness, as if some iron barrier separated them.

'Well then, shall we begin?' she went on. 'Don't mind me. Let yourself go, and sing as loud as you like, for Monsieur Duveyrier isn't here. I'm sure you've heard him boast that he doesn't like music.'

This last sentence was filled with such contempt that Octave ventured to laugh gently. It was, in fact, the only reproach aimed at her husband that guests were sometimes allowed to make; although she had sufficient self-control to hide the hatred and the physical repulsion that he inspired in her, his jokes about her piano were too much to bear.

'How can someone not like music?' said Octave, with enthusiasm, wishing to make himself agreeable.

She sat down at the piano. A volume of old songs lay open before her. She chose one from Grétry's *Zemire et Azor*.* As Octave could barely read music, she went through it with him first, so that he could hum the tune. Then she played the prelude, and he began to sing:

> When Love lights up the heart,
> Life becomes passing sweet!

'That's perfect!' she cried, in rapture. 'A tenor, without question – a tenor! Do go on!'

Octave, quite flattered, sang the next two lines:

> And I, who feel his dart,
> Lie swooning at your feet!

She beamed with delight. For the last three years she had been looking for a tenor! And she recounted all her setbacks – Monsieur Trublot, for instance. It would be worth looking into the reason for such a lack of tenors among society's young men; no doubt smoking had something to do with it.

'Now then, are you ready?' she continued. 'Let's put some expression into it: make a bold start.'

Her cold face became wistful as her eyes turned towards him with a dreamy look. Thinking that she was melting, he himself became more excited and aware of her charms. Not a sound could be heard in the adjoining apartments; the semi-darkness of the large room seemed to envelop them both in a seductive drowsiness. As he bent over her to see the music, his chest touched her hair, adding a thrill of passion to the lines:

> And I, who feel his dart,
> Lie swooning at your feet!

But, the melodious phrase over and done with, she dropped her passionate expression as if it were a mask, to reveal her under-lying coldness. He shrank back in alarm, not wishing to repeat the episode with Madame Hédouin.

'You'll soon get the hang of it,' she said. 'Only you must mark the time more – like this; you see?'

And she sang the line for him, twenty times over, bringing out each note with the austerity of an irreproachable woman whose passion for music was shallow – and only went as far as its execution. By degrees her voice grew louder, and filled the room with shrill cries, until they both heard someone loudly calling out behind them: 'Madame! Madame!'

With a start she recognised Clémence, her maid.

'Well, what is it?'

'Oh, madame, Monsieur Vabre has fallen face down on his writing-desk, and he isn't moving! We're all so frightened!'

Then, without exactly grasping the maid's meaning, she rose from the piano in astonishment, and went out with Clémence. Octave, who didn't dare follow her, remained walking up and down the drawing-room. After some moments of awkward hesitation, however, and hearing the sound of hurrying foot-steps and anxious voices, he decided to see what was happening. Crossing the next room, which was quite dark, he reached Monsieur Vabre's room. All the servants had rushed in – Julie in her kitchen apron; Clémence and Hippolyte, their minds still on a game of dominoes they had just been playing. And there they all stood in bewilderment round the old man while Clotilde, stooping down, shouted in his ear and implored him to speak. But he still wouldn't move his face buried in his papers. His forehead had struck the ink-stand. There was a splash of ink over his left eye, which was trickling slowly down towards his lips.

'He's having a fit,' said Octave. 'It won't do to leave him there. We must move him to the bed.'

Madame Duveyrier, however, was losing control, gradually overcome with emotion. She kept repeating: 'Do you think so? Do you think so? Goodness gracious! Oh, my poor dear father!'

Hippolyte, the footman, was in no hurry to move. He was repulsed by the idea of having to touch the old man who might die in his arms. Octave was forced to ask him for assistance. Between them, they laid him down on the bed.

'Bring some warm water,' the young man said to Julie, 'and bathe his face.'

Clotilde now became angry with her husband. Why did he always have to be away? It was as if he did it on purpose; he was never at home when he was needed, not that that was very often! Octave, interrupting, advised her to send for Doctor Juillerat. No one had thought of it before. Hippolyte started off at once, glad to get away.

'Leaving me alone like this!' Clotilde went on. 'I don't know, there must be all sorts of things to sort out. Oh, my poor dear father!'

'Would you like me to let the other members of your family know?' said Octave. 'I can fetch your two brothers. It might be a good idea.'

She didn't answer. Two large tears filled her eyes, while Julie and Clémence endeavoured to undress the old man. But she stopped Octave; her brother Auguste was out, he had an appointment that evening, and as for Théophile, it would be better if he didn't come up, as the mere sight of him would be enough to finish the old man off. Then she told him how her father had gone personally to Théophile to collect their overdue rent, but they had both given him a most brutal reception, especially Valérie, refusing to pay a single penny, and claiming it as the sum he had promised to let them have when they had got married.

The seizure was doubtless the result of such a scene, for he had come back in a terrible state.

'Madame,' said Clémence, 'one side of him is already quite cold.'

This only served to increase Madame Duveyrier's indignation. She was afraid to say anything more in front of the servants. Her husband obviously wasn't a bit bothered about their interests! Ah, if only she had some knowledge of the law! And she could not keep still, but walked up and down in front of the bed. Octave, noticing the index cards, was drawn to the complicated system spread out across the table. There, in a large oak box, was a whole series of cards, carefully classified, the inane work of a lifetime. Just as he was reading on one of the cards the inscription: 'ISIDORE CHARBOTEL.* Salon of 1857, *Atlanta*; Salon of 1859, *Androcles and the Lion*; Salon of 1861, *Portrait of Monsieur P—*', Clotilde came up to him, and quietly but firmly said: 'Go and fetch him.'

As he seemed surprised, she gave a shrug, implicitly giving her story about a report on the Rue de Provence affair the status of one of those excuses that she used to keep up appearances. Now she was in no mood to do so.

'Yes, as you know perfectly well; from that place in the Rue de la Cerisaie. All our friends know.'

He started to protest. 'I assure you, madame, that—'

'Don't try to protect him,' she went on. 'It doesn't bother me in the slighest; he can stay there, if he likes. If it weren't for my poor dear father!'

Octave bent down as Julie was wiping Monsieur Vabre's eye with the corner of a towel; but the ink had dried on to the skin, leaving a livid mark. Madame Duveyrier advised her not to rub so hard, and then turned back to Octave, who was already at the door.

'Not a word to anyone,' she murmured. 'There's no point upsetting the whole house. Take a cab, knock at the door, and make sure you bring him back with you.'

When Octave had gone, she sank into a chair near the sick man's pillow. He had not regained consciousness; only his slow, painful breathing broke the melancholy silence in the room. Then, as the doctor hadn't arrived, and finding herself alone with two terrified maidservants, she burst into tears, sobbing violently in her grief.

It was at the Café Anglais, for some unknown reason, that Bachelard had invited Monsieur Duveyrier to dine. Perhaps it was for the pleasure of having a distinguished magistrate as his guest, and of showing him that tradespeople knew how to spend their money. He had asked Trublot and Gueulin as well – four men and no women; women don't know how to appreciate a good dinner. They prevent one from enjoying the truffles, and ruin one's digestion. Bachelard, in fact, was well known all along the boulevards for his sumptuous dinners whenever some customer of his turned up from the depths of India or Brazil – dinners at three hundred francs a head, by which he nobly upheld the prestige of French commission agencies. A mania for spending money possessed him; he insisted on having the most expensive dishes, gastronomical rarities that were often unpalatable: sturgeon from Volga, eels from the Tiber; grouse from Scotland; fowl from Sweden; bears' feet from the Black Forest; bison-humps from America; turnips from Teltow; gourds from Greece. Then, too, he had to have everything that was not in season, such as peaches in December, or partridges in July, with an abundance of flowers, silver plate, cut glass, and such monopolising of the waiters that the whole restaurant was turned topsy-turvy; not to mention the wines which the cellar had to be ransacked to find. He always required unknown vintages, nothing being old enough nor rare enough for him, and he dreamed of unique bottles of wine at two louis the glass.

That evening, as it was summer-time, a season when everything is in abundance, he had found it rather difficult to run up an excessive bill. The menu, which had been arranged the day before, was nevertheless exceptional: asparagus cream soup followed by *timbales à la Pompadour*; two *relevés*: trout *à la genevoise*, and fillet of beef *à la Chateaubriand*; two *entrées*: ortolans *à la Lucullus* and a crayfish salad; then, a haunch of venison, with artichokes *à la jardinière*, followed by a chocolate *soufflé* and various fruit. It was simple in its grandeur, and made more imposing by a magnificent choice of wines: old Madeira with the soup, a '58 Château-Filhot with the *hors-d'oeuvres*, Johannisberg and Pichon-Longueville with the *relevés*, a '48 Château-Lafite with the *entrés*; sparkling Moselle with the roast, and iced Roederer with the dessert. He was deeply sad to have missed out on a bottle of Johannisberg, a hundred and five years old, which had been sold, only three days before, to a Turk for ten louis.

'Drink up, sir, drink up!' he urged on Duveyrier; 'when wine is good it never gets into your head. It's like food, which never does you any harm if it's fine.'

He, however, was on his best behaviour, posing as an upstanding gentleman, carefully groomed, with a rose at his buttonhole, refraining from his usual trick of smashing the dishes. Trublot and Gueulin ate everything in sight. The uncle's theory appeared to be correct, for Duveyrier, who was always troubled by indigestion, drank quantities of wine, and then had another helping of crayfish salad without feeling at all uncomfortable; the red blotches on his face merely turned purple.

At nine o'clock the dinner was still in progress. The candles, which flared in the breeze from an open window, made the silver plate and the glass sparkle, while, emerging from the remains of the feast, stood four large baskets filled with exquisite, fast-fading flowers. As well as the two *maîtres d'hôtel*, each guest had a waiter behind his chair, whose special responsibility was to supply him with wine and bread, and change his plates. It was very stuffy in spite of the fresh breeze from the boulevard. Everybody was filled to bursting, amid the spicy aroma of the dishes and the vanilla-like perfumes of the precious wines.

Then, when coffee had been served, with liqueurs and cigars, and all the waiters had withdrawn, Uncle Bachelard, throwing himself back in his chair, heaved a sigh of contentment.

'Ah, I feel good!' he declared.

Trublot and Gueulin, stretching themselves, leaned back in their chairs as well.

'Full up!' said the first.

'Up to the eyes!' added the other.

Duveyrier, puffing, gave a nod of assent and murmured: 'Oh, those crayfish!'

All four of them looked at each other and chuckled. With bellies stretched to bursting point, they slowly, selfishly proceeded to digest, like four middle-class men who had just stuffed themselves, free from all thoughts of their families. It had cost a lot of money; nobody else had dined with them; there were no females to take advantage of their warm-heartedness; so they let themselves go and propped their stomachs against the table. Their eyes half closed, at first they refrained from talking, each absorbed in his own solitary bliss. Then, perfectly at ease, and glad that no women were there, they placed their elbows on the table, moved their red faces close together and talked endlessly about women, and nothing but women.

'I've seen the light!' declared Uncle Bachelard. 'There's nothing to beat virtue.'

Duveyrier nodded in agreement. 'And I've bid goodbye to that sort of fun. I admit I've had my share of it in the past. Why, in the Rue Godot-de-Mauroy,* I know every blessed one of them – fair girls, dark ones and red-haired ones. Sometimes, though not often, there's the odd good-looking one. Then there are those dirty hotels in Montmartre – furnished lodgings, you know; and even filthy little streets in my own neighbourhood, where you can pick up the most amazing creatures ugly as sin but mighty inventive . . .'

'Oh! tarts!' broke in Trublot, in his contemptuous manner. 'What a waste of time! You won't catch me at that sort of game; you never get your money's worth out of them.'

Duveyrier was thrilled by such risqué conversation. He drank his *Kummel* in sips, his stiff magistrate's features distorted now and again by little sensual quiverings.

'I cannot stand vice,' he said; 'it disgusts me. In order to love a woman, you must respect her, mustn't you? It would be quite impossible for me to have anything to do with one of those unfortunate women, unless, of course, she appeared ashamed of her way of life and had been rescued from it with a view to her becoming a decent woman. Love couldn't have a more noble mission than that. In short, a respectable mistress – you understand? In that case I can't say that I'd be able to resist.'

'But I've had no end of respectable mistresses,' cried Bachelard. 'They're a damned sight worse than the others, and such sluts too! Bitches that play around behind your back, and then give you the pox to boot! My last one, for instance – a most respectable-looking little lady that I met outside a church. I rented a milliner's shop for her at Ternes,* just to set her up, you know. She never had a single customer, mind you. Well, sir, would you believe it? She used to have the whole street in to sleep with her!'

Gueulin chuckled, his red hair growing more bristly than usual, while the hot air brought beads of perspiration to his brow. Sucking his cigar, he mumbled: 'And the other one, that tall girl at Passy who had a sweetshop? And the other one in a room near here, with her outfits for orphans? And the captain's widow, do you remember, who used to show the mark of a sword cut on her belly? Every one of them made a fool of you, uncle! I can tell you that now, can't I? Well, one evening I had to be on my guard against the lady with the sword-mark on her belly. She was keen, but I wasn't such a fool! You never know how far women like that may lead you.'

Bachelard seemed vexed. Recovering himself, however, he screwed up his large eyelids and winked hideously.

'My boy, you may have them all if you like. I've got something better than that.'

And he refused to explain himself, delighted to have provoked the others' curiosity. Yet he was dying to tell them, to have them discover his secret.

'A young girl,' he said, at last; 'but the real thing, on my honour!'

'Impossible!' cried Trublot. 'They no longer make such a thing.'

'Respectable family?' asked Duveyrier.

'A most respectable family,' Bachelard confirmed. 'Imagine something stupidly chaste. A chance find – I just had her like that. I firmly believe she thinks nothing has happened!'

Gueulin listened in astonishment. Then with a sceptical gesture, he muttered: 'Ah, yes! I know.'

'Eh? What do you mean, you know?' said Bachelard, angrily. 'You know nothing at all, my boy; no one knows about her. She's Bibi's property; she's not to be looked at, not to be touched – a case of "hands off"!'

Then, turning to Duveyrier, he said: 'You, sir, being kind-hearted, can quite understand my feelings. It has a softening influence, somehow, to go and see her; it almost makes one feel young again. Anyhow, I've got a nice quiet little nook there where I can rest after all that business with those trollops. Ah, and if you knew how sweet and refreshing she is, such a soft white skin, with firm shoulders and strong thighs on her – not a bit scraggy, but round and firm as a peach!'

The counsellor's red blotches glowed again as, in a wave, the blood rushed to his face. Trublot and Gueulin looked at Bachelard, feeling half inclined to hit him as he sat leering there, with his row of glittering false teeth, and saliva dribbling down from either side of his mouth. What! This old wreck of an uncle crawling out of all those Parisian nights, debauched, whose

flaming nose alone remained firm among the drooping flab of
his cheeks, had got hidden away somewhere some flower of
innocence, some soft budding body, whose virginal flesh he
tainted with his stale lust, masking his lechery with a false air of
drunken benevolence!

Meanwhile, growing tender, he continued to elaborate, as he
licked the edge of his liqueur glass: 'After all, my one dream is
to make the dear child happy! But, you know, she's starting to
fill out nicely; I'm like a father to her. If I could only find some
sensible young chap, I'd give her to him, only if he'd marry her,
of course.'

'That way you'd make two people happy,' murmured Duveyrier, sentimentally.

The atmosphere in the little room was almost suffocating. A
glass of chartreuse had been knocked over, making the tablecloth, already blackened by cigar ash, sticky. What these men
needed was some fresh air.

'Would you like to see her?' the uncle asked suddenly as he
got up from the table.

They looked at one another, enquiringly. Certainly they
would love to do him the honour of meeting her, if he so
wished; and behind their feigned indifference they craved the
satisfaction of finishing their dessert in the home of old Bachelard's young girl. Duveyrier merely observed that Clarisse was
expecting them. Then Bachelard, pale and agitated since making
the suggestion, declared that they wouldn't even stop to sit
down. They would merely have a look at her and then leave at
once. They went down and stood outside for a few moments on
the boulevard, while their host paid the bill.

When he reappeared, Gueulin pretended not to know where
the girl in question lived.

'So, let's go then, uncle! Which way is it?'

Bachelard became serious, tortured by the vanity that
prompted him to show off Fifi, and the dread that she might be
stolen from him. For a moment he looked to the left, then to
the right, anxiously. At last he blurted out: 'No! I don't want to
take you there, after all.'

And he obstinately refused, not bothered by Trublot's teasing,
not even deigning to invent a pretext for this sudden change of
mind. They had to go to Clarisse's, and as it was a lovely
evening they decided to be healthy and walk there to help them

digest. So they set off along the Rue de Richelieu, fairly steady on their feet, but so full up that the pavement hardly seemed wide enough. Gueulin and Trublot went in front, followed by Bachelard and Duveyrier, deeply engaged in confiding to one another like brothers. The former was earnestly assuring the latter that it was not that he distrusted him; he would have shown her to him, for he knew he was discreet; but it was always unwise to expect too much from young people, was it not? And the other agreed with him, admitting that he, too, had had his fears concerning Clarisse. At first he had kept all his friends away, and then it had pleased him to invite them there and turn the place into a charming little retreat for himself once she had given him proof beyond doubt of her fidelity. Oh, she was a woman with brains, incapable of forgetting herself; kindhearted and with sound ideas! Of course, there were certain things in her past with which she could be reproached, though mainly due to lack of guidance. Since she had loved him, however, she was back on the straight and narrow. The counsellor talked in this vein all along the Rue de Rivoli, while the uncle, irritated at not being able to put in another word about his own little angel, had to restrain himself from telling Duveyrier that, in fact, his paragon Clarisse slept with all and sundry.

'Yes, yes, I'm sure,' he murmured. 'But, believe me, there is nothing like virtue.'

The house in the Rue de la Cerisaie seemed fast asleep amid the silence of the deserted street. Duveyrier was surprised not to see any lights in the third-floor windows. Trublot suggested, without the slightest hint of irony, that no doubt Clarisse had gone to bed to wait for them. Or, perhaps, added Gueulin, she was playing a game of bézique in the kitchen with her maid. They knocked. The gas on the stairs burned with the straight, motionless flame of a lamp in some chapel. Not a sound, not a whisper. But as the four men passed the concierge, he rushed out of his office saying: 'Sir, sir, the key!'

Duveyrier stopped short on the first step. 'Is madame not at home, then?' he asked.

'No, sir. And wait a moment; you'll need a light.'

As he handed him the candlestick, the concierge, despite the look of exaggerated respect on his pallid face, could not repress a roguish grin. Neither the uncle nor the two young men said a word. So, in silence, with backs bent, they filed up the stairs, the ceaseless beat of their footsteps echoing along the gloomy passages. Duveyrier, trying to make sense of it all, led the way, moving his legs mechanically, almost as if he were sleepwalking, while the candle that he held in his trembling hand projected the four shadows of this weird procession on the wall, like a march of broken puppets.

On the third floor he suddenly grew faint and couldn't find the keyhole. Trublot was obliging enough to open the door for him. The key, as it turned in the lock, made a hollow, reverberating sound, as if beneath the vaulted roof of some cathedral.

'My goodness!' he muttered. 'The place doesn't look as if anybody lives in it!'

'Sounds pretty empty,' said Bachelard.

'Just like a proper family vault,' added Gueulin.

They went in with Duveyrier leading the way, holding the candle up high. The hall was empty; even the hat-pegs had vanished. The drawing-room was empty, as was the parlour; not a single piece of furniture, not a curtain at one of the windows, not even a brass rod. Petrified, Duveyrier glanced down at his feet and then looked up at the ceiling, and then went round examining the walls as if to discover the hole through which everything had disappeared.

'What a clean-out,' said Trublot, involuntarily.

'Perhaps they're having the place done up,' remarked Gueulin gravely. 'Let's look in the bedroom; they may have moved the furniture in there.'

But this room was equally bare, deserted, as hideous in its nudity as plaster walls from which the paper has been stripped. Where the bed had stood, the removal of the iron supports of the canopy had left gaping holes; one of the windows was half open, and the air from the street gave the room the damp, stale smell of a public square.

'Oh! My God!' stammered Duveyrier, as at last he wept, overcome by the sight of the place where the mattresses had rubbed against the wall, taking off some of the paper.

Uncle Bachelard became fatherly, as he repeated: 'Courage, sir! The same thing happened to me, and I survived. Damn it all, your honour is safe!'

Duveyrier shook his head and passed on to the dressing-room, and then into the kitchen. More disastrous revelations!

The oilcloth in the dressing-room had been removed, as well as all the hooks in the kitchen.

'No, really, that's going too far!' said Gueulin. 'Fancy that! She might have left the hooks behind!'

Tired out by the dinner and the walk, Trublot began to find this empty apartment far from amusing. But Duveyrier never put his candle down, and went on roaming about as if he felt the need to surround himself with the extent of his abandonment. The others were forced to follow him. Once more he went through every room, wishing to re-inspect the drawing-room, parlour, and bedroom, looking carefully into each corner, light in hand, while behind him the others, in single file continued the procession of the staircase, with their huge dancing shadows fantastically decorating the barren walls. In this melancholy atmosphere the noise of their footsteps on the boards resounded mournfully and, to put the finishing touch to the general dreariness, the whole place was thoroughly clean, not a scrap of paper or piece of straw to be seen, clean as a well scrubbed bowl, for the concierge had been cruel enough to take a broom to it.

'Do you know, I can't stand any more of this,' cried Trublot, at last, as they were inspecting the drawing-room for the third time.

'I'd give ten sous for a chair. I really would!'

All four of them stood still.

'When did you see her last?' asked Bachelard.

'Yesterday, sir,' exclaimed. Duveyrier.

Gueulin shook his head. My word! she hadn't wasted any time and it was a tidy job. Trublot suddenly called out. He had just spied on the mantelshelf a dirty collar and a damaged cigar.

'You mustn't complain,' he said, laughing; 'she's left you a keepsake, at least.'

Duveyrier, momentarily touched, looked at the collar. Then he murmured: 'Twenty-five thousand francs' worth of furniture. There was twenty-five thousand francs' worth. But it's not even that I regret!'

'Won't you have the cigar?' asked Trublot, interrupting. 'Very well, then allow me. It's broken, but I can stick some cigarette paper round it.'

He used the candle which Duveyrier still held to light it, then, sliding in to a sitting posture against the wall, he said: 'This is better than nothing! I must sit on the floor for a bit; I'm ready to drop!'

'Well,' asked Duveyrier, 'can any of you tell me where she can possibly have gone?'

Bachelard and Gueulin looked at each other. It was a delicate matter. However, the uncle took the brave decision to tell the poor chap everything: Clarisse's pranks and promiscuity, and the lovers she used to pick up behind his back at every one of her parties. No doubt she had gone off with her latest, that big fellow, Payan, the mason, in whose artistic future his native city in the South had invested.

Duveyrier listened to these abominable revelations in horror. At last, he exclaimed in despair: 'There is no such thing as honesty in this world!'

Then, growing suddenly communicative, he told them everything that he'd done for her. He spoke of his kindheartedness, accused her of having shaken his belief in all that was best in human life, thus conveniently keeping under such sentimental wraps his own base appetites. Clarisse had become a necessity to him. But he would find her out, if only to make her blush for her conduct, so he said, and to see if her heart was devoid of every ounce of honour.

'Don't do anything of the sort!' cried Bachelard, secretly delighted at the counsellor's misfortune. 'She will only take you for a ride again. There's nothing like virtue, you know. Get hold of some young girl without any deviousness about her, and as innocent as a new-born child; then there's no danger and one can sleep in peace.'

Trublot, meanwhile, went on smoking, with his back to the wall and his legs stretched out, relaxed and lost in thought. The others had forgotten him.

'I can find out the address for you, if you really want it,' he said. 'I know the maidservant.'

Duveyrier turned round, astonished at hearing this voice that appeared to come out of the floor, and when he saw Trublot smoking what remained of Clarisse, exhaling great clouds of smoke, in which he seemed to see his twenty-five thousand francs' worth of furniture evaporating, with an angry gesture, he exclaimed: 'No; she's unworthy of me! She must beg me to forgive her on her knees!'

'Hey! I think she's coming back!' said Gueulin, straining his ears to listen.

Someone was indeed walking in the hall; and a voice cried: 'Hello there, what's up? Is everybody dead?' And then Octave appeared. These empty rooms and open doors astonished him. But his amazement increased as, in the centre of the bare drawing-room, he saw the four men – one on the floor, and three standing – in the dim light of a single candle, which the counsellor carried like a church taper. It didn't take long to bring him up to date.

'Unbelievable!' he exclaimed.

'Didn't they tell you anything downstairs?' asked Gueulin.

'No, nothing at all. The concierge calmly watched me go upstairs. So she's bolted has she? I am not surprised. She had such funny eyes and hair!'

He asked for details, and talked for a little while, forgetting the sad news he brought. Then suddenly he turned towards Duveyrier.

'By the way, it was your wife who sent me to fetch you. Your father-in-law is dying.'

'Oh, I see,' said Duveyrier, simply.

'What, old Vabre?' muttered Bachelard. 'That's no surprise.'

'Well, he's had a good innings!' remarked Gueulin philosophically.

'Yes, it's time to let go,' added Trublot, in the act of sticking another cigarette paper round his cigar.

At last these gentlemen decided to leave the deserted apartment. Octave kept saying that he had given his word of honour that he would bring Duveyrier back with him at once, no matter what state he was in. The latter carefully closed the door, as if he were leaving his extinguished feelings there. But downstairs, shame suddenly overcame him, and Trublot had to return the key to the concierge. Then, in the street, there was a silent interchange of vigorous handshakes, and, as soon as Duveyrier and Octave had driven off in a cab, Bachelard said to Gueulin and Trublot, as they stood there in the deserted street: 'God damn it! I must let you see her!'

For a minute or so he kept walking up and down, greatly excited at the despair shown by that big idiot Duveyrier, and bursting at his own particular happiness, due, as he thought, to his own profound deviousness, a joy that he could no longer contain.

'Well, you know, uncle,' said Gueulin, 'if you're only going to take us as far as the door again and then change your mind, then . . .'

'No, God damn it! You shall see her! I should like you to. It's nearly midnight, but never mind; she'll get up if she's gone to bed. You know, she's the daughter of a captain – Captain Menu, and let me tell you, she's got a most respectable aunt, born at Villeneuve, near Lille! You can get that confirmed at the Mardienne Brothers', in the Rue Saint-Sulpice. Ah, God damn it! It will do us good! You shall see exactly what virtue is!'

He took them by the arms, Gueulin on the right and Trublot on the left, as he hurried along in search of a cab to get them there more quickly.

Meanwhile, as they drove along, Octave briefly described Monsieur Vabre's seizure to his companion, without concealing the fact that Madame Duveyrier knew the address in the Rue de la Cerisaie.

After a pause, the counsellor asked in a doleful voice: 'Do you think she'll forgive me?'

Octave remained silent. The cab went rumbling along. Only every now and then a ray of light from some gas lamp interrupted the gloom. Just as they arrived, Duveyrier, full of anguish, asked another question.

'The best thing I can do at present is to make it up with my wife, don't you think so?'

'Perhaps that would be the wisest plan,' said Octave, obliged to make some sort of reply.

Then Duveyrier felt that he ought to show some concern for his father-in-law. A man of great intelligence, he said, with a quite incredible capacity for work. They would probably succeed in pulling him round. In the Rue de Choiseul they found the door of the house open and quite a group of people in front of Monsieur Gourd's lodge. Julie, on her way to the chemist's, was ranting about the middle classes who let one another die when they were ill; it was only working folk, she said, who took each other soup or warm towels. The old fellow might have swallowed his tongue twenty times in the two hours since his attack before one of his children took the trouble to shove a bit of sugar into his mouth. A hard-hearted lot, said Monsieur

Gourd – irresponsible. They would be ashamed at the thought of having to give their father an enema. Hippolyte, to cap it all, told them about madame upstairs, how silly she looked with her arms waving about in front of the poor old gentleman, while the servants were running about doing all they could. But they all held their tongues as soon as they saw Duveyrier.

'Well?' he enquired.

'The doctor is just putting on mustard poultices,' said Hippolyte. 'Oh, I had such a job finding him!'

Upstairs, in the drawing-room, Madame Duveyrier came forward to meet them. She had been crying a good deal; her eyes shone beneath their reddened lids. The counsellor, greatly embarrassed, held out his arms and embraced her, murmuring: 'My poor Clotilde!'

Surprised at this unusual display of affection, she drew away.

Octave had dropped back, but heard the husband say in a low voice: 'Forgive me! Let's forget our quarrels on this sad occasion. You see, I've come back to you, for good. Oh, I've been well punished!'

She made no reply, but disengaged herself. Then for Octave's benefit she restored the fiction of what she was supposed to know: 'I shouldn't have disturbed you, my dear, for I know how urgent that report about the Rue de Provence affair is. But I was all alone, and I felt I needed you here. My poor father is dying. Go in and see him; the doctor's there.'

When Duveyrier had gone into the adjoining room, she approached Octave, who, in order to give an impression of composure, was standing by the piano. The instrument was still open, and the piece from *Zémire et Azor* lay there as they had left it on the music-stand. He pretended to be studying it. The soft light from the lamp still only partially illuminated the large room.

Madame Duveyrier looked at the young man for a moment without speaking, tormented by an anxiety which led her to throw off her habitual reserve.

'Was he there?' she asked curtly.

'Yes, madame.'

'Then, what's happened? What's the matter with him?'

'That person has left him, madame, taking all the furniture with her. I found him in the bare rooms with only a candle!'

Clotilde made a gesture of despair. She understood. Her

handsome face displayed a mixture of discouragement and disgust. Not only had she lost her father, but now his death might even serve as a pretext to bring about a reconciliation between herself and her husband! She knew him well enough; he would always be around, now that there was nothing outside to protect her from him; and, mindful of conjugal duties, she trembled at the thought that she would have to submit to the most abominable of them all. For a moment she looked at the piano. Huge tears filled her eyes as she said, simply: 'Thank you, sir.'

Then, one after the other, they both went into Monsieur Vabre's bedroom. Duveyrier, looking very pale, was listening to Doctor Juillerat, who was explaining something in a low voice. It was a very bad attack of apoplexy. The patient might possibly live until the next day, but there was no hope at all. Clotilde entered just at that moment, overheard this last statement and sank down into a chair, wiping her eyes with her tear-soaked handkerchief which she had nervously twisted into a ball. However, she had enough strength to ask the doctor if her poor father would at least regain consciousness. The doctor had his doubts, and, as if he had guessed what lay behind the question, he expressed a hope that Monsieur Vabre had long since put his affairs in order. Duveyrier, who seemed to have left his mind in the Rue de la Cerisaie, now appeared to wake up. He looked at his wife and then remarked that Monsieur Vabre hadn't confided in anyone, so he didn't know. Certain promises had been made in favour of their son Gustave. His grandfather often spoke of helping him as a reward for their having taken him to live with them. At any rate, if there was a will, it would be found.

'Has the family been told?' asked Doctor Juillerat.

'Goodness me, no!' murmured Clotilde. 'It was so dreadfully sudden. My first thought was to send Monsieur Mouret for my husband.'

Duveyrier gave her another look – now they understood each other. Slowly approaching the bed, he examined Monsieur Vabre stretched out and stiff as a corpse, his rigid features streaked with yellow spots. One o'clock struck. The doctor spoke of leaving as he had tried all the usual remedies and could do nothing more. He would call again early in the morning. As he was leaving with Octave, Madame Duveyrier called the latter back.

'Let's wait till the morning,' she said. 'You can make some excuse to send Berthe to me, and I'll call Valérie, and they'll break the news to my two brothers. Poor things! Let them at least sleep well tonight. There are enough of us for the wake; we'll stay up and weep together.'

And there she and her husband remained, watching the old man, whose death-rattle echoed through the room.

CHAPTER II

When Octave came downstairs next day at eight o'clock, he was very surprised to find that the whole household knew about Monsieur Vabre's seizure of the previous night, and of their landlord's desperate condition. The household, however, was not so much concerned about the patient, as what he might be leaving behind.

In their little dining-room the Pichons sat down to cups of hot chocolate. Jules called Octave in.

'Well! What a fine mess there'll be if he dies like that! We'll see some funny goings-on. Do you know if he's made a will?'

The young man, without answering, asked them how they had heard about it. Marie had found out at the baker's; in fact, the news had reached every floor and even to the end of the street, via the servants.

Then, after smacking Lilitte for putting her fingers into the chocolate, Marie added: 'And all that money, too! If only he'd thought of leaving us a sou for each one of his five-franc pieces! Not much fear of that, though.'

And, as Octave was going, she added: 'I've finished your books, Monsieur Mouret. Do come and collect them, won't you?'

Concerned, he hurried downstairs, remembering that he had promised Madame Duveyrier that he would send Berthe to her before there was any gossip, when on the third floor he met Campardon about to go out.

'So,' said the latter, 'your employer is going to inherit a fortune. As far as I can make out, the old boy has got something like six hundred thousand francs, besides this place. Well, he spent nothing at the Duveyriers', and he had a good bit left over from the Versailles property, without counting the twenty-odd thousand francs from the rent on this place. Not a bad sum considering there are only three to share it.'

Still chatting, he followed Octave downstairs. On the second floor they met Madame Juzeur, who had come down to see what her young servant, Louise, had been up to all morning, wasting over an hour in fetching four sous' worth of milk. She naturally joined in the conversation, already up to date.

'No one knows if he's sorted out his affairs,' she said, quietly. 'Perhaps there'll be some problems.'

'Well, well,' said the architect, gaily, 'I wouldn't mind being in their shoes. It wouldn't take long. Divide the whole lot into three equal parts, each takes his share, and be done with it.'

Madame Juzeur leaned over the banisters, and then looked up to be sure that no one was on the stairs. Then, lowering her voice, she said: 'And what if they didn't find what they expected?'

Campardon opened his eyes wide. Then he shrugged his shoulders. No! that was just rubbish. Vabre was an old miser, sitting on a nest egg. Having said so, he left as he had an appointment at Saint-Roch with the Abbé Mauduit.

'My wife has been moaning about you,' he said to Octave, turning round after going down three steps. 'Do go and have a chat with her, some time.'

Madame Juzeur detained the young man for a moment. 'And me! You've neglected me too! I thought you at least liked me a little bit. When you come, I'll let you taste a liqueur from the West Indies – it's quite delicious!'

He promised to call in, and then hurried down into the hall. Before reaching the little side door under the arch, he had to pass a whole group of servants. They too were engaged in distributing the dying man's possessions. There was so much for Madame Clotilde, so much for Monsieur Auguste, and so much for Monsieur Théophile. Clémence stated the figures as fact, claiming she knew exactly what they were, as Hippolyte had seen the money in a drawer. Julie, however, disputed them. Lisa was telling them how her first master, an old gentleman, had done her out of her wages by dying without even leaving her his dirty linen. Adèle listened to these inheritance stories open-mouthed and with arms dangling until she could almost see gigantic piles of five-franc pieces falling into her lap. And in the street, Monsieur Gourd, pompous as ever, was talking to the stationer over the road. For him the landlord was already dead.

'What I'm intrigued about,' he said, 'is who will get the house. They'll divide everything – no problem! But what about the house? They can't cut that up into three.'

Finally Octave entered the shop. The first person he saw

sitting at the cashier's desk was Madame Josserand, hair combed, sparklingly clean and neatly dressed, ready for the onslaught of the day. Berthe, next to her, who had no doubt come down in a hurry, was dressed in a loose-fitting gown. She looked charming and seemed excited. But, on seeing him, they stopped talking. The mother gave him a deadly look.

'So Monsieur Mouret,' she said, 'this is how you show your loyalty to the firm! You conspire with my daughter's enemies!'

He tried to defend himself, to explain what had happened. But she would not allow him to speak, accusing him of having spent the night with the Duveyriers looking for the will in order to change certain clauses.

And, when he laughingly enquired what possible interest he could have in doing such a thing, she replied: 'Your own interest, your own interest! In short, sir, it was your duty to come and tell us, since God willed it that you should be a witness of the sad event. Only to think that, if it hadn't been for me, my daughter would still have been ignorant of the matter! Yes, they would have robbed her if I hadn't rushed downstairs as soon as I heard the news. Eh? Yes, your interest, as far as I know! Madame Duveyrier may not look as good as she once did, but I'm sure there are some less fussy people who would still find her passable.'

'Oh, Mother!' cried Berthe. 'Clotilde's beyond reproach.'

Madame Josserand shrugged her shoulders, pityingly.

'Don't listen to me then, but you know perfectly well that people will do anything for money!'

Octave was obliged to tell them all the details of the attack. They exchanged glances. Obviously, to use the mother's phrase, there had been some scheming going on. It was really too kind of Clotilde to wish to spare her family any unnecessary emotion! However, they allowed the young man to start work, although they still had their doubts as to his part in the affair. And they continued their heated discussion.

'And so who's going to pay the fifty thousand francs agreed on in the contract?' asked Madame Josserand. 'Once he's underground, we can say goodbye to that.'

'Oh, the fifty thousand francs!' murmured Berthe, embarrassed. 'You know that, like yourself, he only agreed to pay ten thousand francs every six months. We don't even know for sure yet. It's best just to wait and see.'

'Wait? Oh, yes! Wait till he comes to life again and brings you the money, I suppose? You fool, you want to be robbed, do you? No, no! You must claim the money at once from the estate. As for us, we're alive, thank God. It may not be certain if we'll pay or not; but, as far as he's concerned, he's dead, so he will have to pay.'

She made her daughter swear not to give in, for she herself wasn't going to be made a fool of by anybody. Carried away, she occasionally cocked an ear as if to hear what was going on overhead at the Duveyriers'. The old fellow's bedroom was just above her. On hearing what had happened, Auguste had gone upstairs immediately. But even that did not pacify her; she longed to be there herself, and imagined all sorts of intricate schemes.

'You go up, too!' she cried at last, in a sudden outburst. 'Auguste is too weak; I'm sure they'll walk all over him.'

So Berthe went upstairs. Octave, who was dressing the shop window, listened to what they were saying. When he saw that he was alone with Madame Josserand, and that she was going to the door, he asked her whether it would be more appropriate to close the shop, hoping to get a day's holiday.

'Why, what for?' she asked. 'Wait till he's dead. It's not worth losing a day's business.'

Then, as he was folding up a piece of crimson silk, she added, in order to qualify her hard-hearted remark: 'But it might be wise not to put anything red in the window.'

On the first floor, Berthe found Auguste with his father. The room had not altered since the evening before; it was still damp, silent, filled with the same noise of long, difficult breathing. The old man lay on the bed completely rigid, having lost all feeling and all movement. The oak box, full of index cards, still lay on the table; none of the furniture seemed to have been moved, nor a drawer to have been opened. The Duveyriers looked more exhausted, however, worn out by a sleepless night; their eyelids twitched convulsively, as if something weighed on their minds. At seven o'clock they had sent Hippolyte to fetch their son Gustave from the Lycée Bonaparte, and the lad, a thin, precocious boy of sixteen, was there, bewildered by this unexpected holiday, which was to be spent at the bedside of a dying man.

'Oh, my dear, what a terrible shock!' said Clotilde, as she went over to embrace Berthe.

'Why didn't you tell us?' replied the latter, with her mother's sour pout. 'We were ready to help you through it all.'

With a look, Auguste begged her to be silent. It wasn't the time to start squabbling. They could afford to wait. Doctor Juillerat, who had already been once, was expected again, but he was still certain that the patient would not live through the day. Auguste was telling all this to his wife, when Théophile and Valérie arrived.

Clotilde came forward at once, saying again, as she embaced Valérie: 'What a terrible shock, my dear!'

But Théophile seemed extremely irritated.

'So now, it seems,' he said, without even lowering his voice, 'when one's father dies, it's the coal-man who lets you know! I suppose you wanted the time to go through his pockets!'

Duveyrier stood up indignantly, but Clotilde motioned him aside. Meanwhile, speaking very quietly, she replied to her brother.

'Miserable man! Isn't even our father's suffering sacred to you? Look at him; see your handiwork? You're the one who brought on the attack by refusing to pay the rent you owed him.'

Valérie began to laugh.

'Come on, you're not serious!' she said.

'What? Not serious?' replied Clotilde, in a tone of disgust. 'You knew how fond he was of collecting his rents. If you had planned to kill him, you couldn't have chosen a better way.'

The argument became increasingly heated, each accusing the other of scheming to get hold of the inheritance, when Auguste, as sullen and impassive as ever, called them to order.

'Stop it! There's plenty of time for that. You shouldn't be discussing it now!'

The other members of the family, realising he was right, gathered around the bed. There was total silence in the damp room, only broken by the death-rattle. Berthe and Auguste stood at the foot of the bed; Valérie and Théophile, having come in last, had been obliged to remain some way off, near the table; Clotilde sat at the head of the bed, her husband standing beside her, while close up to the edge of the mattresses she had pushed her son Gustave, whom the old man adored. They all looked at one another, without uttering a word. But their shining eyes and compressed lips spoke volumes, expressing all the anxiety and aggravation which filled the heads of these next of kin, as they waited there, pale-faced and heavy-eyed. The two young couples were particularly irritated at the sight of the schoolboy close to the bed, for obviously the Duveyriers were counting on Gustave's presence to influence his grandfather in their favour if he regained consciousness.

What's more, this tactic was proof that no will existed; and the Vabres furtively glanced at the old iron safe, which their father had brought from Versailles and had had fixed in a corner of his room. He had a mania for keeping all kinds of things in it. Doubtless the Duveyriers had ransacked the safe during the night. Théophile was keen to find a way to trap them into an admission.

'I say,' he finally whispered to the counsellor, 'suppose we sent for the notary? Papa may wish to make some alterations to his will.'

At first Duveyrier did not hear. He found being in the bedroom extremely tedious, and all night had let his thoughts wander back to Clarisse. Clearly the most sensible thing would be to get back with his wife. And yet the other woman was so enticing when, almost like a child, she pulled her blouse up and over her head; and, as he gazed dreamily at the dying man, he had a vision of her doing just that; and he would have given anything to have her again, just one more time. Théophile had to repeat his question.

'I asked Maître Renaudin,' replied the counsellor, startled. 'There is no will.'

'But what about here?'

'Neither here nor at the notary's.'

Théophile looked at Auguste. That was plain enough, wasn't it? The Duveyriers must have searched the drawers. Clotilde saw the look, and felt annoyed with her husband. What was the matter with him? Had grief robbed him of his senses? And she added: 'Papa will be sure to have done the right thing. Good God, we'll know soon enough!'

She began to cry. At the sight of her grief, Valérie and Berthe also started sobbing gently. Théophile went back on tiptoe to his chair. He had found out what he wanted to know. If his father regained consciousness, he would certainly not allow the Duveyriers to use their brat of a son as a means of turning matters to their own advantage. But, as he sat down, he saw his brother Auguste wiping his eyes, and that moved him so much that he too started to choke back tears. The idea of death stared him in the face; perhaps he would die of a similar seizure; it was awful. Then the whole family dissolved in tears. Gustave was the only one who couldn't cry. He was alarmed by it all, and looked down at the floor, breathing in time with the dying man's death-rattle, in order to have something to do, just as at their gymnastic lessons he and his fellow-pupils were made to keep in step.

Meanwhile, the hours passed. At eleven o'clock the return of Doctor Juillerat provided some distraction. The patient was much worse. It was now doubtful whether he would be able to recognise his children before he died. And the sobbing started again, when Clémence ushered in the Abbé Mauduit. Clotilde, rising to meet him, was the first to receive his condolences. He seemed deeply affected by this family misfortune, and found a word of encouragement for each of them. Then, tactfully, he spoke of the last rites, hinting that this soul should not be allowed to pass away without some comfort from the Church.

'I had thought about it,' murmured Clotilde.

But Théophile raised objections. Their father was not religious; at one time he had held quite radical opinions, for he read Voltaire. The best plan would be to avoid doing anything, as they could not consult him. In the heat of the argument, he even remarked: 'You might as well administer the last rites to that piece of furniture.'

The three women silenced him. They were all overcome by emotion, declaring that the priest was right, and apologised for not having sent for him, having been completely thrown by the distressing situation. Had Monsieur Vabre been able to speak, he would certainly have consented, they said, for he did not like to make himself conspicuous in any way. They were themselves prepared to take on the responsibility.

'If only for our neighbours' sake,' said Clotilde, 'it ought to be done.'

'Of course,' said the Abbé Mauduit, who strongly approved, 'a man in your father's position ought to set a good example.'

Auguste remained indifferent. But Duveyrier, roused from his memories of Clarisse, remembering how she used to put stockings on with one thigh raised in the air, insisted that the last rites should be administered. They were a necessity, and no member of his family should die without them.

Doctor Juillerat, who had discreetly stood aside, not even showing his freethinker's disdain, then went up to the abbé and whispered, as to a colleague often met on occasions of this kind: 'You'd better hurry; there's no time to lose.'

The priest rushed off, saying that he would bring the sacrament and everything necessary for the last rites, so as to be prepared for whatever might happen.

Then Théophile, obstinate as ever, muttered: 'Oh, so now it seems they force the dying to take communion against their will!'

Suddenly there was a great commotion. On going back to her place by the bed, Clotilde found the dying man with his eyes wide open. She could not contain a slight shriek. They all rushed to the bedside, and the old man's gaze slowly wandered from one to another, without moving his head. Doctor Juillerat, visibly surprised, leaned over his patient to watch his final crisis.

'Father, it's us. Do you recognise us?' asked Clotilde.

Monsieur Vabre stared at her; then his lips moved, but uttered no sound.

They pushed each other aside in their eagerness to catch his last word. Valérie, at the back, was obliged to stand on tiptoe, saying bitterly: 'You're suffocating him. Stand back! If he wanted anything, no one could tell what it was.'

So the others had to stand back. Monsieur Vabre's eyes were, indeed, wandering round the room.

'He wants something, that is certain,' murmured Berthe.

'Here's Gustave,' said Clotilde. 'You can see him, can't you? He's come back from school to kiss you. Kiss your grandfather, Gustave.'

As the boy drew back in fear, she pushed him forward with her arm, waiting for a smile to light up the dying man's distorted face. But Auguste, following the direction of his eyes, declared that he was looking at the table. No doubt he wanted to write. This caused great excitement, and everyone rushed to move the table close to the bed, and fetch some paper, an ink-stand and a pen. Finally they lifted him, propping him up with three pillows. The doctor authorised all this with a movement of his eyelids.

'Give him the pen,' said Clotilde, trembling, still holding Gustave towards him.

A solemn moment followed. Crowding round the bed, the whole family waited anxiously while Monsieur Vabre, who did not seem to recognise anyone, let the pen slip from his fingers. He gazed at his box of file-cards on the table. Then he fell forward, off his pillows, like a bundle of rags and, stretching out his arm in a supreme effort, he began fumbling around in the oak box like a happy baby playing in the mud. He beamed, and tried to speak, but could only stammer out one syllable over and over again, one of those monosyllabic cries into which infants can put a whole host of meanings.

'Ga . . . ga . . . ga . . . ga . . .'

It was to his lifetime's work, to his immense statistical study, that he was saying good-bye. Suddenly his head rolled forward. He was dead.

'I feared as much,' muttered the doctor, who, seeing the family's bewilderment, carefully straightened the dead man's limbs and closed his eyes.

Was it possible? Auguste took away the table, and everyone remained chilled and mute. Then they burst into tears. Well, since there was nothing more to be done, they would still try to do what they could to share the fortune. And Clotilde, having hastily sent Gustave away, to spare him from such a harrowing spectacle, wept unrestrainedly, leaning her head on Berthe, who was also sobbing, as was Valérie. Théophile and Auguste, at the window, kept rubbing their eyes. But Duveyrier seemed to be the most inconsolable of all, as he stifled loud sobs with his handkerchief. No, he really couldn't live without Clarisse; he would rather die at once, like Vabre, lying there. The loss of his mistress struck him in the midst of all this mourning and added immense bitterness to his grief.

'Madame,' said Clemence, entering, 'the holy sacraments.'

Abbé Mauduit appeared on the threshold. Behind his back a choirboy's inquisitve face could be seen. Seeing them all in tears, the abbé glanced questioningly at the doctor, who shrugged as if to say that it wasn't his fault. Then, having mumbled a few prayers, the priest withdrew in embarrassment, taking the sacraments with him.

'That's a bad sign,' said Clémence to the other servants, who were grouped round the open door. 'The good Lord shouldn't be disturbed for nothing. I bet he'll be back in this house before the year's over!'

Monsieur Vabre's funeral did not take place for two days. Duveyrier had still somehow managed to get the words 'Blessed with the Holy Sacraments of the Church' printed on the circulars announcing the death. As the shop was closed, Octave was free, delighted by this extra holiday, as he had been wanting to rearrange his room, move the furniture, and put his books together in a little bookcase that he had picked up second-hand. He had got up earlier than usual, and had just finished reorganising everything, at about eight o'clock on the morning of the funeral, when Marie knocked at the door. She had brought him a bundle of books.

'As you never come and collect them,' she said, 'it's up to me to make the effort to return them myself.'

But, blushing, she refused to come in, shocked at the idea of entering a young man's room. Their affair had come to an end quite naturally; he had simply not returned for more. And yet she was as affectionate as ever, always greeting him with a smile when they met.

Octave was in high spirits that morning and began teasing her.

'So it's Jules, is it, who won't let you come to my room?' he kept saying. 'How are you getting on with Jules now? Is he being nice to you? You know what I mean. So, go on tell me.'

She laughed, not shocked at all.

'Why, of course, whenever you take him out, you go and treat him to vermouth, and tell him things that make him come home like a madman ... Oh, he's certainly nice to me! You know, more often than I'd prefer. But I'd rather it happened at home than elsewhere, that's for sure!' She became serious again, and added: 'Look, I've brought back your Balzac; I couldn't finish it. It's too sad; he only talks about unpleasant things, that man!'

And she asked him for stories with more romance, adventures and exotic travels. Then she talked about the funeral. She was going to the church, and Jules would make it to the cemetery. Death had never frightened her; at the age of twelve, she sat up a whole night with an uncle and aunt who had died of the same fever. Jules, on the other hand, hated talking about the dead, so much that he had actually forbidden her, two days ago, to mention the landlord laid out downstairs. But she couldn't find anything else to talk about, and neither could he; so for a whole hour they barely exchanged a dozen words, and did nothing else but think of the poor man. It was becoming tiresome and, for Jules's sake, she would be glad when they took him away. And, relieved to be able to talk about it, she satisfied her curiosity, overwhelming Octave with questions. Had he seen him? Did he look very different? Was it true that something horrible had occurred as he was being placed in the coffin? Was it true that his relatives had ripped up all the mattresses in their eagerness to search everywhere? So many stories went around in a house like this with so many servans! Death, after all, was the only thing that everybody was interested in.

'You're giving me another one of Balzac's,' she said, looking over the fresh batch of books that he was lending her. 'No, take it back: it's too far too lifelike!'

As she held the volume out to him, he caught hold of her wrist and tried to pull her into the room. She amused him with all her questions about death; she suddenly seemed entertaining, more lively, desirable.

But she saw what he had in mind, and blushed bright red. Freeing herself from his grasp, she ran way, saying: 'Thank you, Monsieur Mouret; see you later on at the funeral.'

When Octave was dressed, he remembered his promise to go and see Madame Campardon.

He had two whole hours to spare, as the funeral was at eleven o'clock, and he thought of making the most of his morning by making a few calls in the house. Rose was in bed when he called. He apologised for disturbing her, but she herself called him into her room. They saw so little of him, and she was so glad to have someone to chat to!

'Ah, my dear boy,' she cried; 'it's me who ought to be lying down there, nailed up between four planks!'

Yes, the landlord was very lucky to be finished with his life! And as Octave, astonished to find her so downcast, asked her if she felt worse, she replied: 'No, thank you. It's always the same thing, only there are times when I feel as if I've had enough. Achille has had to put up a bed in his study, as it got on my nerves whenever he moved around at night . . . And, you know, we've persuaded Gasparine to leave the shop. I am so grateful to her for doing this, and she looks after me so well! Ah, if I wasn't surrounded by so much affection and kindness, I wouldn't survive!'

Just then Gasparine, with the submissive air of a poor relation turned servant, brought in her coffee. Helping Rose to raise herself, she propped her up against some cushions and gave her the coffee on a little tray covered with a napkin. Rose, in her embroidered camisole, engulfed by the lace-edged linen, ate her breakfast with a hearty appetite. She looked so fresh, younger than ever and very pretty with her pale skin and little blonde curls.

'Oh, my stomach's all right. There's nothing wrong with that!' she kept saying, as she dunked her slices of bread and butter.

Two tears fell into the coffee and Gasparine scolded her: 'Now, if you cry, I shall call Achille. You should be happy, sitting there like a queen on a throne!'

By the time Madame Campardon had finished and again found herself alone with Octave, her good humour was restored. Coquettishly, she returned to the subject of death, but with the relaxed gaiety of a woman whiling away a whole morning in a warm bed. Well, she'd have to go, too, when her turn came. No, they were right, she wasn't unhappy, and could bear to go on living, since they spared her most of life's worries. So she rambled on in her self-centred manner, lying there like a sexless goddess.

Then, as the young man got up to go, she said: 'Now, do come more often, won't you? Go and enjoy yourself; don't let the funeral get you down. One dies a little every day. You just have to get used to it.'

On the same floor, Louise, the little maid at Madame Juzeur's, let Octave in. She took him into the drawing-room, looking at him for a moment, grinning sheepishly, and at last said that her mistress was dressing. Madame Juzeur, however, appeared almost immediately, dressed in black, and in this mourning outfit she seemed more serene, more refined, than ever.

'I was sure that you would come this morning,' she sighed, feebly. 'All night long I kept dreaming about you. Quite impossible to sleep, you know, with that corpse in the house!'

And she confessed that she had got up three times in the night to look under the furniture.

'You should have called me,' said the young man, gallantly. 'Two in a bed are never afraid.'

She affected a charming air of shame.

'Stop it, you're naughty!'

And she held her hand over his lips. Of course, he was obliged to kiss it. Then she spread out her fingers, laughing as if she were being tickled. Excited by this game, he tried to push matters further. He caught her in his arms and pressed her close to his chest, without her offering any resistance. Then he whispered: 'Come on, why won't you?'

'Well, definitely, not today!'

'Why not today?'

'What, with that dead body downstairs? No, no, it's impossible!'

He tightened his embrace, and she gave in. Their warm breaths mingled.

'When, then? Tomorrow?'

'Never.'

'But you're quite free. Your husband behaved so badly, you don't owe him anything ... What's up? Afraid of getting pregnant?'

'No! The doctors have told me I can't have children.'

'Well, in that case, as there's no reason not to, what's to stop us?'

He tried to force himself on her. But, wriggling, she slipped away from him.

Then, putting her arms around him, she held him tightly so that he couldn't move, and murmured caressingly: 'Anything you like except that! Do you understand me? Not that, never, never! I would rather die! It's one of my principles, that's all. I've sworn to heaven I wouldn't, not that you need know anything about that. So you're just as selfish, it seems, as other men, who are never satisfied if they are refused something. Yet I'm very fond of you. Anything you like, only not that, my sweetheart!'

She allowed him to explore her body more intimately, only pushing him away with a sudden nervous and violent movement when he attempted the only forbidden act. Her obstinacy had in it a sort of Jesuitical reserve, a fear of the confessional, certain of being pardoned for petty sins, while a more serious one might get her into trouble with her spiritual pastor. And there were other hidden motives: a blend of honour and self-esteem; the coquetry of always keeping men on a string by never satisfying them; and the refined pleasure of allowing herself to be kissed all over without having to submit. This was what she enjoyed most, and she was determined to keep it that way. Not a single man could flatter himself that he had had her since her husband's cowardly desertion. She was a virtuous woman.

'No, sir, not one! I can hold my head up high even though many unfortuante women in my position would have behaved differently!'

She gently pushed him aside and got up from the sofa.

'Leave me alone. I can't stop thinking about that corpse downstairs. The whole house seems to smell of it!'

Meanwhile, the time drew near for the funeral. She wanted to get to the church ahead of the procession to avoid seeing all the funeral trappings. But, as she was seeing him out, she suddenly remembered mentioning her liqueur from the West Indies. So she made him come back, and brought the bottle and two glasses herself. It was creamy and very sweet, with a scent of flowers. When she had drunk it, a sort of girlish greediness bathed her face in a dreamy rapture. She could have lived on sugar; sweet things scented with vanilla and rose excited her as much as the touch of a lover.

'That will keep us going,' she said.

In the hall, she shut her eyes as he kissed her on the mouth. Their sugary lips seemed to melt like bonbons.

It was nearly eleven o'clock. They had not yet been able to bring down the coffin, as the undertaker's men, having drunk away several hours at a local wineshop, were taking ages to put up the funeral hangings. Curious, Octave went to have a look. The porch was already closed off at the back by a large black curtain, but the men still had to nail up hangings over the door. And, on the pavement outside, a group of servants were gossiping with their noses in the air, while Hippolyte, in deep mourning, hurried the workers on with an air of dignity.

'Yes, madame,' Lisa was saying to a dried-up-looking widow who had been working for Valérie for a week, 'it's not done her any good at all. The whole neighbourhood knows the story. To make sure of her share of the old man's money, she had that child by a butcher in the Rue Sainte-Anne, as her husband looked as if he might snuff it any minute. But her husband's alive, and it's the old boy that's gone. A lot of good she's done herself with her filthy brat!'

The widow nodded her head in disgust.

'Serves her right!' she answered. 'All her dirty tricks have done her no good. I shan't be working for her any more. I've given her a week's notice this morning. And what with that little monster Camille using my kitchen as a toilet!'

Just then Julie came downstairs to give Hippolyte an order. Lisa ran to question her, and then, after a few moments' conversation, she came back to Valérie's maid.

'It's a funny business,' she said, 'and nobody can make neither head nor tail of it. It seems to me your mistress needn't have had the baby after all and could have let her husband kick the bucket, as they're apparently still hunting for the old boy's dough. The cook says they look in quite a state and thinks they'll end up punching each other by the end of the day.

Adèle came up, with four sous' worth of butter under her apron, Madame Josserand having ordered her always to hide what she'd been to buy. Lisa wanted to see what she was carrying, and then called her a big fool. Who ever heard of anyone being sent to fetch four sous' worth of butter! Ah, well! If it had been her, she would have made those skinflints feed her better, or else she would have helped herself before they got anything; yes, to the butter, the sugar, the meat, anything! For some time the other servants had been inciting Adèle to rebel. It was gradually having an effect. She munched off a corner of the butter and ate it, without any bread, to show the others how little she respected her masters.

'Shall we go up?' she said.

'No,' replied the widow. 'I want to see him brought down; I've delayed an errand on purpose of this.'

'So have I,' added Lisa. 'They say he weighs eighty kilos. If they drop him on their beautiful staircase, he'd do some damage, I bet!'

'Well, I'm going up. I'd rather not see him,' said Adèle. 'I don't want to have a dream like I did last night where he was pulling me out of bed by the heels, and laying into me for making a mess.'

She went off followed by the laughter of her two companions. All night long Adèle's nightmare had been a source of amusement on the servants' floor. In addition the maids had left their doors open so as not to be alone; and a coachman, a practical joker, pretended to be a ghost, and little screams and stifled giggles were heard all along the passage until daybreak. Biting her lips, Lisa declared that she would never forget it. But there'd certainly been a lot of larking about, that's for sure!

But Hippolyte's angry voice brought their attention back to the hangings. Forgetting his dignity, he was shouting out: 'You drunken fool! You're putting it up the wrong way!'

It was true: the man was about to hook the shield bearing the deceased's monogram upside down. The black hangings, edged with silver, were now in their proper place, and only a few curtain hooks still had to be put up, when a cart loaded with a few pieces of cheap furniture pulled up at the entrance. A young boy was pushing it along and a tall, pale girl followed, giving him a hand. Monsieur Gourd, who was talking to his friend, the stationer opposite, rushed forward, forgetting he was in mourning, and exclaimed: 'What on earth is he up to? Can't you see, you fool?'

The tall girl intervened.

'Sir, I'm the new lodger, you know. These are my things.'

'It's impossible! Come back tomorrow!' cried the concierge angrily.

She looked at him and then at the funeral draperies, half dazed. It was plain that this door, covered with black, bewildered her. But, recovering herself, she explained that she couldn't really leave her furniture out in the street. Then Monsieur Gourd began to bully her.

'You're the boot-stitcher, aren't you? The one that's taken the little room up at the top? Another one of the landlord's stubborn ideas! Just for the sake of a hundred and thirty francs, and after all the trouble we had with the carpenter! He promised me, too, that he would never again rent rooms to a worker. And now, damn it! It's started all over again, and this time a woman's involved!'

Then he remembered that Monsieur Vabre was dead.

'Yes, you can see it for yourself. The landlord has just died, and if it had happened a week ago you wouldn't be here today, that's for sure. Come on, hurry up, before they bring him down!'

And, in his exasperation, he himself gave the cart a shove, pushing it through the hangings, which opened and then slowly closed again. The tall, pale girl disappeared behind the mass of black drapery.

'She's come at a nice time!' said Lisa. 'A great day to move in, what with a funeral going on! If that had been me, I'd have socked that old bugger one!'

But she was silent as she saw Monsieur Gourd reappear, for he was the terror of the servants. His bad mood was due to the fact that, as people said, the house would be inherited by Monsieur Théophile and his wife. He would willingly have given a hundred francs, he said, to have Monsieur Duveyrier as landlord. At least he was a magistrate. This was what he was explaining to the stationer. Meanwhile, people now began to come downstairs. Madame Juzeur passed, smiling at Octave, who had met Trublot outside on the pavement. Then Marie appeared, and watched them placing the trestles for the coffin with great interest.

'Those people on the second floor are strange,' remarked Monsieur Gouard as he looked up at their closed shutters. 'It's as if they always manage to avoid doing things like anybody else. Yes, they were off on a journey three days ago.'

At this moment, Lisa hid behind the window, on catching sight of Gasparine, who was bringing a wreath of violets, a thoughtful gesture on the part of the architect, who was hoping to keep on good terms with the Duveyriers.

'God!' exclaimed the stationer, 'the other Madame Campardon has got herself up nicely!'

Without malice, he called her by the name given to her by all the neighbouring tradespeople. Lisa stifled a laugh. Then suddenly the servants realised that the coffin had been brought down, which proved a great disappointment. How stupid of them to be standing out in the street, looking at the black curtains! They quickly went indoors just as the coffin, carried by four men, was being brought out of the hallway. All the hangings made the porch dark and, at the back, one could see the pale daylight of the courtyard, which had been scrubbed that morning. Little Louise, who had followed Madame Juzeur, stood on tiptoe, wide-eyed and pale with curiosity. The coffin-bearers puffed and panted at the foot of the staircase, which, with its gilding and sham marble, seemed inhospitably imposing in the faint light that fell from the frosted glass windows.

'There he goes, without getting his rent for the quarter!' muttered Lisa, with the twisted humour of the landlord hating class.

Madame Gourd, who had remained stuck in her armchair because of her bad legs, now got up with difficulty. As she could not get as far as the church, Monsieur Gourd had instructed her not to let the dead landlord go past their office without some mark of respect. They owed him that much. She came as far as the door in a black cap, and as the coffin passed, she curtseyed.

During the service at Saint-Roch, Doctor Juillerat ostentatiously remained outside the church. There was actually quite a large crowd there, as several of the men preferred to stay in a group on the steps. It was a glorious, very mild June day. As they could not smoke, they talked politics instead. The central door was left open, and at intervals bursts of organ music escaped from the church, all draped in black and ablaze with candles.

'I suppose you know that Monsieur Thiers* is standing as a candidate for our district next year,' remarked Léon Josserand, in his solemn tone.

'Oh! Is he?' replied the doctor. 'Of course, you being a Republican means you won't vote for him, eh?'

The young man, whose opinions had become less radical under Madame Dambreville's tutelage, drily answered: 'Why not? He's quite clearly standing against those supporting the Empire.'

A violent discussion ensued. Léon spoke of tactics; Doctor Juillerat obstinately clung to the principles. According to him, the middle classes had had their day. They only blocked the path of revolution and, now that they had money, they stood in the way of progress more stubbornly and blindly than the old nobility.

'You're afraid of everything. You react violently as soon as you think you're being threatened!'

Suddenly Campardon became angry: 'I, sir, at one time was a Jacobin* and an atheist, like yourself. But I came to my senses, thank God. I certainly wouldn't even consider your Monsieur Thiers; he's muddle-headed and simply toys with ideas!'

However, all the liberals present – Monsieur Josserand, Octave, Trublot, who didn't give a damn – all declared that they would vote for Monsieur Thiers. The official candidate, Monsieur Dewinck, was a successful chocolate manufacturer from the Rue Saint-Honoré, who they often joked about. This same Dewinck didn't even have the backing of the clergy, who were uneasy about his relationship with the Tuileries. Given his own clerical sympathies, Campardon certainly didn't seem very enthusiastic about Dewinck. Then, suddenly changing the sub-

ject, he exclaimed: 'The bullet that wounded your Garibaldi*
on the foot should have struck his heart!'

And to avoid being seen any longer in such company, he went
into the church, where the Abbé Mauduit's harsh voice sang out
with the lamentations of the choir.

'He almost lives in the place now,' muttered the doctor,
shrugging his shoulders. 'They should sweep out the whole lot!'

He was fascinated by what was happening in Rome. Then,
when Léon reminded them of what the cabinet minister had
said* to the Senate, namely that the Empire had sprung from
the Revolution solely in order to keep it in check, they began to
talk about the coming elections again. Everybody agreed that
the Emperor needed to be taught a sound lesson; but they were
growing anxious already, divided in their opinions of the various candidates, whose names even conjured up grisly visions of
revolution. Nearby, Monsieur Gourd, dressed as impeccably as
a diplomat, listened to their debate with icy scorn. He quite
simply believed in the powers that be.

The service, however, was just coming to an end. A long,
melancholy wail from the depths of the church silenced them.

'*Requiescat in pace.*'

'*Amen.*'

At the Père-Lachaise Cemetery,* as the coffin was being
lowered into the grave, Trublot, still arm-in-arm with Octave,
saw him smile at Madame Juzeur.

'Ah, yes!' he muttered. 'What an unfortunate woman! "Anything-you-like-except-that!"'

Octave gave a start. What? Had Trublot tried it on too?
Then, with a gesture of disdain, the latter explained that he
hadn't, but a friend of his had. Plenty of others too, who knew
they'd only get so far, but apparently content just to nibble.

'Excuse me,' he added; 'now the old boy's safely underground, I'm off to see Duveyrier about something that I had to
do for him.'

The relatives, silent and melancholy, were now leaving. Then
Trublot, detaining Duveyrier, told him that he had seen Clarisse's maid, but he hadn't found out the address, as the maid
had left the day before Clarisse moved, after a violent row. The
last ray of hope vanished, and Duveyrier, burying his face in his
handkerchief, rejoined the other mourners.

The quarrelling began that evening. The family had made a

disastrous discovery. With that untroubled scepticism characteristic of some notaries, Monsieur Vabre had left no will.
Cupboards and drawers had been searched in vain, the worst of
it being that they couldn't lay their hands on a single sou of the
hoped-for six or seven hundred thousand francs; not of the
money, the title deeds or the shares. All they found was the sum
of seven hundred and thirty-four francs, in ten-sous pieces – the
hoard of a doddering old fool. Moreover, there was undeniable
evidence – a notebook filled with figures, and letters from
stockbrokers – which convinced his relatives, livid with rage, of
the old man's secret vice, an uncontrollable passion for gam-
bling, an inept, furious craving for dabbling in stocks and
shares, which he hid behind the innocent mania of his statistical
research. Everything had been sacrificed: his Versailles savings,
his rents; even the money squeezed out of his children. During
recent years, indeed, he had even mortgaged the house for a
hundred and fifty thousand francs, at three different periods.
The family, dumbfounded, stood round the famous safe in
which they believed the fortune was locked up. All that it
contained, however, was a lot of odds and ends – scraps picked
up about the house, odd bits of iron and glass, old ribbons and
broken toys stolen from Gustave when he'd been a young child.
    The family's fury was uncontainable. They called the old man
a swindler; it was scandalous to have thrown his money away
like that, like an underhand old devil who doesn't give a damn
about anybody, putting on a shameful act to get people to spoil
him. The Duveyriers were clearly beside themselves for having
put him up for twelve years, without ever once asking him for
the eighty thousand francs of Clotilde's dowry, of which they
had only received ten thousand. At least they'd got ten thousand
francs, Théophile remarked angrily. He hadn't yet got a penny
of the fifty thousand francs promised at the time of his marriage.
Auguste, however, complained even more bitterly, reproaching
his brother who had at least been able to pocket three months'
interest on that sum, whereas he wouldn't ever see any of the
fifty thousand francs specified in his own contract. Then Berthe,
spurred on by her mother, made various cutting remarks, parad-
ing her indignity at having become involved with such a dishonest family; and Valérie went ranting on about the rent that she
had continued paying for so long through fear of being disinherited; but she couldn't take it all in, and talked about the missing

money as though it had been spent on unbridled debauchery.

For a fortnight the whole house was obsessed by these discoveries. Finally it appeared that all that remained was the building, valued at three hundred thousand francs. When the mortgage had been paid off, there would be about half that sum to divide between Monsieur Vabre's three children. Fifty thousand francs each. Not much of a consolation, but this was what they had to be content with. Théophile and Auguste had already decided what to do with their shares. It was agreed that the building should be sold. Duveyrier undertook all the arrangements in his wife's name. First of all, he persuaded the two brothers not to have a public auction; if they were willing, the sale could take place at his notary's, Maître Renaudin, a man whose integrity he could vouch for. Then, acting on the notary's advice, he slyly hinted to them that it would be best to put up the house at a low figure, only a hundred and forty thousand francs to begin with. A very canny strategy, this, which would bring crowds of people to the sale; the bids would mount rapidly, and they would raise far more than they expected. Full of happy confidence, Théophile and Auguste agreed. However, on the day of the sale, after only five or six bids, Maître Renaudin suddenly let the house go to Duveyrier for a hundred and forty thousand francs. There was not even enough to pay off the mortgage! This was the final straw.

No one ever learned the full details of the terrible scene that took place at the Duveyriers' that evening. The solemn walls of the house muffled the shouting. Théophile accused his brother-in-law of being a criminal, openly accusing him of having bribed the notary by promising to appoint him a justice of the peace. As for Auguste, he just talked of the courts and declared that he would drag Maître Renaudin into the dock as well, who the whole neighbourhood knew to be a scoundrel. But even if it never transpired how, as rumour had it, they came to blows, their parting words on the doorstep were overheard; angry remarks which rang out in the austere decorum of the staircase.

'Two-faced bastard!' cried Auguste. 'You sentence people to prison who had not done half as much!'

Théophile, coming out last, and half choked by fury and a fit of coughing, yelled back through the door he was holding open: 'Thief! Thief! Yes, thief! You, too, Clotilde, do you hear? You're a thief!'

Then he slammed the door so violently that all the adjoining ones shook too. Monsieur Gourd, who was listening, became alarmed. He looked up the well of the staircase to see what was going on, but all that he could see was Madame Juzeur's delicate profile. With back bent, he returned on tiptoe to his lodge, once again a model of decorum. He could deny having heard any disturbance. Personally, he was delighted, and sided with the new landlord.

A few days later there was a reconciliation between Auguste and his sister. It surprised everybody. Octave had been seen going to the Duveyriers'. The counsellor, ill at ease, had decided to charge no rent for the ground-floor shop for five years to keep at least one of the inheritors quiet. When Théophile heard this, he and his wife went downstairs to his brother's and made another scene. So he, too, had sold himself to that gang of thieves! However, Madame Josserand happened to be in the shop at the time, and she soon silenced him. She advised Valérie, quite clearly, not to sell out any more than her daughter had done.

And Valérie, forced to retreat, exclaimed: 'So we're the only ones who are to grin and bear it, are we? I'm damned if I'll pay any more rent. I've got a lease, and that criminal won't dare throw us out. And as for you, my little Berthe, one day we'll see how much you'll be killing yourself for.'

Doors were slammed again. A deadly feud now existed between the two families. Octave, who had been of service, was present on this occasion, like one of the family. Berthe almost fainted in his arms, while Auguste made sure that none of his customers had overheard. Even Madame Josserand trusted the young man. Towards the Duveyriers, however, she was very severe.

'The rent is something,' she said, 'but I want those fifty thousand francs.'

'Of course you do, if you pay yours,' Berthe ventured to remark.

Her mother seemed not to understand.

'I tell you, I want them, do you hear? That old villain Vabre must be laughing in his grave. I won't let him boast of having made a fool of me, though. There are some low-lifes in this world, that's for sure! Fancy promising money that one hasn't got! Oh! We'll get it for you all right, my girl, or I'll dig him up myself and spit in his face!'

One morning, when Berthe was at her mother's, Adèle came in, looking very scared, to say that Monsieur Saturnin was there, with a man. Doctor Chassagne, the director of the Moulineaux Asylum, had repeatedly informed the Josserands that he could not keep their son, as his was not a clear-cut case of insanity. And having heard about the papers making over the three thousand francs, which Berthe had cajoled her brother into signing, he wanted to avoid being compromised in the matter, and was sending Saturnin home.

The news terrified them. Madame Josserand, frightened of being strangled, tried to reason with the attendant.

But he just said: 'The director asked me to tell you that when someone is sane enough to give money to his parents, he's sane enough to live with them.'

'But he's mad. He'll murder us.'

'Not so mad that he can't sign his name!' replied the man as he left.

However, Saturnin came in quite calmly, his hands in his pockets, just as if he were returning from a stroll in the Tuileries Gardens. He never even spoke about his stay in the asylum. He embraced his father, who wept, and then kissed his mother and Hortense, who both trembled with fright. He was overjoyed when he saw Berthe, caressing her with all the charm of a schoolboy. She at once took advantage of his affectionate mood to tell him about her marriage. He showed no sign of anger, and didn't seem to understand at first, as if he had forgotten his former fits of rage. But when she was about to go downstairs, he started yelling: married or not married, he didn't care, so long as she stayed where he was, always with him, always close to him. Seeing her terrified mother, who had already rushed away to lock herself in, Berthe thought of taking Saturnin with her. They would find some way to make him useful, in the basement of their shop, even if it was only tying up parcels.

That same evening, Auguste, despite his evident disgust at the idea, gave in to his wife. They had hardly been married three months, yet they already sensed a growing gulf between them.

It was the collision of two completely different individuals, both in temperament and upbringing – a sullen, fastidious and passionless husband and a lively wife who had grown up pampered by fake Parisian luxury, determined to make the most for herself, like a selfish spoiled child. Thus he couldn't understand her need to be continually out and about, her shopping trips, her outings, her visits, rushing to every theatre, exhibition, and other place of amusement. Two or three times a week Madame Josserand came to collect her daughter, staying out till the evening, delighted to be seen in her company, basking in the glory of Berthe's elegant dresses, which she no longer paid for. Auguste's resistance, indeed, was mainly due to these flashy gowns, which he could see no reason for buying. Why dress above one's means and status? Why spend money he so urgently needed in his business on that sort of thing? He had always said that if they were selling silk to other women, they should only wear wool. But Berthe, adopting her mother's vicious tone, would then ask if he would prefer her to be stark naked. She also deflated him further by showing him the poor state of her petticoats and her contempt for underwear out of sight, and always had a set of stock phrases ready to silence him with if he persisted in his objections.

'I would rather be envied than pitied. Money's money, and whenever I had twenty sous I always pretended I had forty.'

Since her wedding, Berthe had put on weight and had gradually begun to look more like her mother. The limp girl putting up with her mother's slaps had vanished. She was now a woman of ever-increasing obstinacy, dominated by a desire to turn everything to her own pleasure. Auguste sometimes looked at her with amazement, so quickly had she matured. At first she had taken a vain delight in enthroning herself at the cashier's desk in a modest and studiously elegant outfit. Then she had quickly acquired an aversion to trade, hating to remain in one place for so long; indeed, it almost made her ill. And, ever since then, a constant battle had been going on between herself and her husband. She shrugged her shoulders behind his back, just as her mother did behind her father's; she repeated all the petty domestic quarrels that had plagued her own childhood; she treated him simply as a person whose duty it was to pay up, showing him her profound contempt for men, a contempt which her entire upbringing had been based upon.

'Oh, Mamma was right, after all!' she would exclaim after one of their rows.

At first, however, Auguste had endeavoured to please her. A peaceful man, he dreamed of having a quiet little home, and clung on to his dream with the obsession of an old man unable to break the habits of his chaste and thrifty bachelor lifestyle. As his old rooms on the first-floor landing were too small, he took a flat on the second floor, facing the courtyard, and thought it wildly extravagant to spend five thousand francs on furniture. Berthe, delighted at first with her bedroom in polished wood and blue silk, showed utter contempt for it later on, after visiting a friend of hers who had married a banker. The first quarrels had been on the subject of servants. Although used to dealing with half-witted maids whose very bread was doled out to them, the chores the young wife forced her servants to perform sent them sobbing to the kitchen for hours on end. Auguste, not usually tender-hearted, once foolishly ventured to comfort one of them, but an hour later was forced to send her packing, amid the sobs of his wife, who furiously demanded him to choose between herself and that creature. A much more robust girl came along next and apparently made up her mind to stay. Her name was Rachel, a Jewess, no doubt, although she denied it, and concealed her nationality. Aged about twenty-five, she had a hard face, a big nose, and coal-black hair. At first Berthe said that she would not put up with her for longer than a couple of days, but the newcomer's mute obedience, her apparently understanding everything and yet saying nothing, gradually satisfied her. It looked as if the mistress, in her turn, had been put in her place, keeping the girl for her merits, though, at the same time, vaguely afraid of her. Rachel, who never refused to do any sort of work, however hard, for just a crust, was gradually taking over the household, with her eyes open and her mouth shut, like an intuitive servant waiting for the fatal moment when Madame would be unable to refuse her anything.

What's more, from top to bottom, a great calm now pervaded the building, after the commotion caused by Monsieur Vabre's sudden death. The staircase was again as peaceful as a chapel and not a sound could be heard from behind those mahogany doors enclosing the profound respectability of the families within. A rumour was going round that Duveyrier and his wife

were back together. As for Valérie and Théophile, they spoke to
no one, as always maintaining their stiff and dignified air. Never
before had the house seemed so strict and principled. Monsieur
Gourd, in cap and slippers, went about the building like some
solemn beadle.

One evening, about eleven o'clock, Auguste kept going to the
shop door every few minutes, looking up and down the street
with ever-increasing impatience. Berthe, who had been collected
by her mother and sister at dinner-time, not even having finished
her dessert, had not yet come back although she had been out
for over three hours, and had promised to return before closing
time.

'Damn it!' he exclaimed at last, clasping his hands so tightly
that his knuckles cracked.

Then he came to a halt in front of Octave, who was ticketing
some remnants of silk on the counter. At this time of the
evening, no one was going to be buying anything at this end of
the Rue de Choiseul. They only stayed open to tidy up the shop.

'I bet you know where they've gone, don't you,' said Auguste.

Octave looked up with an air of innocent surprise.

'But, sir, they told you ... they said they were going to a
lecture.'

'A lecture, indeed, a lecture!' grumbled the husband. 'Their
lecture was over at ten o'clock. Respectable women would be
home by now!'

Then he resumed his pacing, glancing sideways at Octave,
whom he suspected of being in on their plan, or, at least, of
making excuses for them. Octave, feeling ill at ease, watched
him furtively too. He had never seen him so worked up. What
could have happened? Turning his head, he saw Saturnin at the
other end of the shop, cleaning a mirror with a sponge soaked
in spirit. Gradually, they had begun to give the madman housework to do so that at least he earned his keep.

That evening there was a strange glint in Saturnin's eyes. He
crept up behind Octave and said to him in a low voice: 'I'd
watch out! He's found a piece of paper. Yes, he's got a piece of
paper in his pocket. I'd be careful if it's anything of yours!'

Then he hurriedly went back to his mirror. Octave couldn't
make it out. For some time the lunatic had shown an odd
affection for him, like the caress of an animal beneath whose
unerring instinct lay a deeper, more subtle sentiment. What

made him mention a piece of paper? He hadn't written a letter to Berthe, but only allowed himself to look tenderly at her now and again, while waiting for a chance to give her some little present. This was the approach he had decided upon after much thought.

'Ten past eleven, damn it!' exclaimed Auguste, who never usually swore.

At that moment, however, the ladies came in. Berthe wore a charming outfit in pink silk embroidered with white, while her sister, always in blue, and her mother, always in mauve, still wore their gaudy elaborate gowns, which they revived every season. Madame Josserand, large and imposing, came in first to put a stop to any complaints from her son-in-law. This had been pre-planned during a brief council together at the top of the street. She even condescended to explain their late arrival by saying that they had dawdled along, looking in the shop windows. Auguste grew very pale, but he didn't protest. He replied curtly, clearly holding himself back until the right moment. Madame Josserand sensed the calm before the storm after years of experience of family rows. She tried to intimidate him a while longer but, obliged at last to leave, she had to content herself with saying: 'Good-night, my girl, and sleep well if you want a long life.'

Instantly Auguste, no longer able to contain himself and oblivious of the presence of Octave and Saturnin, pulled a crumpled piece of paper out of his pocket and thrust it into Berthe's face, stammering: 'How do you explain this?'

Berthe had not even taken off her hat. She went very red.

'That?' she replied. 'Why, it's a bill.'

'Yes, it's a bill, and for false hair, too! For false hair, of all things; as if you hadn't got any on your head! But that's not the point. You've paid this bill; now, tell me, what did you pay it with?'

Becoming more and more embarrassed, Berthe at last replied: 'With my own money, of course!'

'Your own money! But you haven't got any. Somebody must have given you some, or else you took it from here. I know what you've been up to. You've been running up debts. I'll put up with most things, but not debts, do you hear? Not debts, never!'

He said this with all the horror of a prudent man whose

business principles were based on never owing a penny. He went on reproaching his wife for always gadding about town, complaining about the clothes and all the other luxuries that he couldn't afford. Was it right that people in their position should stay out till eleven o'clock at night, dressed up in pink silk gowns embroidered with white beads? Someone with such a taste for luxury would need to bring a dowry of five hundred thousand francs with them. However, he knew exactly who was to blame; it was that idiot of a mother, who had taught her daughters how to squander fortunes without having so much as a rag to put on their backs the day of their wedding.

'Don't insult my mother!' cried Berthe, who at last became exasperated. 'She's not to blame; she did her duty. What about your family! They're a fine bunch! People who killed their father!'

Octave carried on pricing the silks, and pretended not to hear. But he watched the dispute, and had his eye on Saturnin, who had stopped polishing the mirror and, fists clenched and eyes flashing, stood there trembling, ready to make a spring at Auguste's throat.

'Forget our families!' replied the latter. 'We've got enough problems of our own. Look, you'll have to change your stupid ways, I'm not paying another penny. I've made up my mind about that! Your proper place is here, behind the counter, dressed simply, like any self-respecting woman would be. And if you run up debts, you'll see!'

Berthe was shocked at the brutality with which her husband had put his foot down, forbidding her little ways, her pleasures and her clothes. It was as if everything she enjoyed, everything she had dreamed of finding in marriage had been wrenched away. But, with a woman's cunning, she hid her real wound, finding a pretext for the anger that flushed her face as she indignantly exclaimed: 'I will not permit you to insult my mother!'

Auguste shrugged his shoulders.

'Your mother indeed! You look just like her, and just as ugly when you get yourself into such a state! I hardly recognise you now, it's your mother all over again! God, it's frightening!'

Berthe calmed down instantly, and looked him straight in the face.

'Go and tell Mamma what you've just said. She'll soon send you packing!'

'Will she now?' cried Auguste, beside himself. 'Then I think I'll go and see her right away!'

He turned and left, and not a moment too soon, for Saturnin, with wolfish eyes, was coming up on tiptoe to strangle him from behind.

Berthe sank into a chair, murmuring: 'There's a man I would never marry if I had my time again, by God!'

Upstairs, Monsieur Josserand opened the door, as Adèle had already gone to bed, and was greatly surprised. He was just getting ready to spend that night addressing labels, in spite of having felt so unwell for some time. Somewhat embarrassed, and ashamed of being found out, he took his son-in-law into the dining-room, talking about an urgent deadline – a copy of the inventory of the Saint-Joseph glass works which had to be completed. But when Auguste bluntly accused his daughter of running into debt, and told him about the quarrel caused by the false hair incident, the poor man trembled all over; he stammered incoherently, cut to the quick, and tears filled his eyes. His daughter was in debt, and her life was full of rows and family upsets just like his own! All his own misfortunes had been handed down to his child! Another fear possessed him, that his son-in-law would broach the subject of money, claim the dowry and denounce him as a swindler. No doubt he knew everything, or he would never burst in on them in this way at nearly midnight.

'My wife has gone to bed,' he stuttered in confusion. 'There's no point waking her up, is there? Really, I'm surprised to hear all this! My poor dear Berthe isn't a bad girl, I assure you! Give her a chance. I'll have a word with her. As for ourselves, my dear Auguste, I don't think we've done anything to upset you . . .'

He looked at him enquiringly, feeling reassured; Auguste evidently knew nothing as yet. Then Madame Josserand appeared outside her bedroom door. She stood there in her nightdress looking pale and fearsome. Infuriated though he was, Auguste recoiled. She must have been listening at the door, as she launched straight in.

'It can't be your ten thousand francs that you've come for? The instalment's not due for at least another two months. We'll pay you in two months, sir. We're not in the habit of dying to avoid keeping *our* promises.'

Her astounding assurance completely overwhelmed Monsieur Josserand. Once started, she went on making the most extraordinary statements, to the utter bewilderment of Auguste, who could not get a word in edgeways.

'You haven't got a clue, sir. Once you've finally succeeded in making Berthe ill, you'll have to send for the doctor, and then you'll have a chemist's bill to pay. I left just now because I saw that you were determined to make a fool of yourself. Go ahead! Beat your wife, if you like; my conscience as a mother is clear, for God sees everything, and punishment is never far behind!'

At last Auguste was able to explain his grievances. He complained once more about the perpetual gadding about, the expensive dresses and all the rest of it. He was even bold enough to criticise the way that Berthe had been brought up.

Madame Josserand listened with an air of absolute contempt. Then, when he had finished, she said: 'That, dear son-in-law, is such utter rubbish, it doesn't even deserve an answer. My conscience is clear, that's enough for me. And to think that I entrusted my angel to you! As all you can do is insult me, I shan't have anything more to do with your quarrels. In future you'll have to sort yourselves out!'

'But your daughter will end up by being unfaithful to me, madame!' cried Auguste, in a fresh burst of rage.

Madame Josserand, about to withdraw, turned round and looked him full in the face.

'Sir,' said she, 'you're doing all you possibly can to drive her to it.'

Then she went back to her room, as majestic as some colossal triple-breasted Ceres robed in white.

The father detained Auguste for a few minutes longer. He tried to pacify him, pointing out that with women it's best to put up with everything; and he ended up sending him away much calmer and resolved to forgive Berthe. But as soon as the poor old man found himself alone again in the dining-room, in front of his little lamp, he burst into tears. It was all over. Nothing would ever be right again. He would never find time at night to address enough labels to help his daughter in secret. The thought that she might run into debt overwhelmed him with a sense of personal shame. He felt quite ill after receiving this fresh blow; one of these nights his strength would fail him.

At last, with great difficulty, he forced back his tears and went on with his work.

Downstairs in the shop, Berthe remained motionless for a moment, her face buried in her hands. One of the men, having put up the shutters, went back down into the basement, and it was then that Octave thought he ought to approach the young woman. Ever since Auguste had gone, Saturnin kept making signs over his sister's head, inviting Octave to comfort her. Now, looking radiant, he redoubled his winks, and fearing that he had not been understood, he emphasised his hints by blowing kisses with childish impulsiveness.

'What? Do you want me to kiss her?' Octave asked him, by signs.

The madman vigorously nodded assent. Then as he saw Octave smilingly approach Berthe, who had seen nothing of this, he sat on the floor behind a counter, out of sight, so as not to be in their way. The gas lamps were still burning brightly in the silent, empty shop. There was a sort of deathlike peace, and a stuffy smell from the bales of silk.

'Madame, please don't take it too much to heart,' said Octave tenderly.

She gave a start on seeing him so near to her.

'Please excuse me, Monsieur Octave, I didn't intend you to witness this unpleasant scene. And you must excuse my husband, who must be feeling unwell this evening. Every family has its little upsets, you know . . .'

Her sobs choked her. The mere thought of justifying her husband's faults to outsiders brought on a violent fit of weeping which completely overpowered her. Saturnin peeped anxiously over the counter, but ducked down again as soon as he saw Octave take hold of Berthe's hand.

'Try to be brave, madame, I beg you.'

'But I can't help it!' sobbed Berthe. 'You were there, so you heard it all. All over ninety-five francs' worth of hair! As if every woman didn't wear false hair these days! But he doesn't know anything and doesn't understand! He has no experience of women, Monsieur Octave, none at all! I'm so unlucky!'

In the heat of her anger she blurted out everything. A man she thought had married her for love, but who would soon leave her without a shirt on her back! Didn't she fulfil her duties? He couldn't reproach her with neglecting any of them.

If he hadn't flown into a rage when she asked him to get her some false hair, she would never have been obliged to buy some with her own allowance. For the slightest thing there was always the same fuss; she could never express a wish or say that she wanted some trivial item of clothing without coming up against the same fiercely obstinate opposition. Naurally, she had some pride; she never asked for anything any more, preferring to go without rather than humiliate herself for no purpose. For instance, the last fortnight she had been longing for some ornaments that she and her mother had seen in a jeweller's window in the Palais Royal.

'You know, three paste stars to put on one's hair. Just a little knick-knack – a hundred francs, I think. Well, I must have talked about them from morning till night, but it was no good, my husband didn't take the hint!'

Octave could never have hoped for a better opportunity. He seized it straight away.

'Oh, yes, I know the ones! I often heard you speak about them. Well, madame, your parents have been so kind to me, and you yourself have been so extremely helpful, that I thought I might venture to . . .'

As he spoke, he drew from his pocket a long box containing the three stars, which sparkled on cotton wool. Berthe excitedly jumped up from her chair.

'But, sir, it's impossible for me to . . . I couldn't really . . . you shouldn't have!'

With mock ingenuousness he invented various pretexts. In the South people often did things like that. Besides, the ornaments weren't expensive. Berthe, flushed and no longer crying, was drawn towards the contents of the box, revived by the sight of the sparkling fake gems.

'Please accept them, madame, just to show me that you're satisfied with my work.'

'No, Monsieur Octave, really, you mustn't make me. I'm sorry that you should have . . .'

At this moment, Saturnin came out of hiding and examined the jewellery with as much rapture as if they were holy relics. Soon his sharp ear detected Auguste's returning footsteps. He warned Berthe with a slight click of his tongue. Just as her husband was about to enter she made up her mind.

'Well,' she hurriedly whispered, thrusting the box in her

pocket, 'I'll say that my sister Hortense gave them to me as a present.'

Auguste ordered the gas light to be turned out, and then went upstairs with his wife to bed, without saying a word about their quarrel, being secretly glad to find that Berthe was herself again, as if nothing had happened. The shop was plunged into darkness, and just as Octave was also leaving, he felt two hot hands squeezing his in the gloom. It was Saturnin, who slept in the basement.

'Friend, friend, friend!' repeated the lunatic, in an outburst of wild affection.

With all his plans thwarted, Octave was gradually developing an intense desire for Berthe. If at first he had followed his usual tactics, and his wish to seduce women as a means of self-advancement, he now no longer regarded Berthe merely as his employer, and thus his ticket to gaining control of the entire establishment. What he desired, above all, was to enjoy this pretty little Parisienne, with all her luxury and charm; the sort of dainty crature he'd never had in Marseilles. He felt a sudden craving for her tiny gloved hands, her little feet in their high-heeled boots, her soft bosom concealed beneath frills and flounces, even the hint of off-white beneath her magnificent dresses. This sudden burst of passion had such an effect on him that, throwing his usual caution to the wind, he began showering her with presents, squandering the five thousand francs he had brought with him from the South, savings that had quietly doubled in value as a result of shrewd investment.

But what threw him more than anything was that falling in love had made him timid. He had lost his former assertiveness, his impatience to reach his goal, savouring instead a certain languid pleasure in not rushing things. Moreover, this passing weakness in someone usually so practical-minded, led him to conclude that the conquest of Berthe would be a campaign fraught with difficulties, requiring time and diplomacy. His two failures, with Valérie and Madame Hédouin, doubtless filled him with terror at the thought of yet another rejection. In addition, beneath this agitated hesitation, there lurked a fear of the woman he adored, an absolute belief in Berthe's virtue, and all the blindness of a desperate love paralysed by desire.

Next day, Octave pleased that he had managed to get Berthe to accept his present, thought that it might be useful to be on

good terms with her husband. Accordingly, as they ate together
– Auguste always catered for his staff so as to keep a closer eye
on them – he paid him the utmost attention, listened to him
during dessert and loudly agreed with everything he said. He
even went so far as pretending to share his disapproval of
Berthe's conduct, feigning to play the detective and report
various little incidents to him from time to time. Auguste was
really touched. One evening he confessed to Octave that he had
been on the point of dismissing him, believing him to be in
league with Madame Josserand. But Octave also expressed a
loathing for that awful woman, and this served to seal their
alliance. Deep down, the husband was, in fact, good man. He
might be bad-tempered, but he was easy-going enough as long
as no one put him out by spending his money or by undermining
his values. He vowed that he would never lose his temper again,
for after the quarrel he had suffered from a terrible headache,
which had put him out of action for three days.

'You see what I mean, don't you?' he would observe to
Octave. 'All I want is peace and quiet. Nothing else bothers me,
apart from my honour of course, and provided my wife doesn't
run off with the money in the till. That's reasonable enough,
isn't it? I'm not asking anything out of the ordinary from her,
am I?'

Octave complimented his good sense, and they both sang the
praises of a quiet life, with each year exactly like the last, and
all of them spent measuring yards of silk. To please his
employer, the young man was content to abandon his ideas of
trade on a grandiose scale. One evening he had frightened
Auguste with his dream of huge modern stores, advising him as
he had advised Madame Hédouin, to purchase the adjoining
building, so as to enlarge his shop. Auguste, whose four
counters were already enough to drive him crazy, looked at
Octave with the terrified look of a shopkeeper used to counting
every last penny, so that the young man hastily withdrew his
proposition and went into ecstasies over the sound integrity of
small businesses.

Days passed. Octave was building his nest in the house – a
downy nest, which he found snug and warm. The husband
thought highly of him, and Madame Josserand herself, though
he avoided being too polite to her, even looked at him encour-
agingly. As for Berthe, she treated him with delightful familiar-

ity. His great friend, however was Saturnin, whose mute affection he saw increasing, like the devotion of a faithful dog, as his desire for Berthe grew more intense. The madman appeared intensely jealous of everyone else. No man could go near his sister without him instantly becoming restless and curling his lip as if ready to bite. If, on the other hand, Octave casually bent over her, making her laugh the soft velvety laugh of a contented lover, Saturnin would laugh with joy as well, his face even partly reflecting their sensual delight. This poor creature seemed to experience love via this soft female flesh that instinctively he felt belonged to him, while for the chosen lover he felt nothing but ecstatic gratitude. He would stop Octave in all sorts of corners, look around suspiciously, and then, if they happened to be alone, he would talk about Berthe, always repeating the same stories in disjointed phrases.

'When she was little, she had tiny legs as big as that! She was so chubby, so rosy, so merry! She used to wriggle about on the floor. Then whack! Whack! Whack! She used to kick me in the stomach. That's what I liked! Oh, I used to love it!'

In this way Octave got to know the entire history of Berthe's childhood, of her babyish accidents, her toys, of her gradual growth into a charming, uncontrolled animal. Saturnin's empty brain carefully stored up these insignificant facts, which he alone remembered, such as the day she pricked herself and he sucked the blood, or the morning he held her in his arms when she wanted to get on to the table. But he always harked back to the major drama of her illness.

'Ah, if only you'd seen her! I used to stay with her at night on my own! They beat me to send me back to bed. But I used to creep back barefoot. All by myself. It made me cry, she was so white. I used to touch her to see if she was too cold. Then they left me alone. I looked after her better than they did. I knew about her medicine, and she took whatever I gave her. Sometimes, when she was really suffering, I laid her head on my chest. It was so nice being together. Then she got better, and I wanted to go back to her, but they beat me again!'

His eyes sparkled, he laughed and wept, just as if the whole thing had happened only the day before. From these broken phrases of his, the whole story of this strange attachment became clear; the devotion of this poor halfwit, keeping watch at the young patient's bedside after all the doctors had given up on her, devoting body and soul to his beloved sister, who lay there dying, and whom he nursed in her nakedness with a mother's tenderness – all his affection and all his male desire arrested and withered once and for all by this drama of suffering, the shock of which he had never recovered from. Ever since that time, despite the ingratitude which had repaid such devotion, Berthe became everything to him, a mistress in whose presence he trembled – a daughter and a sister he had saved from death, an idol he jealously adored. And so he purused her husband with the wild hatred of a thwarted love, full of abuse for him, while unburdening his soul to Octave.

'He still can't see out of his eye! That headache of his is so annoying. Did you hear him shuffling about yesterday? Look! There he is staring out of the window. What an idiot! Oh, you filthy animal, you filthy animal!'

Auguste could hardly move without making him angry. Then he would come up with worrying suggestions.

'If you like, we could get him and bleed him like a pig!'

Octave tried to calm him down. Then, on his quiet days, Saturnin would go from Octave to Berthe, delighted to repeat what one had said about the other, running errands for them, acting as an adoring go-between. He would willingly have flung himself down as a carpet for them to walk on.

Berthe had never mentioned the present again. She appeared not to notice Octave's trembling attentions, treating him as a friend, apparently unconcerned. Never before had he taken such pains with his appearance, and he was for ever gazing at her, with his eyes the colour of old gold, whose velvety softness he considered irresistible. But she was only grateful to him for the lies that he told on her behalf when helping her to escape from the shop now and again. The two thus became accomplices, and he made it easier for her to go out with her mother, putting her husband off the scent if ever he showed the slightest suspicion. Her mania for such frivolous excursions made her absolutely reckless, and she relied entirely on his tact and intelligence to cover for her. Then, on her return, if she found him behind a pile of goods she rewarded him with the hearty handshake of a comrade.

One day, however, she was greatly upset. She had just come back from a dog show, when Octave beckoned her to follow him downstairs into the basement, where he gave her an invoice which had arrived during her absence – sixty-two francs for embroidered stockings.

She had turned quite pale, exclaiming: 'Oh, God! Did my husband see this?'

He hastened to reassure her, telling her what a job it had been to smuggle the bill away from under Auguste's very nose. Then, in an embarrassed tone, he added: 'I paid it.'

She at once pretended to feel in her pockets, and, finding nothing, merely said: 'I will pay you back. Oh, thank you so much, Monsieur Octave! I would be dead if Auguste had seen that!'

And this time she took hold of both his hands, and for an instant pressed them in her own. But the sixty-two francs were never mentioned again. She had an ever-increasing desire for freedom and pleasure – everything that, as a girl, she had expected from marriage and all that her mother had taught her to exact from a man. She brought with her an appetite as yet unappeased, taking her revenge for her deprived youth spent with her parents; for all the dry scraps of meat and having to go without butter in order to buy boots; for all the shabby gowns that had to be patched up a dozen times; for their fabricated social position, maintained at the price of squalid misery and filth. Most of all she wanted to make up for those three winters spent in traipsing the length and breadth of muddy streets in ball slippers in search of a husband; boring evenings during which she did her best to stave off hunger pains by guzzling syrup, bored to tears with having to smile and play the charming innocent for the benefit of stupid young men, inwardly exasperated at being obliged to affect ignorance despite being well aware of what was going on. On top of that, she had to make up for all the dreadful treks home in the pouring rain without a cab; for having shivered in an ice-cold bed, and the maternal slaps that made her cheeks glow. At the age of twenty-two, she believed she would be left on the shelf, reduced to the status of a hunchback, looking at herself in her nightdress to see what was wrong with her. But now she finally had a husband and, like the hunter who brutally delivers the final blow to the hare he has breathlessly pursued, so Berthe showed herself to be merciless, treating Auguste like the vanquished enemy.

Gradually the breach grew ever wider between the two, despite the husband's efforts in the interests of a quiet life. He made desperate attempts to preserve the drowsy monotony of his little home, closing his eyes to trivial misdemeanours and even tolerating the more serious ones, always afraid of making some appalling discovery that might drive him insane. All Berthe's lies about little gifts which, she alleged, were tokens of sisterly or motherly affection, he now calmly accepted; he did not even grumble too much if she went out in the evening. Thus Octave was secretly able to take her to the theatre twice in the company of Madame Josserand and Hortense, delightful outings which made the ladies agree that Octave really knew how to live.

Until now, at the slightest word, Berthe had always flaunted her virtue in her husband's face. At least she led a virtuous life, and he should consider himself lucky, for, in her opinion, and in that of her mother, a husband was only within his rights to be bad-tempered when his wife had proved herself unfaithful. Such chastity, genuine enough at first when greedily indulging her appetite for frivolous amusement, was no great sacrifice on her part. She was by nature cold, sheer egotism predominating over passion, and preferred indulging herself in ways that were not entirely virtuous. Having suffered so many rejections as a single woman, who thought that men would never be interested in her, she was merely flattered by Octave's attentions, and she took care to make the most of them, calmly reaping the benefits, having grown up with a frenzied desire for money. One day she allowed her clerk to pay a five-hour cab fare for her; another time as she was about to go out, she talked him into lending her thirty francs behind her husband's back, saying that she had forgotten her purse. She never repaid him.

The young man was of little importance to her, she had no designs on him; she merely made use of him, without premeditation, just to pander to her whims and fancies. And all the while she posed as an ill-used wife, as a martyr who fulfilled her duties without fail.

One Saturday a fearful quarrel occurred between the young couple, over a deficit of twenty sous in Rachel's household accounts. As Berthe used to pay this account, Auguste always handed over the money necessary to meet the household expenses for the following week. That evening the Josserands were coming to dinner, and the kitchen was littered with provisions – a rabbit, a leg of mutton, and cauliflowers. Near the sink, Saturnin squatted on the floor blacking boots. The quarrel was provoked by attempts to explain the missing twenty-sous piece. What could have become of it? How could one lose twenty sous? Auguste wanted to check the bill, to see if it was added up correctly. Meanwhile Rachel, hard-faced but compliant, calmly carried on skewering her piece of lamb, with mouth shut and eyes for ever on the watch. At last Auguste parted with fifty francs, and was going downstairs, when he suddenly came back, tormented by the thought of the lost coin.

'It will have to be found,' he said. 'Perhaps you borrowed it from Rachel and have forgotten about it.'

Berthe was deeply hurt. 'So now you're accusing me of making a bit from the shopping money, are you? Well, thank you for the compliment.'

This was the start of it, and harsh words soon followed. Auguste, despite his desire for peace at any price, became aggressive, exasperated by the sight of the rabbit, the leg of mutton, and the cauliflowers – a whole pile of provisions that his wife was going to stuff under her parents' noses in one go. He looked through the account book, exclaiming at every item. Good heavens! It was monstrous! She must be in league with the maid to make a profit on the housekeeping.

'What!' cried Berthe, beside herself with anger. 'You accuse *me, me* of being in league with the maid? Why, it's you, sir, who pays her to spy on me! Yes, she's always on my back, I can't move a step without her watching me. She can look through the keyhole as much as she likes when I'm changing my underwear; I don't do anything to be ashamed of and I don't give a damn for your detectives! But don't you dare go as far as to accuse me of being league with my maid!'

For a moment this unexpected onslaught completely dumfounded Auguste. Without relinquishing her leg of lamb, Rachel turned round, and, with her hand on her heart, protested her innocence.

'Oh, madame, how could you believe that? Especially of me, who respects madame so highly!'

'She's off her head!' exclaimed Auguste, shrugging his shoulders. 'Don't you even feel you have to make any excuses, my girl. She's off her head!'

Suddenly a noise from behind startled him. It was Saturnin, who had thrown down one of the half-cleaned shoes and was coming to his sister's rescue. His face wore a furious expression and, with clenched fists, he stammered that he would throttle the filthy animal if he dared to say she was mad again.

Auguste, terror-stricken, rushed behind the water-inlet, shouting: 'This is just too much! I can't say a word to you without him interfering! It's true I took him in, but on condition that he behaved himself. He's another nice present from your mother! She was terrified of him, and so she saddled me with him, preferring to let me be murdered instead of her. I'm greatly obliged to her! Look, he's got hold of a knife. For God's sake, stop him!'

Disarming her brother, Berthe pacified him with a look, while Auguste, turning deadly pale, continued muttering incoherently. Always brandishing knives! One false move and it could all be over! And you wouldn't get redress from the courts where a madman was involved. It simply wasn't fair to keep a brother like that as a bodyguard, ready to stop a husband venting his justified indignation, and forcing him to swallow his anger.

'You've got absolutely no tact!' cried Berthe, scornfully. 'No gentleman discusses matters of this sort in the kitchen!'

She withdrew to her room, slamming the doors behind her. Rachel went back to her spit, as if she'd heard nothing. Aware of everything but knowing her place, she discreetly refrained from looking at madame as she left the room; and when her master stamped about, she never moved a muscle. Almost immediately, however, Auguste rushed out after his wife, and then Rachel, impassive as ever, put the rabbit on to boil.

'Please understand, my dear,' said Auguste, on joining Berthe in her bedroom, 'that remark was not for your benefit. I meant it for the girl who is clearly stealing from us. Those twenty sous will have to be found somehow.'

Berthe shook with nervous exasperation as, pale and resolute, she glared at him.

'Will you ever stop going on about your twenty sous? It's not twenty sous I want – it's five hudnred francs. Yes, five hundred francs a month for clothes. Since you decided to talk about money in the kitchen in front of the maid, then I want to raise the subject too! I've kept quiet about it for long enough. I want five hundred francs!'

Auguste's jaw dropped. But Berthe went on to rehearse the arguments with which her mother had attacked her father every fortnight for twenty years. Did he intend her to go barefoot?

When a man married a wife, he should, at least, manage to clothe and feed her properly. She would rather beg than lead such a poverty-stricken exisence. It wasn't her fault if he was incompetent at managing his business; yes, incompetent, wanting in ideas, in enterprise, knowing merely how to make ends meet. A man whose goal in life should have been to amass a fortune as rapidly as possible, in order to dress her like a queen, and make the people from 'Au Bonheur des Dames' green with envy! Nothing of the sort! With his feeble brain, bankrupty would not be far off. This outburst brought out a veneration and thirst for money handed down to her by her family and born of the first-hand experience of seeing how far they would stoop in order to appear to have it.

'Five hundred francs!' said Auguste, at last. 'I'd rather close the shop down.'

She looked at him coldly.

'You refuse? Very well, then I'll run up debts.'

'You mean more debts, you wretch!'

He grabbed her roughly by the arms and pushed her violently against the wall. Choking with silent anger, she rushed forward and flung open the window as if she were going to jump into the street; but, instead, she turned round and pushed her husband out of the room, stammering: 'Get out, before I do something you'll regret!'

And she noisily bolted the door behind him. For a moment, hesitating, he stood and listened. Then he hurried downstairs to the shop, seized with renewed terror at the sight of Saturnin, whose eyes glittered in the gloom. The noise of their brief wrangle had brought him out of the kitchen.

Downstairs, Octave was selling some scarves to an old lady. He immediately noticed Auguste's agitation; and, out of the corner of his eye, he watched him restlessly pacing up and down in front of the counters. As soon as the customer had gone, Auguste could no longer contain his feelings.

'My friend, she's going mad!' he said, without mentioning his wife. 'She's locked herself in. Will you do me a favour and go up and speak to her? I'm really afraid she might do something silly!'

Octave pretended to hesitate. It was such a delicate matter! However, out of loyalty, he consented. Upstairs, he found Saturnin keeping guard outside Berthe's door. Hearing footsteps, the madman grunted menacingly. But, on recognising Octave, his face brightened.

'Oh, it's you!' he murmured. 'You're all right. She mustn't cry. Be nice to her, think of something. And stay with her, you know. Don't worry about anybody coming. I'm here. If the maid tries to peep, I'll hit her.'

And, sitting down, he kept guard in front of the door. As he was holding a boot in his hand, he began polishing it just to pass the time.

Octave had decided to knock. No answer, not a sound. Then he called out his name. The bolt was immediately drawn back. Berthe, half opening the door, begged him to come in. Then she nervously bolted it again.

'I don't mind *you*,' she said, 'but I won't let *him* in!'

She furiously paced up and down, from the bed to the window, which was still open. She was muttering away incoherently: he could entertain her parents himself, if he felt like it; and explain her absence to them as well, for she certainly wouldn't eat with them; she'd rather die first! She would prefer to go to bed. So saying, she excitedly flung back the cover, shook the pillows and turned down the sheets, so forgetful of Octave's presence that she even began undoing her dress. Then she went off at a tangent to something else.

'Would you believe it? He beat me, yes, beat me! And just because I was ashamed of always going about in rags and asked him for five hundred francs.'

Standing in the middle of the room, Octave tried to find words to pacify her. She shouldn't let herself get so upset. It would work itself out. Then he timidly ventured to help.

'If you're short of money, why not turn to your friends? I should be happy to help. Just a loan, you understand, and you can pay me back.'

She looked at him. After a pause, she replied: 'No, it would never do. What would people think, Monsieur Octave?'

Her refusal was so firm that the question of money was dropped. Her anger, however, seemed to have subsided. Breathing heavily, she dabbed her face, and became very pale, very calm, looking somewhat drained, her eyes large and resolute. As he stood there looking at her, he was overcome by a timidity for which he normally had nothing but scorn. Never before had he felt so in love; the very intensity of his desire made the handsome sales assistant unusually awkward. All the time he was uttering vague suggestions about how Berthe and her husband might patch up their quarrel, he was really debating in his own mind whether he should take her in his arms. But the fear of another rejection held him back. She sat there watching him in silence and looking determined as lines of concentration spread across her brow.

'Heavens!' he falteringly continued. 'You must have patience. Your husband's not a bad sort. If you learn how to manage him, he'll let you have what you want.'

Beneath the empty words, they were both seized by a quite different idea. There they were, alone, free, where no one could find them with the door bolted. Such a secure feeling and the warm atmosphere of the room was getting to them. And yet he didn't dare; the feminine side of him, his womanly intuition heightened in that moment of passion to the point of making him the woman in their encounter. Then, Berthe, as if suddenly remembering her early lessons, dropped her handkerchief.

'Oh, thank you so much!' she said to the young man as he picked it up.

Their fingers touched and this momentary contact brought them closer to each other. She gave him a tender smile; her body relaxed, for she remembered that men hate boards. A girl should not behave like a naïve idiot; she should submit to a little playfulness without seeming to do so, if she wanted to ensure a catch.

'It's getting quite dark,' she said, as she went to close the window. He followed, and in the shadow of the curtains she allowed him to take her hand. She began to laugh louder – a silvery laugh that stunned him; wooing him with all her pretty gestures. Then, as he gradually grew bolder he threw back her head to reveal her soft, youthful neck, palpitating with excitement. Losing control, he kissed her under the chin.

'Oh, Monsieur Octave!' she chided, taken aback, pretending gently to put him in his proper place.

But, instead, catching hold of her, he threw her backwards on the bed, which she had just turned down; and, with his desire satisfied, his callousness reappeared – his ferocious disdain for the female which lurked beneath a semblance of respectful adoration. She submitted tacitly, without pleasure. When she got up again, her wrists bruised and her face drawn by a spasm

of pain, all her contempt for the male became apparent in the
black look which she flung at him. Not a sound could be heard.
Only the regular beat of Saturnin's brush as he sat outside
cleaning the husband's boots disturbed the silence.

Meanwhile Octave, exhilarated by his conquest, kept thinking
of Valérie and of Madame Hédouin. Finally, he was now
something more than that little Pichon woman's lover! It was as
if he were reinstated in his own eyes. Then, noticing Berthe's
pained movements, he felt somewhat ashamed, and kissed her
with great tenderness. She soon recovered her composure, however, as her face resumed its resolute, oblivious expression. With
a gesture she seemed to say, 'Never mind, what's done is done.'
Yet she felt the need to express her sadness.

'Ah, if only you'd married me!' she murmured.

Her words surprised, almost troubled him; but, kissing her
again, he answered: 'Yes, that would have been nice!'

That evening, the dinner with the Josserands proved perfectly
charming. Berthe had never seemed so sweet and gentle. She
never said a word to her parents about the quarrel, and greeted
her husband with becoming deference. The latter, delighted,
took Octave aside to thank him. He did this with such warmth,
and shook his hand so vigorously to show his gratitude, that
the young man felt quite embarrassed. In fact, they were all
especially nice to him. Saturnin, whose table manners were
impeccable, also looked at him with loving eyes, as if he had
shared in sinful pleasure. Hortense even deigned to listen to
him; while Madame Josserand, full of motherly zeal, kept filling
his glass.

'Why, yes,' said Berthe, during dessert, 'I've decided to take
up painting again. I've wanted to decorate a cup for Auguste
for a long time.'

Auguste was greatly touched. Meanwhile, under the table,
Octave kept his foot on Berthe's all through dinner as a kind of
token of possession in the midst of this little bourgeois occasion.
Rachel's searching gaze, however, always made Berthe feel
uneasy. Was it obvious? Clearly, the maid had to be dismissed
or bought.

Monsieur Josserand, sitting next to his daughter, managed to
take her mind off it by slipping her nineteen francs, wrapped up
in paper, under the tablecloth. Leaning towards her, he whis-

pered: 'That's out of my private work, you know. If you've any
debts, you ought to pay them.'

Between her father nudging her, and her lover, who kept
gently stroking her foot, she felt thoroughly relaxed. Life was
going to be less tedious for her. They all let themselves go,
determined to enjoy this peaceful family gathering. It was really
almost too good to be true; their luck must have changed. Only
Auguste was out of sorts, with a splitting headache, as was to
be expected after getting himself so upset. And, at around nine
o'clock, he was forced to go to bed.

CHAPTER 13

For some time now, Monsieur Gourd had taken to prowling about, looking mysteriously ill at ease. One met him moving noiselessly along with eyes peeled and ears strained, forever up and down both staircases, where the tenants had even seen him on his rounds in the middle of the night. It was clear that the moral tone of the house was a matter of concern to him; he sensed a breath of scandal disturbing the bare walls of the icy courtyard, ruffling the claustral serenity of the entrance hall, and menacing the spotless virtue of every hearth on every floor.

One evening Octave found the concierge standing motionless in the dark at the end of his corridor, pressed against the door that opened on to the back stairs. Surprised, he asked him what he was doing there.

'I want to know what's going on, Monsieur Mouret' replied Gourd, simply, as he shuffled off to bed.

The young man was greatly alarmed. Did the concierge have suspicions about him and Berthe? Perhaps he was spying on them. Obstacles were always being put in the way of their affair in a house as carefully supervised as this, whose inhabitants all professed to be so strictly moral. He could therefore only be with his mistress infrequently, notably if she went out in the afternoon without her mother, when he would find a pretext to leave the shop and join her at the end of some street, so that he could stroll with her arm-in-arm for an hour. Since the end of July, Auguste spent every Tuesday night in Lyons, where he had been foolish enough to buy into a silk factory which was in difficulties. Until now, however, Berthe had refused to make the most of this night of liberty. The thought of Rachel made her tremble, and she feared that she might be careless enough to put herself in this girl's power.

It was precisely on a Tuesday evening that Octave caught Monsieur Gourd on the watch near his room. This redoubled his fears. For a whole week he had been vainly imploring Berthe to come upstairs to his room at night when everybody was asleep. Is this what Gourd suspected? Octave went to bed tortured by both passion and fear. His romance was turning

into an insane passion; and he angrily saw himself succumbing
to every sort of sentimental absurdity. As it was, he could never
meet Berthe in a shopping arcade without buying for her
whatever took her fancy. For instance, only the day before, in
the Passage de la Madeleine, she had looked so avidly at a little
bonnet in a window, that he went into the shop and bought it
for her as a present – plain white chip, with just a wreath of
roses – something delightfully simple, but two hundred francs!
A bit steep, he thought.

Towards one o'clock he fell asleep, after feverishly tossing
about for a long while between the sheets. Then he was roused
by a gentle tapping at his door.

'It's me,' faintly whispered a woman's voice.

It was Berthe. Opening the door, he clasped her passionately
to him in the dark. But she had not come upstairs for that.
Having lit a candle, he saw that she was in a state about
something. The day before, as he hadn't had enough money on
him, he couldn't pay for the bonnet at the time, while she was
so delighted that she actually gave the shop her name; and
accordingly they had just sent her the bill. And she was so
worried at the thought that they might call on her husband to
pay it, in the morning, that she had risked coming upstairs,
reassured by the profound silence of the house and feeling
certain that Rachel was asleep.

'Tomorrow morning, without fail!' she said, cajolingly, while
trying to escape his embrace. 'It must be paid tomorrow
morning!'

But he again put his arms around her.

'I want you to stay!'

Only half awake and shivering, he whispered the words close
to her neck as he drew her nearer to the warm bed. She was
only wearing a petticoat and a camisole; to his touch she seemed
naked, with her hair already up for the night, and her shoulders
still warm from the gown she had only just taken off.

'I promise to let you go in an hour. Please stay!'

She stayed. Slowly the clock chimed away the hours in the
voluptuous warmth of the room; and at each stroke he held her
back, pleading so tenderly that she could do nothing but give
in. Then, at about four in the morning, when she was finally
going, they both fell sound asleep in each other's arms. When

they opened their eyes, broad daylight was streaming through the window. It was nine o'clock. Berthe shrieked.

'My God! I'm done for!'

Then came a moment of panic. She leaped out of bed, her eyes heavy with sleep and exhaustion, groping about blindly, throwing on her clothes, gasping with terror. Octave, equally desperate, was blocking the door. She couldn't go out dressed like that at this hour. Was she mad! Somebody might meet her on the stairs; it was far too dangerous. They must find a way for her to get downstairs unobserved. But she obstinately persisted in trying to leave the room there and then, trying to push past him as he barred the doorway. Then he thought of the back staircase. Nothing could be more convenient, and she could sneak back to her own apartment through the kitchen. Only, as Marie Pichon was always in the corridor in the mornings, Octave thought it best, for safety's sake, to go and engage her in conversation while Berthe made her escape. He hurriedly put on his trousers and an overcoat.

'My God! You're taking so long,' muttered Berthe, to whom the bedroom had become like an insufferable furnace.

At last, Octave went out in his quiet, everyday fashion. To his surprise, he found Saturnin with Marie, calmly watching her doing her housework. The madman was glad to hide away here, as he used to, since she left him entirely alone; and he was sure not to get pushed about. He didn't bother Marie, and she willingly tolerated his presence, despite his lack of conversation. He was company in a way, and she went on singing her love song in a low, mournful voice.

'Hello! There you are with your sweetheart!' said Octave, as he skilfully managed to keep the door behind him closed.

Marie turned scarlet. Poor Monsieur Saturnin! Was it likely? Why, if you even touched his hand it seemed to hurt him! The idiot got angry too. He never wanted to be in love, never, never! Anybody who told his sister such a lie would have him to deal with. Surprised at his sudden rage, Octave had to pacify him.

Meanwhile Berthe was making her way down the servants' staircase. There were two floors to negotiate. On the very first step, she was stopped in her tracks by the sound of coarse laughter coming up from Madame Juzeur's kitchen, and, trembling, she paused by the open window overlooking the narrow courtyard. Then, all at once, there was a babel of voices; the morning sewage surged up in waves from this fetid drain. It was the maids, furiously accusing little Louise of spying on them through the keyhole as they were undressing. A fine thing for a dirty little brat like that, not yet fifteen, to do! Louise only laughed louder. She didn't deny it. She'd seen Adèle's backside often enough. What a sight! Lisa was awful skinny and Victoire's belly was the shape of an old cask. To shut her up, the others attacked her with even filthier insults. Then, to divert attention from their nakedness publicised for all to see, they started on their mistresses, stripping them naked this time. Ah, yes Lisa might be skinny, but not as skinny as that second Madame Campardon, a right old dried shark; quite a tasty morsel for an architect. As for Victoire, in her view the Vabres, Duveyriers, and Josserands would be bloody lucky to have a belly as good as hers when they reached her age. And Adèle certainly wouldn't have wanted to exchange her behind for those pathetic little bums on madame's daughters. Thus Berthe, standing motionless and amazed, received this kitchen filth full in the face. She had never dreamed of such a cesspool before stumbling on the maidservants washing their dirty linen in public, at the very moment their masters were busy shaving.

Suddenly a voice exclaimed: 'There goes the bell for sir's hot water.'

Immediately, windows were closed and doors slammed. There was a ghostly silence. Berthe didn't dare move yet. But when she finally started down again, it occurred to her that Rachel might be in the kitchen waiting for her. This made her even more afraid. She dreaded going in now! She would rather have headed for the street, and have run away, never to return. However, she pushed the door half open, and was relieved not to find the maid behind it. Then, as triumphantly as a child finding its way home, she hurried to her room. But there, beside the unslept-in bed, stood Rachel, silent and impassive. She glanced first at the bed, then at madame. Panicking, Berthe stammered out some excuse about her sister being unwell upstairs. Then, appalled at her feeble lie, and aware that the game was up, she burst into tears. Sinking into a chair, she sobbed bitterly.

This lasted a whole minute. Not a word was exchanged; the tranquil silence of the room was broken only by the sound of weeping. Rachel, playing the model of discretion to perfection,

knowing everything, but whose lips are sealed, had turned away
and pretended to be smoothing the pillows, as if she had just
finished making the bed. Then, as the silence seemed only to
distress Berthe even more, Rachel said respectfully, while she
went on with her dusting: 'Madame shouldn't get herself so
worked up, monsieur's no angel.'

Berthe stopped crying. She would tip the girl, that would be
the best thing to do. So she gave her twenty francs on the spot.
Then, somehow, that seemed rather mean, and feeling uneasy,
when she fancied she saw the girl's lip curl disdainfully, she
brought her back from the kitchen to make her a present of a
nearly new dress.

While all this was going on, Octave, for his part, was again
seized with a fear of Monsieur Gourd. On leaving the Pichons,
he had found him standing in exactly the same place as the
night before, spying behind the door of the servants' staircase.
Without daring to speak, he followed Gourd gravely down the
front staircase. On the floor, below, the concierge took out a
key, and went into the room that was let to the distinguished
gentleman who came there one night a week to work. Through
the half-open door Octave got a good view of it; it normally
remained as firmly shut as a tomb. That morning the room was
in a terrible mess, as the man had doubtless been working there
the night before; a large bed with the sheets ripped off it, an
empty wardrobe with a mirrored door which revealed the
remains of a lobster, several opened bottles, and two basins full
of dirty water, one near the bed and the other on a chair. As
calmly as a retired magistrate, Monsieur Gourd proceeded to
empty the basins and rinse them out.

While hurrying to the Passage de la Madeleine to pay for the
hat, Octave was still haunted by the fear of discovery. On his
return, he resolved to sound out the concierge and his wife.
Stretched out in her spacious armchair, Madame Gourd was
taking the air in front of the open window, flanked by two
flower-pots. Near the door mère Pérou, looking humble and
anxious, stood waiting.

'Isn't there any post for me?' asked Octave, as a way of
starting a conversation.

Just then Monsieur Gourd came down from the third-floor
room. Keeping it tidy was the only work in the house that he
continued to do, and he appeared flattered that the gentleman

should confide in him, paying him well, on condition that nobody else touched those basins.

'No, Monsieur Mouret, nothing at all!' he replied.

Though perfectly aware of mère Pérou's presence, Gourd pretended not to see her. The previous day, he had almost thrown her out in his fury at her having spilled a bucket of water in the hall. Now she had come for her wages, trembling at the very sight of him, and cowering against the wall.

While Octave lingered to sweet-talk Madame Gourd, the concierge brutally addressed the poor old woman: 'So you've come for your money, I suppose. How much is it?'

But Madame Gourd interrupted. 'Look, my love; there goes that girl again, with her nasty little beast of a dog.'

It was Lisa, who, a few days ago, had picked up a stray spaniel in the street. Ever since, there had been words exchanged with Gourd and his wife. The landlord would not have animals in the house. Absolutely not! No animals and no women! The little dog was already banned from the courtyard; it did what it had to do in the street. As it had been raining that morning, and the dog's paws were all wet, Monsieur Gourd rushed forward, shouting: 'It's not to run up the stairs, do you hear? Carry it in your arms!'

'Oh, yes! And get myself in a right mess!' said Lisa insolently. 'How tragic, if the back stairs were to get a bit damp! Up you go now, my pet!'

Monsieur Gourd tried to grab the animal, nearly slipped in doing so, and vented his fury on all those filthy maids. He kept up a war of attrition, seething with the rage of a former servant now in a position to give orders.

Lisa suddenly turned round, and, with the sharp tongue of a girl reared in the gutters of Montmartre, shouted: 'Get off my back! You're nothing more than an old flunkey who got the boot! Why don't you go and empty the duke's piss-pots?'

It was the only taunt that could silence Monsieur Gourd, and all the maids made the most of it. He withdrew, fuming, muttering incoherent threats, and saying that he had been proud to serve the duke, while the rotten baggage that she was wouldn't have lasted even a couple of hours in his service. Then the shaking mère Pérou became his target.

'Well, how much do we owe you then? What? Twelve francs sixty-five? That's not possible! Sixty-three hours at twenty centimes an hour ... Oh, you added on the extra quarter of an hour! Not on your nelly! I've told you already, I never pay for extra quarters of an hour.'

And he didn't even give the poor woman her money there and then; instead, he left her shaking with fear, and joined in the conversation between his wife and Octave. The latter skilfully turned to all the worries that a house like this must cause them, hoping to make them talk about the various tenants. Some odd goings-on at times behind those doors, eh?

Then the concierge gravely observed: 'There are things that concern us, Monsieur Mouret, and things that don't. Look over there in the archway, for example. That just drives me mad! Just look at that!'

He pointed to the boot-stitcher, who was passing, the tall, pale girl who had arrived in the middle of old Vabre's funeral. She walked with difficulty, weighed down by her enormous belly, which seemed even bigger in contrast to her scraggy neck and skinny legs.

'What do you mean?' asked Octave, naïvely.

'Why, can't you see? That belly of hers, that belly!'

It was that belly that so exasperated Monsieur Gourd. A single woman with a stomach like that, and Lord knows where she'd got it from, for she was quite flat when she first handed over her money as innocently as in a church. Oh, we would never have rented her a room had we known. And now she had begun to swell out of control, indecently huge!

'You can understand how annoyed I was, sir,' he said, 'and the landlord, too, when I first realised! She should have told us about it, shouldn't she? You don't go barging into a respectable house hiding something like that. But, at first, it was hardly noticeable, it was posible to ignore it, so I kept quiet. I hoped that at any rate she would be discreet. Well, I kept watching her, and she was getting bigger before my very eyes so quickly that it quite alarmed me. Now look at her! She doesn't even try to hide it, but shows it off. She can barely get through the porch now!'

He pointed theatrically at her as she headed towards the backstairs. That belly of hers seemed to cast its shadow over the stony cleanliness of the courtyard, as far as the sham marble and gilded zinc decorations of the hall. It seemed to bring disgrace to the whole building, tainting the very walls and, as it swelled, undermining family values on every floor.

'Upon my word, sir, if this carries on, we would rather retire to Mort-la-Ville, wouldn't we, Madame Gourd? For, thank goodness, we've got enough to live on, and depend on nobody. A house like ours advertised by that kind of belly! It's the talk of the street! Everybody stares when she comes in now!'

'She looks very ill,' said Octave, following her with his eyes, and afraid to show much sympathy. 'She always seems so sad, so pale, so forlorn . . . Yet she must have a lover.'

Gourd reacted violently to this: 'There we have it! Do you hear Madame Gourd? Monsieur Mouret also thinks she's got a lover. Such things obviously don't just happen! Well, sir, I've been watching her for a couple of months, but I've never spotted a man! What a bad lot she must be! Just let me catch her chap and chuck him out! But I can't catch a glimpse of him, and that's what worries me!'

'Perhaps nobody comes to see her?' Octave ventured to suggest.

The concierge looked at him in amazement.

'That wouldn't be natural. Oh, I'm still determined to catch him! I've another six weeks now she's had notice to quit in October. Can you imagine if she gave birth here! And you know, though Monsieur Duveyrier indignantly insisted in her clearing off before that happens, I can hardly sleep myself at night for thinking that she might do the dirty on us, and not wait till then. Well, all these misfortunes would have been avoided if it hadn't been for that old miser Vabre! Just for the sake of an extra hundred and thirty francs, and in spite of my advice. The carpenter ought to have been a lesson to him. But no, not a bit of it; he had to go and take in this boot-stitcher, a a tenant! Go ahead then and ruin your house with labourers, and let lodgings to a bunch of filthy workers. When you get the lower class into your house, sir, you're asking for it!'

And again he pointed to the poor woman's belly, as she struggled up the backstairs. Madame Gourd had to calm her husband down; he took the decency of the house too much to heart. One day it would make him ill. Then, as mère Pérou dared to make her presence known by coughing discreetly, he turned on her once more, calmly deducting the sou she had charged for her extra quarter of an hour. Having at last got her twelve francs sixty, she was just leaving when he offered to take her on again, but at the rate of only three sous an hour. She began to weep, and accepted.

'I can always get someone else to do the work,' he said. 'You're no longer strong enough for it. You don't even do two sous worth.'

Going up to his room again for a moment, Octave felt reassured. On the third floor he caught up with Madame Juzeur, who was returning home. Every morning now she had to come down and look for Louise, who wandered off when sent to the different shops.

'How pleased with yourself you look!' she said, with her subtle smile. 'It's obvious that someone somewhere is spoiling you.'

The remark served to reawaken the young man's fears. He followed her into her drawing-room, pretending to joke with her. Only one of the curtains was pulled back; the carpets and hangings softened the intimate lighting, and in this room, as soft as an eiderdown, one scarcely caught a sound from the outside world. She made him sit next to her on the low, wide sofa. But, as he did not take her hand and kiss it, she asked, coquettishly: 'So you don't love me any more?'

Blushing, he declared that he adored her. Then, smothering a nervous giggle, she offered him her hand. He was obliged to raise it to his lips, so as to quash any suspicions that she might possibly have. But she withdrew it at once.

'No, no! don't pretend to get excited . . . It doesn't give you any pleasure at all. I can feel that it doesn't. Besides, it's only natural.'

Whatever did she mean by that? He caught her by the waist; but, however much he questioned her, she wouldn't answer, yielding to his embrace but shaking her head. In order to make her speak, he began tickling her.

'Why, it's because . . . because you're in love with somebody else,' she murmured.

She mentioned Valérie, and reminded him of the evening at the Josserands', when he devoured her with his eyes. Then, when he swore that he had never had her, she laughingly replied that she was only teasing him. Only there was another whose favours he had enjoyed, and this time she named Madame Hédouin, growing more amused at his energetic protests. Who

was it, then? Was it Marie Pichon? Well, he couldn't deny
having had her. But he did so nevertheless; she shook her head
and assured him that the little bird that had told her was never
wrong. Then, to get the names of these women out of her, he
had to go further, caressing her all over to get her to speak.

However, she had not yet mentioned Berthe's name. He was
about to let her go when she said: 'Then there's one last one.'

'Which last one?' he anxiously enquired.

Tightening her lips, she obstinately refused to say more until
he had unsealed them with a kiss. She couldn't mention the
name, for that person getting married had been her idea.
Without actually naming her, she spoke of Berthe. Then, into
her soft bosom, he made a full confession, experiencing a certain
cowardly pleasure as he did so. How silly of him to hide it from
her! Perhaps he had thought she would be jealous! Why should
she be? She hadn't granted him her favours, had she? Oh,
nothing but a little childish fun, like now, but not that, oh, not
that! For, after all, she was a virtuous woman, and she was
almost vexed that he should have thought her likely to be
jealous.

All the while she lay back languidly in his arms, talking about
her cruel husband, who, after one week of marriage, had
deserted her. An unfortunate woman like herself knew all too
much about the tempests of the heart! She had guessed what
she called Octave's 'goings-on' a while ago, for nobody could
be kissed in the house without her hearing it. Ensconced on the
broad sofa, they shared their secrets, unconsciously breaking off
for an intimate caress now and again. She told him he was an
idiot, for it was entirely his fault he hadn't succeeded with
Valérie; she could have helped him to have her long ago, if only
he had asked her advice. Then she questioned him about little
Marie Pichon, hideous legs and nothing much between them,
eh? Yet she always came back to Berthe, charming with lovely
skin, and the feet of a princess. But it wasn't long before she
had to put an end to this little game, pushing him away.

'No, leave me alone! I have my principles! And it doesn't give
you any pleasure either. Ah, you say it does; but I know better!
It's all your nonsense just to flatter me! It would be dreadful if
it did give you any pleasure. You keep that for her. Now, be off
with you, you naughty man!'

And she sent him away after making him solemnly promise

to come and confess himself often to her, hiding nothing if he wished her to take charge of his love affairs.

On leaving her, Octave felt more at ease. She had restored his good humour, and her complicated notion of virtue positively amused him. As soon as he went down to the shop, he gave Berthe, interrogating him with her eyes, a reassuring nod about the hat bill. Thus the whole dreadful panic of the morning was forgotten. When Auguste came back, shortly after lunch, he found them both as usual: Berthe bored to death at the cashier's desk, and Octave gallantly measuring silk for a lady.

From then on, however, the lovers' rendezvous became less frequent still. He, full of passion, followed her despairingly into every corner, begging her to meet him, whenever and wherever she liked.

She, on the other hand, with the indifference of a spoiled child, took no pleasure in such a guilty passion, except for the secret outings, the presents, and the hours of forbidden luxury spent in cabs, theatres and restaurants. She was the product of her education, with her lust for money, pretty clothes and expensive treats; and she had soon grown as tired of her lover as she had of her husband, finding him far too demanding for what he gave her in return: it required no special effort, on her part, not to satisfy him. Exaggerating her fears, she constantly kept refusing him. Never again in his room; oh, no! She would die of fright! And her apartment was out of the question, for someone might come in. And when, to get around the problems of the house, he begged her to let him take her to a hotel for an hour, she then began to cry, saying that he really couldn't have much respect for her. However, the expenditure went on regardless, and her whims only increased. After the hat, she had wanted a lace fan; not to mention the numerous other little things that took her fancy here and there, in the shop windows. Though he didn't yet dare say no to her, his sense of thrift came back to him as he saw all his savings being frittered away. Like the practical man he was, it seemed to him to be pretty stupid to be paying out, when all that he got from her in return was her foot under the table. Clearly Paris had brought him bad luck; first rejections, and then this silly love affair, which was draining his wallet. He certainly couldn't be accused of using women to succeed. He found a certain sense of humour in this;

it was consolation for his hidden anger at a scheme which, so far, had proved such a dismal failure.

Auguste certainly didn't get in their way. Ever since getting involved in the disastrous business venture in Lyons, he had been racked more than ever by his neuralgic headaches. Berthe had felt a sudden thrill of delight as, on the first of the month, she saw him one evening put three hundred francs under the bedroom clock for her clothes allowance. And, despite the fact that it was less than she'd asked for, she lovingly flung herself into his arms with gratitude. On this occasion, the husband enjoyed a night of passion such as the lover never obtained.

And that was how September passed, as tranquil as the house itself, emptied by the summer. The second-floor people had gone to the coast in Spain, earning a contemptuous shrug of the shoulders from Monsieur Gourd. How absurd! Really distinguished people were quite content to go to Trouville!* Ever since the beginning of Gustave's holidays, the Duveyriers had been staying at their country house at Villeneuve-Saint-Georges.* Even the Josserands had gone to stay for a fortnight with friends near Pontoise,* while letting it be rumoured that they were going to some fashionable spa. With the house empty, the apartments deserted, and the staircase wrapped in an even drowsier silence, Octave seemed to think that there would be less danger; and he kept on at Berthe until, from sheer weariness, she allowed him in, one evening, when Auguste was away at Lyons. But this almost came to a sorry end as well. Madame Josserand, who had returned two days before, was seized with such violent indigestion after dining out, that Hortense rushed downstairs to fetch her sister. Fortunately, Rachel was just finishing clearing her pots and pans, so she was able to let Octave slip out by the servants' staircase. After this scare, Berthe took advantage of it to refuse him everything, as she had before. And they made the mistake of not keeping the maid sweet. She waited on them with her coldly respectful air, deigning neither to see nor hear what was going on around her. However, as madame was always hankering after money, and as Monsieur Octave had already spent far too much on presents, she could hardly contain her scorn for this dump where the lady's lover did not even tip her ten sous when he slept there. If they thought that they'd bought her for all eternity with twenty francs and an old gown, they were greatly mistaken. She was worth a lot more than that! From then on, she was less obliging, no longer sweeping over their tracks, although they were never aware of her ill-humour; tipping was the least of their worries, given how often they fought over a time and a place to steal a kiss. The silence of the house grew even more pervasive; and Octave, in his search for some safe corner, was always bumping into Monsieur Gourd, on the watch for shameful things that made the very walls blush, creeping about surreptitiously, haunted by the bellies of pregnant females.

Madame Juzeur often had to console this lovesick young man who could never be with his mistress, and gave him the very best advice. At one point, Octave's desire reached such a pitch that he thought of asking her to lend him her apartment. No doubt, she wouldn't have refused, but he feared Berthe would be disgusted if she knew he had confided in Madame Juzeur. He also thought of making use of Saturnin; perhaps the madman, like a faithful dog, could stand guard over them in some secluded room. But lately his mood had been somewhat strange, sometimes displaying exuberant affection for his sister's lover, while at others staring at him sulkily, with fiery glances of sudden hatred and suspicion. They were like the nervous and violent ourbursts of jealousy of a woman. He had noticed this particularly on mornings when Saturnin had come across him laughing and joking with little Marie Pichon. As a matter of fact, Octave never passed Marie's door now without going in, unconsciously drawn back in by some strange fancy, a pang of reawakened desire. He was passionately in love with Berthe; but frustration renewed his feelings for Marie, more tender than they'd ever been during their affair. It was wonderful to look at her, to touch her, to exchange pleasantries with her, all those playful manoeuvres of a man wanting to repossess one woman while secretly embarrassed about loving another. On the days when Saturnin caught him hovering round Marie, the madman glared at him wolfishly, ready to bite; not ready to forgive him and kiss his hand like some tame animal until he saw that he was back at Berthe's side, her loving, faithful slave.

As September drew to an end and the residents were about to return, Octave, in his torment, had a mad idea. It so happened that Rachel, whose sister was getting married in the provinces, had asked to be away the Tuesday night Auguste was in Lyons. Octave's idea was that they should sleep together in the maid's room, where no one would ever dream of looking for them. Offended by such a proposal, Berthe immediately rejected it; but, with tears in his eyes, he begged her to agree, and spoke of leaving Paris and his suffering once and for all. At last, worn down by his entreaties, but in such a state that she hardly knew what she was doing, she consented. Every detail of the plan was fixed. On Tuesday evening, after dinner, they had tea at the Josserands' to allay any suspicion. Trublot, Gueulin and Uncle Bachelard were all there. Even Duveyrier dropped in, much later, as he occasionally slept in town now, allegedly because of early business appointments. Octave made a point of chatting to each of them and then, at the stroke of midnight, he slipped away and locked himself into Rachel's room, where Berthe was to join him an hour later, when everybody was asleep.

Upstairs, he spent the first half-hour getting the room ready. In order to overcome Berthe's revulsion, he had promised her that he would change the sheets and bring all the necessary linen himself. Thus he proceeded to make the bed, slowly and clumsily, fearing that someone would hear him. Then, like Trublot, he sat down on a trunk and tried to wait patiently. One by one the servants came up to bed; and, through the thin partitions, he could hear the sounds of women undressing and relieving themselves. It struck one o'clock, then quarter past, then half past. He grew anxious; why was she so late? She must have left the Josserands at one o'clock, at the very latest; and it would not take her more than ten minutes to get back to her apartment, and leave it again by the servants' staircase. When it struck two, he imagined all sorts of disaster. At last, thinking that he recognised her footsteps, he heaved a sigh of relief. As he opened the door to give her some light, he froze. Outside Adèle's door, Trublot, bent double, was looking through the keyhole; and, terrified by this sudden shaft of light, he jumped back.

'What! You here again?' said Octave, in a tone of annoyance.

Trublot began to laugh, without seeming in the least astonished at finding Octave there at that time of night.

'Just imagine,' he whispered, 'that idiot Adèle didn't give me her key, and now she's gone down to be with Duveyrier ... You look surprised. Didn't you know that Duveyrier was sleeping with her? Well, it's true my friend. He's made it up with his wife, who lets him have his way now and again; however, as she keeps him on short rations, he has to fall back

on Adèle. It's convenient for him, you see, when he comes up to
Paris.'

Then, breaking off, he bent down again to take another look,
muttering between clenched teeth: 'No, there's nobody there!
He's keeping her longer this time ... What an empty-headed
slut that Adèle is! If she had only given me the key, I could have
waited for her in bed, in the warmth.'

Then he went back to the attic where he had been hiding,
taking Octave with him, who wanted to know how the evening
had ended at the Josserands'. But Trublot never let him get a
word in, for he went on talking about Duveyrier, in the inky
darkness and stuffy atmosphere under the rafters. Yes! The
brute had wanted Julie, at first, but she was a bit too fussy for
that sort of thing, and besides, in the country, she had taken a
fancy to little Gustave, a lad of sixteen, who seemed promising.
His nose thus put out of joint, Duveyrier, who dared not to try
it on with Clémence because of Hippolyte, had thought it wise
to choose someone outside his own household. How on earth
he had ever managed to pounce on Adèle nobody knew: behind
some door no doubt, for the dirty creature backed up with as
little resistance as she did when slapped, so she was hardly likely
to refuse the landlord.

'For the last month he's never missed one of the Josserands'
Tuesdays,' said Trublot. 'I shall have to find Clarisse for him,
so as to make him leave us in peace.'

Octave finally managed to ask him how the evening had
ended. Berthe had left before midnight, apparently quite composed. No doubt she was waiting for him in Rachel's bedroom.
But Trublot, delighted to have met him like this, wouldn't let
him go.

'It's stupid of her to keep me hanging about for so long,' he
continued. 'I'm half asleep as it is. My boss has put me into the
liquidation department. Up all night three times a week, my
friend! If only Julie were here, I know she'd make room for me;
but Duveyrier has only brought Hippolyte with him from the
country. By the way, you know Hippolyte, that great lout who's
sleeping with Clémence? Well, I just caught him in his shirt,
sneaking into Louise's bedroom, that ugly brat whose soul
Madame Juzeur is so anxious to save! What a triumph for
Madame Anything-you-like-except-that! A puny fifteen-year-
old, a filthy bundle picked up off a doorstep, what a dainty

morsel for that strapping, big-boned fellow, with his damp
hands and his bull neck! I don't give a damn myself, but it's
disgusting all the same!'

Bored as he was, Trublot that night seemed full of philosophical insights. He went on muttering: 'Well, well, like master, like
servant! When filthy landlords set the example, the staff may be
forgiven for doing likewise. There's no doubt about it, France is
a bloody shambles!'

'Good-bye. I'm off,' said Octave.

But Trublot still wouldn't let him go, insisting on going
through each and every maid's room in which he might have
slept if the summer season had not emptied so many of them.
The worst of it was that they all double-locked their doors, even
when they just went along to the end of the corridor, as they
were all so frightened of being robbed by each other. There was
no point in trying it on with Lisa, who seemed to have rather
odd tastes. He hadn't been tempted by Victoire, though ten
years ago she might have been a bit spicy. What he most
deplored was Valérie's mania for changing her cook; it was
becoming positively unbearable. He counted them on his fingers,
a whole string of them. One who asked for chocolate in the
mornings; one who didn't like her master's eating habits; one
carted off by the police just as she was roasting a piece of veal;
one who was so strong that she broke everything she touched;
one who had a maid to wait on her; one who went out in her
employer's gowns, and who slapped her mistress when she
ventured to comment on it. All these within a month! Why there
wasn't even time to go into the kitchen and touch them up!

'Oh! And then,' he added, 'then there was Eugénie. You must
have noticed her, a tall fine girl, a real Venus, my dear chap. No
joke! People used to turn round in the street to look at her.
Well, for ten days the whole house was upside down. All the
women were furious; the men could hardly contain themselves.
Campardon was licking his lips and Duveyrier's ploy was to
come up here and see if the leaks were coming from the roof.
You've never seen anything like it; the whole damned place fired
up from cellar to attic! But I have my doubts. She was a bit too
smart. Believe me, my dear chap, the ugly and the stupid are
best, as long as you get enough of them, that's my opinion, and
what I like myself. And how right I was. Eugénie was sent
packing when madame finally found out, on seeing her sheets,

which were black as soot, that she entertained the coal-merchant from the Place Gaillon every morning; sheets so black that to wash them must have cost a small fortune. Well, and what happened? As a result of it, the coal-merchant was more than a little off-colour; and the coachman, left behind by the people on the second floor, that great oaf who's had every one of them, he had a dose of it too. He had it so badly, he still limps because of it. But I don't feel sorry for him. He's loathsome!'

At last Octave managed to escape, and as he was leaving Trublot there in the deep gloom of the attic, the latter suddenly exclaimed: 'But I say, what are you doing up here in the maids' quarters anyway? Ah, you rogue! So you come for some too!'

And he laughed gleefully. Promising not to tell, he sent him on his way, wishing him a pleasant night. He himself was determined to wait for that ragbag Adèle, who tended to stay if she was in a man's bed. But Duveyrier surely wouldn't dare to keep her till the morning.

On getting back to Rachel's room Octave was once more disappointed. Berthe hadn't come. He had now become angry; she had simply fooled him; her promise had simply been a tactic to put an end to his pleas. While he worked himself into a state, waiting for her, she was calmly sleeping, glad to be alone and have the large broad marital bed to herself. However, instead of going back to his own room to sleep, he stubbornly lay there in his clothes and spent the night planning his revenge. This bare, cold maid's room irritated him, with its dirty walls, its squalor, and its insufferable smell of slovenly females; he shrank from admitting to himself to what depths his frenzied passion had lowered him in his craving to appease it. Far away in the distance, he heard it strike three. Strapping maidservants snored away to his left; occasionally, bare feet made the boards creak, and then a splashing sound, like a fountain, rippled along the floor. But what most unnerved him was an endless moaning to his right, the feverish cry of someone in pain, and unable to sleep. Was she in labour? That poor woman! All alone in her agony, cooped up under the roof in one of those miserable closets hardly big enough for her belly.

About four o'clock, Octave was again disturbed, this time by Adèle coming to bed and Trublot joining her. They very nearly had a quarrel. She protested that it wasn't her fault; the landlord had kept her, and she couldn't help it. Then Trublot accused her of becoming arrogant. But she began to cry, she wasn't arrogant at all. What sin had she committed that God allowed every man in the place to have her! When one had finished there was another; there seemed no end to it. She never tried to lead them on, and she got so little pleasure out of it that she went around looking sluttish on purpose, so as not to give them any encouragement. And yet they always wanted more, adding to everything else she had to do. It was killing her, not to mention Madame Josserand, bullying her to scrub the kitchen every morning.

'You lot,' she stammered out between her sobs, 'can sleep as long as you like afterwards. But I have to work like a slave. No! There's no justice in this world. I'm fed up with it all.'

'There, there, don't upset yourself,' Trublot said gently in a sudden burst of fatherly tenderness. 'Mind you, some women would be glad to be in your place! As the men like you, you great silly, you should let yourself be liked!'

At daybreak, Octave fell asleep. There was a deep silence everywhere. Even the boot-stitcher no longer groaned, as half-dead she lay holding her belly with both hands. The sun was shining in through the narrow window when the young man was awoken by the door being opened. It was Berthe, who had come up just to see, unable to resist. At first she had dismissed the idea, and then had invented various pretexts, like needing to tidy the room if, in his rage, he had left it in a mess. She certainly hadn't expected to find him there. When she saw him get up from the little iron bedstead, looking pale and threatening, she was taken aback, and, with head lowered, listened as he vented his fury. He urged her at least to offer some sort of explanation.

After a long pause, she murmured: 'At the last moment I couldn't; it was too vulgar . . . I do love you, I swear I do! But not here, not here!'

Then, as he approached her, she drew back, fearing that he might want to make the most of this opportunity. This was indeed what he had in mind. It struck eight; all the servants had gone down, and Trublot had also just left. Then, as he caught hold of her hands, saying that when one loves a person one doesn't mind anything, she complained of the smell of the room, and went to open the window. But he again drew her towards him and, affected by his distress, she was about to give in when a torrent of filthy language rose up from the courtyard below.

'Oh, you cow! You slut! I've had enough! Your rotten dishcloth has fallen on my head again!'

Berthe, trembling, broke away from his embrace, whispering: 'There! Do you hear that? Oh, no, not here, I beg you! I would be so ashamed of myself. Do you hear those girls? They make my blood run cold. The other day they really upset me. No! leave me alone, and I promise you that you can have it, next Tuesday, in your own room.'

Standing there, not daring to move, the two lovers were forced to overhear everything.

'Just let me catch sight of you,' Lisa angrily continued, 'and I'll chuck it back in your face.'

Then, leaning out of her kitchen window, Adèle replied: 'What a row about a little bit of rag! Why, I only used it yesterday for washing up with, and it fell out the window quite by accident.'

So a truce was declared, and Lisa asked her what they had had for dinner the night before. What! Another stew? What skinflints! If she lived in a dump like that she'd buy herself cutlets, see if she wouldn't! And she kept on urging Adèle to pinch the sugar, the meat, and the candles, just to show her independence; as for her, she was never hungry, so she let Victoire rob the Campardons, without even claiming her share.

'Oh! cried Adèle, who was gradually being corrupted. 'The other night I hid some potatoes in my pocket, and they burned my thigh. Oh, it was fun! And, you know, I love vinegar! I don't care a bit, I just drink it out of the cruet now!'

It was then Victoire who leaned out, after finishing a glassful of the cassis and brandy to which Lisa sometimes treated her in the mornings, as a reward for making sure nobody found out where she went at all hours of the day and night. Standing at the back of Madame Juzeur's kitchen, Louise stuck out her tongue at them and Victoire turned on her.

'Wait a bit, you guttersnipe; I'll stuff that tongue of yours somewhere in a minute!'

'Come on, then, you drunk old cow!' cried Louise. 'I saw you yesterday throwing up all over your plates.'

Immediately a fresh wave of filth surged up against the walls enclosing the stinking hole. Even Adèle, now well versed in

Parisian patter, hurled abuse at Louise, while Lisa cried out: 'I'll shut her up if we've any of her cheek! Yes, yes, you little bitch, I'll tell Clémence. She'll sort her out. Isn't it disgusting at her age? Licking men's balls when she still needs her own arse wiped! But hush! There's the chap himself, and what a filthy swine he is!'

Hippolyte had just poked his head out of the Duveyriers' window. He was cleaning his master's boots. In the spite of everything, the others greeted him politely, for he was an aristocrat among servants; and as he despised Lisa, so she despised Adèle, looking down on her from a greater height than the rich dismiss those of their class fallen of hard times. They asked Hippolyte for news of Mademoiselle Clémence and Mademoiselle Julie.

Good Lord! They were bored to death down there in the country, but they were both pretty well. Then, changing the subject, he said: 'Did you hear that woman last night, tossing and turning with her stomach pains? Didn't it get on your nerves? It's a good job she's leaving. I'd half a mind to call out, "push hard and get it over with!"'

'Monsieur Hippolyte is absolutely right,' said Lisa. 'Nothing is worse than a woman who's always got the stomach-cramps. Thank God, I don't know what it's like, but I think I should try and bear it so that other folk might sleep.'

Then Victoire, wanting some fun, turned to Adèle: 'You great clot! When you had your first baby, did it come out in front or behind?'

They all shook with laughter at such a crude joke, while Adèle, looking scared, replied: 'A baby? No, that mustn't happen! It's not allowed, and besides I don't want one.'

'My girl,' said Lisa, gravely, 'it happens to everyone. And I don't suppose the Lord made you different from anyone else!'

Then they talked about Madame Campardon: at least she didn't have any fears on that score; in her state, it was the only thing she could count her blessings for. All the ladies of the house were discussed in this respect, Madame Juzeur, who took her own precautions; Madame Duveyrer, who was disgusted by her husband; Madame Valérie, who got her babies made for her elsewhere, because her husband wasn't man enough to make even a bit of one. And gales of laughter rose up from the fetid depths of the courtyard.

Berthe turned paler. She waited, afraid to leave the room. She looked down at the floor, as if violated in Octave's presence. As for him, he realised the maids had ruined his chances; to make love with that filthy commentary going on would be impossible. His desire ebbed away, leaving him weary and extremely sad. Berthe trembled. Lisa had just mentioned her by name.

'Talking of high jinks, I know someone who seems to be having a whale of a time! Adèle, isn't it true that your mademoiselle Berthe was already up to all sorts of little private games, when you were still washing her petticoats?'

'And now,' said Victoire, 'she gets her husband's clerk to give her a quick once over. No danger of any dust settling there!'

'Keep your voice down!' warned Hippolyte.

'What for? Her pig of a maid isn't there today. Sly devil, she is, that looks as if she'd eat you if you mention her mistress! She's a Jewess, you know, and they say she murdered somebody once at her place . . . Perhaps the handsome Octave dusts her off in a quiet corner too. His boss must have employed him just to make babies for him, the great imbecile!'

Then Berthe, in unbearable anguish, looked up at her lover, imploringly, as she stammered out: 'Good God! Good God!'

Octave caught hold of her hand and pressed it. He too was choking with helpless anger. What was to be done? He dared not show his face and silence those hussies. The filth bubbled on, of a kind Berthe had never heard, while the cesspool brimmed over, as it had done each morning, without her having any suspicion of its existence. Their affair, so carefully concealed, was now trailed through all the garbage and slops of the kitchen. Nobody had ever suspected it, but the maids knew everything. Lisa related how Saturnin played the gooseberry; Victoire made fun of the husband's headaches; he would do well to keep his good eye on the look-out. Even Adèle had a go at her mistress's daughter, letting the others in on Berthe's ailments, soiled undergarments and the intimacies of her dressing-table.

And their kisses too were tainted by the gleeful tide of muck; and their secret meetings; in fact, everything about their love that had been theirs alone.

'Look out, down below!' cried Victoire suddenly. 'There goes them stinkin' carrots from yesterday. They'll do for that old sod Gourd!'

Out of sheer spite, the maids used to throw down left-overs into the courtyard, which the concierge had to sweep up.

'And there goes a lump of rotten kidney!' cried Adèle, in her turn. All the dregs of their saucepans, all the scum from their pots, were flung out too, while Lisa went on about Berthe and Octave, tearing apart all the lies they used to hide their bare-faced adultery. Hand in hand, and looking into each other's eyes, the lovers stood there aghast; and their fingers grew icy cold, confronted as they were by the sordid nature of their liaison, and feeling impotent and exposed in the face of the hatred of their servants. So this was what it had all come to, fornication amid a pelting rain of rotten vegetables and putrid meat!

'And, you know,' said Hippolyte, 'the young chap don't care a damn for his missis. He's only got hold of her to help him get on in the world . . . At heart, he's a right old miser, a chap without any scruples whatever, who, while pretending to love women, wouldn't mind giving them a jolly good beating!'

Berthe, looking at Octave, saw him turn pale. He was so distressed and his expression so changed that it frightened her.

'My word! They deserve each other!' replied Lisa. 'I wouldn't give much for her, either. Badly brought up, a heart of stone, utterly selfish, sleeping around for money; yes, for money! I know that kind of woman, and I wouldn't mind betting that she doesn't even enjoy it!'

Berthe's eyes overflowed with tears. Octave watched her face crumble. It was as if they had both been flayed alive, stripped naked in front of each other, without being able to protest. The young woman, stifled by the rising stench of this cesspool, needed to escape. He made no attempt to stop her; their mutual self-disgust made being near each other excruciating, and they longed for the relief of being out of sight.

'Next Tuesday then, in my room. You promised!'

'Yes, yes!'

In turmoil, she fled, He stayed behind, pacing up and down, his hands twitching nervously as he rolled the bedlinen he'd brought upstairs into a bundle. He shut out the maid's gossip until one phrase suddenly caught his ear.

'I tell you Monsieur Hédouin died last night . . . If only the good-looking Octave had foreseen that, he might have perse-vered with Madame Hédouin, for she's loaded.'

This news, leaking from the cesspit, touched him to the core. So Monsieur Hédouin was dead! He was filled with regret and, thinking aloud, couldn't refrain from responding: 'Yes, dammit! I was a fool.'

When Octave finally went downstairs with his bundle of sheets, he met Rachel coming up to her room. A few minutes earlier she would have caught them. Downstairs, she had found her mistress in tears again; however, this time she had got nothing out of her, neither a confession nor a sou. She was furious, convinced that they had used her absence to get together, and thus cheated her of her little extras. She gave Octave a black, threatening scowl. A strange schoolboy bashfulness prevented him from giving her ten francs, while, anxious to show that he had nothing on his conscience, he went into Marie Pichon's. But a grunt from the corner made him turn around. Saturnin got up, exclaiming, in one of his jealous fits: 'Watch out! We're enemies from now on!'

That very morning happened to be 8 October, and the boot-stitcher had to get out before noon. For a week, Monsieur Gourd had been watching her stomach with increasing unease. That belly would surely never wait until the 8th. The poor woman had begged the landlord to let her stay a few days longer and wait for the birth, but her request had been met with an indignant refusal. At every moment she was seized with pains; on the last night, she was afraid she would give birth all by herself. Then, about nine o'clock, she began to move her things out, helping the lad, who had his hand-drawn cart in the courtyard below, leaning against the furniture or sitting down on the staircase when bent double by a particularly excruciating cramp.

Monsieur Gourd, however, hadn't found out anything; there was no man, after all. He had been made a fool of. All that morning he went wandering about, angry and glum. When Octave ran into him, the thought that he, too, knew about his affair filled him with dread. If he did know about it, his greeting was no less polite than usual, for, as he had already said, what did not concern him did not concern him. That morning, he had also raised his cap to the mysterious lady as she noiselessly hurried away from the gentleman's on the third floor, leaving only a faint perfume of verbena behind her. He had also greeted Trublot, as well as the other Madame Campardon and Valérie.

Those were all gentry. If the young men were caught coming
out of the maidservants' bedrooms, or the ladies tripping downstairs, in tell-tale dressing-gowns, why, that was none of his
business. What concerned him did concern him, and he kept his
eye on the few miserable bits of furniture belonging to the boot-
stitcher, as if that elusive man were making his escape in one of
the drawers.

At quarter to twelve the girl appeared, her face as white as
wax, looking as sad and as despondent as ever. She could hardly
walk and, until she got out into the street, Monsieur Gourd was
all of a tremble. Just as she was giving up her key, Duveyrier
came through the hall, so feverish after his night that the
blotches on his brow were blood-red. He assumed a haughty
and implacably virtuous demeanour, as the poor thing and her
belly went past him. Shameful and resigned, she bowed her
head; and following behind the little cart she left with the same
despairing gait with which she had arrived on the day that the
black funeral hangings had enveloped her.

It was only then that Monsieur Gourd had his triumph. As
though it was that belly that had removed all the unhealthiness
from the house, all those shameful goings-on that caused the
very walls to blush, he exclaimed to the landlord: 'Well, good
riddance! We'll be able to breathe again now, for, upon my
word, it was getting positively disgusting! It's like a hundred-
weight off my chest . . . You see, sir, in a respectable house like
this, there shouldn't be any women, and least of all labouring
women.'

CHAPTER 14

The following Tuesday, Berthe did not keep her promise. She had, in fact, told Octave beforehand not to expect her, during a hurried meeting that same evening after closing up the shop; she sobbed bitterly, for she had been to confession the day before, feeling the need of religious solace, and was still under the influence of the Abbé Mauduit's solemn exhortations. Ever since her marriage she had given up going to church; but, having been splattered by the maids' foul language, she had become so sad, so forlorn, and felt so tainted, she had returned to her childhood faith for an hour, ardently longing to be made pure and good. When she got back, after she and the priest had wept together, she was appalled that she had sinned. Octave shrugged his shoulders, powerless and enraged.

Then, three days later, she again promised to see him the Tuesday afterwards. At one of their rendezvous, in the Passage de Panoramas, she had noticed some Chantilly lace shawls, and went on about them, her eyes full of desire. Thus, on the Monday morning, the young man told her, laughingly, so as to soften the brutality of such a bargain, that if she really kept her word she would find a little surprise waiting for her in his room. She guessed what he meant and again began to cry. No, no, she couldn't possibly come now; he was ruining everything. She had simply mentioned the shawl on a whim; in fact, she would throw it into the fire if he gave it to her as a present. Nevertheless, the next day they came to a satisfactory arrangement; at half past twelve that night she was to knock three times very gently on his door.

That day, as Auguste was leaving for Lyons, Berthe thought that he looked somewhat strange. She had caught him whispering with Rachel behind the kitchen door; what's more, his face was all yellow, he was shaking violently, and one of his eyes was closed up. But, as he was complaining about his headache, she thought he must be unwell, and assured him that the journey would do him good. No sooner had he gone than she went back to the kitchen, and feeling uneasy, tried to sound Rachel out. The maid, however, maintained her respectful demeanour, as

severe and as discreet as she'd been when she first came to work
for them. Berthe, somehow, sensed that she was dissatisfied, and
felt how stupid it had been to give the girl twenty francs and a
dress, and then suddenly stop all such extras, even though she
couldn't do much about it, given that she was always in want
of a five-franc piece herself.

'My poor girl,' she said, 'I've not been over-generous to you,
have I? But that isn't my fault. I haven't forgotten you, and I'll
make it up to you some day.'

Rachel coldly replied: 'Madame owes me nothing.'

Then Berthe went to fetch two of her old blouses, as proof of
her good intentions. But when the maid took them from her,
she said she would use them as kitchen cloths.

'Much obliged, madame, but calico gives me a rash; I only
wear linen.'

However, she seemed so polite that Berthe was reassured; she
confided in her that she would be sleeping away from home,
even asking her to leave a lamp on just in case. The front door
was to be bolted, and she would go out by the back stairs and
take the key with her. Rachel received her instructions as calmly
as if she had been told to cook a beef stew for the following
day.

That evening, as a tactical ploy, because Berthe was dining
with her parents, Octave accepted an invitation from the Campardons. He counted on staying there until ten o'clock, and
then going up to his room to wait as patiently as possible until
half past twelve.

The meal at the Campardons' was a patriarchal occasion.
Seated between his wife and her cousin, the architect lingered
lovingly over the food, plain, homely fare, as he termed it,
wholesome and copious. That evening there was chicken with
rice, a joint of beef and some fried potatoes. Ever since cousin
Gasparine had taken to managing everything, the whole household lived in a perpetual state of indigestion, for she was so
good at economising, paying less money and getting twice as
much meat as anybody else. Campardon had three helpings of
the chicken, while Rose stuffed herself with rice. Angèle only
had the beef; she adored the blood, and Lisa slyly gave her extra
spoonfuls of it. Gasparine, on the other hand, hardly touched a
thing, saying her stomach had shrunk.

'Eat up!' cried the architect to Octave. 'You never know if this meal will be your last!'

Madame Campardon, in a whisper, told the young man yet again what a brilliant idea it was to have their cousin come and live with them: she had made it a happy home; and there had been at least a hundred per cent reduction in their expenditure; the servants had been brought into line; Angèle was being set a wonderful example.

'And, above all,' she murmured, 'Achille's always as happy as a fish in water, and I have to do absolutely nothing ... Just fancy! She actually washes and dresses me now. I don't have to lift a finger; she's taken over absolutely everything that used to be such a chore.'

Then the architect entertained them with how he had got the better of 'those clowns at the Ministry of Education'.

'As you can imagine, my dear boy, they caused me no end of bother about the Evreux job ... Of course, all I wanted to do was please His Grace. However, the new kitchens and the heating apparatus came to more than twenty thousand francs. No funds had been made available, and it wasn't easy to squeeze twenty thousand francs out of the slender sum allowed for repairs. Not to mention the pulpit, for which I had a grant of three thousand francs, but which came to nearly ten thousand, making another seven thousand to be accounted for ... somehow. So, this morning, I was summoned to the ministry, where a big lanky chap began to give me a dressing-down. But I'm not the type to stand for that sort of thing! So I flatly told him that I would send for His Grace himself, who would soon come to Paris to explain matters. He suddenly became so polite, it was incredible; it makes me laugh now to think of it! They're scared stiff of the bishops at the moment. If I had a bishop to back me, why, I could demolish Notre-Dame and rebuild it, if I wanted to, and spit in the government's face!'

They all had a good laugh at the minister's expense, talking about him disdainfully, with their mouths chock-full of rice. Rose declared that it was best to be on the side of religion. Ever since his restoration of Saint-Roch, Achille had been overwhelmed with work. The most important families clamoured for his services; he couldn't get through it all, and had to work through the night. God certainly was well disposed towards them, and they gave Him thanks both morning and evening.

During dessert, Campardon suddenly exclaimed: 'By the way, my friend, I suppose you've heard that Duveyrier has found . . .' he was going to say Clarisse. But he remembered that Angèle was present so, with a side glance at his daughter, he added: 'He found his relative, you know.'

By biting his lip and winking, he at last made Octave understand, who at first quite failed to catch his meaning.

'Yes, Trublot told me. The day before yesterday, when it was pouring with rain, Duveyrier is sheltering in a doorway, and there she is, there was his relative, just opening her umbrella . . . For the last week, Trublot had been on the look-out for her, so as to bring her back to him.'

Angèle modestly looked down at her plate, filling her mouth with food. The family were most careful that the conversation should never transgress the bounds of decency.

'Is she pretty?' asked Rose of Octave.

'That's a matter of taste,' he replied. 'Some people might think so.'

'She had the cheek to come to the shop one day,' said Gasparine, who, thin as she was, detested skinny people. 'She was pointed out to me . . . a real beanpole!'

'Never mind,' said the architect; 'Duveyrier's back in harness. His poor wife, you know . . .'

He was going to say that the poor wife was probably overjoyed and greatly relieved. But he remembered that Angèle was there, so he remarked solemnly: 'Relations don't always get on together . . . Well, well, every family has its troubles!'

Lisa with a napkin over her arm, looked across the table at Angèle who, so as not to laugh out loud, hastily began to take a long drink, concealing her face with her glass.

Shortly before ten o'clock, Octave professed to be so tired that he simply had to go to bed. Despite Rose's tender attentions and the general bonhomie, he felt ill at ease, aware of Gasparine's ever-increasing hostility. He had done nothing, however, to provoke this. She merely hated him because he was a good-looking fellow who, she suspected, had had all the women in the house; and this exasperated her, although she herself didn't fancy him in the least. It was merely the thought of his conquests that instinctively roused her feminine wrath, now that her own looks had faded all too soon.

Directly after he left, the Campardons talked of going to bed.

Every evening, before getting into bed, Rose spent a whole hour getting ready, using face washes and scents, doing her hair, checking her eyes and mouth, and ears; even putting a little patch under her chin. At night she replaced her sumptuous gowns by equally sumptuous nightcaps and chemises. On this particular evening she chose a nightdress and cap trimmed with Valenciennes lace. Gasparine had been helping her, holding basins for her, mopping up the water she had spilled, drying her with a face-towel, tending to her needs with far greater skill than Lisa.

'Ah! Now I feel comfortable,' said Rose, at last, stretching herself out in her bed, while her cousin tucked in the sheets and raised the bolster.

She smiled contentedly as she lay there alone in the middle of the large bed. With her plump, soft body swathed in lace, she looked like some beautiful woman about to welcome the lover of her dreams. When she felt pretty, she could sleep better, so she said. Well, it was her only remaining pleasure.

'Everything all right, eh?' said Campardon, as he came in. 'Well, good-night, my pet.'

He pretended that he had got some work to do. He would have to stay up. Rose got cross, insisting that he get some rest; it was so foolish of him to wear himself out in this way!

'Now, listen to me, you just go to bed! Gasparine, promise me you'll make him go to bed!'

Gasparine put a glass of sugar and water and one of Dickens's novels by the bed. She looked at Rose, without replying, and then, bending over her, whispered: 'You do look nice tonight!'

Then she kissed her on both cheeks, with dry lips and bitter mouth, with the subdued air of a poor, plain relation. Flushed, and suffering from frightful indigestion, Campardon, too, looked down at his wife. His moustache quivered slightly as, in his turn, he stooped to kiss her.

'Good-night, my dear!'

'Good-night, my love! Now, mind you go to bed at once.'

'Don't worry,' said Gasparine, 'if he's not in bed and asleep by eleven o'clock, I'll get up and turn the lamp out.'

About eleven o'clock, after yawning over some plan for a Swiss cottage that a tailor in the Rue Rameau had taken into his head to have built, Campardon slowly undressed, thinking meanwhile of Rose lying there so clean and pretty. Then, after

turning down his own bed, because of the servants, he went and
joined Gasparine in hers. It was most uncomfortable for them,
as there was no elbow-room, and he, in particular, had to
balance himself on the edge of the mattress, so that the next
morning one of his thighs was quite stiff.

Just then, as Victoire, having washed up, had retired for the
night, Lisa came in to see if Angèle needed anything. Her young
mistress was waiting for her in bed; and it was there that,
unknown to her parents, they played endless games of cards on
the bedspread. And as they played, they inevitably talked about
Gasparine, that dirty creature, whom the maid coarsely laid
bare before little Angèle. In this way they made up for their
humble, hypocritical demeanour during the day; and Lisa took
a certain base pleasure in corrupting Angèle, satisfying the girl's
morbid curiosity now that she was on the verge of puberty.
That night they were furious with Gasparine because for the
last two days she had locked up the sugar which the maid
usually filled her pockets with, afterwards emptying them on to
the child's bed. Nasty old cow! They couldn't even get a lump
of sugar to munch when they went to sleep!

'And she gets loads of sugar from your father anyway,' said
Lisa, laughing knowingly.

'Oh, yes, I bet she does!' murmured Angèle, also laughing.

'What does he to do her, your father? Show me again . . .'

The young girl threw her bare arms around the maid's neck
and squeezed her, kissing her violently on the mouth, repeating
'Yes, like that . . . yes, like that!'

It struck midnight. Campardon and Gasparine were moaning
in the discomfort of their narrow bed, while Rose, ensconced in
the centre of hers stretched out her limbs and read Dickens till
tears filled her eyes. A deep silence filled the house; the chaste
night cast its shadows over this virtuous family.

On going upstairs, Octave found that the Pichons had company. Jules called to him, saying that he must come in and have
a glass of something with them. Monsieur and Madame Vuillaume were there; they had made their peace with Jules and
Marie after her pregnancy. Her confinement had taken place in
September. They had even consented to come to dinner on
Tuesday to celebrate the young woman's recovery. She had only
been out the day before for the first time. Eager to appease her
mother, who was annoyed by the very sight of yet another baby

girl, Marie had sent the child out to nurse, not far from Paris.
Lilitte was asleep with her head on the table, knocked out by a
glass of wine, which her parents had forced her to drink to toast
her little sister.

'Well, one can manage with two,' said Madame Vuillaume,
after clinking glasses with Octave. 'Only that's the last one, my
dear son-in-law, do you understand?'

They all began to laugh but the old lady remained perfectly
serious, saying: 'I can't see what there is laugh at. We'll put up
with this baby, but I swear that if another one comes along . . .'

'Oh, if another one comes along,' cried Monsieur Vuillaume,
completing her sentence, 'you'll prove yourselves to be both
heartless and stupid. Damn it! Life's a serious matter, and one
must exercise restraint when one hasn't got a fortune . . .'

Then, turning to Octave, he added: 'As you know, I've been
decorated. Well, I can assure you that, in order not to dirty too
many ribbons, I never wear my Légion d'Honneur when I'm at
home. Now, if I'm ready to deprive my wife and myself of that
pleasure, I'm sure that our children can deprive themselves of
the pleasure of producing more daughters. No, sir, it's not just
a question of money.'

The Pichons obediently promised that they would behave
themselves from now on. If they didn't, they knew there would
be real trouble.

'Why, rather than go through what I've gone through,' cried
Marie, pale as death . . .

'I'd sooner have my leg cut off,' declared Jules.

The Vuillaumes gave a nod of satisfaction. As they'd given
their word, they would be forgiven. Then, as it was just striking
ten, they all embraced one another affectionately, and Jules put
his hat on to see them to their omnibus. So touching, indeed,
was this return to their old habits that, on the landing, they
kissed again.

After, leaning over the banisters, standing next to Octave, to
see them go, Marie took him back with her to the dining-room,
saying: 'Mamma doesn't mean to be unkind; and, after all, she's
right. Children are no joke!'

Having shut the door, she began to remove the glasses, which
were still on the table. The small room, with its smoking lamp,
was still quite warm from this little family gathering. Lilitte was
still sleeping, her head resting on a corner of the oilcloth.

'I'm off to bed,' said Octave, sinking back comfortably into a chair.

'What! So early?' she replied. 'It's not like you to be so conscientious. Have you got something to do early tomorrow morning?'

'No, I haven't,' he said. 'I'm sleepy, that's all. But I can stay another ten minutes or so.'

He remembered that Berthe would not be coming up till half past twelve. There was plenty of time. He had been so obsessed for weeks by the thought of having her in his arms for a whole night, that now he was no longer pulsating with excitement. The feverish impatience of waiting all day, as he counted every minute bringing him nearer to satisfying his tormented desire, had worn him out, leaving him empty.

'Another glass of cognac?' asked Marie.

'I don't mind if I do.'

He thought that it might perk him up. As she took the glass from him, he seized her hands and held them in his, while she smiled, unafraid. Pale as she was after what she had been through physically, he found her very attractive; surging within him, the rising tide of his former passion took over his whole body. Yes, he had given her back to his husband that evening long ago, having placed a fatherly kiss on her brow; now he wanted to have her again, an urgent and violent desire extinguishing a longing for Berthe who suddenly seemed remote.

'You're not afraid today then?' he asked, as he squeezed her hand tighter.

'No, because from now on it's impossible. But we'll always be good friends.'

With that she let him understand that she knew everything. Saturnin must have told her. Moreover, she always noticed on what nights Octave received a certain person in his room. Observing his pallor and anxiety, she hurriedly assured him that she would never tell anyone. She wasn't angry; on the contrary, she wished him every happiness.

'Why, I'm married, you know,' she said; 'so I couldn't hold it against you.'

Taking her on his knee, he exclaimed: 'But it's you I love!'

He spoke the truth, for at that moment it was Marie that he loved, with a deep and infinite passion. Thoughts of his new affair, and the two months spent hankering after another woman, had vanished. Once more he saw himself in the little apartment, kissing Marie on the neck when Jules's back was turned, with her as tender as ever, offering no resistance. That was real happiness. Why had he ever turned it down? It filled him with regret. He still desired Marie and felt that he would be eternally unhappy if he could never have her again.

'Leave me alone,' she murmured, trying to get away from him. 'You're being silly, and you'll only hurt me . . . Now that you're in love with somebody else, what's the point of tormenting me?'

She tried to say no in her gentle, languid way, simply put off by something that she didn't very much enjoy. But he lost his head, and squeezed her more vigorously, kissing her breasts through her coarse woollen bodice.

'It's you I love, can't you see that? I swear on my life I'm not telling you a lie. Open my heart, and you'll see. Now, please be nice! Just this once, and then never again, if you don't want to. You really are too cruel; if you don't let me, I shall die!'

Marie became powerless, paralysed by the dominating force of this man's will. She was a mixture of kindness, fear and stupidity. She moved away, as if anxious first to carry the sleeping Lilitte into the other room. But he held her back, afraid she would wake the child. And she surrendered, in the same place where a year ago she had passively fallen into his arms. There was a sort of buzzing silence throughout the little apartment as the whole house lay submerged in the peace. Suddenly the lamp grew dim, leaving them nearly in darkness, as Marie got up and just turned up the wick in time.

'You aren't cross with me?' asked Octave, with tender gratitude; never before had he experienced such bliss.

She had stopped winding up the lamp, and with her cold lips gave him one last kiss, as she said: 'No, because you enjoy it. But, all the same, it's not right, on account of that other person. With me, it doesn't mean anything any more.'

Her eyes were wet with tears and, though not annoyed, she seemed sad. After leaving her, he felt dissatisfied with himself; he would have preferred to go straight to bed and sleep. He had satisfied his appetite but it had left a disagreeable after-taste; a stale lust that left a lingering bitterness. The other woman was now coming, and he would have to wait for her; it was a thought that weighed terribly on his mind; if he was lucky, she might not be able to come. And after all those frenzied nights dreaming up wild schemes as to get her into his room for just an hour. Perhaps she would again fail to keep her word. It was almost too much to hope for.

It struck midnight. Tired as he was, Octave sat up and waited, dreading hearing the rustle of her skirts along the narrow passage. By half past twelve, he was in a real state; and at one o'clock he thought he was safe, though his relief was mixed with the vague irritation of a man who has been fooled by a woman. Then, yawning vigorously, and just as he was about to undress, there were three gentle knocks at the door. It was Berthe. Both put out and flattered, he met her with outstretched arms; but trembling she pushed him aside and listened at the door which she hastily closed behind her.

'What is it?' he asked, lowering his voice.

'I don't know,' she stammered, 'but I'm frightened. It's so dark on the staircase; I was convinced someone was following me. How stupid this all is! I'm sure something terrible is going to happen.'

This had a chilling effect on both of them. They didn't even kiss each other. However, she looked enchanting in her white gown with her golden hair twisted up into a coil at the back of her head. As he gazed at her, she seemed to him far prettier than Marie; but he no longer desired her; the whole thing was a bore. She sat down, to recover her breath, and then she suddenly pretended to be furious as she caught sight of a box on the table, which she was sure contained the lace shawl she'd been going on about for the last week.

'I'm going,' she said, without moving from her chair.

'What do you mean?'

'Do you think I'm for sale? You always manage to hurt my feelings. Now, tonight, you've spoiled everything. Why did you go and buy it, after I told you not to?'

However, she got up and finally consented to look at it. But she was so disappointed on opening the box, that she couldn't stop herself from indignantly exclaiming: 'What, it's not the Chantilly one, it's llama!'

Trying to cut back on his present-giving, this time Octave had been unable to resist being mean. He tried to explain to her that some llama was splendid, just as good as Chantilly, and he launched into his sales patter, just as if he were standing behind the counter, making her feel the lace, while assuring her that it would last for ever.

But she shook her head disdainfully, saying: 'The fact is, this only cost one hundred francs, whereas the other would have come to three hundred.'

Then, noticing that he turned pale, she attempted to mend matters by adding: 'Of course, it's very kind of you, and I'm much obliged. It's not what a gift costs, but the thought behind it, that counts.'

Then she sat down again, and there was a pause. After a while he asked if she was going to get into bed. Of course she was; but she was still shaken after her fright on the stairs. Then she told him how worried she was about Rachel, and how she had caught Auguste whispering with her behind the door. Yet it would have been so easy for them to bribe the girl by giving her a five-franc piece now and again. But you had to get the five-franc pieces first, and she never ever had any money for herself. As she spoke, her voice grew harsher; the despised llama shawl exasperated her so much, that in the end, she began berating her lover in exactly the same terms as she used to with her husband.

'What kind of a life is this? Never a penny to spare, always being refused the slightest thing! Oh, I'm sick to death of it!'

Octave, who was unbuttoning his waistcoat as he paced the room, stopped and said: 'What's the point of telling me all this?'

'The point, my dear sir? The point? Well, there are certain things that anybody with any sensitivity would do without my having to raise the matter ... Don't you think you ought to have put me at ease by bribing that girl from the start?'

She paused, adding ironically: 'It wouldn't have ruined you, I'm sure!'

There was another silence. Octave went on walking up and down. At last he said: 'I'm sorry for your sake that I'm not rich.'

The quarrel became more heated, reaching the levels of a marital row.

'Go on! Tell me that I'm after you for your money!' she cried, with all the bearing of her mother, whose very words seemed to leap to her lips. 'I'm a mercenary woman, am I not? Well, I admit it. I am mercenary because I'm a sensible woman. It's no use denying it, money's money; and when I only had twenty

sous I always said that I'd got forty, because it's far better to be
envied than pitied.'

As this point he interrupted her, saying wearily, like a man
suing for peace: 'Look, if you're that upset about the llama
shawl, I'll get you a Chantilly one!'

'Your shawl!' she went on in a fury. 'I wasn't even thinking
about your shawl! It's everything else that drives me mad, don't
you see? Oh! You're just like my husband! If I walked around
the streets barefoot, you wouldn't care the least bit! Yet, if a
man's fond of a woman, mere decency ought to make him feel
bound to clothe and feed her. But that's what no man will ever
understand. Why, between the pair of you, you'd let me go out
with nothing on but a nightdress, if I was quite content to do
so.'

Worn out by this domestic quarrel, Octave decided not to
respond, having noticed that Auguste sometimes got rid of her
in this way. He slowly undressed and let the storm pass over,
reflecting how unlucky he had been in his love affairs. Yet he
had felt a passionate desire for Berthe, so passionate, in fact,
that it had interefered with all his plans, and now that she was
here in his bedroom, all she could do was quarrel with him, and
give him a sleepless night, just as if they had been married for
six months.

'Let's go to bed, now,' he said, at last. 'We thought we were
going to be so happy together. It's silly to waste our time
arguing like this!'

Then, anxious to make up, feeling no desire, yet wishing to
be polite, he tried to kiss her. But she pushed him aside and
burst into tears. Seeing that reconciliation was hopeless, he
began furiously taking off his boots, determined to get into bed
whether she did so or not.

'Go ahead! Complain about my outings too!' she sobbed.
'Tell me that I cost you too much! Ah, I see it all now! It's
because of that wretched present! If you could shut me up in a
box, you'd do it. Going out to see my friends isn't a crime. And
as for Mamma . . .'

'I'm going to sleep,' he said, jumping into bed. 'I wish you'd
undress, and forget that mother of yours. She's given you a
damned nasty temper, let me tell you.'

Mechanically, she began undressing herself, raising her voice
as she became more and more excited.

'Mamma has always done her duty. It's not for you to discuss her here. How dare you mention her name? That's just about the last straw, to begin abusing my family!'

The tie of her skirt had got into a knot, and she snapped it viciously. Then, sitting down on the bed to pull off her stockings, she exclaimed: 'How I regret ever having been so weak! One would be far more careful if one could foresee how things would turn out!'

She had nothing on but her underwear. Her legs and arms were naked, the nakedness of a soft, plump little woman. Her breasts heaving in anger, peeped out of their lace covering.

Lying with his face to the wall, Octave suddenly turned round exclaiming: 'What's that? You're sorry you ever loved me?'

'Of course I am. A man like you, incapable of understanding a woman's feelings.'

As they glared at each other, their faces assumed a hard, loveless, expression. She was resting one knee on the edge of the mattress, her breasts thrust forward, her thigh bent, in the pose of a pretty woman just getting into bed. But he had no eyes for her rosy flesh and the supple fleeting outline of her back.

'Good God! If I could have my time again!'

'You mean you'd have somebody else, I suppose?' he said brutally.

She had stretched out alongside him under the bedclothes, and was just about to reply in the same tone, when suddenly there was a violent knock at the door. Struck dumb with fear, hardly understanding at first, they both remained motionless, then they heard a muffled voice.

'Open the door! I can hear you, doing all those filthy things! Open the door, or I'll smash it in!'

It was Auguste's voice. Yet the lovers still didn't move. There was such a buzzing in their ears that they could think of nothing. They felt very cold lying there next to each other, as cold as corpses. Finally, Berthe jumped out of bed with the instinctive need to escape from her lover; while Auguste, outside, kept repeating: 'Open the door! Open the door, I say!'

A moment of terrible confusion and unspeakable anguish followed. Berthe, deathly pale, rushed around the room, desperately looking for a way out. Octave's heart was in his mouth at each blow on the door, against which he had automatically gone to lean, as if to reinforce it. The noise grew unbearable, the idiot would soon rouse the whole house; they would have to open up. But when she realised what he was going to do, Berthe clung to his arms, begging him not to with her terrified eyes. No, no; for mercy sake! He would burst in on them, armed with a knife or a pistol! Growing as pale as she was, as her fear rubbed off on him, he hurriedly pulled on his trousers, whispering to her to get dressed. She sat there naked, doing nothing, unable to even find her stockings. Meanwhile, Auguste grew even more serious.

'Ah, so you won't open and you won't answer! Very well, you'll see!'

Ever since paying last quarter's rent, Octave had been asking the landlord to have two new screws fixed to the staple of his lock, as it had worked loose. Suddenly the wood cracked, the lock gave way, and Auguste, losing his balance, fell sprawling into the middle of the room.

'Damn it!' he cried.

He was holding merely a key, and his hand, grazed by his fall, was bleeding. He got up, livid with shame and fury at the thought of so absurd an entry. Waving his arms about wildly, he tried to launch himself on Octave. But the latter, despite the embarrassment of being caught barefoot with trousers buttoned awry, caught him by the wrists and, being the stronger, held these as in a vice.

'Sir,' he cried, 'you are violating my home. It's disgraceful, and ungentlemanlike!'

And he very nearly struck him. During their brief struggle, Berthe rushed out through the shattered door in her chemise. In her husband's bloody fist she thought she saw a kitchen knife, and she seemed to feel the cold steel between her shoulders. As she fled along the dark passageway she fancied she heard the sound of blows, though unable to tell by whom these were dealt or received. Voices, half unrecognisable, exclaimed: 'Whenever you please, I'm at your service!' 'Very good; you'll be hearing from me.'

She made it to the back stairs at a run. But after rushing down two flights as if pursued by tongues of flame, she found her kitchen door locked and remembered that she had left the key upstairs in the pocket of her dressing-gown. Besides, there was no lamp, not a ray of light from beneath the door; it was obviously the maid who'd betrayed them. Without stopping to get her breath back, she flew upstairs again and passed along the corridor leading to Octave's room, where the two men were still shouting furiously.

They were still at it; perhaps, she would have time. And she ran down the front staircase, hoping that her husband had left the door of their apartment ajar. She would lock herself into her bedroom and not let anybody in. But once again she found herself confronted by a closed door. Finding herself locked out of her own home and naked, she lost her head, and rushed from floor to floor like some hunted animal in search of a hiding-place. She would never dare to knock at her parents' door. For an instant she thought of taking refuge in the concierge's lodge, but the shame of it made her turn back. Then, leaning over the banisters, she stopped to listen, deafened by the beating of her heart in that great silence, and her eyes dazzled by lights that seemed to rise up out of the inky darkness. The knife, that awful knife in Auguste's bloody fist! Its icy blade was about to be buried in her flesh! Suddenly there was a noise. She imagined he was coming after her, and she shivered with fright to the very marrow of her bones. Then, as she was just outside the Campardons' door, she rang wildly, desperately, almost breaking the bell.

'Goodness gracious! Is the house on fire?' cried a voice anxiously from within.

The door was immediately opened by Lisa, who had only just left Angèle's bedroom, on tiptoe, carrying a candlestick. The furious tug at the bell had made her jump, just as she was crossing the hall. The sight of Berthe in her chemise utterly amazed her.

'Whatever's the matter?' she asked.

Berthe came inside, slammed the door, and leaning against the wall, gasped: 'Shh! Don't make a noise! He wants to murder me!'

Lisa was unable to get a more rational explanation out of her before Campardon, looking very worried, appeared on the scene. This extraordinary noise had disturbed Gasparine and himself in their narrow bed. He had only put on a pair of underpants, his puffy face was sweating, with his yellow beard flattened and covered with white fluff from the pillow, as he breathlessly sought to put on the bold front of a husband who sleeps in his own room.

'Is that you, Lisa?' he cried, from the drawing-room. 'What's going on? Why aren't you upstairs?'

'I was afraid that I hadn't locked the door properly, sir, and that stopped me from going to sleep, so I just came down to make sure. But it's madame . . .'

At the sight of Berthe in her nightgown, leaning against the wall, Campardon was also frozen with fear. A sudden sense of propriety made him feel to check that his underpants were buttoned up. Berthe seemed to have forgotten that she was not wearing any clothes.

'Oh, please, monsieur, let me stay here . . . He wants to murder me!'

'Who does?'

'My husband.'

But now, behind the architect, Gasparine had arrived. She had taken the time to put on a dress, though her unkempt hair was also covered with fluff. Beneath the material you could see the outline of her bony shoulders and flat chest. She was angry that her pleasure had been interrupted. The sight of Berthe, soft, plump and virtually stark naked, only served to make it worse.

'Well, whatever have you been doing to your husband?' she asked.

At this simple question, Berthe was overcome with shame. Suddenly conscious of her nakedness, she blushed from head to foot and held both arms across her bosom, shielding herself from scrutiny, and stammering: 'He found me . . . he caught me . . .'

The other two understood, and exchanged a look of disgust. Lisa, lighting up the scene with her candle, pretended to share the indignation of her superiors. However, that was as far as they got by way of finding out what was going on, for Angèle came running in, pretending to have just woken up, rubbing her eyes all heavy with sleep. This lady in her nightdress brought her to a sudden halt, sending a shiver through every muscle of her slender, girlish frame.

'Oh!' she cried, in surprise.

'It's nothing. Go back to bed!' shouted her father.

Then, aware that he must invent some tale or other, he said the first thing that came into his head, an utterly ludicrous lie at that.

'Madame's sprained her ankle coming downstairs, and has asked us to help her. Go back to bed or you'll catch cold.'

Lisa almost laughed as her eyes met Angèle's eager stare, and the child went back to bed, flushed and rosy, delighted to have been treated to such a sight. At that moment, Madame Campardon could be heard, calling to them from her room. She had been so engrossed by her Dickens that she still had not put her light out, and wanted to know what was the matter. What was going on? Who was there? Why didn't they come and tell her?

'Come this way, madame,' said Campardon, taking Berthe in. 'You wait there a moment, Lisa.'

Rose lay there in the broad bed, spread out luxuriously like a queen, looking as tranquil and as serene as some idol. She had been greatly moved by her bedtime reading, and had placed the Dickens on her bosom, and as she breathed it rose and fell. When Gasparine briefly explained matters, she also appeared to be extremely shocked. How could anyone go and sleep with a man who wasn't her husband? She was repelled by the very idea of what she herself was no longer in the habit of doing. But the architect was by now glancing furtively at Berthe's breasts. For Gasparine this was the last straw.

'I can't have this,' she cried. 'Really, madame, it's too disgraceful! Cover yourself up at once!'

She herself flung one of Rose's shawls round Berthe, a large knitted shawl which was lying about. It hardly reached her thighs, and Campardon, in spite of himself, kept his eyes on her legs.

Berthe was still trembling from head to toe. Though safe enough where she was, she still glanced at the door and shuddered. Her eyes filled with tears as she begged the lady, who looked so calm and comfortable, to protect her.

'Oh, madame, hide me! Save me! He's going to murder me!'

There was a pause. They all looked questioningly at each other, without attempting to conceal their disapproval of such scandalous behaviour. Imagine rushing in like that after midnight in your nightwear and waking people up! No, such things were not done; it showed a lack of tact, and placed them in a far too embarrassing position.

'We have a little girl in the house,' said Gasparine at length. 'Please consider our moral duty, madame.'

'The best thing would be for you to go to your parents,'

suggested Campardon. 'If you would allow me to accompany you, I . . .'

Berthe was again filled with terror.

'No, no! He's on the stairs. He'll kill me!'

And she begged to be allowed to stay, anywhere, on a chair, till morning, when she would slip out quietly. To this the architect and his wife were inclined to consent, he being perfectly happy to carry on feasting on her charms, and she being interested in such a midnight drama. Gasparine, however, remained firm. Yet her curiosity finally got the better of her.

'Wherever were you?'

'Upstairs, in the room at the end of the passage, you know.'

Campardon instantly threw up his arms, exclaiming: 'What! With Octave? Impossible!'

Such a pretty, plump woman with that puny little Octave. The thought of it vexed him. Rose, too, felt annoyed, and she immediately became severe. As for Gasparine, she was beside herself, stung to the quick by her instinctive hatred of that young man. So he'd been at it again. He'd had them all, she was convinced of that, but she wasn't going to be stupid enough to keep them warm for him in her own apartment.

'Put yourself in our place,' she said, sternly. 'As I said before, we have a little girl in our home.'

'Then there's the house,' Campardon chimed in. 'There's your husband, too, with whom I have always been on the best of terms. He would have a right to be astonished. We can't be seen to approve of your conduct, madame, conduct that I do not presume to judge, yet which is perhaps, shall I say, somewhat . . . er . . . thoughtless, don't you think?'

'Of course, it's not that we're judging you,' continued Rose. 'But people are so spiteful! They might say that you used to meet here. And my husband, you know, does work for such a narrow-minded lot. The least stain on his good name, and he would lose everything. But, madame, if you don't mind my asking you, how is it that religion did not prevent you from doing such a thing? Only the other day the Abbé Mauduit was talking to us about you in such affectionate and fatherly terms.'

Berthe looked first at one, then at another, as they spoke, utterly dazed and bewildered.

In her terror she was beginning to realise what she had done, and was surprised to find herself there. Why had she rung the bell? Why had she disturbed them all at that time of night? Now she saw plainly who they were: the wife, taking up the whole bed, the husband in his underwear, their cousin in a thin petticoat, both covered with white feathers from the same pillow. They were right, she should never have burst in on them like that. Then, as Campardon gently pushed her towards the hall, she left without even replying to Rose's question on religion.

'Would you like me to accompany you as far as your parents' door?' asked Campardon. 'You should be with them.'

She refused, with a terrified gesture.

'Then wait a moment; I'll just see if there's anybody on the stairs. I'd be terriby upset if anything happened to you.'

Lisa had stayed in the hall holding a light. He took it from her, and went outside on to the landing, coming back at once.

'There's no one there, I assure you. Make a run for it.'

Whereupon Berthe, who so far had not uttered another word, threw off the woollen shawl and flung it on the floor, saying: 'Here, take this, it's yours. He's going to murder me, so what's the use?'

Then, in her nightdress, she ran out into the dark, just as she had come.

Campardon, furious, double-locked the door, mumbling: 'We don't want any blood spilled here, thank you.'

Then, as Lisa sniggered behind him, he added: 'It's true; they'd be coming here every night if we let them in. It's every man for himself. I wouldn't mind giving her a hundred francs, but with my good name, not on your life!'

In the bedroom, Rose and Gasparine were regaining their composure. Such brazen behaviour! Running up and down stairs stark naked! Really, some women lost all self-respect when the mood took them! But it was nearly two o'clock, they must get to sleep. So they all kissed again. 'Good-night, my love.' 'Good-night, my sweet.' Ah, how nice it was to love one another and always to get along, when one saw what awful things happened in other people's homes! Rose went back to her Dickens, which had slipped on to her stomach. He was all she needed; she would read another page or two and then fall asleep, emotionally exhausted, letting the book slide under the sheets as she did every night. Campardon followed Gasparine, making her get into bed first. Then he lay down beside her, and they both grumbled, for the sheets had got cold and they felt most uncomfortable, and it would take them a good half-hour to get warm.

Meanwhile Lisa, before going upstairs, went back to Angèle's room and said to her: 'The lady sprained her ankle, so . . . show me how you think she did it!'

'Why, like this, like this!' replied the child, as she flung her arms round the maid's neck and kissed her on the lips.

On the staircase Berthe shivered. It was cold there, as the hot-air stoves were never lit before the 1st of November. However, her terror subsided. She had gone down and listened at the door of her apartment; nothing, not a sound. Then she had come up again, not daring to go as far as Octave's room, however, but listening at a distance. There was a deathly silence everywhere, not a whisper to be heard. She squatted down on the mat outside her parents' door, with a vague intention of waiting for Adèle. The thought of having to confess everything to her mother tormented her as much as if she were still a little girl in disgrace. Gradually, however, the solemn staircase filled her with anguish once again; it was so dark, so austere. No one could see her; and yet she was overcome with embarrassment sitting there in her nightdress amid such respectable gilt and fake marble surroundings. It was as if she were subject to the dignified displeasure of the conjugal alcoves behind those broad mahogany doors. Never had the house appeared to her so saturated with purity and virtue. A ray of moonlight streamed through one of the windows on the landing, giving it the appearance of a church. From basement to attic the peace was all-pervasive; traces of middle-class virtue floated everywhere in the gloom, while her naked body gleamed in the eerie light. The very walls seemed scandalised, and she drew her nightdress closer around her, covering up her feet, terrified at the thought of seeing the spectre of Monsieur Gourd emerge in velvet cap and slippers.

Suddenly a noise made her jump up in a fright; and she was about to thump with both fists at her mother's door, when the sound of someone calling stopped her in her tracks.

It was a voice faintly whispering: 'Madame! Madame!'

She looked over the banisters, but could see nothing.

'Madame! Madame, it's me!'

And Marie appeared, also in her nightdress. She had heard

the commotion, and had slipped out of bed leaving Jules fast asleep, while she stopped to listen in the darkness of her little dining-room.

'Come in. You're in trouble, and I'm on your side.'

She gently comforted her, telling her everything that had happened. The two men had not hurt each other. Octave, cursing horribly, had pushed the chest of drawers in front of his door, to shut himself in, while the other had gone down carrying a bundle with him, some of her things that she had left, her shoes and stockings, which he must have automatically rolled up in her dressing-gown on seeing them lying around. Anyhow, it was all over. Next day they would prevent them from fighting their duel.

But Berthe wouldn't go beyond the doorway, still frightened and abashed at entering a stranger's home. Marie had to take her by the hand.

'You can sleep here, on my sofa. I'll lend you a shawl, and I'll go and see your mother. My goodness, what a dreadful thing! But when you're in love, you never stop to think of the consequences!'

'Not that we get much pleasure out of it!' said Berthe, as she heaved a sigh of regret for all the emptiness and absurdity of her night. 'It's not surprising that he cursed and swore. If he's like me, he must have had more than enough of it!'

They were both going to speak about Octave, when suddenly they stopped, and feeling their way in the darkness, fell into each other's arms, sobbing bitterly. Semi-naked, they clasped each other convulsively, with their hot tears streaming passionately over their nightdresses in disarray. It was a sort of final collapse, an overwhelming sorrow – the end of everything. Nothing more was said, but they continued to weep in the darkness amid the profound silence of the respectable, sleeping household.

That morning, as the house awoke, it wore its most majestic air of middle-class decorum. On the staircase there was not a trace of the scandals of the night; the stucco panelling no longer reflected a lady scampering past in her nightshirt, nor did the carpet reveal the spot where the odour of her white body had evaporated. Only Monsieur Gourd, going on his rounds at about seven, sensed something as he passed the walls. However, what did not concern him did not concern him, and when, as he came down, he saw Lisa and Julie evidently discussing the scandal, for they seemed so excited, he fixed them with an icy stare, separating them at once. Then he went outside, to be sure that everything was quiet in the street. It was. However, the maids must already have been gossiping, for the neighbours kept stopping, and tradesmen stood at their shop doors looking up at the different floors, just as people stare open-mouthed at houses where some crime has been committed. On seeing so handsome a façade, however, the curious were silenced, and politely went on their way.

At half past seven Madame Juzeur appeared in her dressing-gown; she was looking for Louise, or so she said. Her eyes glittered; her hands were feverishly hot. She stopped Marie, who was coming upstairs with her milk and tried to make her talk. But she got nothing out of her, even failing to learn how the mother had received her errant daughter. Then, pretending to wait a moment for the postman, she stopped at the Gourds', asking, at last, why Monsieur Octave hadn't come down. Perhaps he was unwell? The concierge said that he didn't know, but Monsieur Octave never came down before ten minutes past eight anyway. Just then, the other Madame Campardon passed by, pale and stiff; they all greeted her. Madame Juzeur, with no option but to go back upstairs, was lucky enough to catch Campardon just coming out, buttoning his gloves. At first they exchanged rueful glances; then he shrugged his shoulders.

'Poor things!' she murmured.

'No, no! It serves them right!' he said, viciously. 'They deserve to be made an example of. A fellow I introduced into a respectable house, begging him not to bring in any women; and just to show what he thinks of my advice, what does he do? He goes to bed with the landlord's sister-in-law! It makes me look such a fool!'

Nothing further was said. Madame Juzeur went back indoors while Campardon hurried downstairs in such a rage that he tore one of his gloves.

As it struck eight, Auguste, worn out and his features contorted by a severe migraine, crossed the courtyard on his way to the shop. He had come down by the back stairs, ashamed and dreading the thought of meeting anyone. However, he couldn't let his business drop. At the sight of Berthe's empty desk in the middle of the counter, his feelings almost overcame him. The assistant was taking down the shutters, and Auguste was giving the orders for the day, when Saturnin appeared, coming up from the basement, and gave him a dreadful fright. The madman's eyes were ablaze; his white teeth glittered like those of some ravenous wolf. With clenched fists, he came straight up to Auguste.

'Where is she? If you dare touch her, I'll kill you.'

Auguste recoiled.

'Now this one too,' he muttered, barely concealing his fury.

'Shut up, or I'll kill you!' cried Saturnin once more, as he made a rush at him.

Auguste judged it wise to retreat. He had a horror of lunatics; there was no reasoning with such people. Having shouted to the assistant to lock Saturnin in the basement, he was just going out the archway, when he suddenly found himself face to face with Valérie and Théophile. The latter, who had a terrible cold, was swathed in a thick scarf, and kept coughing and groaning. They both must have heard what had happened, for they both looked sympathetically at Auguste. Since the quarrel about their inheritance, the two families were sworn enemies, no longer on speaking terms.

'You've still got a brother,' said Théophile, shaking Auguste by the hand as he recovered from a fit of coughing. 'Remember that in your misfortune.'

'Yes,' added Valérie, 'this ought to pay her back for all the nasty things she said to me. But we're awfully sorry for you, we're not utterly heartless.'

Greatly touched by their kindness, Auguste took them into

the back of the shop, while keeping his eye on Saturnin, who was prowling about. Here they made their peace. Berthe's name was never mentioned; Valérie merely remarked that that woman had been the cause of all the ill-feeling, for there had never been a single disagreeable word in their family until she had joined it and brought it into disrepute. Auguste, listening, looked down and nodded. There was a certain glee in Théophile's sympathy, for he was delighted that he was not the only one, and he scrutinised his brother to see how people looked in that predicament.

'Well, what have you decided to do?' he asked.

'Why, challenge him to a duel, of course!' the husband replied firmly.

That put an end to Théophile's amusement. Auguste's courage made them both shudder. Then their brother described the awful encounter of the previous night; how, having foolishly hesitated to buy a pistol, he had been forced to content himself with punching the man. True, he had received a blow in return, but all the same, he had given him what for. A villain who had been deceiving him for the last six months, pretending to side with him against his wife, even to the point of reporting back to him on what she did when she went out. As for her, the wretched creature had taken refuge with her parents; and she could stay there as long as she liked, as he would never take her back.

'Would you believe it? Last month I let her have three hundred francs to spend on clothes!' he cried. 'I've always been so good-natured, so tolerant, ready to put up with anything rather than make myself ill! But that's more than anyone can stand. I can't put up with that! Never!'

Théophile's thoughts turned to death. He shook feverishly, his voice strangled: 'It's ridiculous; you'll be thrashed. I wouldn't challenge him to a duel if I were you.'

Then, as Valérie looked at him, he sheepishly added: 'If such a thing ever happened to me.'

'Ah, that wretched woman!' exclaimed his wife. 'To think that two men are going to kill each other on her account! If I were her, I could never get that off my conscience.'

Auguste remained resolute. He was going to fight. What's more, he had already made all the arrangements. As he was determined to have Duveyrier as his second, he was now about to go up and tell him what had happened, and get him to go and get Octave immediately. Théophile would act as the other second, if he was willing. Théophile had no choice; but his cold seemed to get worse, and he became irritable, like a sickly child in need of sympathy. However, he offered to accompany his brother to the Duveyriers'. They might be thieves, but there were times when all that had to be forgotten; both he and his wife seemed anxious to patch up their differences with the Duveyriers, having doubtless reflected that it wasn't in their best interests to carry on sulking. Valérie obligingly offered to look after the cashier's desk for Auguste, to give him time to find some suitable new shop-girl.

'Only,' she said, 'I have to take Camille for a walk in the Tuileries Gardens at about two.'

'Oh, just leave it this once,' said her husband. 'Besides, it's raining.'

'No, no; the child needs fresh air. I must go out.'

As last the two brothers went upstairs to the Duveyriers. Théophile had to stop on the first step, overcome by a frightful fit of coughing. He caught hold of the handrail and when he could speak again, he gasped: 'You know, I'm much happier now, I trust her completely. No; I can't reproach her on that account. Besides, she's given me proof.'

Auguste, not understanding, looked at his brother's yellow, jaded face and the sparse bristles of his beard, which showed up on his flabby flesh.

Théophile was annoyed by his look, his brother's gall quite disconcerted him, and he continued: 'I'm talking about my wife, you know. Poor old chap, I pity you with all my heart! You remember what a fool I made of myself on your wedding-day. But, in your case, it's quite clear, for you actually saw them at it.'

'Bah!' cried Auguste, putting on a bold face. 'I'll soon put a bullet through him. My word! I wouldn't care a damn about the whole thing, if only I hadn't got this confounded headache'

Just as they rang at the Duveyriers', Théophile suddenly realised that the counsellor probably wouldn't be there; ever since he'd found Clarisse again, he had let himself go completely, not even pretending to sleep at home. Hippolyte, who opened the door, avoided giving any information about his master's whereabouts, but said that they would find madame practising her scales. They went in to find Clotilde, tightly corseted, at her piano, her fingers running up and down the keyboard with regular precision. As she dedicated two hours a day to this exercise to preserve her lightness of touch, she used her brain at the same time by reading the *Revue des Deux Mondes*, which lay open on the stand in front of her, her moving fingers losing nothing of their mechanical speed.

'Ah, it's you!' she exclaimed, as her brothers rescued her from the hailstorm of notes. She showed no surprise at seeing Théophile, who just remained there very stiffly, as if he were standing in for somebody else. Auguste had his story ready, suddenly feeling ashamed to tell his sister what had really happened and afraid that the news of the duel might frighten her. But she didn't allow him the chance to lie and, after looking fixedly at him, said, in her quiet way: 'What do you intend to do now?'

He gave a start, blushing violently. So everybody knew about it apparently. And he replied with the same bravado with which he had already silenced Théophile: 'Why, fight, of course!'

'Oh!' she said, greatly surprised this time.

However, she didn't express her disapproval. True, it would only increase the scandal, but honour had its price. She was content merely to remind him that she had been against the marriage from the start. One couldn't expect anything from a girl who seemed to be totally ignorant of a wife's duties.

Then, as Auguste asked her where her husband was: 'He's travelling,' she replied, without a moment's hesitation.

This news distressed him as he didn't wish to do anything until he had consulted Duveyrier. She listened, never mentioning the new address, as she didn't want her relatives to know about the state of her own marriage. At last she thought of a way out, and advised him to go and see Monsieur Bachelard, in the Rue d'Enghien; he might know something. Then she went back to her piano.

'It was Auguste who asked me to come with him,' said Théophile, who had remained silent until then. 'Shall we kiss and be friends, Clotilde? We're all in trouble.'

Holding out her cold cheek, she said: 'My poor brother, those in trouble have only themselves to blame. I'm willing to forgive everybody. Now, you make sure you take care of yourself, you seem to me to have a nasty cold!' Then, calling Auguste back, she added: 'If this isn't settled soon, let me know, as I shall only worry about it.'

Then the hailstorm of notes started again, surrounding her, drowning her, and her fingers mechanically ran up and down, hammering out scales in every key, while she gravely continued reading the *Revue des Deux Mondes*.

Downstairs Auguste debated for a moment whether to go to Bachelard's or not. How could he say to him: 'Your niece has cheated on me'? He finally decided to get Bachelard to give him Duveyrier's address without filling in the details of the whole story. So everything was agreed: Valérie would stay in the shop, and Théophile would look after the house until his brother's return. Auguste sent for a cab and was about to leave when Saturnin, who had momentarily vanished, suddenly rushed up from the basement, brandishing a large kitchen knife, and screaming: 'I'll kill him! I'll kill him!'

Terrified once again and white as a sheet, Auguste hastily jumped into the cab and shut the door, exclaiming. 'He's got hold of another knife! Where on earth does he find them all! For goodness sake, Théophile, send him home and make sure he's not there when I get back. As if I haven't got enough to worry about as it is!'

The shop assistant caught hold of the madman's shoulders. Valérie gave the address to the cabman, a hulking dirty fellow, with a face the colour of raw beef. Still recovering from the previous night's drinking, he was in no hurry and took up the reins in leisurely fashion, having made himself comfortable on the box.

'By distance, guv?' he asked, in a hoarse voice.

'No, by the hour, and look sharp. There'll be a good tip in it for you.'

The cab moved off. It was a huge, filthy old landau which rocked fearfully on its worn-out springs. The gaunt white skeleton of a horse ambled along, in spite of all the energy expended in shaking its mane and kicking up its hoofs. Auguste looked at his watch; it was nine o'clock. By eleven the duel might be arranged. At first, the dawdling carriage annoyed him. Then drowsiness gradually overcame him; he hadn't had a wink of sleep all night and this dreadful cab only made him feel more depressed. Finding himself alone now, rocked by the motion of the cab and deafened by the rattling of the cracked panes, the fever that had kept him going all morning subsided. How stupid the whole thing was, after all! His face grew grey, as he put both hands to his head, which ached horribly.

In the Rue d'Enghien there was more to annoy him. To begin with, Bachelard's doorway was so choked with vans that he was almost run over; then, in the glass-roofed courtyard, he came across a group of packers vigorously nailing up cases. Not one of them knew where Bachelard was, and their hammering went right through his head. However, he had decided to wait for the uncle when an apprentice, touched by his obvious suffering, whispered an address in his ear: Mademoiselle Fifi, Rue Saint-Marc, third floor. He would probably find Bachelard there.

'What d'ye say?' asked the cabman, who had fallen asleep.

'Rue Saint-Marc, and drive a bit quicker, if you can.'

The cab jogged on at its funereal pace. On the boulevards, one of the wheels got jammed up against an omnibus. The panels cracked, the springs groaned and Auguste was gripped by an ever-darkening melancholy as he continued the search for his second. Finally, however, they reached the Rue Saint-Marc.

On the third floor, a pale, plump little old woman opened the door. She seemed very upset; and when Auguste asked for Monsieur Bachelard, she let him in at once.

'Oh, sir, I'm sure you're one of his friends! Please try and calm him down. Poor man, he's put out about something that happened earlier. You must know who I am, I'm sure he's mentioned me to you; I'm Mademoiselle Menu.'

Bewildered, Auguste found himself in a narrow room overlooking the courtyard; a room which had the cleanliness and the deep peace of some country cottage. The whole place spoke of the innocent toil of ordinary people. By an embroidery frame, on which there was a priest's stole, a pretty, fair-haired, naïve-looking girl was weeping bitterly, while Uncle Bachelard, with his bulbous nose and bloodshot eyes, stood seething with fury and despair. He was so upset that Auguste's entrance didn't appear to surprise him. He immediately appealed to him as a witness, and the scene went on.

'Now, look here, Monsieur Vabre, you're an honest man; now, what would you say in my place? I got here this morning rather earlier than usual, went into her room with my lumps of sugar from the café, and three four-sous pieces as a surprise, and I found her in bed with that pig Gueulin! Now, tell me, frankly, what would you say to that?'

Auguste grew scarlet with embarrassment. At first he imagined that Bachelard knew of his own problems and was making fun of him.

However, without waiting for a reply, the uncle went on: 'Ah, my girl, you don't know what you've done, that's for certain! I was just beginning to feel young again and was so glad to have a nice, quiet little place where I thought I could be happy! To me you were an angel, a flower; in short, something sweet and pure, to console me after all those filthy women, and now you go and sleep with that dirty beast Gueulin.'

Genuine emotion choked him; his voice quavered with the intensity of his grief. His whole world was shattered; and he wept for his lost ideals, still hiccuping from last night's drinking.

'I didn't know, dear uncle,' stammered Fifi, whose sobs grew louder. 'I didn't know that it would upset you so much.'

And, in fact, she really didn't look as if she knew what she'd done. Her eyes, with their ingenuous look, her scent of chastity, her lack of guile, all seemed to belong to a little girl still ignorant of the difference between a gentleman and a lady. Moreover, her aunt Menu swore that she was just as innocent as before.

'Please calm down, Monsieur Narcisse. She's very fond of you, all the same. I was sure that you wouldn't like it. I says to her, I says: "If Monsieur Narcisse hears about it, he'll be angry." But she don't know what life is yet, she don't, nor what pleases, and nor what doesn't please. Don't cry any more, it's you she loves deep down.'

As neither Bachelard nor Fifi were listening to her, she turned to Auguste to tell him how worried she was about how all this would affect her niece's future. It was so difficult to find a respectable home for a young girl nowadays. She, who for thirty years had worked at Mardienne Brothers', the embroiderers, in the Rue Saint-Sulpice, where any enquiries concerning her might be made, she well knew how hard it was for a girl working in Paris to make both ends meet if she wanted to keep herself respectable. Good-natured though she was, and though she had received Fifi from the hands of her own brother, Captain Menu, on his death-bed, she could never have managed to bring the child up on her thousand-francs life annuity, which had allowed

her to give up her needlework. And, seeing her cared for by
Monsieur Narcisse, she had hoped to die happy. Not a bit of it!
Fifi had gone and made her uncle angry, just over a silly thing
like that.

'I dare say you know Villeneuve, near Lille?' she ended.
'That's where I come from. It's a biggish town . . .'

Auguste ran out of patience. Shaking off the aunt, he turned
to the uncle, whose noisy grief had now become somewhat
subdued.

'I came to ask you for Duveyrier's new address. I expect you
know it.'

'Duveyrier's address? Duveyrier's address?' stammered Bachelard. 'You mean Clarisse's address. Just wait one minute!'

And he opened the door of Fifi's room. To his great surprise
Auguste saw Gueulin emerging from it, whom Bachelard had
locked in so as to give him time to dress himself, and also in
order to detain him until he had decided what to do with him.
At the sight of the young man, looking thoroughly sheepish and
with his rumpled hair, Bachelard's anger returned.

'Ah, you wretch!' he cried, 'you, my own nephew, have
disgraced me! You've blackened your family's good name, and
have dragged my reputation through the mud! Ah, but you'll
come to a bad end, and one day we'll see you in the dock!'

With bowed head, Gueulin listened, both embarrassed and
furious.

'Look here, uncle,' he muttered, 'you're going too far. There's
a limit to everything. Not much fun for me, I can tell you. Why
did you take me to see the girl? I never asked you to. It was you
who dragged me here. You drag everybody here!'

But Bachelard, sobbing afresh, went on: 'You've taken everything from me. She was all I had left . . . You'll be the death of
me, you will, and I won't leave you a penny, not a single bloody
penny!'

Then Gueulin, unable to control himself any longer, burst
out:

'For God's sake, shut up! I've had enough. What did I always
tell you? One always pays for these kinds of things! Look what's
happened to me on the one occasion I thought of taking
advantage of an opportunity. The night was pleasant enough,
of course, but afterwards there's the very devil to pay!'

Fifi had dried her tears. At a loss at what to do, and feeling awkward, she went back to her embroidery, raising her large, guileless eyes now and again to look at the two men, apparently dazed by their anger.

'I'm in a great hurry,' Auguste ventured to remark. 'If you could kindly give me the address, just the street and the number, that's all I need.'

'The address?' said Bachelard. 'Let me see! Just one minute!'

Then, overcome with emotion, he seized Gueulin by both hands. 'You ungrateful fellow. I was keeping her for you, for goodness sake! I said to myself: now, if he's good, I'll give her to him . . . With a nice little dowry of fifty thousand francs. But, you dirty swine, you couldn't wait, but you had to go and have her right away!'

'Get your hands off!' cried Gueulin, but touched by the old fellow's kindheartness. 'It's obvious I'm not going to get out of this mess in a hurry.'

But Bachelard led him across to the girl, asking her: 'Now, Fifi, look at him, and tell me if you would have loved him.'

'Yes, uncle, if it pleased you,' she replied.

This gentle answer touched him to the core. He rubbed his eyes and blew his nose, choked with emotion. Well, well, he would see what could be done. All he'd wanted was to make her happy. Then he hurriedly dismissed Gueulin.

'Be off with you! I'll think the matter over!'

Meanwhile, Aunt Menu had taken Auguste aside again, in order to explain her views. A workman, she argued, would have beaten the young girl; a clerk would have gone on endlessly getting her pregnant. With Monsieur Narcisse, however, there was the chance of having a dowry, which would allow her to make a suitable marriage. Thank God, theirs was a good family, and she would never have let her niece go wrong, nor fall from the arms of one lover into those of another. No, it was with her wish that Fifi should have a respectable position.

Just as Gueulin was about to go, Bachelard called him back.

'Kiss her on the forehead; I give you my permission.'

He himself let Gueulin out; and then came back and stood in front of Auguste, holding his hand to his heart.

'It wasn't a joke,' he said. 'Upon my honour, I meant to give her to him later on!'

'What about this address?' asked Auguste impatiently.

Bachelard seemed surprised, as if he had answered that question already.

'Eh? What's that? Clarisse's address? But, I don't know it!'

Auguste looked as if he were about to explode with rage. Everything was a mess, and everybody seemed to be conspiring to make him look foolish! Seeing how upset he was, the uncle made a suggestion: Trublot, no doubt, knew the address, and he could be found at Desmarquay's, the stockbroker who he worked for. Bachelard, obliging rogue that he was, even offered to accompany his young friend, who accepted.

'Look,' he said to Fifi, after kissing her himself on the forehead, 'here's the sugar for you from the café all the same, and three four-sous pieces for your money-box. Be a good girl until I tell you what to do.'

The girl modestly continued her needlework with exemplary diligence. A ray of sunlight, reflecting off a neighbouring roof, brightened up the little room, touching with its gold this innocent nook, which even the noise of traffic below didn't disturb. It roused the poet in Bachelard.

'May God bless you, Monsieur Narcisse!' said Aunt Menu, as she showed him out. 'You've put my mind at rest . . . simply listen to what your heart tells you; that will inspire you.'

The cabman had again dropped off to sleep, and grumbled when Bachelard gave him Monsieur Desmarquay's address in the Rue Saint-Lazare. No doubt, the horse had gone to sleep too, for it needed several blows to make it move. At length the cab jolted uncomfortably along.

'It's tough, all the same,' continued Bachelard, after a pause. 'You can't imagine how upset I was at finding Gueulin there in his shirt . . . No, that's something you have to experience before you can understand it.'

So he went on, going into every detail without ever noticing Auguste's increasing uneasiness. The latter, who felt his position becoming more and more false, finally told him why he was in such a hurry to find Duveyrier.

'Berthe with that shop assistant!' cried Bachelard. 'I'm astounded!'

His astonishment seemed to be due to his niece's choice more than anything. But, after reflecting a while, he grew indignant. His sister, Eléonore, had a lot to answer for. He meant to drop the family altogether. Of course, it wouldn't do for him to be mixed up with this duel; but, nevertheless, he regarded it as essential.

'Like me, just now, when I saw Fifi with a man in his shirt, my first impulse was to murder everybody! If it had happened to you . . .'

Auguste shuddered painfully, and Bachelard stopped short.

'True, I wasn't thinking . . . You don't seem to be enjoying my story very much.'

They relapsed into silence as the cab swayed dismally from side to side. Auguste, whose valour ebbed with each turn of the wheels, submitted resignedly to the jolting, looking sallow, with his left eye closed in pain. Why did Bachelard think that a duel was indispensable? As the guilty woman's uncle, it was not his place to insist on bloodshed. His brother's words buzzed in his ear: 'It's ridiculous; you'll be thrashed!' They kept on obstinately coming back to him, until they seemed part and parcel of his neuralgia. He was sure to be killed: he had a sort of inkling that he would be; a sense of lugubrious foreboding completely overwhelmed him. He saw himself as a corpse, and mourned his fate.

'I told you Rue Saint-Lazare,' cried Bachelard, to the cabman. 'It's not in Chaillot. Turn up to the left.'

At last the cab stopped. So as to be careful, they asked to see Trublot, who came out bare-headed to talk to them in the doorway.

'Do you know Clarisse's address?' asked Bachelard.

'Clarisse's address? Of course! It's in the Rue d'Assas.'*

They thanked him, and were about to get into the cab again, when Auguste enquired: 'What's the number?'

'The number? Oh, I don't know the number!'

At that point, Auguste declared that he would rather give the whole thing up. Trublot tried his best to remember; he had dined there once, just behind the Luxembourg Gardens it was; but he couldn't recollect if it was at the end of the street, or on the right or on the left. But he remembered the door well, and could have recognised it at once. Then Bachelard had another idea and begged Trublot to accompany them, despite Auguste's protests that he didn't want to trouble anybody else and that he'd rather return home. As for Trublot, he refused, seeming somewhat strained. No; he wasn't going to that hole again. But he avoided giving the real reason: flabbergasting it had been, that tremendous slap that he'd got from Clarisse's new cook one evening when he'd gone to pinch her backside as she stood over her oven. It was incredible! A slap like that in return for the accepted way of getting to know each other! It had never happened to him before; it amazed him.

'No,' he said, trying to find an excuse, 'I'll never set foot in such a boring house again. Clarisse, you now, has become simply impossible; her temper's worse than ever, and she's more bourgeois than the bourgeois themselves. She's got all her family with her, ever since her father died, a whole tribe of pedlars; mother, two sisters, a great lout of a brother; even an old invalid aunt, with a face like one of those hags selling dolls in the street! You wouldn't believe how miserable and under the weather Duveyrier looks among them all!'

And he went on to tell them of that rainy day when the counsellor had found Clarisse standing in a doorway, she had been the first to get angry, sobbing that he had never had any respect for her. Yes, she had left the Rue de la Cerisaie, she had been so hurt, though for a long while she had hidden her feelings. Why did he always take off his decoration whenever he came to see her? Did he think that she would sully it? She was ready to make it up with him, but first he had to swear on his honour that he would always wear his decoration, for she wanted to be respected and was not prepared to suffer such indignities. Shaken by this quarrel, Duveyrier swore that he would do as she asked. He was completely under her power again, and deeply moved; she was right; what a noble-spirited creature.

'Now he never takes his ribbon off,' added Trublot. 'I think she even makes him sleep with it on. It flatters her, in front of her family, too. And, as that big chap Payan had already spent her twenty-five thousand francs' worth of furniture, this time she's got Duveyrier to buy her thirty thousand francs' worth. Oh, he's had it! She walks all over him while he sniffs around her skirt. There's no accounting for taste!'

'Well, I must be off, as Monsieur Trublot can't come,' said Auguste, whose misery was only increased by what he'd heard.

Trublot, however, suddenly changed his mind; he would accompany them after all; only he wouldn't go upstairs, he'd just show them the door. After fetching his hat and making some excuse, he joined them in the cab.

'Rue d'Assas,' he shouted to the driver. 'Go right along it, and I'll tell you when to stop.'

The driver swore. Rue d'Assas, of all places! Some people liked driving about, damned if they didn't! Well, they'd get there when they'd get there. The big white horse, as it ambled, steaming along, made hardly any headway, its neck arched at every step in a sort of excruciating nod.

Meanwhile, Bachelard had already begun to tell Trublot about his misfortune. Bad news made him talk. Yes, that swine Gueulin with a delicious little girl like that! He'd caught them both in their shirts. But, at this point in the story, he suddenly remembered Auguste who, looking glum and doleful, had collapsed in a corner of the cab.

'Ah! Of course; I beg your pardon,' he muttered. 'I keep forgetting.' Then, turning to Trublot: 'Our friend here has just had a spot of bother in his own home; and that's why we're trying to find Duveyrier. Yes, you know, last night he caught his wife with . . .' And with a gesture he completed his sentence, adding simply: 'Octave, if you didn't already know.'

Tending to be rather blunt, Trublot was about to say that this didn't surprise him in the least. But he checked himself and, instead, said something quite different, but with a contempt leaving the husband unsure of what exactly he meant: 'What an idiot that Octave is!'

At this commentary on the adultery there was a pause. Each of the three men was deep in thought. The cab was getting nowhere. It seemed to have been lumbering along for hours on a bridge, when Trublot, the first to awake from his reverie, remarked discerningly: 'This cab doesn't go very fast.'

But nothing could quicken the horse's pace; by the time they got to the Rue d'Assas it was eleven o'clock. There they wasted nearly another quarter of an hour for, despite Trublot's boast, he didn't recognise the door after all. First he let the cabman drive right along the street without stopping him, and then he made him come back again. He did this three times running. Acting on his precise instructions, Auguste called at ten different houses, but the concierges replied that they 'hadn't got such a person'. At last, a fruitseller told him the right number. He went upstairs with Bachelard, leaving Trublot in the cab.

It was the great lout of a brother who opened the door, a cigarette between his lips, puffing smoke in their faces as he

showed them into the drawing-room. When they asked for
Monsieur Duveyrier, he first stared mockingly at them, without
answering, and then slouched off, presumably to find him. In
the middle of the drawing-room, draped in luxurious new blue
satin and already stained with grease, one of the sisters, the
youngest, was sitting on the carpet, wiping out a kitchen
saucepan, while the elder girl, having just found the key to a
splendid piano, thumped on it with clenched fists. On seeing the
gentlemen enter, they both looked up, but didn't stop, as they
went on thumping and scrubbing with renewed energy. Five
minutes passed, and nobody came. Deafened by this din, the
visitors looked at each other, until shrieks from an adjoining
room filled them with terror. It was the invalid aunt being
washed.

At last an old woman, Madame Bocquet, Clarisse's mother,
peeped round the door, dressed in such a filthy gown that she
dared not show herself.

'Who do the gentlemen wish to see?' she asked.

'Why, Monsieur Duveyrier, of course!' cried Bachelard, losing
his patience. 'We've told the servant already! Tell him it's
Monsieur Auguste Vabre and Monsieur Narcisse Bachelard.'

Madame Bocquet shut the door again. Meanwhile, the elder
of the sisters, standing on a stool, thumped the keyboard with
her elbows; while the younger scraped at the bottom of the
saucepan with a steel fork. Another five minutes elapsed. Then,
in the midst of this din, which seemingly had no effect upon
her, Clarisse appeared.

'Oh, it's you!' she said to Bachelard, without even looking at
Auguste.

Bachelard was quite taken aback. She had put on so much
weight he would never had recognised her. The tall, slender she-
devil, with her fluffy mop of hair like a poodle's, had been
transformed into a dumpy matron, with her hair neatly plas-
tered and all shiny with pomade. But instead of giving him the
chance to say anything, she immediately told him, and with
brutal frankness, that she didn't want a gossip like him at her
place, who went and told Alphonse all sorts of horrid stories.
Yes, yes, that's exactly what he'd done; he'd accused her of
sleeping with Alphonse's friends, and of carrying on with scores
of men behind his back. It was no use his saying he hadn't, and
Alphonse had told her so himself.

'Look here,' she added, 'if you've come here to booze, you may as well clear out. The old days are over. From now on I mean to be respectable.'

She paraded her growing desire for decency and honour which had almost become an obsession. In these fits of high-mindedness she had driven away her lover's guests one by one, by forbidding them to smoke, by insisting on being called Madame and on receiving formal visits. Her former superficial, second-hand self had vanished; all that remained was her exaggerated attempt to play the fine lady, sometimes punctured by foul language and fouler gestures. Bit by bit, Duveyrier found himself once again totally alone; instead of it being an amusing escape for him, it had become a grisly middle-class kind of place, amid whose dirt and din he encountered all the worries of his own home. As Trublot remarked, the Rue de Choiseul was no more boring, and it was certainly far less filthy.

'We've not called to see you,' replied Bachelard, recovering himself, being used to more welcoming greetings from such ladies. 'We want to speak to Duveyrier.'

Then Clarisse glanced at his companion. She thought he was a bailiff, knowing that Alphonse's business was in a terrible state lately.

'Well, what do I care, after all?' she said. 'Take him and keep him if you like. It's not much fun for me to have to look after him all the time.'

She no longer even tried to hide her disgust, convinced, in fact, that her cruelty only made him more attached to her. Opening a door, she exclaimed: 'Come out then, as these gentlemen insist on seeing you.'

Duveyrier, who apparently had been waiting behind the door, came in, shook hands with them, and tried to smile. He no longer had the youthful air of former days, when he used to spend the evening with her in the Rue de la Cerisaie. He was worn down, and looked thin and depressed. He trembled nervously now and again, as if alarmed by something behind him.

Clarisse stayed to listen, but Bachelard was reluctant to speak in front of her, so he invited the counsellor to lunch.

'Say you'll come, because Monsieur Vabre needs to see you. Madame will be good enough to excuse you . . .'

At that moment Clarisse caught sight of her youngest sister thumping on the piano. Slapping her violently, she drove her out of the room, and she boxed the other child's ears and packed her off with her saucepan too. There was a terrible row. The invalid aunt in the next room started screaming again, thinking they were about to beat her.

'Do you hear, my love?' murmured Duveyrier. 'These gentlemen have asked me to lunch.'

She was not listening, but shyly, tenderly touched the keys. For the last month she had been learning to play the piano. This had been the unconfessed longing of her whole life, a remote ambition which, if attained, could alone stamp her as a woman of high society. After making sure that nothing was broken, she was about to stop her lover from going, merely in order to be disagreeable with him, when Madame Bocquet once again popped her head round the door, still hiding her gown.

'Your piano teacher's here,' she said.

Clarisse instantly changed her mind, and called out to Duveyrier: 'That's fine, you bugger off! I'll have lunch with Théodore. We don't need you.'

Théodore, her piano teacher, was a Belgian, with a big rosy face. She immediately sat down at the piano, and he placed her fingers on the keyboard, rubbing them to make them less stiff. For an instant Duveyrier hesitated, clearly put out. But the two men were waiting for him. He had to go and put on his boots. When he came back she had launched haphazardly into her scales, coming out with a cacophony of notes which Bachelard and his companion found unbearable.

Yet Duveyrier, driven mad by his wife's Mozart and Beethoven, stood still for a moment behind his mistress, apparently enjoying the sound, despite his nervous facial twitchings. Then, turning to the other two, he whispered: 'Her talent for music is quite amazing.'

After kissing her hair, he withdrew discreetly, and left her alone with Théodore. In the hallway the great lout of a brother impudently asked him for a franc to buy some tobacco. Then, as they went downstairs and Bachelard expressed surprise at his conversion to the charms of the piano, Duveyrier swore that he had never hated it; and he went into raptures, saying how greatly Clarisse's simple scales stirred his soul, giving in to his need to bring a touch of romance to his baser appetites.

Downstairs Trublot had given the driver a cigar, and was listening to his life-history with undisguised interest. Bachelard insisted on having lunch at Foyot's; it was in fact lunchtime, and they could talk better while they were eating. Then, when the cab finally managed to move off, he brought Duveyrier up to date, who at once became very serious. Auguste's discomfort seemed to have increased during the visit to Clarisse, where he had not uttered a single word. Now, completely exhausted by this interminable drive, his head throbbing, he sat slumped in a corner. When Duveyrier asked him what he meant to do, he opened his eyes, paused for a moment as if in anguish, and then repeated: 'Fight, of course!' His voice, however, sounded fainter; and, closing his eyes, as if asking to be left in peace, he added: 'Unless you can suggest anything else.'

So, as the vehicle lumbered along, the men deliberated. Duveyrier, like Bachelard, favoured a duel. The thought of bloodshed did upset him as he pictured a dark stream staining the staircase of his own house. But honour demanded it, and honour was at stake, no compromise was possible. Trublot took a broader view of the case; it was all too silly, he said. Simply for what he politely termed a woman's frailty. With a faint movement of his eyelids, Auguste agreed with him, exasperated by the warlike fury of the other two, who certainly ought to have been in favour of reconciliation. Despite his tiredness, he was obliged to tell the story of that night once again, the punch he had given Octave and the one he had received in return. Soon the question of the adultery was forgotten; the sole topic of discussion was the ensuing duel. This was what was commented on and analysed in order to try and find a satisfactory solution.

'Talk about splitting hairs!' cried Trublot contemptuously. 'If they exchanged punches, then they're quits.'

Duveyrier and Bachelard looked at each other aghast. But by this time they had reached the restaurant, and Bachelard declared that, first of all, they had better have lunch. It would clear their heads. He invited them to a hearty lunch at his expense, ordering extravagant dishes and wines, so that for three hours they sat over their meal in a private room. The duel was not mentioned even once. Immediately after the *hors-d'oeuvres* the conversation inevitably turned to women; Fifi and Clarisse were held up for inspection, turned over and dissected. Bachelard now admitted that he'd been in the wrong, so as not to give Duveyrier the impression that he'd been jilted, while the

latter, to make up for having let Uncle Bachelard see him
weeping on that night in the empty apartment in the Rue de la
Cerisaie, went on and on about his present happiness, until he
actually began to believe in it, and became quite sentimental.
Prevented by his migraine from eating or drinking, Auguste sat
there, apparently listening, with one elbow on the table, looking
wretched. During dessert, Trublot remembered the driver, who
had been left downstairs. Feeling sorry for him, he sent him the
remains of the meal and the dregs of the bottles; for, from
certain remarks that the fellow had made, he had sensed in him
a former priest. It struck three. Duveyrier grumbled at having to
be an assessor at the next court sitting. Bachelard, now very
drunk, spat sideways on to Trublot's trousers, who didn't even
notice it; and amid the liqueurs, the day would have ended
there, if Auguste hadn't roused himself with a sudden start.

'So, what's going to be done, then?' he enquired.

'Look here, my lad,' replied Bachelard, familiarly, 'if you like,
we'll sort the whole thing out nicely for you. It's stupid, you
can't possibly fight a duel.'

No one seemed surprised at this conclusion. Duveyrier nodded approvingly.

Bachelard went on: 'I'll go with Monsieur Duveyrier and see
the chap, and make the brute apologise, or my name isn't
Bachelard. The mere sight of me will make him knuckle under,
just because I'm an outsider. I don't give a damn for anybody, I
don't!'

Auguste shook him by the hand, but didn't seem completely
relieved, for he had such a splitting headache. At length they left
the private dining-room. Beside the kerb, the driver was still
having his lunch inside the cab. He was quite drunk, and had to
shake all the crumbs out, even giving Trublot a fraternal punch
in the stomach. It was only the poor horse that had had nothing,
and, with a despairing wag of the head, it refused to budge.
After some encouragement, however, it reeled forward, along
the Rue de Tournon. It had struck four before they stopped at
the Rue de Choiseul. Auguste had had the cab for seven hours.
Trublot, who remained inside, said that he would hire it for
himself, and would wait for Bachelard, whom he was going to
invite to dinner.

'Well, you *have* been a long while!' said Théophile to his
brother, as he ran forward. 'I began to think you were dead!'

And, as soon as the others had come into the shop, he gave a full report on the day's events. Ever since nine o'clock he had been watching the house, but nothing had happened. At two o'clock, Valérie had gone with Camille to the Tuileries. Then, about half past three, he had seen Octave go out. Nothing else; nothing had stirred, not even at the Josserands; to the point where Saturnin, who had been looking under all the furniture for his sister, had at last gone up to ask for her, and Madame Josserand, to get rid of him, had slammed the door in his face, saying that Berthe wasn't there. Since then the madman had gone prowling about, grinding his teeth.

'All right!' said Bachelard. 'We'll wait for Monsieur Octave. From here we'll be able to see when he comes back.'

Auguste, his head in a whirl, tried his best to keep on his feet, until Duveyrier advised him to go to bed. It was the only cure for migraine.

'Just you go upstairs; we shan't need you any more. We'll let you know the outcome. My dear friend, it's no good getting in a state about it.'

So the husband went upstairs to bed.

At five o'clock the two others were still waiting for Octave. He had gone out for no particular reason, other than to get some fresh air and forget the unpleasant events of the night. He walked past 'Au Bonheur des Dames' where Madame Hédouin, dressed in mourning, stood at the door, and he stopped to greet her. On telling her that he had left the employment of the Vabres, she quietly asked him why he didn't come back to her. Without thinking, the whole thing was settled there and then. After bowing to her once more, and promising to come the next day, he wandered off, full of vague regrets. Chance always seemed to upset his calculations. Absorbed by various schemes, he roamed about the neighbourhood for more than an hour; then looking up, he saw that he was in the shadowy alley of the Passage Saint-Roch. In the darkest corner opposite to him, at the door of a dubious-looking lodging-house, Valérie was saying goodbye to a man with a big beard. She blushed and tried to get away through the padded door of the church. Then, seeing that Octave was following her and smiling, she decided to wait for him at the entrance, where they chatted amiably to each other.

'You're avoiding me,' he said. 'Are you angry with me?'

'Angry?' she rejoined. 'Why should I be angry with you? They can scratch each other's eyes out, if they like, I don't care!'

She was referring to her family. She immediately gave vent to her old spite against Berthe, sounding out the young man through various allusions. Then, sensing that he was secretly tired of his mistress and still furious about the events of the previous night, she no longer restrained herself, but blurted out everything. To think that that woman had accused her of selling herself, when in fact she never took a penny, nor accepted a present! Well, perhaps a few flowers sometimes, a bunch or two of violets. Everybody knew now which of the two sold herself. She had predicted that some day he would discover how much it cost to have her.

'It cost you more than a bunch of violets, didn't it?'

'Yes, it did,' he muttered, like a coward.

Then, in his turn, he let slip some rather disagreeable things about Berthe, saying how spiteful she was, even declaring that she was overweight, as if avenging himself for all the turmoil that she had caused him. All day long he had been expecting her husband's seconds, and he was now going home to see if anybody had called: the whole idea of a duel was ridiculous and she could easily have put a stop to it. He finished up by giving an account of their absurd rendezvous, their quarrel, and Auguste's arrival on the scene before they had so much as touched each other.

'I swear on my life!' he said. 'I hadn't laid a finger on her at that point!'

Valérie laughed excitedly. And she drew closer to Octave in this tender intimacy of shared secrets, as if to some female friend who knew everything. Occasionally some devout worshipper coming out of church disturbed them; then the door closed again gently and they found themselves alone, safely shrouded in the green baize hangings of the porch as if in some secure and saintly refuge.

'I don't know why I live with such people,' she continued, referring to her relatives. 'Oh, I'm not blameless, certainly! But, frankly, I can't feel sorry for them at all because I care so little for them. And as far as love is concerned, if only you knew how tiresome I find it!'

'Come on, it's not that bad,' cried Octave, cheerfully. 'People aren't always as stupid as we were yesterday . . . They have a good time now and then!'

Then she told him everything. It wasn't just hatred for her husband, or his feverish shivering, his impotence, and his endless snivelling, that had driven her to be unfaithful only six months after marrying him; no, she did it often without planning to, simply because things came into her head, for which she could give no sort of explanation. Everything was falling apart, and she felt so wretched that she could have committed suicide. Since there was nothing to stop her, it didn't much matter who she went to bed with.

'Really, were there never any good times?' asked Octave again, who only seemed to be interested in this particular point.

'Well, not like they describe,' she answered. 'I swear.'

He looked at her, full of compassion. All for nothing, and without getting any pleasure out of it! Surely it wasn't worth all the trouble she took, in her perpetual fear of being caught. But, above all, his self-esteem was restored, for he hadn't got over being turned down by her. So that was why she wouldn't let him have her that evening! He reminded her of the incident.

'Do you remember, after one of your turns?'

'Yes, yes; I do remember. It's not that I didn't like you, but I just didn't feel like it! But listen, it's better this way, otherwise we would have hated each other by now.'

She gave him her little gloved hand. Squeezing it, he repeated: 'You're right. It's better this way . . . In fact, you only really love the women you've never had!'

It was an emotional moment. Touched, they stood there for a while, hand in hand. Then, without another word, they pushed open the padded church door, as she had left her son Camille inside with the woman who hired out chairs. The child was asleep. She made him kneel down, and herself knelt for a moment, her head in her hands, as if deep in prayer. Just as she was about to rise, the Abbé Mauduit, coming out of a confessional, greeted her with a fatherly smile.

Octave merely walked across the church. When he returned home, it caused a stir. Only Trublot, asleep in the cab, didn't catch sight of him. Tradespeople at their shop doors eyed him gravely. The stationer opposite was still gazing at the front of the house, as if to discover something from the stones themselves. The coal-merchant and the greengrocer, however, had

already calmed down and the neighbourhood had relapsed into
its frigidly dignified state. Lisa, who was gossiping with Adèle
in the doorway as Octave passed, merely stared at him, and
then they both went on complaining about the cost of poultry,
watched sternly by Monsieur Gourd who greeted the young
man. As he proceeded up the stairs, Madame Juzeur, on the
look-out since that morning, opened her door slightly and,
catching hold of his hands, drew him into her hallway, where
she kissed him on the forehead, murmuring: 'Poor boy! Go on,
I won't keep you now. But come back for a chat when it's all
over.'

He had hardly got to his room before Duveyrier and Bachelard called. Astonished at seeing the latter, he initially tried to
give them the names of two of his friends. But, without replying,
the two men spoke of their age and gave him a lecture on his
bad behaviour. When, in the course of the conversation, he
announced his intention of leaving the house as soon as possible,
his two visitors both solemnly declared that this proof of his
tact would suffice. There had been enough scandal, and it was
time for him to forego his own pleasures in the interest of
respectable residents. Duveyrier accepted Octave's notice to quit
there and then, and left, while Bachelard, behind his back, asked
the young man to dine with him that evening.

'Look, I'm counting on you. We're going to live it up.
Trublot's waiting for us downstairs . . . I don't give a damn
about Eléonore, but I don't want to see her. I'll go on ahead so
that they don't catch us together.'

He went downstairs. Five minutes later Octave joined him,
delighted at the way things had turned out. He slipped into the
cab, and the melancholy horse, which for seven hours had been
dragging the husband about, now limped along with them to a
restaurant near Les Halles, where they served incredibly good
tripe.

Duveyrier went back to Théophile in the shop. Valérie had
just come in, and they were all chatting, when Clotilde herself
appeared, on her return from some concert. She had gone there,
however, in a perfectly calm frame of mind, convinced, she said,
that a solution that suited all concerned would be found. There
was a pause; and a moment of embarrassment for both families.
Théophile, seized by a terrific fit of coughing, was almost
choking to death. As it was in their mutual interest to make it

up, they took advantage of the emotion stirred up by these fresh family troubles. The two women hugged each other; Duveyrier swore to Théophile that the Vabre inheritance was ruining him. However, by way of compensation, he promised to waive his rent for three years.

'I must just go up and reassure poor Auguste,' said Duveyrier, finally.

On the staircase he heard hideous cries, like those of an animal about to be slaughtered, coming from the bedroom. Saturnin, armed with his kitchen knife, had silently crept into the apartment, where, with eyes like gleaming coals, and frothing at the mouth, he had launched himself at Auguste.

'Tell me where you're hiding her!' he cried. 'Give her back to me, or else I'll kill you.'

Startled out of a fitful sleep, Auguste was trying to escape. But Saturnin, with all the strength of an obsessed maniac, had caught hold of him by the tail of his shirt and, throwing him backwards, placed his neck at the edge of the bed, with a basin immediately underneath it, holding him there like an animal in a slaughter-house.

'Ah! I've got you this time . . . I'm going to cut your throat, yes, just like a pig!'

Luckily, the others arrived just in time to release the victim. Saturnin had to be locked up, for he was raving mad. Two hours later, the superintendent of police having been summoned, they took him away a second time to the asylum at Les Moulineaux with his family's consent. Poor Auguste was still shaking.

He remarked to Duveyrier, who had informed him of the arrangement made with Octave: 'No, I'd rather have fought a duel. It's impossible to defend yourself against a madman. Only a maniac would try to cut my throat because his sister's been unfaithful to me! I've had enough of it, my friend! I swear, I've had enough!'

On the Wednesday morning, when Marie had brought Berthe to Madame Josserand, the latter, aghast at what this scandal would do to her standing, turning very pale and didn't say a word. She grabbed hold of her daughter's hand as if she were a schoolteacher showing some guilty pupil into a corner. Leading her to Hortense's bedroom, she pushed her in, and at last exclaimed: 'Hide in here, and don't show yourself . . . You'll be the death of your father.'

Hortense, who was washing, was astounded. Red with shame, Berthe flung herself on the unmade bed, sobbing violently. She had expected an instant and blazing row, and had prepared her defence, having resolved to shout back the minute her mother went too far; but this mute severity, this way of treating her as if she were a naughty little girl who had been eating jam on the sly, left her feeling helpless, and brought back all the terrors of her childhood and the tears shed in corners when she penitently made solemn vows of obedience.

'What's the matter? What have you been doing?' asked her sister, whose amazement increased on seeing that she was wrapped in an old shawl lent to her by Marie. 'Has poor Auguste been taken ill in Lyons?'

But Berthe wouldn't answer. No, later on; there were things that she couldn't talk about and she begged Hortense to leave her alone so that she could at least cry in peace. The day went by in this fashion. Monsieur Josserand had gone to his office, without the slightest idea that anything had happened, and when he came home that evening Berthe was still in hiding. Having refused any food, she avidly devoured the small dinner that Adèle secretly brought her. The maid stayed to watch her and, noticing how hungry she was, said: 'Don't get in such a state. You must keep your strength up. The house is quite calm, and as for the dead and wounded, nobody's even been hurt.'

'Oh!' said the young woman.

She questioned Adèle, who gave her a lengthy account of the day's proceedings, telling her about the duel which had not come off, what Auguste had said, and what the Duveyriers and the Vabres had done. And Berthe breathed a sigh of relief, devoured everything, and asked for some more bread. It was really too silly to let the whole thing distress her so much when the others had apparently got over it already.

So when Hortense joined her at about ten o'clock, she gaily greeted her, dry-eyed. Smothering their laughter, they had great fun, especially when Berthe tried on one of her sister's dressing-gowns and found it too tight for her. Her bosom, which marriage had developed, almost split the material. Never mind, if she moved the buttons she could put it on tomorrow. They both seemed to have returned to their childhood, there in that same room which for years they had shared. This touched them, and brought them closer to each other than they had been for a long while. They were obliged to sleep together, as Madame Josserand had got rid of Berthe's old bed. As they lay there side by side, with outstretched limbs, after the candle was out, they talked on and on, their eyes wide open in the dark, unable to sleep.

'So you won't tell me?' asked Hortense once again.

'But you're not married,' replied Berthe. 'I really can't . . . It's a row that I had with Auguste. He came back, you see and—'

Then, as she broke off, her sister carried on impatiently: 'Go on, go on! Why stop? Good God, as if at my age I wouldn't understand!'

So Berthe confessed everything, choosing her words carefully at first, but finally telling her all there was to know about Octave and about Auguste. Lying there on her back in the dark, Hortense listened, uttering a word or two every now and then to question her sister or express an opinion: 'Well, what did he say then?' 'And how did you feel?' 'That's a bit odd; I wouldn't like that!' 'Oh, really! So that's how it happens, does it?' Midnight struck, then one o'clock, then two o'clock, and still wide awake they kept talking the thing over as their limbs grew warmer and warmer beneath the bedclothes. In this sort of semi-trance, Berthe forgot she was with her sister and began to think aloud, unburdening her heart and soul of the most intimate details.

'As for Verdier and me,' said Hortense, suddenly, 'things will be much simpler, because I'll do whatever he wants me to.'

At the mention of Verdier, Berthe was startled. She thought the engagement had been broken off as the woman he had lived

with for fifteen years had recently had a child just as he was on
the point of leaving her.

'Do you mean to say that you'll marry him, after all?' she
asked.

'Well, why shouldn't I? I was stupid to wait so long. The
child won't live long. It's a sickly girl.'

In her disgust, like a respectable middle-class spinster, she
almost spat out the word 'mistress', revealing all her hatred for
a creature who'd been living with a man for that long. It was
just a cheap trick, nothing else, her having a baby; she'd worked
out that Verdier, having bought her some clothes so as not to
throw her out with nothing on her back, was trying to accustom
her to a separation by sleeping elsewhere more and more. Ah,
well! We'll just have to wait and see.

'Poor thing!' exclaimed Berthe.

'What do you mean, poor thing?' cried Hortense, bitterly.
'It's obvious you've been no angel either.'

But she immediately regretted such a cruel outburst; and,
putting her arms round her sister, she kissed her and declared
that she hadn't meant it. They both fell silent, but still they
couldn't sleep, going over what had happened again and again,
their eyes wide open in the dark.

Next morning Monsieur Josserand felt unwell. He had carried
on working away at his labels until two in the morning, despite
the fact that for several months he had felt exhausted and was
suffering from a gradual loss of strength. He got up, however,
and dressed himself; but, just as he was leaving for his office, he
felt so worn out that he sent a delivery boy with a note
informing Bernheim Brothers of his ill-health.

The family were just about to have their coffee, at a bare
table in the dining-room, still reeking of the greasy residue of
last night's meal. The ladies appeared in dressing-gowns, wet
from their ablutions and with hair twisted up any old how.
Seeing that her husband was going to stay home, Madame
Josserand had resolved to bring Berthe out of hiding, for she
was already sick of all this mystery, and fearful that at any
moment Auguste would come up and make a scene.

'Hello! You're here for breakfast? Why's that?' exclaimed the
father, in surprise, on seeing his daughter, her eyes puffy with
sleep and her bosom squeezed tightly into Hortense's robe.

'My husband wrote to say that he would be staying in Lyons,' she replied, 'so I thought that I'd spend the day with you.'

The sisters had arranged to stick to this story. Madame Josserand, still looking like a severe schoolteacher, refrained from saying anything to the contrary. But Berthe's father eyed her uneasily, as if aware that something was wrong. As the tale seemed to him somewhat unlikely, he was about to ask how the shop would get on without her when Berthe came and kissed him on both cheeks in her old smiling, seductive way.

'You're sure you're not hiding anything from me?' he murmured.

'What an idea! Why should I hide anything from you?'

Madame Josserand merely shrugged her shoulders. Why bother with all these precautions? To gain an hour, perhaps, not more. It wasn't worth it. Sooner or later the father would have to receive the shock. However, breakfast passed off merrily. Monsieur Josserand was delighted to find himself once more with his two girls; it seemed to him like old times when, only just awake, they used to amuse him by recounting their childish dreams. For him they still had the fresh scent of youth about them, with their elbows on the table as they dipped their bread in their coffee, laughing aloud with their mouths full. All the past came back, too, as opposite them he was faced with their mother's rigid countenance, her enormous body bursting out of an old green silk dress which she wore in the mornings without a corset.

Breakfast, however, was marred by an unfortunate episode. Madame Josserand suddenly shouted at the maid: 'What's that you're eating?'

She had been watching Adèle, still in slippers, plodding heavily round the table.

'Nothing, madame,' she replied.

'What do you mean nothing? You're chewing something; I'm not blind. Look, you've still got some of it in your mouth. Ah, it's no good your trying to suck your cheeks in, I can still see . . . You've got something in your pocket, too, haven't you?'

Adèle got flustered and tried to step backwards, but Madame Josserand caught hold of her skirt.

'For the last quarter of an hour I've watched you taking something out of here and stuffing it into your mouth, hiding it

in the palm of your hand. It must be something very good. So
show me, then.'

Thrusting her hand into the girl's pocket, she pulled out a
handful of stewed prunes, with all the syrup dripping from
them.

'What on earth is this?' she furiously exclaimed.

'They're prunes, madame,' said Adèle, realising that she had
been found out and growing insolent.

'Oh! So you eat my prunes, do you? That's why they disappear so quickly. Well, I never! Prunes! And in your pocket, too!'

She also accused her of drinking the vinegar. Everything
vanished in the same way; one couldn't leave a cold potato out
without being sure that it would never be seen again.

'You're a real pig, my girl.'

'If you gave me enough to eat,' replied Adèle, rudely; 'then
I'd leave your cold potatoes alone.'

This was the last straw. Madame Josserand rose, majestic and
menacing.

'Be quiet; don't you dare answer me like that! I know what it
is; it's the other servants that have spoiled you. As soon as some
stupid twit of a girl fresh from the country arrives in the house,
all the other trollops in the place put her up to every trick in the
book. You never go to church any more, and now you've begun
to steal!'

Spurred on by Lisa and Julie, Adèle was not going to give in.

'If I was such a stupid twit, as you put it, you shouldn't have
taken advantage of me. It's too late now.'

'Get out! You're fired!' cried Madame Josserand, pointing to
the door dramatically.

She sat down, shaken, while the maid, in no hurry, dawdled
about in her slippers, and munched another prune before going
back to her kitchen. She was sent packing in this way at least
once a week; it no longer even worried her. At the table an
awkward silence prevailed. Finally Hortense remarked that it
was no good firing her one day, only to take her back the next.
There was no question, she was a thief, and had become quite
insolent; but they might as well have her as anybody else; at
least she condescended to wait on them, whereas any other
maid would not tolerate them for as long as a week, even with
the added complication of her drinking the vinegar and stuffing
her pockets full of prunes.

Their breakfast ended, however, in cosy intimacy, despite this episode. Monsieur Josserand, feeling quite emotional, spoke of poor Saturnin, who had had to be taken away again last night in his absence, and he believed the tale they had told him about an attack of raving madness in the middle of the shop. Then, when he complained of never seeing Léon, Madame Josserand, previously silent, curtly remarked that she was expecting him that very day. He was probably coming to lunch. A week ago the young man had broken off with Madame Dambreville, who, to keep her promise to him, wanted him to marry some stale old widow. He, however, had undersatood he would be marrying a niece of Monsieur Dambreville's, a creole, of great wealth and dazzling looks, who had only arrived at her uncle's house last September, after the death of her father in the West Indies. So there had been terrible scenes between the two lovers. Consumed with jealousy, Madame Dambreville refused to give her niece to Léon, not wishing to take second place to such a budding and youthful beauty.

'What's happening about this marriage then?' asked Monsieur Josserand, discreetly.

At first the mother answered in a roundabout way, because of Hortense. She now worshipped her son, a young man who would go far. Sometimes she even flung his triumph in his father's face saying that, thank God, at least he took after his mother, and wouldn't let his wife go without. Gradually, she picked up steam.

'Well, he's had enough of it all! It's all right for now, it hasn't done him any harm yet. But if she doesn't hand over her niece soon it'll be good-bye and he'll break it off! And I agree with him actually.'

For decency's sake, Hortense began to drink her coffee, pretending to hide behind her cup; while Berthe, who could now understand what was going on, looked vaguely disgusted at her brother's success. They all got up from the table, and Monsieur Josserand, feeling much better, had perked up and talked of going to the office after all, when Adèle brought in a calling card. The lady in question was waiting in the drawing-room.

'What? She's here, at this hour?' cried Madame Josserand. 'And me without my corset on! Never mind; it's about time I told her a few home truths.'

It was, in fact, Madame Dambreville. So the father and his two daughters remained chatting in the dining-room, while the mother made for the drawing-room. Before pushing the door open she uneasily surveyed her old silk gown, tried to button it, removed some stray threads that had got on to it from the floor, and, with a shove, forced her exuberant bosom back into place.

'Please, excuse me, madame.' said the visitor, smiling. 'I was just passing and thought I would call in to see how you were.'

Corseted and with her hair done, she was groomed to perfection, and her relaxed and friendly manner was that of someone who had just dropped in to say hello to a friend. Her smile, however, wavered, and beneath this blasé appearance, one could sense the terrible anguish shaking her whole being. At first she talked of a thousand trivial matters, avoided mentioning Léon's name, but eventually made up her mind to pull out of her pocket a letter which she had just received from him.

'What a letter! It's awful!' she mumbled, her voice changing and choked with tears. 'What has he got against me, madame? He won't even come and see me any more.'

And she feverishly held out the letter, her hand trembling. Madame Josserand coolly took it and read it. It was to break off the relationship and its three lines were cruelly concise.

'Well, for God's sake,' she said, handing back the note, 'I can't say I blame Léon . . .'

Straight away, Madame Dambreville began to sing the praises of the widow; she was only just thirty-five, very respectable, fairly well off, and so energetic that she couldn't rest until her husband had become a minister. She had kept her promise she said; after all she had found a good match for Léon; so why should he be angry with her? Then, without waiting for an answer, in a sudden nervous impulse she mentioned her niece, Raymonde. Surely he didn't think that would be possible? An uncontrollable sixteen-year-old tomboy who knew nothing about life.

'Why not?' Madame Josserand kept repeating in reply to each question. 'Why not, if he's fond of her?'

'No! He's not fond of her, he can't be fond of her!' Madame Dambreville cried, losing all control of her feelings. 'Listen to me!' she exclaimed. 'All I ask from him is a little gratitude. I made him what he is today. He has me to thank for his job, and, as a wedding present, he'll be appointed a government counsel. Madame, please! Tell him to come back; ask him to do it for my sake. I implore him, and you as his mother, to find it in your heart to . . .'

She clasped her hands together, and her voice faltered. There was a silence as they both sat facing each other. Then, all of a sudden, she burst into tears, sobbing hysterically: 'Not with Raymonde; oh, no, not with Raymonde!'

It was the fury of passion, the cry of a woman who refuses to grow old, clinging desperately to her last lover as she slips past her prime. She grabbed hold of Madame Josserand's hands, soaking them with tears, and confessed everything, humiliating herself, repeatedly saying that she, and she alone, could influence her son, swearing to be at her beck and call if only she would return Léon to her. Doubtless she hadn't come there to say all this; on the contrary, she had resolved to give nothing away; but her heart was breaking and she couldn't stop herself.

'Hush, my dear! You're making me feel ashamed,' replied Madame Josserand, who seemed angry. 'My girls there might overhear you. As for me, I don't know anything, and I don't want to know anything. If you've had any differences with my son you'd better sort it out between you. I could never take sides.'

She overwhelmed her with good advice, however. At her time of life one ought to be resigned. God could become a great source of comfort to her. But she ought to hand over her niece, if she wanted to offer a sacrifice to heaven in repentance. Besides, this widow wouldn't suit Léon at all, who needed a good-looking wife to preside at his dinner table. And she spoke admiringly of her son, full of maternal pride, listing his good qualities and showing him to be worthy of the most charming of brides.

'Just think, my dear friend, he's not even thirty yet. I should hate to seem disobliging, but you're old enough to be his mother, you know. Oh! He knows how much he owes to you, and I'm extremely grateful myself. You will always be his guardian angel. But, you know, when something's over, it's over. Surely you didn't imagine that you could keep him for ever, did you?'

Then, as the unhappy woman refused to listen to reason, only wishing to get back her lover at once, the mother lost her temper.

'Look here, madame, you'd better be off! I've been far too nice over all this ... He's had enough and that's that! It's obvious. Just take a look at yourself! I'll be the one reminding him of his duty from now on if he gives in to your demands again. I ask you, what is there in it for either of you now? He'll be here himself soon; and if you were counting on me ...'

Madame Dambreville only took in the very last part of this speech. She had been pursuing Léon for a whole week, without ever getting to see him. Her face brightened as she uttered the heartfelt cry: 'If he's coming, I shall stay here!'

Whereupon she sank back heavily into a chair, gazing vacantly into space and making no further reply, as stubborn as some animal that even blows can't budge. Distressed at having said too much, and exasperated at this woman who was fast becoming a fixture in her drawing-room, and yet whom she didn't dare throw out, Madame Josserand finally went out of the room and left her there. In fact, a noise in the dining-room had made her uneasy; she thought she could hear Auguste's voice.

'All I can say, madame, is that I've never seen such behaviour!' she exclaimed, as she slammed the door violently. 'It's most indiscreet!'

As it so happened, Auguste had come upstairs determined to have with his wife's parents the discussion he'd been planning since the previous evening. Monsieur Josserand, becoming more and more lively at the prospect of having some fun, had given up all thoughts of going to the office. He had just suggested a walk to his daughters when Adèle announced the arrival of Madame Berthe's husband. There was general astonishment at this; the young wife turned pale.

'What! Your husband here?' said the father. 'I thought he was in Lyons! So you lied to me? Something's wrong. I've thought as much for the past two days!'

Then, as she got up to go, he stopped her.

'Talk to me. Have you had another row of some sort? Is it about money? About the dowry of ten thousand francs that we haven't paid him?'

'Yes, yes, that's what it was!' stammered Berthe, as she stepped aside and escaped.

Hortense also got up. She ran after her sister, and they both took refuge in her bedroom. The rustle of their skirts left behind them a trail of panic which swept over their father, suddenly finding himself seated alone at the table in the middle of the silent dining-room. He felt unwell again. His ghastly pallor and world-weary look returned. The moment he had dreaded, awaiting it with shame and anguish, had come; his son-in-law was going to mention the insurance; and he would have to admit the dishonesty of the scheme to which he had consented.

'Come in, come in, my dear Auguste,' he said, barely getting the words out. 'Berthe has just told me all about your quarrel. I'm not very well, so they're humouring me. I'm truly sorry that I can't give you the money. I should never have promised to, I know.'

So he faltered on, like some guilty party confessing a crime. Auguste listened to him in surprise. He had already learned the truth about the bogus insurance, but had never dared ask for the ten thousand francs; that terrible Madame Josserand might have reacted by sending him to old Vabre's tomb to get his own paternal inheritance of ten thousand francs.

As the subject had been brought up, however, Auguste used this as a starting point. It was his first grievance.

'Yes, yes, sir,' he said; 'I know all about it; I've had it up to here with all your fine tales and promises. I wouldn't have minded so much about not having the money but it's the hypocrisy of the whole thing that makes me so angry! Why all this complication about an insurance policy that never existed! Why pretend to be so kindhearted and sympathetic, offering to advance sums which, as you said, couldn't be touched for three years, when all the while you hadn't got a penny! There's only one word for such behaviour!'

Monsieur Josserand was on the point of replying, 'It wasn't me, it was the others!'

But a sense of family honour restrained him, and he hung his head in shame, while Auguste went on: 'Besides, everybody was against me; Duveyrier, with his scoundrel of a lawyer, was no better. I asked them to insert a clause in the contract, guaranteeing the payment of the insurance money, but they told me to keep quiet about it . . . If I had insisted on that, you could have been guilty of forgery, sir, yes, forgery!'

White as a sheet, this accusation brought the father to his feet; and he was about to reply, offering to work hard for the rest of his life, if this would buy his daughter's happiness, when

Madame Josserand rushed in like a whirlwind, beside herself
with anger at Madame Dambreville's stubbornness and unaware
that the bodice of her old green silk dress was splitting open
under the weight of her heaving bosom.

'Eh? What's that?' she cried. 'Who's talking of forgery? You,
sir? You'd better go to Père-Lachaise first, sir, and see if your
father's cash-box is open yet!'

Auguste was expecting this, but he was extremely annoyed
nevertheless.

However, with head held high, she went on with astonishing
composure: 'We've got your ten thousand francs all safe. Yes,
it's all in that drawer over there. But we're not going to give
you the money until Monsieur Vabre comes back to give you
your inheritance. A nice family, indeed! The father a gambler,
who swindles us all, and the brother-in-law a thief, who collars
the inheritance!'

'Thief? Thief?' spluttered Auguste, beside himself with rage.
'The thieves are here, madame!'

With their red faces almost touching, they confronted each
other; Monsieur Josserand, unable to bear such scenes, strove
to separate them, begging them to stay calm. His whole body
quivered, and he was obliged to sit down.

'In any case,' said Auguste, after a pause, 'I don't want a slut
like that in my house. You can keep your money and your
daughter, too. That's what I came to tell you.'

'You're changing the subject,' remarked Madame Josserand
coolly. 'Very well, we'll talk about that.'

But the father, too weak to get up, looked at them aghast. He
could no longer understand what was going on. What did they
say? Slut? Who was the slut? Then, listening to them, he realised
that it was his daughter; and the rest of his life ebbed away
through the gaping wound. So his own daughter would be the
death of him! He would thus be punished for all her faults
which he'd never corrected while bringing her up! The thought
that she was living in debt and always quarrelling with her
husband had already saddened his old age, making him relive
all the suffering he himself had had to put up with. And now
she was an adulteress, having sunk to that lowest level of infamy
for a woman. The idea was revolting to his simple, honest soul.
He grew cold as ice, listening, mute, while the others argued.

'I told you that she'd be unfaithful to me!' cried Auguste, in a tone of indignant triumph.

'And I told you that you were driving her to it!' screamed Madame Josserand, exultantly. 'Oh, I'm not saying Berthe was right to do what she did; in fact, she's behaved like an idiot, and she's about to know exactly what I think about it all . . . But, as she's not here, I'll say it again: you, and you alone, are to blame!'

'What do you mean? I'm to blame?'

'Of course you are, my dear! You haven't got the slightest idea how to treat a woman . . . Now, listen to me, here's an example. Did you ever condescend to come to one of my Tuesdays? No. And if you did, you only stayed half an hour at the most, and then you only came three times during the whole season. It's all very well to say you've always got a headache. Manners are manners, that's all . . . I don't say it's a great crime, no; but there it is, you don't know how to behave!'

She hissed out the words with a venom that had gradually accumulated, for when her daughter had got married she had counted on her son-in-law to fill her drawing-room for her with desirable guests. But he had brought no one, and never even came himself; thus another of her dreams vanished, realising that she could never hope to rival the Duveyrier choruses.

'However,' she added, with a touch of irony, 'I don't force anybody to enjoy themselves in my home.'

'That fact is, nobody ever *does* enjoy themselves,' he retorted, irritated.

She lost her temper instantly.

'That's right, go ahead, insult me as much as you like! I'd have you know, sir, that, if I chose, I could get the very best of Parisian high society to come to my parties, and I certainly never depended on you for my social position.'

It was no longer a question of Berthe's misconduct; in this personal quarrel her adultery wasn't an issue. As if the victim of some hideous nightmare, Monsieur Josserand sat there listening to them. It wasn't possible; his own daughter could never have caused him this kind of grief. At last, rising with difficulty, he went out, without saying a word, to find Berthe. As soon as she came, he thought, she would fling her arms round Auguste's neck; everything would be explained, everything would be forgotten. He found her having a row with Hortense, who kept urging her to ask her husband's forgiveness, for she was already tired of her, fearing that she might have to share her room with her for some time to come. At first Berthe refused, but finally followed her father.

As they came back to the dining-room, where the dirty breakfast cups were still lying around, Madame Josserand was shouting: 'No, I meant it, I don't feel at all sorry for you!'

Then, seeing Berthe come in, she was silent, relapsing into her severe, majectic pose, while Auguste made a grand gesture of protest, as if to sweep his wife from his sight.

'Now, look,' said Monsieur Josserand, in his low, tremulous voice, 'What's the matter with all of you? You're driving me crazy with this bickering. I don't know what's going on. Tell me, my child, your husband's mistaken, isn't he? You explain it to him, go on. Show some compassion for your poor old parents. Now, kiss and make up, for my sake.'

Berthe, who would have embraced Auguste, stood there trussed in her dressing-gown, looking very awkward as she saw her husband recoil from her with a look of tragic repugnance.

'What? You won't kiss him, my darling?' continued the father. 'You ought to make the first move. And you, my dear boy, you should encourage her, and show a little understanding.'

Finally Auguste exploded: 'Be understanding! I like that! I caught her in her nightdress, sir, with that man! Are you making fun of me, suggesting that I should embrace her? In her night-dress, do you hear, sir?'

Monsieur Josserand was thunderstruck. Then, seizing Berthe's arm, he exclaimed: 'You're not saying anything. So it's true, is it? On your knees, then!'

But Auguste had reached the door; he was about to escape.

'It's no good. Your old tricks won't work this time! Don't think you can saddle me with her again. Once was more than enough. Never again, do you hear? I'd rather get a divorce. Hand her on to someone else, if you find her a nuisance. And, as it happens, you're no better than she is.'

He waited until he had got into the hall before relieving his feelings in one final taunt: 'Yes, if you've turned your daughter into a tart, you shouldn't shove her on to an honest man.'

The front door was slammed, and there was a profound silence. Berthe mechanically sat back down at the table with downcast eyes, examining the dregs in her coffee cup, while her mother paced up and down, carried away by the strength of her emotions. The father, utterly worn out, his face white with pain, sat alone in the far corner of the room, leaning against the wall. The room reeked of rancid butter, the cheap kind of butter on sale at Les Halles.

'Now that insolent man has gone,' said Madame Josserand, 'we can sort this out. You see, monsieur, this is all the result of your incompetence. Now do you see how wrong you were? Do you think that this sort of thing would ever have occurred in the home of one of the Bernheim brothers, to one of the owners of the Saint-Joseph glass factory? No, I should think not! If you'd listened to me, if you'd managed to twist your employers round your little finger, this insolent person would be grovelling at our feet now, for, obviously, he's only after money. If you've got money, people think you're somebody, monsieur. Far better be envied than pitied. Whenever I had twenty sous, I always pretended I had forty. But you, sir, you don't give a damn whether I go barefoot or not; you've let your wife and daughters down in a most disgraceful fashion, dragging them down to a life of misery. Oh, it's no good protesting! That's the cause of all our troubles.'

Monsieur Josserand stared blankly, without moving. His wife stopped in front of him, fired up and ready for a scene. Then, seeing that he was motionless, she resumed her pacing.

'That's it, show your contempt. You know it doesn't affect me in the slightest. Just you dare say anything against my family after what's happened in your own! Uncle Bachelard might be an old buzzard, but my sister's polite enough. Do you want to know what I think? Had my father not already died, you would have been the death of him. As for yours—'

Monsieur Josserand's pallor increased, as he gasped: 'Eléonore, I beg you. Say what you want about my father, about my whole family; but please, I beg you, leave me in peace; I don't feel well!'

Berthe looked up compassionately.

'Mamma, leave him alone,' she said.

Then, turning on her daughter, Madame Josserand went on with greater fury: 'As for you, I was saving you till last. Ever since yesterday I've been keeping it in. But I'm warning you, I can't control myself any longer! With that shop assistant of all

people! Have you lost all sense of pride? I thought that you
were simply making use of him, being just friendly enough to
keep him keen as a salesman at the counter downstairs. And I
helped you. I encouraged him! Now, tell me, what did you hope
to gain from it all?'

'Nothing at all; that's for sure!' stammered Berthe.

'So why did you carry on with him? Forget the scandal; it
was more stupid than anything else!'

'You are funny, Mamma! It's not as if one stops to think
about that sort of thing!'

Madame Josserand resumed her pacing.

'Don't stop to think! Well that's just what you ought to do.
Fancy behaving like that! Why, there's not an ounce of common
sense about the whole thing, that's what makes me so angry!
Did I ever tell you to cheat on your husband? Did I ever cheat
on your father? There he is; ask him. Let him tell you if he ever
caught me with another man.'

She slowed down, seeming almost majestic, rearranging her
bosom in the green bodice of her dress.

'No, never; not a slip, not an indiscretion, nor the thought of
one even! I've led a chaste life, and yet the Lord knows what
I've had to put up with from your father! I have every excuse,
and lots of women would have taken their revenge. But I had
common sense; that's what saved me. There, you see, he's
speechless! He's there in his chair with nothing to say. As a
virtuous woman, I'm beyond reproach. Oh, you great idiot,
surely you see what a fool you've made of yourself.'

Then she delivered a long lecture on morality as far as
adultery was concerned. Hadn't she now given Auguste the
right to lord it over her? She had given him a terrible weapon.
Even if they were to make it up, she would never be able to
have the slightest row with him without that being instantly
flung in her face. A great state of affairs, eh? How delightful it
would be for her always to eat humble pie! It was all over, and
she could say good-bye to any of the little privileges to be
obtained from a dutiful husband, such as any little kindnesses
and considerations. No! Better to live a virtuous life than not be
able to have the last word in one's own home!

'Before God, I swear,' she cried, 'I would have shown restraint
myself, even if the Emperor himself* had tried it on with me!
There's too much to lose!'

She strode on, silent for a time, as if lost in thought, and then added: 'Besides, it's the most shameful thing of all.'

Monsieur Josserand looked at her, and then at his daughter, moving his lips without speaking, his whole dejected frame beseeching them to put an end to this savagery. But Berthe, though usually daunted by violence, had been so wounded by her mother's moral lecture that she finally rebelled; what she had been taught while looking for a husband had left her unaware of the gravity of what she had done.

'For God's sake!' she cried, planting both elbows on the table, 'you shouldn't have made me marry a man I didn't care for . . . I hate him now, and so I've found somebody else.'

And it all came out; in fragments and then suddenly a rush of words: the story of her marriage; the three winters devoted to man-hunting; the various youths at whom she'd been hurled; these failed attempts to sell her body on the streets of middle-class drawing-rooms; what mothers taught their penniless daughters, a complete course in polite and acceptable prostitution, the lightest of touches during a dance, the surrendering of hands behind a door, the shamelessness of innocence speculating on the lustful appetites of the foolish; then, one fine evening, a husband picked up just like a whore picks up a client; the husband trapped behind a curtain, falling into the snare of his feverish desire.

'Anyway, he can't stand me, and I can't stand him!' she exclaimed. 'It's not my fault that we don't understand each other. The day after our wedding he seemed to think that we'd swindled him; yes, he had the same cold and disagreeable look on his face as he does when he loses a sale. As for me, I was never smitten with him. If that's all that marriage has to offer! It started from that moment. Never mind, it was bound to happen, and it's not all my fault.'

She was silent; and then; with an air of profound conviction, she added: 'Ah, Mamma, how well I understand you now! Do you remember how you told us you'd had more than enough of it?'

Standing in front of her, Madame Josserand listened to her, indignant and aghast.

'*I* said that?' she screamed.

But Berthe was worked up and wouldn't stop.

'Yes, you did, lots of times. And I'd like to see how you'd

have behaved in my place. Auguste is not easy-going, like Papa.
You'd have had a fight about money before the week was out.
It's men like him that make you realise that all men are good
for nothing but to be used.

'*I* said that?' cried the mother, beside herself with rage.

She approached her daughter so threateningly that the father
held out both hands, as if begging for mercy. Their endless
shouting struck him to the core; each fresh outburst seemed to
widen the wound. Tears filled his eyes as he stammered out:
'Please stop it. Spare me all this!'

'What! No, it's shocking,' continued Madame Josserand,
raising her voice. 'The wretched girl actually blames me for her
promiscuous conduct! She'll tell me next that it was I who
helped her to be unfaithful to her husband! So it's my fault,
then? After all, that's what it comes down to. Well, is it?'

Berthe sat there, her elbows on the table, looking pale but
resolute.

'Well obviously if you had brought me up differently—'

She never finished the sentence. Her mother gave her such a
hard slap that it knocked her forward on to the oil-cloth table-
cover. Since last night this smack had lurked in her palm, her
fingers itching, as when her little girl used to oversleep.

'There, take that for your education!' she cried. 'Your husband ought to have knocked you senseless!'

Without raising her head, Berthe burst into tears, resting her
cheek on her arm. She forgot that she was twenty-four; this slap
reminded her of the past, and of all the timorous hypocrisy of
her growing-up. The independence of the adult crumbled in her
childhood pain.

Hearing her sob so violently, her father was overcome with a
terrible grief. Tottering forward, he pushed his wife aside,
saying: 'Tell me, do you both want to be the death of me? Must
I get down on my knees and beg you?'

Having unburdened her feelings, and finding nothing further
to say, Madame Josserand withdrew in regal silence. Opening
the door suddenly, she caught Hortense listening behind it. This
caused a fresh outburst.

'So you've been listening to all this filth, have you? One of you
does shocking things, and the other gloats over them! You're
two of a kind! Good God! Whoever could have brought you
up?

Hortense came in calmly, and said: 'I didn't need to listen; we can hear you from the far end of the kitchen. The maid is in fits. Besides, I'm old enough to get married now, and so there's no reason why I shouldn't know.'

'Verdier, I suppose!' was the mother's biting reply. 'That's the sort of satisfaction I can expect from you too. Now you're waiting for the little brat to die; but you'll have to wait because I've heard it's a big, fat baby. Serves him right!'

A flood of bile turned the girl's gaunt face yellow, as she replied through clenched teeth: 'If it's a big, fat baby, Verdier can get rid of it. And I'll make him get rid of it quicker than you think, just to teach you all. Yes, yes; I'll find myself a husband, since the matches that you make are always a sham!'

Then, as her mother approached:' You're not hitting me, oh no! So you'd better watch it!'

They glared at each other, and Madame Josserand was the first to give in, masking her retreat with an air of disdainful superiority.

The father, however, thought that the fight was about to start again. Caught between these women, the mother and her daughters, the three human beings he'd loved and who now were ready to murder one another, he felt as if the whole world were giving way under his feet; and he, too, escaped to his room as if he had received the final blow and wanted to die alone. He repeatedly sobbed out: 'I can't bear it, I can't bear it any more!'

Silence reigned once more in the dining-room. Berthe, still letting out long sighs, with her cheek resting on her arm, had calmed down. Hortense sat peacefully at the other end of the table, buttering a piece of toast to regain her composure. She then drove her sister deeper into despair with her gloomy reasoning, saying that life at home had become unbearable and that if she were in her place she would prefer to be slapped by her husband rather than by her mother; that, at least, was far more normal. What's more, when she married Verdier, she would simply throw her mother out, as she was not going to have rows of this sort in her home. Just then Adèle came in to clear the table; but Hortense went on, saying that if there was any more of this she should hand in her notice; and the maid agreed with her. She had been obliged to shut the kitchen window because Lisa and Julie had both been prying. The whole thing, however, had amused her greatly, and she was still laughing about it. What a fine slap Madame Berthe had got! She was the worst off, after all. And as she waddled around, Adèle became quite philosophical: after all, she said, what did the people in the house care? The world went on, and before the week was out nobody would even remember madame and her two gentlemen. Hortense, who nodded her approval, interrupted her to complain about the butter; it had left a vile taste in her mouth. Goodness gracious! Butter at twenty-two sous! Why, it could only be poison! And, as it left a revolting scum in the saucepans, the maid proceeded to explain that it was not even economical to buy such stuff; but then a dull sound, a sort of thud on the floor, made them all stop and listen.

Berthe, alarmed, finally raised her head. 'What's that?' she asked.

'Perhaps it's madame and the other lady in the drawing-room,' suggested Adèle.

On going through the drawing-room, Madame Josserand had received a shock. A lady was sitting there, all by herself.

'What? You're still here?' she exclaimed, on recognising Madame Dambreville, whose presence she had entirely forgotten.

The visitor didn't move. The family rows, raised voices, the banging of doors, seemed to have passed her by, and she was completely unconscious of it all. She remained there, motionless, gazing vaguely into space, absorbed in passionate despair.

But something was at work within her; this advice of Léon's mother had upset her, and she had half decided to pay dearly for the last few fragments of happiness.

'Come, now,' cried Madame Josserand, with brutal candour. 'You can't very well sleep here. I've heard from my son, and I'm no longer expecting him.'

Then, with a parched tongue, as if she had just woken up, Madame Dambreville spoke.

'I'm leaving now. Please excuse me. Tell him from me that I've thought the matter over, and I consent. I'll think it over further, and perhaps I'll arrange for him to marry that girl, as he wants to. But I'm the one giving her to him, and I want him to come and ask me for her; ask me, just me, do you see? Oh, make him come back to me, make him come back!'

She went on imploringly, and then, lowering her voice, like a woman who, having sacrificed everything, still obstinately clings to one last consolation, she added: 'He can marry her, but he must live with us. Otherwise, there's nothing doing. I'd rather lose him altogether.'

Then she left. Madame Josserand became charming once again, making various consoling noises in the hall. She promised to see Léon that very evening, in a humble, affectionate frame of mind, declaring that he would be delighted to live with his new aunt. Then, having shut the door behind Madame Dambreville, full of pity and tenderness, she thought to herself: Poor boy! He'll pay dearly for that.

But at that moment she, too, heard the dull thud which shook the floorboards. What on earth could that be? Had the maid smashed all the crockery?

She rushed back to the dining-room and questioned her daughters.

'What's the matter? Did somebody drop the sugar bowl?'

'No, Mamma, we don't know what it is.'

Turning round to look for Adèle, she caught her listening at the bedroom door.

'What are you doing?' she cried. 'Everything's being smashed to bits in your kitchen while you stand there spying on your master. Yes, yes, it started with the prunes and now it's ended with something very different. For some time past, my girl, I haven't liked the way you look: you smell of men—'

Wide-eyed, Adèle looked at her, and interrupted: 'It's nothing like that. I think it's the master who's collapsed in there.'

'My God, I think she's right!' cried Berthe, turning pale. 'It was just as if someone had fallen over.'

So they went into the room. Lying on the floor, near the bed, Monsieur Josserand had fainted. His head had struck a chair, and a thin stream of blood trickled from his right ear. The mother, her two daughters and the maid stood in a circle examining him. Only Berthe burst into tears, sobbing convulsively, as if still smarting from the slap she'd received.

And as the four of them lifted up the old man and placed him on the bed, they heard him murmur: 'It's all over. They've killed me.'

Months passed, and spring had come. In the house in the Rue de Choiseul everybody was talking of the approaching marriage of Octave and Madame Hédouin.

That, however, was rather premature. Octave had gone back to his old job at 'Au Bonheur des Dames', where every day turnover was increasing. Since her husband's death, Madame Hédouin had not been able to manage an ever-growing business on her own. Old Deleuze, her uncle, was crippled with rheumatism and couldn't do anything at all; so, as a matter of course, Octave, young, active and full of ideas about expansion, didn't take long to take over major responsibilities in the firm. Still unnerved by his stupid love affair with Berthe, he now no longer dreamed of making use of women and even feared them. The best thing, he thought, would be for him quietly to become Madame Hédouin's partner, and then to enjoy the life of a millionaire. Remembering, too, his grotesquely unsuccessful attempt to seduce her, he treated her as if she were a man, which was exactly what she wanted.

From then on their relationship became very intimate. They would shut themselves for hours together in the little back room. It was here where, having sworn to possess her, he had previously engaged in all kinds of tactical manoeuvres, trying to take advantage of her love of business, caressing numbers into her ear, ready to pounce in the excitement of takings high enough to put her off her guard. Now he was merely good-natured, with no ulterior motive, thoroughly engrossed in the business itself. Even his desire seemed to have subsided, although he still remembered the tingle in her spine as she leaned against him when they waltzed together on the evening of Berthe's wedding. Perhaps she had felt something for him after all? Anyhow, it was best to remain as they were; for, as she rightly observed, the firm needed their full attention, and it was foolish to want things that would only have taken their minds off it from morning till night.

Seated together at the narrow desk, they often forgot themselves after going through the books and settling the orders.

Octave reverted to his dreams of expansion. He had sounded out the owner of the next house, who was quite ready to sell. The umbrella-maker and the second-hand dealer must be forced to quit, so that they could open a special silk department. She listened intently, still not daring to take such a step. But she warmed increasingly to Octave's talent for business, recognising in him her own drive and taste for making money, and the serious, practical side of her character beneath his debonair exterior of a polite shop-assistant. What's more, he had such boldness and flair, qualities lacking in herself, that she was filled with admiration. It was imagination applied to trade, the only sort of imagination that ever stirred her. He was becoming her master.

At length, one evening, as they sat side by side, looking over some invoices, under the hot flame of the gas flame, she said slowly: 'I've spoken to my uncle, Monsieur Octave. He's consented, so we'll buy the house next door. Only—'

But, merrily interrupting her, he cried: 'The Vabres will go under then!'

She smiled, and murmured reproachfully: 'So you hate them, do you? It's not right, you should be the last person to wish them any harm.'

She had never once made a remark about his affair with Berthe, so this sudden allusion to it made him very embarrassed, without exactly knowing why. He blushed and stammered out some excuse.

'No, no! That doesn't concern me,' she continued, still smiling and very calm. 'Forgive me; I didn't mean to mention it. I'd promised myself never to say a word about it . . . you're young. Serves these women right, doesn't it, if they're willing. It's up to the husbands to look after their wives if they can't look after themselves.'

He felt relieved to see that she wasn't angry. He had often feared that if she got to know about his past romance she might disapprove.

'You interrupted me, Monsieur Octave,' she went on gravely. 'I was about to add that, if I purchase the adjoining house, thus doubling the size of my present business, I can't possibly remain a widow. I shall be obliged to marry again.'

Octave was astonished. So she had already got a husband in

mind, and he knew nothing about it. At once his position there seemed to him compromised.

'My uncle,' she continued, 'told me as much himself. Oh, there's no hurry about it just yet! I've only been in mourning eight months and would wait until the autumn. But, if one's in commerce, all matters of the heart must be subordinate to the imperatives of the situation . . . It's absolutely essential to have a man here.'

She discussed this in a matter-of-fact way as if it were a business deal, while he watched her, with her beautiful regular features, clear healthy complexion, and neat wavy black hair. And he regretted not having tried to become her lover again since she'd lost her husband.

'It's a very serious matter,' he faltered. 'It needs a lot of thought.'

Of course, she agreed with him entirely. And she mentioned her age.

'I'm getting on, you know. I'm five years older than you, Monsieur Octave—'

Then, overcome, he interrupted her, thinking he understood her. Seizing her hands, he exclaimed: 'Oh, madame! Oh, madame!'

But she got up and freed herself. Then she turned down the gas.

'Well, that'll do for today . . . Some of your ideas are excellent, and it's only natural that I should have thought of you as the right person to carry them out. But there'll be a few problems and we must think the whole thing through . . . I know that deep down you're very responsible. Just think the matter over carefully and I will too. That's why I mentioned it to you. We can discuss it some other time, later on.

And things remained this way for weeks. Business went on as usual. As Madame Hédouin always maintained her calm and smiling demeanour towards him, never once hinting at anything more romantic, Octave at first affected a similar peace of mind, as glowingly happy as she was trusting implicitly in the logic of things. She would often remark that if things were meant to be, they would be. So she was never in a hurry to move things forward. None of the gossip concerning her and the young man bothered her in the slightest. All they had to do was wait.

Everyone in the house in the Rue de Choiseul declared that

the match was made. Octave had given up his room there and had got lodgings in the Rue Neuve-Saint-Augustin, close to 'Au Bonheur des Dames'. He no longer visited anyone, and never went to the Campardons' nor the Duveyriers', who were still outraged by his scandalous behaviour. Even Monsieur Gourd pretended not to recognise him when he saw him, to avoid having to greet him. Only Marie and Madame Juzeur, when they bumped into him in the neighbourhood, would stop to have a chat; Madame Juzeur, who eagerly questioned him about his reported engagement to Madame Hédouin, wanted him to promise that he would come and see her and tell her all about it. Marie was in despair at finding herself pregnant again, and told him of Jules's amazement and of her parents' dreadful anger. However, when the rumour of his marriage was confirmed, Octave was surprised to be greeted so warmly by Monsieur Gourd. Campardon, though still not offering to make it up, nodded cordially to him across the street, while Duveyrier, when looking in one evening to buy some gloves, was very friendly. Gradually, the whole household seemed ready to forgive and forget.

Moreover, the middle-class respectability of the building had been restored. Behind the mahogany doors, little corners of virtue reasserted themselves; the gentleman from the third floor came to work one night a week as usual; the other Madame Campardon passed by, as inflexible as her principles; the maids sported dazzling white aprons; and, in the warm silence of the staircase, the pianos on every floor played out the same waltzes, music at once mystic and remote.

Yet the taint of adultery still lingered, imperceptible to the ill-bred among them, but disagreeable to those with high moral standards. Auguste obstinately refused to take his wife back, and as long as Berthe lived with her parents the scandal would not go away; tangible evidence of it would remain. Yet not one of the tenants openly told the real story, as it would have been embarrassing for everybody. By common and, as it were, unspoken consent, they had agreed that the quarrel between Berthe and Auguste had been provoked by the ten thousand francs, a mere squabble about money; it was a much nicer version of events; and it could even be talked about in the presence of young ladies. Would the parents pay up, or wouldn't they? The whole thing became so perfectly simple, for not a soul in the

neighbourhood was either amazed or indignant at the idea that
money problems should lead to blows. Deep down, of course,
this polite arrangement hadn't changed anything; and despite
the apparent calm in the presence of this misfortune, the whole
house had suffered a cruel shock to its dignity.

It was Duveyrier in particular who, as landlord, bore the
brunt of this misfortune so persistent and so undeserved. For
some time past Clarisse had been worrying him so much that he
often returned to his wife in tears. The scandal of the adultery
had stung him to the quick; for, as he said, he saw passers-by
looking the building up and down, the house that he and his
father-in-law had tried so hard to enhance with every domestic
virtue; and it couldn't go on; the whole place would have to be
decontaminated to satisfy his personal honour. So, for the sake
of public decency, he urged Auguste to effect a reconciliation.
Unfortunately he refused, his anger still stoked by Théophile
and Valérie, who had taken over permanently at the cashier's
desk and who continued to revel in the whole fiasco. Then, as
the business in Lyons was in a bad way, and the silk warehouse
likely to collapse for lack of capital, Duveyrier had had an idea.
The Josserands were doubtless anxious to get rid of their
daughter: Auguste should offer to take her back, but only on
condition that they paid the dowry of fifty thousand francs.
Possibly, if they pleaded with him, Uncle Bachelard would end
up giving them the money. At first Auguste vehemently refused
to be a party to any such arrangement; even if it were a hundred
thousand francs, he would still have been robbed. However,
feeling very worried about his April outgoings, he finally
allowed himself to be persuaded by Duveyrier, the latter arguing
in the name of morality, his sole aim being, as he said, to do a
good deed.

When everything was settled, Clotilde chose the Abbé Mauduit to negotiate matters. It was rather delicate; only a priest
could intervene without compromising himself. As it so happened, the abbé had been greatly upset by the shocking things
that had occurred in one of the most valuable households of his
parish. Indeed, he had already offered to use all his wisdom,
experience and authority to put an end to a scandal over which
enemies of the Church would only gloat. But when Clotilde
mentioned the dowry, and asked him to inform the Josserands

of Auguste's conditions, he bowed his head and maintained a painful silence.

'It's money that my brother claims is due to him, you understand,' said Clotilde. 'It's not a deal. My brother's absolutely clear about that.'

'Then it's my duty to go,' said the abbé, at last.

For days on end the Josserands had been waiting for a proposal of some kind. Valérie must have said something, for everyone in the house was talking about it: were they so hard up that they'd have to keep their daughter? Would they manage to find the fifty thousand francs in order to get rid of her? Ever since the subject had been broached, Madame Josserand had been in a terrible rage. What! After the lengths to which they'd had to go to get Berthe married once, now they had to marry her off a second time? Nothing had been settled, a dowry had to be found, and all their money worries were beginning all over again. Surely no mother had ever had to go through this twice over. And it was all that trollop's fault who had been stupid enough to forget her vows! The house became a sort of hell on earth; Berthe was given no respite, for even her sister, Hortense, furious at not having the bedroom to herself, never opened her mouth now without making some cutting remark. Even her meals were a cause for reproach. It seemed rather off, when one had a husband somewhere, to come and sponge off one's parents for a meal, when they themselves had barely enough to eat! Then, in despair, poor Berthe slunk away, sobbing, calling herself a coward, too afraid to go downstairs and throw herself at Auguste's feet begging for mercy: 'Here I am. Beat me, for I can't possibly be more miserable than I am already.' Only Monsieur Josserand treated his daughter with kindness. But her faults and tears were killing him; the cruelty of his family had dealt him a final blow; on permanent sick-leave, he remained almost constantly in bed. Doctor Juillerat, who was looking after him, said it was blood-poisoning; it was actually the entire break-up of his whole body, each organ being affected in turn.

'When you've made your father die of grief, you'll be happy, won't you?' cried the mother.

Berthe, indeed, was afraid to go into her father's room now, for all they did was weep together, only doing each other further harm.

At length Madame Josserand came to a big decision: she

invited Uncle Bachelard for dinner, resigned to having to humiliate herself yet again. She would gladly have paid the fifty
thousand francs out of her own pocket, if she had had the
money, rather than be saddled with this grown-up married
daughter of hers, whose presence brought disgrace on her
Tuesday gatherings. What's more, she'd been told some monstrous things about her brother, and if he didn't cough up, she
was going to give him a piece of her mind once and for all.

Bachelard behaved in a particularly disgusting way at dinner.
He had arrived half drunk: since losing Fifi, he had sunk to the
very lowest depths. Luckily Madame Josserand hadn't invited
anyone else; her good name would have been at risk. He fell
asleep during dessert, in the middle of regaling them with his
incomprehensible and obscene tit-bits, and they had to wake
him up before taking him into Monsieur Josserand's room.
Here, signs of skilful stage-management were evident; in order
to work on the old drunkard's feelings, two chairs had been
placed beside the bed, one for the mother, the other for the
uncle, while Berthe and Hortense were to stand. Let's just see if
he dared renege on his promises again when faced with a dying
man, in such a mournful room, half lit by a smoky lamp.

'Narcisse,' said Madame Josserand, 'this is a serious
situation . . .'

Then, in low, solemn tones, she explained what the situation
was, explaining her daughter's deplorable misfortune, Auguste's
revolting greed, and her painful decision to pay the fifty thousand francs to put an end to this scandal shaming their family.
Then she said, severely: 'Remember what you promised, Narcisse. The night the contract was signed, you put your hand on
your heart and promised that Berthe could rely on her uncle's
kindness. Well, where is that kindness? The moment has come
for you to show it . . . Monsieur Josserand, join me in showing
him what his duty is, if, in your ailing state, you can do so.'

Deeply repugnant though it was to him, the father, from sheer
love for his daughter, murmured: 'It's quite true; you did
promise, Bachelard. Now, before I'm gone, please act like an
honourable man.'

Berthe and Hortense, however, hoping to soften their uncle,
had filled his glass somewhat too frequently. He was in such a
state that they couldn't get anything out of him.

'Eh? What?' he stuttered, without needing to exaggerate his

drunken air. 'Never promise . . . don't know what you mean! Just tell me that again, Eléonore.'

So Madame Josserand went over it all again, and made Berthe, sobbing, embrace him, begging him to keep his word for the sake of her sick husband, and proving to him that in giving the fifty thousand francs, he was fulfilling a sacred duty.

Then, as he dropped off to sleep again, without apparently being affected in the least by the sight of the sick man or the mournful bedroom, Madame Josserand suddenly exploded: 'Look here, Narcisse, this has gone on far too long; you're a swine! I've heard all about your disgusting behaviour. You've married off your mistress to Gueulin, and given them fifty thousand francs, exactly the sum that you promised us. Nice, isn't it? And that beast Gueulin plays a fine part in it all, doesn't he? As for you, you're far worse, you take the very bread out of our mouths, and squander your fortune; that's right, squander it, robbing us of money that was rightfully ours for the sake of that little bitch!'

Never before had she gone so far. To hide her embarrassment, Hortense had to busy herself with her father's medicine. Getting worse by the minute, the sick man tossed about restlessly on his pillows, repeating in a trembling voice, 'Eléonore, be quiet, I beg you! He won't give us anything. If you want to have it out with him, take him away, so that I can't hear you!'

Berthe began to sob loudly as she joined in her father's entreaties.

'That's enough, Mamma; for Father's sake, please stop! My God! I can't bear it! To think that I'm responsible for all this! I'd rather go away somewhere and die quietly!'

Then Madame Josserand bluntly put the question to Bachelard: 'So, will you or will you not give us the fifty thousand francs, so that your niece may hold her head up?'

In his bewilderment, he tried to explain.

'Listen to me a moment. I caught Gueulin and Fifi together. What could I do? I had to marry them. It wasn't my fault!'

'Will you or will you not give the dowry that you promised us?' she furiously reiterated.

His speech faltered, so fuddled now that words failed him.

'Can't do it, swear I can't! Utterly ruined! Else I would, right now! Cross my heart, I would!'

She cut him short with a terrible gesture.

'Very well!' she exclaimed. 'I shall call a family meeting, and pronounce you incapable of managing your own affairs. When uncles become doddering idiots, it's time to have them shut up in some asylum.'

Suddenly Bachelard was overcome with emotion. The room seemed to him very gloomy, with its one flickering lamp; he looked at the sick man, supported by his daughters, who was about to swallow a spoonful of some black liquid, and he immediately burst into tears, accusing his sister of never having understood him. Gueulin's betrayal had been painful enough for him, he said. They knew how sensitive he was, and it was wrong to have asked him to dinner, only to upset his feelings directly afterwards. Instead of the fifty thousand francs, they could have every drop of blood in his veins; there, that was all he could say!

Utterly worn out, Madame Josserand gave up persecuting him when the maid announced Doctor Juillerat and the Abbé Mauduit. They had met on the stairs, and they came in together. The doctor found Monsieur Josserand much worse, for he was still distressed by the scene in which he'd had to play a part. The abbé wanted to take Madame Josserand into the drawing-room, as he had a message for her. She instinctively guessed where he had come from, and majestically replied that she was among family and they should hear everything; even the doctor wouldn't be in the way, for a physician was a confessor as well.

'Then, Madame,' said the priest, calmly but somewhat awkwardly, 'please understand that my actions are the result of an ardent wish to reconcile two families.'

He spoke of God's mercy, and of his joy in being able to reassure honest hearts by putting a stop to so intolerable a state of affairs. He alluded to Berthe as an unfortunate child, which drew from her fresh tears, and there was such fatherly tenderness in everything he said, and his words were so carefully chosen, that Hortense was not obliged to leave the room. Finally, however, he had to bring up the subject of the fifty thousand francs: it seemed that it only needed husband and wife to kiss and make up; but then he mentioned the formal condition of the payment of the dowry.

'My dear abbé, excuse my interrupting you,' said Madame Josserand, 'we are deeply touched by your efforts. But that's out of the question, you understand! We can never bargain with our daughter's honour . . . I can hardly believe that some people would use our child to do a deal . . . Oh! I know all about it; before they were at daggers drawn, and now they're inseparable and insult us from morning to night. No, my dear abbé, that kind of bargain would be outrageous.'

'But, madame,' the priest ventured to observe, 'it seems to me—'

She cut him short, as she went on, with glorious assurance: 'Listen! Here's my brother, ask him what he thinks. Only a moment ago he said to me: "Here, Eléonore, I've brought you the fifty thousand francs. Do settle this wretched business." Well, just ask him what my answer was. Wake up, Narcisse! Wake up, and tell him the truth!'

Bachelard had gone to sleep again in an armchair at the end of the room. He stirred and uttered a few incoherent words. Then, as his sister continued to address him, he placed his hand on his heart, and stammered out: 'When duty calls, we must act. Family comes first!'

'There, you hear what he says!' cried Madame Josserand, triumphantly. 'No money! It's a disgrace! Just tell those people that we'd rather die than pay up. The dowry is here, and we would have paid it; but when it's demanded to buy back our daughter, that really is too disgusting. First let Auguste take Berthe back, and then we'll see what can be done afterwards.'

She had raised her voice to such a pitch that the doctor, examining his patient, had to tell her to be quiet.

'Quietly, please, madame,' he said. 'Your husband is in pain.'

The Abbé Mauduit, becoming more and more embarrassed, approached the bed, and made a few sympathetic remarks. He then withdrew, without mentioning the matter further, hiding his abject failure beneath a good-humoured smile, while his lip curled with wounded disgust. As the doctor also went on his way he bluntly informed Madame Josserand that there was no hope and that they should be extremely careful, as the slightest upset might prove fatal. Appalled at the news, she went into the dining-room to join Bachelard and the girls, leaving Monsieur Josserand in peace, as he seemed inclined to go to sleep.

'Berthe,' she murmured, 'you've just managed to finish off your father. The doctor has just told me so.'

Then the three of them, sitting at the table, began to cry, while Bachelard, also weeping, mixed himself a grog.

When Auguste was told of the Josserands' reply he became even more furious with his wife, and swore that he would kick her out if ever she came and asked to be forgiven. But, in actual fact, he missed her greatly. There was a void in his life, he felt lost, and the aggravations of his solitude were quite as serious as those of his married life. Rachel, whom he had kept on to annoy Berthe, robbed him and scolded him now with the same cool impudence of a wife; and he missed the little pleasures of their shared life, the evenings of mutual boredom, followed by costly reconciliations beneath warm sheets. Above all, he was tired of Théophile and Valérie, who had installed themselves downstairs, and filled the whole shop with their importance. He even suspected them of openly helping themselves to the takings in the till. Valérie was not like Berthe; she enjoyed sitting enthroned at the cashier's desk; only it seemed to him that she had a way of attracting men, right under the nose of her imbecile husband, whose perpetual cold blurred his eyes with tears. He would rather have had Berthe there. At least she never brought half the street traipsing in through the shop. There was something else that worried him. 'Au Bonheur des Dames' was prospering, and threatening to rival his own business, where the takings diminished daily. True, he didn't regret the loss of that wretched Octave, but he was fair-minded, and fully recognised his flair for business. How well things would have worked out if only they had got on better! Waves of nostalgia came over him, and there were moments when, sick of solitude, and feeling his life crumbling away beneath him, he would have gone upstairs to the Josserands and taken Berthe back from them for nothing.

Duveyrier, however, didn't give up hope, constantly urging Auguste to make up, increasingly distressed by the moral blemish that the whole affair had cast on his property. He even pretended to believe what Madame Josserand had told the abbé: if Auguste would take his wife back unconditionally, her dowry money would be paid the very next day. Then, as the very idea made Auguste terribly angry again, the counsellor would appeal to his better nature; he would walk with him along the quays, on his way to the Palais de Justice, teaching him to forgive such wrongs in a voice half choked with tears, and getting him to subscribe to the view, both dismal and cowardly, that happiness could only be found in putting up with a wife, as one couldn't really manage without one.

Duveyrier was in decline; the whole of the Rue de Choiseul was worried by the sight of his sorry gait and pallid face, on which the red blotches grew larger and more inflamed. Some hidden grief seemed to be weighing him down. It was Clarisse who was growing fatter, more insolent, and more presumptious by the day. As her middle-class plumpness increased, he found her fine airs and affected good breeding ever more intolerable. She now forbade him to address her familiarly when members of her family were present; and she flirted in most outrageous fashion with her piano teacher right before his eyes, much to his grief. Twice he had caught her in bed with Théodore, had lost his temper and then had gone down on his knees to beg her forgiveness, accepting that he could only have a share of her. Then, to ensure he remained meek and submissive, she would constantly express her disgust at his blotchy face; and said that she had even thought of handing him on to one of her cooks, a buxom wench accustomed to the most menial of jobs; but even the cook couldn't stomach the idea. Every day, life became more and more unbearable for Duveyrier at his mistress's which now resembled a more hellish version of his own household. The tribe of parasites, the mother, the big blackguard of a brother, the two little sisters and even the invalid aunt, all robbed him unmercifully, living off him shamelessly, and even emptying his pockets at night when he was asleep. His whole life was falling apart: he was almost broke and his legal career was at risk. True, they couldn't dismiss him from his post as a magistrate; but young barristers looked at him roguishly, which embarrassed him when he sat there on the bench administering justice. And when he fled in self-disgust from the din and the filth in the Rue d'Assas and took refuge in the Rue de Choiseul, his wife's cold hatred finished him off. It was then that he would lose his head, glancing towards the Seine on his way to the court, planning to throw himself into it the night his suffering gave him the courage to do so.

Clothilde had, indeed, noticed her husband's emotional state with some anxiety, incensed that that mistress of his, however immoral, couldn't make a man happy. She was also deeply disturbed by an incident, the consequences of which had shaken the whole house. On going upstairs one morning to get a handkerchief, Clémence had caught Hippolyte with that little wretch Louise, on her own bed; since then she boxed his ears in the kitchen at the least provocation, which had unsettled the other servants. The worst of it was, madame could no longer turn a blind eye to the fact that her chambermaid and her footman were living in sin: that other maids laughed at them, the scandal spread along the shops in the street, and if she wished to keep the guilty couple she would have to force them to get married; and as she still found Clémence a most satisfactory maid, that's what she resolved to do, thinking of nothing else. To negotiate matters, however, seemed a somewhat delicate task, especially with lovers who were always scratching each other's eyes out; so she decided to entrust the Abbé Mauduit with it; under the circumstances, he seemed to be marked out for the part of moral mediator. For some time past, indeed, her servants had caused her enormous anxiety. While in the country, she had become aware of the affair between her great lout of a son Gustave and Julie; at first she thought of dismissing the girl, but on the other hand she did like her cooking; so, after much careful reflection, she kept her on, preferring the young rascal to have a mistress in her own home, a decent girl, who wouldn't cause trouble. Elsewhere, there was no way of knowing what sort of woman a lad could get hold of; especially when they started so early. So she kept her eye on them, without saying anything; and now the other two had to come and plague her with their wretched affair!

One morning it so happened that, as Madame Duveyrier was about to go and see the Abbé Mauduit, Clémence informed her that the priest was just on his way to administer the last rites to Monsieur Josserand. The maid, having bumped into this divine presence on the staircase, rushed back to the kitchen, exclaiming: 'I knew that He would be back again this year!'

Then, alluding to the various misfortunes that had befallen the various residents of the house, she added: 'That brought us all bad luck!'

This time the Holy Ghost had not arrived too late: it was a good omen. Madame Duveyrier hastened to Saint-Roch, where she awaited the priest's return. He listened to her, sadly and silently; but he certainly couldn't refuse to enlighten the footman and the chambermaid as to the immorality of their situation. Besides, he would have to get back to the Rue de Choiseul very shortly, as poor Monsieur Josserand could surely never live through the night; and he hinted that, distressing though it was, it was precisely that fact that might make it possible for there to be a reconciliation between Auguste and Berthe. He would endeavour to arrange both matters at the same time. It was high time that the Almighty gave their efforts His blessing.

'I have prayed, madame,' said the priest. 'The Lord will triumph.'

That very evening, at seven o'clock, the whole family assembled around Monsieur Josserand's death-bed; the only ones missing were Uncle Bachelard, who couldn't be found in any of his regular cafés and Saturnin, who was still in the asylum at Les Moulineaux. Léon, whose marriage had unfortunately to be postponed due to his father's illness, looked suitably grief-stricken; Madame Josserand and Hortense bore up bravely. It was only Berthe who sobbed so loudly that, out of consideration to the dying man, she had to withdraw to the kitchen, where Adèle, making the most of the general muddle, was drinking mulled wine. Monsieur Josserand, however, died very quietly. He was the victim of his own integrity. He had lived a useless existence and he slipped away like an honest man weary of all life's evils, strangled by the calm ruthlessness of the only human beings he'd ever loved. At eight o'clock he stammered out Saturnin's name; then, turning his face to the wall, he expired.

No one thought he was dead, for everybody had feared he would go slowly and painfully. They waited a while, letting him sleep. But on finding that he was already cold, Madame Josserand, amid the general sobbing, began to scold Hortense, whom she had instructed to fetch Auguste, counting on giving Berthe back to the latter at the most intense moment of her own husband's suffering, just as he was about to pass away.

'You never think of anything!' she exclaimed, wiping her eyes.

'But, Mamma,' said the girl, weeping, 'none of us thought Papa was going to die so soon! You told me not to go down and fetch Auguste before nine o'clock, to make sure that he was there at the end!'

The quarrel helped to distract the family in their grief. Another thing that had gone wrong! Somehow, they never managed to get anything right! Fortunately, though, there was

still the funeral, which might serve to reconcile husband and
wife.

The funeral was a fitting one, yet not on such a grand scale
as Monsieur Vabre's. Nor did it create nearly as much interest
either in the house or in the neighbourhood, for Monsieur
Josserand was not a landlord, but merely an easy-going old soul
whose death had not even troubled Madame Juzeur's sleep:
Marie who, since the day before, was about to go into labour
at any moment, was the only one who said how sorry she was
not to be able to help the ladies in laying out the poor old
gentleman. Downstairs Madame Gourd thought it sufficient to
stand up and bow from her lodge as the coffin passed, without
coming to the door. All the residents, however, went to the
cemetery: Duveyrier, Campardon, the Vabres, and Monsieur
Gourd. They talked about the spring and how the crops had
been affected by the recent heavy rains.

Campardon was surprised to see Duveyrier looking so ill and,
noticing his ghastly pallor as the coffin was lowered into the
grave, the architect whispered: 'Now he's smelled the earth . . .
God save our house from further bereavements!'

Madame Josserand and her daughters had to be supported as
far as their carriage. Léon, with Uncle Bachelard's help, proved
most attentive, while Auguste sheepishly brought up the rear,
getting into another carriage with Duveyrier and Théophile.
Clotilde went with the Abbé Mauduit, who had not officiated,
but put in an appearance at the cemetery so as to give the
mourners proof of his sympathy. The horses set off homewards
more gaily; and Madame Duveyrier begged the priest to come
straight back to the house with them, deeming the moment a
favourable one. So he consented.

The three funeral carriages silently deposited the relatives at
the Rue de Choiseul. Théophile immediately went back to
Valérie who had stayed to supervise a grand cleaning-up; with
the shop shut, it was too good an opportunity to miss.

'You might as well start packing,' he exclaimed furiously.
'They're all egging him on. I bet you anything that he'll beg her
forgiveness!'

Indeed, they all felt it was high time to put an end to this
deplorable business. At least something good might come of all
this sadness. Auguste, in their midst, could easily see what it
was they wanted; and he sat alone there, exhausted and con-

fused. One by one the mourners slowly passed in under the porch, draped with black. No one spoke. On the staircase there was a silence fraught with deliberation as the crêpe petticoats sadly and softly went up the steps. In a last attempt at revolt, Auguste hurried on ahead, intending to shut himself up in his own rooms; but Clotilde and the abbé, who had followed him, detained him just as he was opening the door. Behind them, on the landing, stood Berthe, in deep mourning, accompanied by her mother and her sister. The eyes of all three were red; Madame Josserand's condition was, indeed, quite distressing to behold.

'Come, now, my friend,' said the priest, simply, with tears in his eyes.

That was enough. Auguste immediately gave in, aware that there was no more appropriate moment than this in which to make his peace. His wife sobbed, and he too wept as he stammered: 'Come home . . . We'll try not to have any more of it.'

The family hugged and kissed one another while Clotilde congratulated her brother, saying that she had always known his kindness of heart would prevail. Madame Josserand displayed a sort of crushed satisfaction, looking like a widow no longer affected by even the most unhoped-for of joys. And she brought her poor dead husband into the general happiness.

'You are doing your duty, my dear son-in-law. He who has gone to heaven thanks you for this.'

'Come on in!' repeated Auguste, quite unnerved.

Hearing a noise, however, Rachel came out into the entrance to their apartment; and, noticing the maid's silent look of rage, Berthe momentarily hesitated. Then she sternly went in, and her black mourning dress disappeared into the gloom. Auguste followed her, and the door closed behind them.

All along the staircase there floated a deep sigh of relief, filling the whole house with joy. The ladies shook their pastor by the hand; God had answered his prayers. Just as Clotilde was leading him away to settle the other matter, Duveyrier, who had stopped behind Léon and Bachelard, wearily came up. They had to explain the good news to him; yet he hardly seemed to take it in, though for months he'd been hoping for just that. His face wore a strange expression, as if he were haunted by one idea, the effect of which was taking its toll. As the Josserands went back to their apartment, he followed his wife and the abbé. They were still in the hall when the sound of stifled screams made them tremble.

'Don't be alarmed, madame,' explained Hippolyte, smugly. 'It's the little lady upstairs and her pains ... I saw Doctor Juillerat run up just now.' Then, left alone he added philosophically: 'One leaves and another one arrives.'

Clotilde took the abbé into the drawing-room and invited him to be seated; she would send Clémence to him first. She gave him a copy of the *Revue des Deux Mondes* to read while he waited, in which there were some really charming verses. She must first of all prepare her maid for what was coming. But, in her dressing-room, she found her husband sitting on a chair.

Ever since the morning Duveyrier had been in a terrible state. For the third time he had caught Clarisse with Théodore; and when he protested, all her parasite relatives, mother, brother and little sisters, had turned on him, driving him downstairs with kicks and blows, while Clarisse shouted obscenities at him, threatening in her fury to send for the police if he ever dared to set foot in her home again. It was all over; the concierge had told him downstairs that for the past week a very rich old fellow had been offering to look after madame. Having been thrown out like this, with no warm place to call his own, Duveyrier, after wandering about the streets, had gone into a back-street shop and bought a small revolver. Life for him had become too unbearable; at least he could now leave it as soon as he found a suitably quiet spot. All he could think of was finding one, as mechanically he went back to the Rue de Choiseul to attend Monsieur Josserand's funeral. Following the hearse, he came up with the idea of suicide in the cemetery; he would withdraw to a secluded corner behind a tombstone. This flight of fancy appealed to his sense of the romantic, to his yearning for a sentimental ideal at odds with his dreary and strait-jacketed bourgeois existence. But as the coffin was lowered into the grave he began to quake in every limb, shuddering at the chill of the earth. This was certainly not the right spot; he must find one somewhere else. Then, coming home more distressed than ever, still obsessed by this one idea, he sat meditating on a chair in the dressing-room, trying to choose the best place in the house, the bedroom, perhaps, near the bed, or here in the dressing-room, just where he was.

'Would you be good enough to leave me alone?' Clotilde asked him.

He already had the revolver in his pocket.

'Why?' he asked, speaking with difficulty.

'Because I want to be alone.'

He thought she wanted to change her dress, and that he revolted her so much that she would no longer even let him see her bare arms. For a moment, bleary-eyed, he looked at her, standing there so tall and beautiful, her complexion the hue of marble and her hair bound up in tawny-coloured coils. Ah, if only she had been willing, everything might have been sorted out! Tottering forward, he stretched out his arms and attempted to embrace her.

'What is it?' she murmured, in surprise. 'What's got into you? You can't do that in here . . . Haven't you still got that other person? Are you telling me we've got to start doing that horrible thing again?'

She seemed so nauseated that he recoiled. Without another word, he went out into the hall, where he stopped for a moment; opposite him he saw a door, the door of the toilet, which he pushed open; and, without hurrying, he went and sat on the seat. It was a nice quiet spot; nobody would come and disturb him here. Putting the barrel of the little revolver into his mouth, he pulled the trigger.

Meanwhile Clotilde, who had felt uneasy at his strange manner all morning, listened to see if he was going to do her the favour of going back to Clarisse. As the creak peculiar to that door told her where he had gone, she paid no further attention to him, but rang for Clémence, when the dull crack of the pistol startled her. What could it be? It sounded like a gunshot. She ran out into the hall, not daring at first to ask him what was the matter; then, as a strange gurgling sound came from within, she called to him and, getting no answer, pulled the door open. It wasn't even bolted. Duveyrier, stunned by fright more than by actual pain, was huddled on the toilet-seat in a lugubrious posture, his eyes wide open, and with blood streaming from his face. He had failed in his suicide attempt. The bullet, having followed the line of his jaw, had passed through his left cheek. He no longer had enough courage to fire a second shot.

'So that's what you've been up to in here, is it?' cried Clotilde, beside herself with rage. 'Why don't you go outside and shoot yourself?'

She was indignant. Instead of softening her attitude, the whole scene utterly exasperated her. Catching hold of him, she roughly pulled him up, trying to get him out of there before anybody saw him. In the toilet of all places! And to have missed as well! It really was too much!

Then, as she supported him back to the bedroom, Duveyrier, half-choked with blood and spitting out his teeth, stammered out between groans: 'You never loved me!'

And he burst into tears, lamenting his lost ideals and the romance that it had never been his lot to experience. When Clotilde had got him to bed, she finally broke down, as her anger gave way to hysterics. The worst of it was that both Clémence and Hippolyte came to answer the bell. At first she told them it was an accident, that their master had fallen down and hurt his chin; but she couldn't sustain this fiction for long for when Hippolyte went to wipe up the blood on the seat, he found the revolver, which had fallen behind the little brush. Meanwhile, the wounded man was bleeding profusely, and the maid suddenly remembered that Doctor Juillerat was upstairs with Madame Pichon, so she ran out and caught him on the stairs just as he was coming down after a successful delivery. The doctor reassured Clotilde; there might possibly be some disfigurement of the jaw, but his life was not in danger. He hastily proceeded to dress the wound, amid basins of water and bloodstained rags, when the Abbé Mauduit, alarmed at all the commotion, let himself into the room.

'What's happened?' he asked.

This question was enough to set off Madame Duveyrier, bursting into tears as soon as she tried to explain. The priest, however, had already guessed, knowing as he did all the secrets of his flock. When he'd been in the drawing-room, he'd felt deeply uneasy, almost wishing he hadn't been able to reunite that wretched young woman with her husband; she hadn't shown the slightest sign of remorse. Awful doubts assailed him; maybe God wasn't on his side, after all. Seeing Duveyrier's fractured jaw, he felt even worse. Approaching the bed, he was about to denounce suicide vehemently, when the doctor, busy with his bandaging, pushed him aside.

'Wait a bit, my dear abbé! Can't you see that he's passed out?'

Indeed, no sooner had the doctor touched him, than Duveyrier lapsed into unconsciousness.

Then Clotilde, to get rid of the servants, who were no longer serving any useful purpose and whose staring eyes disconcerted her greatly, murmured, as she dried her eyes: 'You two, go into the drawing-room. The Abbé Mauduit has something to say to you.'

The priest had to lead them away, another disagreeable task. Hippolyte and Clémence, taken aback, followed him. When they were alone, he came out with a series of incoherent admonishments: heaven awaited those who stayed on the straight and narrow, while to sin just once meant eternal damnation; but it was never too late to turn back and seek salvation. As he meandered on, their surprise changed to bewilderment; with arms dangling at their sides, she, with her slight figure and screwed-up mouth, and he, with his flat face and hulking limbs, exchanged mutual glances of alarm: had madame found some of her napkins upstairs in a trunk? Or was it because of the bottle of wine that they took up with them every night?

'My children,' said the priest, finishing off his sermon, 'you're setting a bad example. The greatest evil of all is to corrupt others, to bring one's own household into disrepute. Yes, you're living in sin, and unfortunately everybody knows about it, as you've been fighing for a whole week.'

He blushed; a certain prudish hesitation made him pick his words. The two servants heaved sighs of relief. They smiled and relaxed, looking cheerful. So that's all it was! They needn't have got themselves so worked up!

'But that's all over, holy father,' declared Clémence, glancing at Hippolyte like a woman who has been won back. 'We're back together now . . . Yes, he explained everything.'

This time it was the priest's turn to look bewildered and miserable.

'You don't understand me, my children. You can't go on living together like this; it's an offence to God and man. You must get married.'

Their astonishment returned. Get married? What on earth for?

'I don't want to,' said Clémence. 'I don't hold with that idea at all.'

Then the abbé tried to convince Hippolyte.

'Look here, my friend, you're a man; you persuade her. Tell her that her reputation is at stake . . . It won't alter your life in any way. You must get married.'

The servant laughed a mischievous, awkward laugh. Finally, looking down at his boots, he blurted out: 'That's quite right; I dare say we should, but I'm married already.'

This reply stopped the priest's moralising in its tracks. Without another word, he withdrew his arguments, putting the hand of God back in his pocket, and regretting his attempt to invoke divine aid to confront such barefaced debauchery. Clotilde, coming into the room had overheard them; and, with one gesture, she exploded. Obeying her, the footman and maid left the room one behind the other, chuckling inwardly, though looking very serious. After a pause, the abbé complained bitterly: why put him in such a position? Why stir up things best left alone? Now the situation was absolutely scandalous. Clotilde simply repeated her gesture: it didn't matter; that was the least of her worries. But she certainly couldn't dismiss the servants here and now or else the whole neighbourhood would immediately get to know about the attempted suicide. She'd have to wait.

'Now, remember, he mustn't be disturbed,' advised the doctor, as he was leaving the bedroom. 'He'll soon be all right again, but he has to rest. Don't lose heart, madame.'

Then, turning to the priest:

'You can do your bit later on, my dear abbé. I can't hand him over to you just yet. If you're going back to Saint-Roch, I'll come with you and keep you company.'

They both went downstairs together.

Gradually the whole house regained its calm. Madame Juzeur had lingered at the cemetery, flirting with Trublot as they deciphered the inscriptions on the gravestones together; and although such dallying, leading nowhere, was a waste of his time, he had to drive her back in a cab to the Rue de Choiseul. That business with Louise filled the poor lady with sorrow. As they reached their destination she was still talking about the wretched girl she had sent back yesterday to the home for destitute children: it was a bitter experience for her, a final disillusion, which dashed all her hopes of ever finding a respectable maid. Then, at the door, she asked Trublot to drop in and see her some time to have a chat. Yes, he would like to, but he was always so busy.

Just then the other Madame Campardon went by. They said hello. Monsieur Gourd informed them of Madame Pichon's successful delivery. They all agreed with Monsieur and Madame Vuillaume: three children for a mere clerk was sheer madness; and the concierge even hinted that, if a fourth baby came along, the landlord would give them notice, as too many children in a house gave a bad impression. But their conversation was cut short by a lady, wearing a veil and leaving behind her a faint scent of verbena, who passed swiftly through the lobby, without speaking to Monsieur Gourd, who pretended not to see her. That morning he had prepared the distinguished gentleman's room on the third floor, getting everything ready for a night's work.

He just had time to call out to the other two: 'Look out! They'll run us over like dogs!'

It was the people on the second floor driving past in their carriage. The horses pranced under the vaulted doorway and, leaning back in the landau, the father and mother smiled at their two pretty fair-haired children fighting over a large bunch of roses.

'What strange people they are!' muttered the concierge, furiously. 'They never went to the funeral; they'd have had to be polite, like everybody else. They smear your good name, but I could tell you a thing or two . . .'

'What do you mean?' asked Madame Juzeur, very interested indeed.

Monsieur Gourd told them that he had had a visit from the police, yes, the police! The second-floor tenant had written such a dirty novel that they were going to imprison him in Mazas.*

'Absolutely outrageous!' he went on in disgust. 'It's full of filth about decent folk. They even say our landlord's in it, yes, Monsieur Duveyrier himself. What a nerve, eh? They've got good reason to keep themselves to themselves! Now we know what they're up to, pretending to stay quietly at home, and not mixing with the other tenants. But as you can see, they can afford to run their carriage as the trash they sell is worth its weight in gold!'

That's what really exasperated Monsieur Gourd. Madame Juzeur only read poetry, and Trublot admitted that he didn't know much about literature. That didn't stop them accusing the novelist of dishonouring, with his writing, the very house in which he and his family lived; and then suddenly they heard wild shrieks coming from the far end of the courtyard.

'You old cow! You were glad enough to have me when your lovers had to be smuggled out! You know exactly what I mean, you cow.'

It was Rachel, whom Berthe had sent packing, and who was giving vent to her feelings on the servants' staircase. This quiet, respectful girl, whom the other servants could never get to gossip, was now like a raging sewer. She had barely been able to contain herself before: Berthe's return had put a stop to her calmly stealing from the master since the estrangement. Being told to get a porter to bring down her trunk sent her into an uncontrollable paroxysm of fury. Berthe stood cowering in the kitchen, while Auguste, wanting to look in charge, remained at the door, receiving the full torrent of abuse.

'Yes!' the infuriated maid went on. 'You never kicked me out when I used to hide your underwear from your cuckold of a husband! No, nor that night when your lover had to put on his socks in my kitchen, while I prevented the old cuckold from coming in, to let you cool down. Ah, you bitch!'

Berthe rushed away to the far end of the appartment in a terrible state. But Auguste was obliged to show a bold front: he turned pale, shaking as each sickening revelation hit him in the face before echoing down the back stairs; all he could say was 'You wretch! You wretch!', torn apart by crude details of the adultery he had just forgiven.

Meanwhile all the servants had come out of their kitchens and leaned over the railings, not missing a single word; even they were amazed by Rachel's fury. Gradually they drew back, appalled by the whole scene. She'd gone too far. Lisa spoke for them all: 'Well, well! gossiping's one thing, but you shouldn't do that to your masters.'

Everyone slipped away, leaving that girl to vent her anger by herself, for it was becoming embarrassing to have to listen to all those awful things, which made everybody uncomfortable, all the more so as she was now beginning to abuse the whole house. Monsieur Gourd was the first to withdraw to his room, remarking that nothing could be done with a woman when she was in a temper. Madame Juzeur's sensitivity about matters of the heart was profoundly wounded by such cruelly intimate disclosures; she seemed so upset that Trublot, much against his will, had to see her safely to her own apartment, in case she fainted. Wasn't it unfortunate? Everything had been so nicely patched up, there was no longer even a hint of scandal; the house had returned to its tranquil decency; and now this vile creature had to go and stir up everything that they'd put out of their minds!

'I may only be a servant, but I'm respectable,' she screamed with all her might, 'and I'm worth more than any of you posh bitches in this damned house! Don't you worry, I'm leaving you. You all make me sick!'

The abbé and Doctor Juillerat quietly came down stairs. They had all heard this, too. Then there was peace: the courtyard was empty, the staircase deserted; the doors seemed hermetically sealed; not a curtain twitched; every apartment seemed shrouded in majestic silence.

In the doorway the priest stopped, as if exhausted.

'So much misfortune!' he murmured, sadly.

The doctor, nodding answered: 'Such is life!'

They would often make this kind of remark as they came away together from a birth or a death. Despite their opposing beliefs, they occasionally agreed upon the subject of human frailty. Both were privy to the same secrets; if the priest heard the confessions of these women, the doctor, for the last thirty years, had delivered their children and looked after their daughters.

'God has forsaken them,' said the abbé.

'No,' replied the doctor; 'don't drag God into it. It's a question of bad health or bad education, that's all.'

Then, going off at a tangent, he violently began to attack the Empire; under a republic things would surely be better. But mixed in with the ramblings of a man of limited intelligence, there were also the wise observations of the experienced physician, well aware of everything that really went on in the neighbourhood. Ah! those women! Some of them were brought up as dolls which made them either corrupt or stupid; others had their feelings and passions perverted by hereditary neurosis; none of them could resist, however dirty or senseless it was, feeling neither desire nor pleasure. He was just as hard on the men lustfully ruining their health while hypocritically pretending to lead sober, virtuous and godly lives. And in all this Jacobin frenzy, the inexorable death-toll of a whole class could be heard; the collapse and decomposition of the bourgeoisie, whose rotten structure was cracking of its own accord. Then, getting out of his depth again, he involved the barbarians, predicting an era of universal happiness.

'I'm really far more religious than you are,' he said, as his diatribe came to an end.

The priest appeared to be listening quietly. But he'd taken nothing in, completely absorbed as he was in his own melancholy. After a pause he murmured: 'If they know not their sin, may heaven have mercy upon them!'

Then, leaving the house, they walked slowly along the Rue Neuve-Saint-Augustin not speaking; too much had already been said; and they had to be careful; their positions demanded discretion. At the end of the street they spotted Madame Hédouin, who smiled at them from the door of 'Au Bonheur des Dames'. Octave stood behind her, smiling too. That very morning, after a serious talk, they had decided to get married. They were going to wait until the autumn. And they were both delighted that the matter had at last been settled.

'Good-day, my dear abbé,' said Madame Hédouin, gaily. 'Still on your rounds, eh, doctor?'

And as he told her how well she was looking, she added: 'Oh, if you only had me as a patient, you wouldn't do much business!'

They stood chatting for a moment. When the doctor mentioned Marie's delivery, Octave seemed delighted to know that his former neighbour had come through safely. And when he heard that number three was a girl too, he exclaimed: 'So her husband can't manage to produce a boy then? She was hoping to get Monsieur and Madame Vuillaume to put up with a boy; but they'll never stand another girl.'

'I think you may be right,' said the doctor. 'They've both gone to bed, they're so upset by the news. And they've sent for a lawyer so that their son-in-law won't inherit even one item of their furniture.'

Then there was more joking. Only the priest was silent, keeping his eyes on the pavement. Madame Hédouin asked if he were unwell. Yes, he was very tired; he was going to rest for a little while. Then, after polite farewells, he walked down the Rue Saint-Roch, still accompanied by the doctor.

At the church door the latter abruptly said: 'That's the worst kind of patient, that one.'

'Which one?' asked the abbé, in surprise.

'That lady who sells calico. She doesn't give a damn for either of us. She doesn't need God or medicine. There's not much to be got out of people like that, who are always well!'

A bright light fell through the broad windows with their white panes edged with yellow and pale blue. Not a sound nor a movement disturbed the deserted nave. Marble facings, crystal chandeliers, and gilded pulpit all slumbered in the peaceful light. It might have been, in its drowsy quietude, some middle-class drawing-room, when the dust-covers have been removed for some grand evening party. Only a woman, in front of the Chapel of Our Lady of the Seven Sorrows, stood watching the tapers which flickered and gave off an odour of melted wax.

The abbé thought of going straight up to his room. Yet, so great was his agitation that he felt impelled to enter the church and remain there. It was as if God were calling to him, vaguely and in a far-off voice, so that he couldn't quite hear the summons. He slowly crossed the church, trying to read the thoughts that arose within him and allay his fears, when suddenly, as he passed behind the choir, an unearthly sight shook his whole being.

Behind the lily-white marble of the Lady Chapel and the Chapel of the Adoration, gleaming with its seven golden lamps, golden candelabra, and golden altar glittering in the dusky light cast by the gold-stained windows, there in this mystic gloom beyond the tabernacle, he saw a tragic apparition, the enactment of a harrowing yet simple drama. It was Christ, nailed to the cross between the weeping Virgin and Mary Magdalene. The white statues illuminated from above stood out against the bare wall, moved forward and grew larger, making this human tragedy in its blood and tears the divine symbol of eternal sorrow.

Devastated, the priest fell to his knees. It was he who had whitened that plaster, contrived that lighting, and prepared so awesome a scene; and now that the hoarding had been removed and the architect and workmen were gone, he was the first to be thunderstruck at the sight. From that austere and terrible Cavalry there came a breath knocking him back. It seemed as if God swept past his face, and he bowed beneath His exhalation, tortured by doubts, by the hideous thought that possibly he was a wicked priest.

Oh, Lord! Had the hour come when all the wounds of this festering world could no longer be hidden by the mantle of religion? Should he no longer sustain the hypocrisy of his flock, nor always be there, like some master of ceremonies, to regulate its vices and its follies? Should he let everything collapse, even at the risk of burying the church itself in the ruins? Yes, this must surely be God's command, for the strength to go on battling against human misery was deserting him, and he was overcome by impotence and disgust. All the corruption that had been stirred up that morning seemed to choke him. Stretching his hands out before him, he asked for forgiveness for his lies, for his cowardly complacency and shameful indifference. Fear of divine wrath shook him to the core. He seemed to see God disowning him, forbidding him to continue taking His name in vain, a jealous God bent upon the destruction of the guilty. His worldly tolerance could not survive such stabs of conscience; all that remained was a believer's terror-stricken faith, struggling in the uncertainty of salvation. Oh, Lord God! What road should he take? What should he do in the midst of this crumbling world, where even the priests were rotten?

Gazing up at the Calvary, the Abbé Mauduit burst into tears. He wept, just as the Virgin and Mary Magdalene wept; he wept for truth which was dead, for heaven which was void. Beyond the marble walls and gleaming jewelled altars, the huge plaster Christ no longer had a single drop of blood in its veins.

It was in December, having been in mourning for eight months, that Madame Josserand consented to dine out for the first time. The Duveyriers had invited her, so it was almost a family occasion to celebrate the start of Clotilde's new season of Saturday evenings. On the previous day, Adèle had been told that she would have to go down and help Julie with the washing-up. When giving parties, the ladies often lent each other their servants in this way.

'Now, above all, try and show a bit more stamina,' was Madame Josserand's advice to her maid. 'I don't know what's up with you lately. You're like a limp rag. Yet you're round and plump enough.'

Adèle was quite simply nine months pregnant. For a long while she thought she was getting fatter, and this astonished her somewhat; famished as she always was, it made her furious when madame triumphantly singled her out in front of all her guests: anyone who accused her of starving her maid should come and see what a greedy thing she was; you didn't get a belly like that by eating scraps! When the slow-witted girl finally realised her misfortune, she often came close to coming out with the truth to spite her mistress, since the latter was taking advantage of her maid's condition to make all the neighbours believe that she was feeding her up.

From that moment onwards however, she was numb with fear. Her uncomprehending brain conjured up all the beliefs of her native village. She believed that she was done for, that the police would come and carry her off if she confessed she was pregnant. So she used all her primitive cunning to hide her condition. She was careful to conceal her unbearable headaches, sickness and terrible constipation, although on more than one occasion she thought she was going to drop down dead while preparing sauces at the stove. Fortunately, it was her hips that widened; though her stomach became larger, it didn't stick out too much, so madamé, exulting over her astounding plumpness, never suspected anything. And the poor girl squeezed in her waist till she could scarcely breathe. Her stomach seemed to her fairly well proportioned, but, all the same, it was terribly heavy when she was scrubbing her kitchen. The last two months had been agony, borne in stubborn and heroic silence.

That night Adèle went up to bed about eleven o'clock. The thought of tomorrow's dinner party terrified her. More slaving away and more bullying from Julie! And she could hardly stand; her limbs felt like jelly! Yet the birth seemed to her vague and a long way off; she preferred not to think about it. She'd rather carry that around for a good while longer, hoping that, somehow, things might sort themselves out. Nor had she made the slightest preparation, being ignorant of any symptons, incapable of remembering or of calculating a date, devoid of any idea, any plan. She was only comfortable when she was in bed, lying on her back. As it had been freezing since the previous day, she kept her stockings on, blew out her candle, and waited until she could get warm. She fell asleep; but then slight pains woke her up again; these first twinges felt like needles; it was as if some insect were stinging her stomach close to her navel; then the pricking pains ceased but she didn't let it worry her, as she was used to all the strange, unaccountable things that went on inside her. Yet suddenly, after half an hour's uneasy sleep, a dull throb woke her up again. This time she grew quite angry. Was she going to have diarrhoea now? How fit would she feel next day if she had to spend all night running back and forth to her chamber pot? Throughout the evening she had been thinking of nothing but this heavy feeling in her gut, expecting a catastrophe. She tried to fight it, rubbing her stomach, and felt that she had soothed the pains. But in a quarter of an hour they returned with greater violence.

'Damn!' she muttered, under her breath, deciding to get up this time.

Groping about in the darkness for the chamber-pot, she squatted down, and exhausted herself by fruitless efforts. The room was icy cold; her teeth chattered. After ten minutes the pains ceased, and she got back into bed. But ten minutes later they returned. She got up again and tried once more without success, going back to bed chilled through, where she enjoyed a moment's rest. This was stupid! Did she need to go or didn't she? Now the pains became persistent, almost continuous and more excruciating, as if some hand were ruthlessly squeezing the inside of her stomach. And then she understood; shivering beneath the cover, she muttered: 'Oh, my God! Oh, my God! That's what it is!'

She was gripped with fear and had to get up and walk about in her agony. She couldn't stay in bed any longer, so she relit her candle and began to pace up and down the room. Her tongue grew parched, she was seized by a burning thirst, and her cheeks grew red as fire. When some sudden spasm bent her double, she leaned against the wall and caught hold of the back of a chair. Hours passed in this way as she tramped relentlessly up and down, never daring to put on her boots for fear of making a noise. Her only protection from the cold was an old shawl, which she wrapped round her shoulders. Two o'clock struck; then three o'clock.

'There's no such thing as God!' she muttered to herself, needing to hear the sound of her own voice. 'It's taking to long; it'll never be over!'

The first stage of labour had, however, been reached. The weight had moved down towards her hips and backside. And, when her belly gave her a moment's respite, she felt a constant gnawing pain there. To get some relief she grasped her buttocks with both hands, supporting them as she waddled about bare-legged, with only coarse stockings on up to her knees. No, there was no such thing as God! Her trusting patience, submitting to His will like an unquestioning beast of burden for whom her pregnancy was merely one more misery, deserted her. So it wasn't enough to be starved to death, and the dirty trollop bullied by all and sundry; but her masters had to go and get her pregnant as well! Filthy swine! She couldn't say if it was the young one or the old one that had done it, because the old one had had another go at her after Shrove Tuesday. Neither of them gave a damn; they'd had their fun, and now she had to suffer for it! If she went and had her baby on their doormat, wouldn't it be nice to see their faces! Then her old fears returned; she would be put in prison; it was best to say nothing. And between two spasms she kept repeating in a choked voice: 'Bastards! How could they do this to me! Oh, my God! I'm going to die!'

And, with hands clenched, she grasped her buttocks more firmly, her poor aching buttocks, stifling her cries of pain as she rocked from side to side. Next door no one stirred; everybody was snoring; she could hear Julie's loud droning, while Lisa's breathing whistled like a shrill fife.

Four o'clock struck, when suddenly she thought that her belly had burst. During one of the spasms something had given, followed by a rush of liquid, which trickled down and soaked her stockings. For a moment she remained motionless, terror-struck and bewildered: a funny way to empty yourself; perhaps she'd never been pregnant after all. Then, fearing there was something else wrong with her, she checked that she wasn't, in fact, bleeding to death. Feeling somewhat relieved, she sat down for a few moments on her trunk. The mess on the floor worried her, and the flickering candle was on the point of going out. Unable to walk about, and aware that the crisis was near, she had just enough strength left to spread out on the bed an old piece of oilcloth that Madame Josserand had given her for her dressing-table. Hardly had she laid down than the final stage of labour began.

For nearly an hour and a half the pains assailed her continu-ally and with increasing violence. The internal spasms had ceased; now she was the one straining every muscle in her stomach and lower back, wanting to free herself from this intolerable weight. Twice more, the feeling that she needed to use the chamber pot made her get up, and she reached out for it, her hand groping about feverishly; the second time she almost remained collapsed on the floor. Each fresh effort was accom-panied by shivering; her face grew burning hot, perspiration broke out on her neck, as she bit the bedclothes to stifle her groaning, the grim, involuntary gasp of a woodcutter felling an oak. After each push she murmured as if addressing someone: 'It isn't possible . . . It'll never come out . . . It's too big . . .'

Arched backwards and with her legs wide apart, she clutched hold of the iron bedstead, which shook as she struggled. Fortu-nately it was an uncomplicated birth with the baby's head in line. Each time it emerged it kept slipping back again, sucked in by the elasticity of the surrounding tissues stretched to breaking-point. As the labour proceeded, she was seized with excruciating cramps which tightened around her middle like an iron girdle. Finally her bones cracked and it was as if everything had been broken. She was terrified by the feeling that she had burst back and front, leaving a hole through which life was ebbing away.

Then the child rolled out on to the bed between her thighs in a pool of excrement and bloody placenta.

She uttered the loud, wild cry of a triumphant mother. Those in the adjoining rooms began to stir and drowsy voices asked, 'Hey! What's going on in there? Is someone being murdered or raped? Don't shout out in your sleep like that!'

Alarmed, she thrust the blanket between her teeth, squeezed her thighs together, and pulled the cover up over the baby, which cried plaintively like a little kitten. Soon she could hear Julie snoring again after turning over in bed; Lisa had fallen asleep again, and this time not even her shrill breathing could be heard. Then, for about a quarter of an hour she felt indescribable relief, a sense of infinite calm. She lay there as if dead, enjoying this state of nothingness.

But then the pains started again. She woke in a fright. Was she going to have another? On opening her eyes she found herself in pitch darkness. Not even a tiny bit of candle! There she lay, all by herself, in a pool, with something slimy between her thighs that she didn't know what to do with. There were doctors for dogs, but not one for her. She and her brat might snuff it for all anyone cared! She remembered having lent a hand when Madame Pichon, the lady opposite, was giving birth. The things that had to be done so as not to let it come to harm! It had stopped crying now. She stretched out her hand and caught hold of a cord that hung out of her stomach. Vaguely she seemed to recollect having seen this cut and tied in a knot. Her eyes had got used to the gloom and the garret was now dimly lit by the rising moon. Then, groping about blindly, half guided by instinct and without getting up, she performed a tedious and painful operation. Pulling down an apron from a hook behind her, she tore off one of its strings, tied the cord in a knot, and cut it with a pair of scissors which she got out of the pocket of her skirt. The effort made her perspire and she lay down again. Poor little thing! She didn't want to kill it, after all!

The griping pains continued. Something uncomfortable was still there which the contractions were trying to force out. She tugged at the cord, first gently, then with all her might. Something was coming away. It fell out in a great lump, and she got rid of it by throwing it into the chamber pot. Thank goodness,

this time it really was over and she wouldn't suffer any more!
Tepid blood trickled down her legs.

She must have dozed for nearly an hour. It struck six, when,
conscious of her state, she awoke. There was no time to lose.
Rising with difficulty in the cold moonlight, she began to do
whatever came into her head first. After dressing herself, she
wrapped the child in some old linen and rolled it up in two
sheets of newspaper. It was quiet now, but its little heart was
still beating. As she had forgotten to look if it were a boy or a
girl, she undid the parcel. It was a girl! Another poor wretch! A
tasty morsel for some brawny groom or footman, like that
Louise, whom they'd found on a doorstep! The servants were
still asleep, and after waking a sleepy Monsieur Gourd to pull
back the front-door latch, she managed to go out and deposit
her bundle in the Passage Choiseul just as the gates were being
opened. Then she crept upstairs again, without meeting a soul.
For once in her life, luck was on her side!

She immediately began to put the room to rights. She rolled
up the oilcloth under the bed, emptied the chamberpot, and
sponged the floor. Then, worn out, white as wax, and with
blood still streaming down her thighs, she lay down again after
wiping herself with a towel.

This was how Madame Josserand found her when, at about
nine o'clock, she decided to go upstairs, amazed that Adèle
wasn't down. As the maid complained of a violent attack of
diarrhoea which had kept her awake all night, her mistress
exclaimed: 'Ah, I expect you've been over-eating again! You
only think about stuffing yourself!'

Alarmed at the girl's pallor, however, she talked of sending
for a doctor, but was glad enough to save the three francs when
Adèle declared that all that she wanted was rest. Since her
husband's death, Madame Josserand lived with Hortense, on a
pension paid to her by the Bernheim brothers. This didn't
prevent her from denouncing them as cheats, and she was now
more penny-pinching than ever, rather than lose face by leaving
her apartment and giving up her Tuesdays.

'Yes, that's what you need, sleep,' she said. 'There's some
cold beef left, which will do for lunch, and tonight we're dining
out. If you can't come down and help Julie, she'll have to do
without you.'

That evening the Duveyriers' dinner passed off very pleasantly. The whole family was there, the two Vabres and their wives, Madame Josserand, Hortense, Léon, and even Uncle Bachelard, who was on his best behaviour. They had also invited Trublot to make up the numbers, and Madame Dambreville, so as not to separate her from Léon, who, after marrying the niece, had fallen back into the aunt's arms again, as he still needed her. They went everywhere together as before, making excuses for the young bride. She had a cold; she was tired; she was sorry she couldn't come, they would say. Everyone around the table expressed regret at not seeing her more often, for they were all so fond of her; she was so charming! They talked of the chorus which Clotilde was going to have at the end of the evening. It was the 'Consecration of the Swords' again, but with the full five tenors this time; it would be magnificent. For the last two months, Duveyrier himself, restored to his former self, went about accosting all his friends, repeating the same set phrase to each of them, 'We haven't seen you for a while. You must come and see us; my wife's going to begin her choruses again.' Thus, by the time the dessert was served, all they could talk about was music. A light-hearted and friendly atmosphere prevailed right through to the champagne.

Then, after the coffee, while the ladies sat round the drawing-room fire, the gentlemen gathered in the dining-room and began to engage in serious debate. Meanwhile, other guests were arriving. The group included Campardon, the Abbé Mauduit, Doctor Juillerat, as well as those who had dined, with the exception of Trublot, who had disappeared as soon as the meal was over. They immediately began to talk politics; for these men were deeply interested in the parliamentary debates, and continued to discuss the recent success of the opposition candidates, who had all been returned for Paris at the May elections. This triumph of the Fronde party vaguely alarmed them, despite their apparent satisfaction.

'Good Lord,' said Léon, 'Monsieur Thiers has many gifts, certainly. But his speeches about the Mexican Expedition are so bitter that they're counter-productive.'

Thanks to Madame Dambreville, Léon had just secured his appointment as a government counsel, and he had immediately joined the establishment party. There was nothing of the hungry revolutionary about him, save an absolute contempt for all doctrine.

'You used to say it was all the government's fault,' remarked the doctor, smiling. 'I hope that you have at least voted for Monsieur Thiers.'

The young man avoided making any reply.

Théophile, suffering from indigestion and troubled by fresh doubts as to his wife's fidelity, chipped in: 'Well, I voted for him. If men refuse to live together as brothers, why, so much the worse for them.'

'Exactly, and so much the worse for you, eh?' remarked Duveyrier, who, though he said little, made his words count.

Théophile stared at him, aghast. Auguste no longer dared admit that he too had voted for Monsieur Thiers. Then, to their surprise, Bachelard professed to be a Legitimist; there was something distinguished about that, he thought. Campardon warmly agreed with him; he himself had abstained from voting, as the official candidate, Monsieur Dewinck, did not offer sufficient guarantees as far as the Church was concerned. He broke out into a wild attack on the *Life of Jesus** which had just appeared.

'It's not the book that ought to be burned, it's the author,' he repeated.

'Perhaps you're too much of a radical, my friend,' interposed the abbé, in a conciliatory voice. 'Yet certainly the signs of the times are dreadful. They talk of deposing the Pope; parliament is in revolt. We're heading for disaster.'

'So much the better,' said Doctor Juillerat, drily.

At this time they were all scandalised. Once again he attacked the middle classes, declaring that once the masses got the upper hand the bourgeoisie would soon be swept away; but the others, interrupting, loudly protestesd that the bourgeoisie incarnated the moral values, the hard work, and prosperity of the nation.

Duveyrier at last made himself heard above the commotion. He boldly confessed that he had voted for Monsieur Dewinck, not because that candidate exactly represented his own opinions, but because he stood for law and order. Yes, the violent orgies of the Terror could be just around the corner. Monsieur Rouher,* that very remarkable statesman, who had just replaced Monsieur Billault, had formally prophesied as much in the Chamber. Then, with this graphic metaphor, he ended: 'The triumph of the opposition is just the first shock to the whole edifice. Beware that it doesn't crush you to death as it falls!'

The others were silent, vaguely afraid that they had let themselves be so carried away that now their own personal safety was in jeopardy. They imagined workmen, blackened with powder and soaked in blood, breaking into their houses, raping their maidservants, and drinking up their wine. Doubtless, the Emperor deserved a lesson; yet they began to be sorry for having given him so severe a one.

'Never fear,' added the doctor, mockingly, 'you'll be rescued again at gunpoint.'

However, he always exaggerated, and they regarded him as an eccentric. It was precisely this reputation that kept him from losing his patients. He then returned to his on-going quarrel with the Abbé Mauduit about the imminent disappearance of the Church. Léon was now on the priest's side; he talked of divine providence, and on Sundays went with Madame Dambreville to nine o'clock Mass.

Meanwhile, more guests kept arriving, and the large drawing-room was filling up with ladies. Valérie and Berthe were exchanging confidences like old friends. The architect had brought the other Madame Campardon with him, doubtless in place of poor Rose, who lay upstairs in bed reading Dickens. She was giving Madame Josserand an economical recipe for bleaching linen without soap, while Hortense, sitting alone to one side, waited for Verdier, with her eyes fixed on the door. Suddenly Clotilde, while chatting to Madame Dambreville, got up and held out both her hands. Her friend, Madame Octave Mouret, had just arrived. She had been married early in November, as soon as her period of mourning had come to an end.

'And where's your husband?' asked the hostess. 'I hope he won't let me down.'

'No, no,' replied Caroline, smiling. 'He's on his way; something detained him at the last moment.'

Everybody, whispering, surveyed her curiously. She was so calm, so striking and always the same with the charming assurance of a woman who succeeds in everything she does. Madame Josserand shook hands with her as if delighted to see her again. Berthe and Valérie stopped talking to examine the details of her dress, which was straw-coloured and covered with lace. But just when it seemed that the past had been calmly forgotten, Auguste, whom politics had left cold, began to show signs of indignant amazement as he stood at the dining-room

door. What! His sister was going to welcome to her home
Berthe's former lover? He felt not only the bitter grudge of a
wronged husband, but also the angry jealousy of a businessman
ruined by a successful rival; as 'Au Bonheur des Dames', now
that it was even bigger and had opened a special silk department, was crippling him financially, he had had to find a
partner. While everyone was congratulating Madame Mouret,
he approached Clotilde and whispered: 'I'm not going to stand
for that, you know!'

'Stand for what?' she asked, in surprise.

'I don't mind the wife; she's done nothing to me. But if the
husband comes, I shall grab Berthe by the arm and leave the
room in front of everybody.'

Clotilde stared at him, and then shrugged her shoulders.
Caroline was her oldest friend, and she certainly wasn't going
to give up seeing her merely to satisfy one of his whims. As if
anybody even remembered the incident now! Far better not to
stir up things that everyone but him had forgotten. He began to
get agitated; but as he turned to Berthe to back him up,
expecting her to rise and leave with him there and then, his wife
tried to pacify him with a frown. Was he crazy? Did he want to
look a bigger fool than ever?

'But it's just because I don't want to look a fool!' he
exclaimed, in despair.

Then Madame Josserand, leaning forward, said severely: 'This
is positively indecent; people are looking at you. For goodness
sake, behave yourself for once!'

Though silent, he had not given in and there was a certain
uneasiness among the ladies. Madame Mouret alone, as she sat
opposite Berthe and next to Clotilde, remained cheerfully calm.
They watched Auguste, who had disappeared into the bay
window, the very place where his marriage had been decided.
Anger had brought on the beginning of a migraine, and every
now and then he pressed his forehead against the icy window-
panes.

Octave, however, didn't arrive until very late. He had met
Madame Juzeur on the landing. She was coming downstairs,
wrapped in a shawl. She complained of a cold on her chest, and
had only got up so as not to disappoint the Duveyriers. Her
feeble state didn't prevent her from flinging herself into the
young man's arms as she congratulated him on his marriage.

'I'm so pleased at the way everything's worked out, my friend! I was beginning to worry about you; I never thought that you'd manage it. Tell me, you naughty boy, how did you get round her in the end?'

Octave smiled and kissed her fingertips. Just then someone running swiftly and lightly up the stairs disturbed them. To Octave's astonishment it was Saturnin. He had left the asylum at Les Moulineaux a week ago, as Doctor Chassage again refused to keep him there any longer, having decided that his madness was not at a sufficiently advanced state. No doubt he was going to spend the evening with Marie Pichon, just as he always used to do when his parents were entertaining. All of a sudden those bygone days came flooding back. Octave seemed to catch the sound of Marie's voice upstairs, as she quietly sang some ballad in her solitude; in his mind's eye he saw her always alone by Lilitte's cot waiting for Jules to return, with her sweet smile and resigned air.

'I wish you every happiness in your married life,' said Madame Juzeur, as she tenderly squeezed Octave's hand.

In order not to enter the room with her, he was loitering behind and taking off his overcoat, when Trublot, in evening clothes, without his hat and looking ruffled, emerged from the kitchen passage.

'She's not at all well, you know!' he whispered, while Hippolyte was announcing Madame Juzeur.

'Who's that?' asked Octave.

'Why, Adèle, the maid, upstairs.'

On hearing of her indisposition, he had gone up in fatherly fashion to see her as soon as dinner was over. It was probably a violent attack of colic. What she needed was a good stiff glass of mulled wine; but she didn't even have a lump of sugar. Then, noticing Octave's indifferent smile, he added: 'Oh, I forgot! You're married now, you sly dog! You're not interested in that sort of thing any more, I'd almost forgotten, catching you just now in the corner with Madame Anything-you-like-except-that.'

They went into the drawing-room together. The ladies were so busy talking about their servants that they didn't even notice them at first. They were quite willing to accept Madame Duveyrier's faltering explanation as to why she was keeping on Clémence and Hippolyte: he was a brute, it was true; but Clémence was such an excellent maid that she was prepared to turn a blind eye to everything else. Valérie and Berthe both declared that they simply couldn't find a decent girl anywhere. They had given it up as a bad job as the agencies had sent them no end of useless sluts, come one day and gone the next. Madame Josserand tore Adéle to shreds, with yet more instances of her filthy habits and unbelievable stupidity; it was a wonder she didn't fire her. The other Madame Campardon praised Lisa to the skies: she was a gem who couldn't be faulted. She was one of those rare servants that are worth their weight in gold.

'She's like one of the family now,' said Gasparine. 'Our little Angèle attends lectures now at the Hôtel de Ville, and Lisa always goes with her. Oh! They could stay out together for days, and we wouldn't worry in the least.'

Just then they caught sight of Octave. He came forward to shake hands with Clotilde. Berthe looked at him, and she coolly went on talking to Valérie, who smiled at him affectionately, as a friend. The others, Madame Josserand and Madame Dambreville, without being too gushing, surveyed him with kindly interest.

'Well, you're here at last!' said Clotilde, in her most gracious voice. 'I was starting to worry about our chorus.'

And when Madame Mouret gently scolded her husband for being so late he made his excuses.

'But, my love, I couldn't get away. Madame, I'm so sorry. I'm entirely at your disposal now.'

The ladies were glancing uneasily at the bay window, where Auguste was hiding. They had a moment of fright when they saw him turn round on hearing Octave's voice. Evidently his migraine was worse; his eyes were all blurred after gazing out into the gloomy streets. But, making up his mind, he came up behind his sister, and said: 'Get rid of them, or we'll be the ones to leave.'

Clotilde again shrugged her shoulders. Auguste seemed to wish to give her time to consider the matter. He would wait a few minutes longer, particularly as Trublot had taken Octave into the other room. The ladies were still uneasy as they'd heard the husband whisper to his wife: 'If he comes back here, get up and follow me immediately. If you don't, you can go back to your mother's.'

Octave's reception by the gentlemen in the parlour was equally cordial. If Léon's manner was somewhat cool, Uncle

Bachelard, and even Théophile, seemed anxious to show, as they shook hands, that the family was ready to forget everything. Octave congratulated Campardon; two days ago he'd been decorated, and was now wearing a broad red ribbon. The architect, beaming, scolded him for never coming to see them to spend an hour or two with his wife, now and then. It was all very fine to say he'd got married; all the same, it wasn't very nice of him to forget his old friends. But at the sight of Duveyrier, Octave was quite startled. He hadn't seen him since his recovery, and he looked uneasily at his distorted jaw, slewed to the left, which gave a lopsided look to his whole face. His voice, too, was disconcerting; deeper by a couple of tones, it sounded cavernous.

'Don't you think he's much improved?' said Trublot, as he led Octave back to the drawing-room door. 'It makes him positively majestic. I heard him the day before yesterday at the Assizes. Listen! They're talking about it now.'

The gentlemen had, indeed, moved from politics to morals. They were listening to Duveyrier, who was giving details about a case in which his attitude had been greatly remarked upon. It was even proposed to appoint him President of the Court and an officer in the Légion d'Honneur. It was a case of infanticide which had occurred more than a year before. The mother, an unnatural creature, a real savage as he described her, was none other than the boot-stitcher, his former tenant, that tall, pale, sad-looking girl whose enormous belly had provoked Monsieur Gourd's fury. And stupid too! Not only had she failed to realise that a belly like that would betray her, but she had actually cut the child in two and hidden it in a hat box! Of course, she told the jury a ridiculous tale: how her seducer had deserted her, and how, hungry and destitute, the sight of the baby that she couldn't feed had driven her to despair; in a word, the usual story. But an example must be made of such people. Duveyrier congratulated himself on a summing-up of such striking clarity that the verdict was a foregone conclusion.

'What did you give her?' asked the doctor.

'Five years,' replied the counsellor, in his new voice, which sounded deep and hoarse. 'It's high time we put a stop to the tide of debauchery that threatens to swamp Paris.'

Trublot nudged Octave, for they both knew about the failed suicide attempt.

'There, you hear what he says?' he whispered. 'Joking apart, it really does improve his voice. It's more moving, isn't it? It goes straight to the heart now. And if you'd only seen him standing there in his long red robes, with his face all twisted! My word! He quite frightened me, he looked so odd; so solemn, too! He really gave me the shivers.'

Here he stopped to listen to what the ladies were saying in the drawing-room. They had started on the servants again. That very day Madame Duveyrier had given Julie a week's notice. Certainly she had nothing to say against the girl's cooking, but in her view good conduct was the most important thing. The truth was that, acting on the advice of Doctor Juillerat, and anxious about her son's health, whose goings-on at home she tolerated so as to control them better, she had had a show-down with Julie, who for some time past had been unwell. Julie, as was fitting for a first-class cook who would never quarrel with her employers, had accepted her week's notice without even condescending to reply that, yes, maybe she had misbe-haved herself, but, all the same, she wouldn't be suffering from what she was suffering from if it hadn't been for the unclean state of Master Gustave, her son. Madame Josserand was quick to share in Clotilde's indignation: yes, where morality was concerned one had to be absolutely inflexible; take Adèle; if she kept that girl on, with all her filthy and stupid habits, it was only because the idiot was so thoroughly virtuous. Oh! On that score she had nothing to complain about!

'Poor Adèle! Spare her a thought,' muttered Trublot, touched by the image of the poor wretch lying half-frozen upstairs under her thin covers.

Then he whispered in Octave's ear sniggering: 'I say, Duvey-rier might at least send her up a bottle of claret.'

'Yes, gentlemen,' continued the counsellor, 'statistics show that infanticide is assuming alarming proportions. Sentimental reasons nowadays carry far too much weight; people trust too much in science, in your so-called physiology, which before long will prevent us from distinguishing good from evil. For debauch-ery there's no cure; we must destroy it at its very root.'

This retort was mainly directed at Doctor Juillerat, who had sought to give a medical explanation of the boot-stitcher's case.

All the other gentlemen, however, were very severe; they were disgusted: for Campardon vice was incomprehensible; Uncle

Bachelard spoke in defence of children; Théophile asked for an enquiry; Léon was concerned about prostitution in its relation with the state; and Trublot, in reply to Octave, told him all about Duveyrier's new mistress, who this time was quite a presentable person, somewhat elderly, but of romantic disposition, able to understand that ideal which the counsellor considered integral to the purity of love; in short, a worthy woman, who would ensure that his married life was tranquil while exploiting him and sleeping with his friends, but never kicking up a row. Only the abbé remained silent, with downcast eyes and a troubled soul, in an enormous sadness.

They were now going to sing the 'Consecration of the Swords'. The drawing-room had filled up; there was a crush of dresses under the bright light from chandeliers and lamps, and laughter rippled along the rows of chairs. Amid the general murmur, Clotilde roughly remonstrated with Auguste as he caught hold of Berthe's arm and tried to make her leave the room when he saw Octave and the other chorus singers enter. But his resolution wavered as his migraine grew, while the silent disapproval of the ladies served to increase his embarrassment. Madame Dambreville's austere gaze utterly disconcerted him; even the other Madame Campardon sided against him. Madame Josserand completed his defeat. She abruptly came into the fray, threatening to take back her daughter and never to give him that dowry of fifty thousand francs she continued to hold out brazenly as a promise. Then, turning to Bachelard, seated behind her and next to Madame Juzeur, she made him renew his promises. Hand on heart, the uncle declared that he would do his duty; family before everything. Auguste, with no fight left in him, was obliged to beat a retreat; he fled to the bay window, where he pressed his burning brow against the ice-cold panes.

Then Octave had a strange feeling as if everything were beginning again. The two years of life in the Rue de Choiseul were a blank. There sat his wife, smiling at him, yet his life hadn't changed; today was like yesterday, seamlessly the same. Trublot pointed out Vabre's new partner to him, a dapper little fellow with fair hair, sitting next to Berthe. He was said to give her heaps of presents. Uncle Bachelard, in poetic mood, was revealing the sentimental side of himself to Madame Juzeur, who was quite moved by certain confidential details about Fifi and Gueulin. Théophile, in despair and doubled up by violent

fits of coughing, took Doctor Juillerat aside and begged him to
give his wife something to soothe her nerves. Campardon,
watching cousin Gasparine, talked about the Evreux diocese,
and the huge upheavals caused by the development of the new
Rue du Dix-Décembre. God and art; nothing else mattered; he
was an artist! Behind a flower-stand, a gentleman's back could
be seen, which all the young laides contemplated with the
utmost curiosity. It was that of Verdier, who was talking to
Hortense. They were having a somewhat acrimonious discussion
about the wedding, which they again postponed until the spring,
so as not to turn the woman and her brat into the street in mid-
winter.

Then suddenly the chorus started. With mouth wide open,
the architect declaimed the opening phrase, Clotilde struck a
chord, and uttered her usual cry. Then the voices became an
ever-increasing uproar; so great was the din that the candles
flickered and all the ladies grew pale. Trublot, found wanting as
a bass, made another sally as a baritone. The five tenors,
however, were the most impressive, especially Octave; Clotilde
was sorry that she had not entrusted him with a solo. As the
voices fell and, with the aid of the soft pedal, as she imitated
the footfall of a patrol departing into the distance, there was
loud applause, and both she and the gentlemen were showered
with compliments. Meanwhile, in the room beyond, behind a
triple row of black coats, one could see Duveyrier clenching his
teeth to keep from shouting out in anguish, with his jaw all
awry and his blotches inflamed and bleeding.

Then, when tea was served, there was a procession of teacups
and sandwiches. For a moment the Abbé Mauduit stood alone
in the middle of the empty drawing-room. Through the wide-
opened door he watched the throng of guests, and, in his defeat,
he smiled as once more he flung the mantle of religion over this
corrupt middle class, as if he were some master of ceremonies,
delaying the final moment of decomposition by throwing a veil
over it. Then, like every Saturday, when it struck twelve the
guests departed one by one. Campardon was one of the first to
leave, accompanied by the other Madame Campardon; Léon
and Madame Dambreville were not long in following, quite like
husband and wife. Verdier's back had long since vanished, when
Madame Josserand took Hortense off with her, scolding her for
what she called her sentimental obstinacy. Uncle Bachelard,

who had got very drunk on punch, kept Madame Juzeur talking at the door for a moment. Her advice, based on wide experience, he found quite refreshing. Trublot, who had pocketed some sugar to take to Adèle, was going to make a bolt by the backstairs but, seeing Berthe and Auguste in the hall, he was embarrassed, and pretended to be looking for his hat.

Just at this moment Octave and his wife, accompanied by Clotilde, also came and asked for their wraps. There was an awkward pause. The hall was not large; Berthe and Madame Mouret were squeezed against each other, while Hippolyte frantically searched for their things. They smiled at each other. Then, as the door was opened, the two men, Octave and Auguste, brought face to face, stepped aside and bowed civilly. They made way for Berthe, bowing slightly. Then Valérie, who, with Théophile, was also leaving, gave Octave another glance, the glance of an affectionate, disinterested friend, as much as to say that only they had no secrets from each other.

'Goodbye!' said Clotilde, blandly, to the two couples before going back to the drawing-room.

Octave suddenly stopped in his tracks. Downstairs he caught sight of Auguste's new partner leaving, the dapper little man with fair hair. Saturnin, who had come down from Marie's, was squeezing his hands in a wild outburst of affection, as he stammered, 'My friend, my friend!' At first he felt a strange twinge of jealousy; then he smiled. The past flooded back, with memories of his love affairs and of his whole Parisian campaign: the willingness of that nice little Madame Pichon; Valérie's rebuff, which he remembered fondly; his stupid affair with Berthe on which he had wasted so much time. Now he had done what he had come to do. Paris was conquered; and he gallantly followed the woman who, deep down, he still thought of as Madame Hédouin, stooping at times to prevent her train from catching in the stair-rods.

Once again the house wore its grand, dignified, middle-class air. He seemed to hear a faint echo of Marie's lullaby. In the porch he met Jules coming home; Madame Vuillaume was dangerously ill, and refused to see her daughter. Everybody had gone; the doctor and the abbé were the last to leave, arguing as they went. Trublot slyly crept up to see Adèle; and the deserted staircase slumbered in its stifling warmth, with its chaste hearths behind virtuously closed doors. One o'clock struck, when Monsieur Gourd, whose buxom spouse awaited him in bed, extinguished the gas light. Then the whole building was plunged into a solemn darkness and innocent sleep, excluding everything except the crushing weight of apathy.

Next morning, when Trublot had gone, after watching over her like a tender parent, Adèle languidly tottered down to her kitchen to allay suspicion. During the night it had thawed, and she opened the window for some air, when Hippolyte shouted up, furiously from the bottom of the narrow courtyard: 'Now then, you pack of sluts! Who's been emptying the slops out again? Madame's dress is done for!'

He had hung one of Madame Duveyrier's gowns out to dry after getting the mud off it, and now found it splashed with greasy slops. Then all the maids from the top of the house to the bottom looked out of the windows and violently denied the accusation. The floodgates were opened, and foul language surged up out of this stinking sewer. When it thawed the walls dripped with damp, and a stench rose from the little dark quadrangle. All the hidden filth of each floor seemed to leak out into this fetid drain.

'It wasn't me,' said Adèle, leaning out. 'I've only just come down.'

Lisa looked up sharply.

'Hello! You back on your feet again? Well, what was it? Did you nearly croak?'

'Yes, I had a terrible stomach-ache, I can tell you.'

This interruption put a stop to the quarrel. The new maids taken on by Berthe and Valérie, and christened 'The Big Camel' and 'The Little Donkey' respectively, stared hard at Adèle's pale face. Victoire and Julie both wanted to have a look at her, and they craned their necks in the attempt. They both suspected something, for it wasn't usual for anyone to wriggle about and groan like that.

The others burst out laughing, and there was another flood of filth, while the unfortunate girl stammered out in her fright: 'Do be quiet with your jokes; I'm sick enough as it is. Do you want to finish me off?'

No, not they. They certainly didn't want to do that. She was the biggest fool going, and utterly disgusting; but they stuck together. They didn't want to do her any harm. So, naturally, they vented their spite on their employers, and discussed last night's party with an air of profound distaste.

'So it seems they've all made it up again, eh?' asked Victoire, as she sipped her syrup and brandy.

Hippolyte, sponging Madame's gown, answered: 'They've none of 'em any more feelings than my old boot! When they spit in each other's faces they wash themselves with the spittle, to make believe that they're clean.'

'It's better they should be on friendly terms,' said Lisa, 'or else it would soon be our turn.'

Suddenly there was a panic. A door opened and the maids rushed back to their kitchens. Then Lisa said it was only little Angèle. Nothing to worry about, the child was all right. And from the black hole all their spite welled up amid the stale, poisonous smell of the thaw. All the dirty linen of the last two years was now being washed. How glad they were not to belong to the middle class when they saw their masters living in this filthy state, and liking it too, for they were always starting over again.

Brutal giggles echoed through the stinking cesspool. Hippolyte actually tore madame's dress; but he didn't care a damn; it was far too good for her as it was. 'The Big Camel' and 'The Little Donkey' split their sides as they looked out over their windowsill. Meanwhile, Adèle, terrified and dizzy with weakness, reeled backwards.

Above the coarse shouting came her answer: 'Bugger off, you heartless things! When you're dying I'll come and dance round your beds, I will!'

'Ah, Julie,' continued Lisa, leaning out to address her, 'how happy you must be to be leaving this rotten house in another week! You can't avoid being infected by it. I hope you'll find something better.'

Julie, with bare arms, covered in blood from cleaning a turbot for dinner, leaned out again, next to the footman. She shrugged her shoulders, and concluded philosophically: 'Dear God, whether it's one dump or another it doesn't matter. They're all the same. Once you've seen one you've seen them all. It's one great pigsty.'

NOTES

p.3 **the Rue Neuve-Saint-Augustin:** now called simply the Rue Saint-Augustin, this reference (for the French reader) immediately identifies the novel's Parisian setting; all the subsequent street-names mentioned here locate it in the second *arrondissement*, in the triangle formed by the Boulevard des Italiens and the Avenue de l'Opéra and intersected by the Rue du 4 Septembre.

p.3 **the Gare de Lyon:** the main Paris station serving the South of France, from which Octave has arrived.

p.3 **Plassans:** Zola's fictionalised version of Aix-en-Provence is the setting for the provincial novels of the *Rougon-Macquart* series, most obviously *La Conquête de Plassans* (1874). Zola re-read that novel during the composition of *Pot-Bouille* to remind himself of the details of Octave's background mentioned in this opening chapter.

p.4 **the *Moniteur*:** the *Moniteur universel* was the official government newspaper; it published the authorised accounts of parliamentary debates.

p.4 **Mort-la-Ville:** a provincial backwater almost certainly invented to underline the deathly connotations of its name.

p.9 **the new opera house:** there are anachronisms here: the novel supposedly begins in October 1861; work on the new Opera started on 21 July 1862. The 'broad thoroughfare' is later referred to [p. 170] as the Rue du Dix–Décembre (changed to the present-day Rue du 4 Septembre which celebrates the Second Empire's fall in 1870 as surely as 10 December does Louis-Napoléon's triumph in the presidential elections of 1848); this was only approved, however, in August 1864 and completed between 1868 and 1869.

p.9 **Evreux:** administrative capital of the *département* of the Eure, 102km. north-west of Paris, with its twelfth century Notre-Dame Cathedral, it was a major ecclesiastical centre.

p.10 *à la* Henri IV: a full but clipped beard characteristic of Henri IV (1553–1610), also famed for his architectural initiatives. So the architect Campardon sporting such a beard does not seem a coincidence.

p.10 the *Gazette de France*: the newspaper supporting the Legitimists, i.e. the party advocating the restoration of the branch of the Bourbon monarchy deposed in 1830, 'legitimate' in their eyes by contrast with the Orléanist heirs of Louis-Philippe (on the French throne between 1830 and 1848).

p.12 the Var and the Basses-Alpes: *départements* of the South of France, between Marseilles and the Italian border.

p.15 'Au Bonheur des Dames': this is sometimes translated as 'The Ladies' Paradise'; it is left in the original here, not least because this shop will become the department store that gives its name to Zola's *Au Bonheur des Dames* of 1883. That novel is, in many ways, the sequel to *Pot-Bouille*.

p.21 the Rue de l'Oratoire: just off the Rue de Rivoli at the eastern end of the Louvre, and (if dressed in evening clothes) a long walk back to the Rue de Choiseul. Any street-map of central Paris will allow the reader to track precisely the Josserand ladies' difficult return home at the beginning of this chapter.

p.24 *Le Temps*: moderate opposition newspaper re-established on 25 April 1861. During the Second Empire it expressed the views of the liberal bourgeoisie.

p.27 Lamartine: Alphonse de Lamartine (1790–1869) was one of the best known of Romantic writers. He also had a political career, culminating in his appointment as Foreign Minister in the short-lived government of February 1848.

p.27 *Jocelyn*: nine-part poem (in versified prose) published by Lamartine in 1836. With its bucolic setting, it is a deeply sentimental account of the priest-hero's renunciation of his worldly love.

p.29 Clermont: i.e. the major city of Clermont-Ferrand, 382 km. south of Paris.

p.29 around the Panthéon: i.e. in the fifth *arrondissement*, with all its educational institutions, including the most famous Parisian schools as well as the Sorbonne.

p.30 **Les Andelys:** a small town on the Seine, now part of the western suburbs of Paris.

p.30 **commission agency:** Zola asked his friend Henri Céard to provide him with details about these agencies (some of them employing over thirty people) which charged their clients for all manner of financial transactions and services which would nowadays be dealt with by banks.

p.38 **Louis Quinze shoes:** an exotic style associated with the reign of Louis XV (1710–74), in the shape of a very high heel with a concave profile.

p.53 *Dame Blanche*: comic-opera by François Boieldieu (1775–1834) first performed in 1825; and a work considered suitable for respectable young ladies.

p.54 **Greuze's *Girl with a Broken Pitcher*:** the *Jeune Fille à la cruche cassée* is one of the best-known paintings of Jean-Baptiste Greuze (1725–1805); his failings were artificiality and hints of misplaced voluptuousness designed to pander to popular taste. When Zola himself was a young man, however, he confessed to Cézanne (in a mawkish letter of 1860) that Greuze was his favourite painter.

p.56 **Lyons silks:** Lyons had been the centre of the French silk industry since 1467; but it was during the Second Empire that its decline began, thus explaining the subsequent reference to Vabre's journeys and commercial difficulties there.

p.61 **Opéra-Comique:** the Théâtre de l'Opéra-Comique, dating from 1783 and rebuilt (after a fire) in 1840, was the principal venue for staging lyric art.

p.64 **the Légion d'Honneur:** France's highest award, created by Napoléon Bonaparte in 1802, with a hierarchy of ranks and decorations; the most common is that of *officier*, often rewarding long-serving senior civil servants.

p.66 **George Sand:** pseudonym of Aurore Dupin (1804–76) whose *André* was published in 1835. George Sand was one of the most widely read of contemporary novelists; her work is characterised by a mixture of rural realism and romantic idealism. The latter is the target of Zola's satire here.

p.69 **Saint-Roch:** the church of Saint-Roch is at no. 286 Rue St-

Honoré. Some of it dates from the sixteenth century, though the main part of it was built between 1653 and 1740; it contains many sculptures and works of art from that period. Zola took extensive notes on the church while preparing *Pot-Bouille*.

p.83 annual Salon: from 1791 to 1880 (although it had existed since the early eighteenth century), the major state-sponsored exhibition of the year, held in May, to which artists submitted their new work in the hope of public recognition. Protests from painters refused entry to this conservative institution reached such proportions that in 1863 Napoléon III ordered a special Salon des Refusés for those who were rejected, including many of the early Impressionists. The scale of old Vabre's labours can be measured by the fact that, at the 1857 Salon (to take one example), the official jury accepted 3,483 works by 1,454 artists.

p.84 the Roman question: in both 1861 and 1862 newly restored parliamentary debate divided those advocating Rome as the capital of a unified Italy and the Catholic lobby insisting that France support the Vatican's claim to temporal as well as spiritual power.

p.85 an Orléanist family: the Orléanists were the supporters of the branch of the Bourbon monarchy represented by Louis-Philippe, Duc d'Orléans (1773–1850), the last French king (cf. note to the *Gazette de France* on p. 10).

p.85 the Mexican Expedition: in January 1862, in an attempt to divert attention from his domestic policies and in the face of virulent liberal opposition, Napoléon III sent French troops to install the Archduke Maximilien of Austria as Emperor of Mexico. This disastrous military campaign resulted in the latter's execution in 1867 (immortalised in Manet's painting of the subject) at the hands of Mexican revolutionaries.

p.88 the 'Consecration of the Swords': 'La Bénédiction des Poignards' is one of the most famous scenes of *Les Huguenots* (1836) by Giacomo Meyerbeer (1791–1864). This kind of opera, the musical equivalent of historical melodrama, enjoyed an immense popularity until the end of the century; it also explains the resistance to Wagner whose cause was championed by the contemporary *avant-garde*. Where Zola stands in this respect is not in doubt. For further information on the precise ways in which Zola parodically counterpoints such librettos and the plot of *Pot-Bouille*, see Nicholas White, 'Carnal Knowledge in French Naturalist Fiction', in *Scarlet Letters. Fictions of Adultery from*

Antiquity to the 1990s ed. by him and Naomi Segal (London: Macmillan, 1997), p. 132, n. 11.

p.93 The *Revue des Deux Mondes*: the most prominent literary periodical of the time. It had been founded as far back as 1829 and was seen by young writers as stuffily conservative; but its Orléanist and parliamentary sympathies, justifying its place in this liberal bourgeois drawing-room, meant that it was viewed with suspicion by the imperial authorities.

p.119 the Rue d'Enghien: this is in the tenth *arrondissement*, about 1 km. north-east of the Rue de Choiseul.

p.123 the Rue de la Cerisaie: this is at the eastern end of Paris, near the Place de la Bastille, and thus at an appropriate distance from the 'respectable' bourgeois district which is the setting for the novel.

p.136 Les Moulineaux: i.e. Issy-les-Moulineaux, once a small town to the south-west of the capital, now part of the sprawling Parisian suburbs.

p.148 the Hôtel du Louvre: opened in 1855, the Grand Hôtel du Louvre enjoyed a contemporary reputation for its most fashionable of restaurants.

p.155 a play that attacked modern society: while this chapter supposedly takes place in May 1862, this is a reference to *Le Fils Giboyer* by Émile Augier (1820–89), actually performed in December 1862 at the Comédie Française; it caused a minor scandal because of its anticlericalism and its satire of the bourgeoisie. That the Emperor had authorised the production was a mere rumour, but one that surfaced again in Zola's work-notes for *Pot-Bouille*.

p.163 the École des Beaux-Arts: since 1816, in the Rue Bonaparte, the established training college for the artistic professions.

p.164 Vichy: 329km. to the south-east of Paris, the premier French spa town until 1914.

p.177 the Fountain of Vaucluse: a massive underground spring, 25km. east of Avignon, immortalised by Petrarch and now a tourist site.

p.182 Grétry's *Zémire et Azor*: comic-opera (1771) by André Grétry (1741–1813) with a libretto by the celebrated playwright and novelist Jean-François Marmontel (1723–99).

p.185 Isidore Charbotel: almost certainly an invention of Zola's, allowing him to satirise a typically conventional and eminently forgettable *oeuvre* consecrated by regular admission to the Salon. One such real painter was Jean-Louis Charbonnel whose work appeared at Salons between 1868 and 1882, including his *Apothéose de sainte Marguerite* (1868), *La Sortie du Bain* (1873), *Aspasie* (1874), *Vie et innocence* (1880) and *Portrait de Mgr Lamouroux* (1878).

p.188 the Rue Godot-de-Mauroy: the added irony of this is that this particular street is not very far (barely 500m.) from the Rue de Choiseul.

p.188 Ternes: this area, in the seventeenth *arrondissement*, was only incorporated within the city limits in 1860.

p.217 Monsieur Thiers: Adolphe Thiers (1797–1877) had come out of political exile to stand successfully as an Orléanist candidate in the elections of 31 May 1863. He subsequently fronted liberal opposition to Napoléon III's régime. After the fall of the Second Empire, he became head of the provisional government and was responsible for crushing the Commune in 1871.

p.217 Jacobin: a reference to the most fervent of the supporters of the French Revolution, banded together in the *club des Jacobins* between 1789 and 1794.

p.218 Garibaldi: this is a further reference to the Roman question (cf. note to **p. 84**; while leading troops fighting for the unification of Italy, Giuseppe Garibaldi (1807–82) was wounded in the foot at the Battle of Aspromonte on 30 August 1862.

p.218 what the cabinet minister has said: in the Senate, on 22 February 1862, Adolphe Billaut (1805–63) had said: 'Yes, certainly the Empire has sprung from the Revolution, but it has done so to further its cause, to direct its progress and to moderate its directions.' Billaut had been Minister of the Interior (1854) and Minister without Portfolio (1860), before becoming Minister of State shortly before his death in October 1863.

p.218 Père-Lachaise Cemetery: the main Parisian cemetery, named after, and built within the gardens of, the Jesuit confessor of Louis XIV. It was also known as the Cimetière de l'Est, which the characters could reach only by crossing the whole city.

p.256 Trouville: the fashionable resort of Trouville-sur-mer, opposite Deauville, on the Normandy coast.

p.256 Villeneuve-Saint-Georges: small town in the Val de Marne, now part of the south-eastern suburbs of Paris.

p.256 Pontoise: small town to the west of Paris to which the court was exiled on more than one occasion in the seventeenth and eighteenth centuries, generating the French expression *revenir de Pontoise*, meaning to 'have a bewildered look' (i.e. as if returning from exile). That Madame Josserand should go there, given how often she is described as regal or majestic, seems entirely appropriate.

p.301 the Rue d'Assas: Clarisse's new address is in the sixth *arrondissement*, near the Luxembourg Gardens (as Trublot correctly recalls).

p.328 the Emperor himself: Napoléon III had a well-deserved reputation as a womaniser.

p.355 Mazas: located on the Boulevard Mazas (now the Boulevard Diderot), the Mazas was the first French prison with a cellular system. Not a single prisoner escaped from it during its existence (1850–98).

p.368 *Life of Jesus*: by adopting a historical rather than sacred perspective, *La Vie de Jésus*, by Ernest Renan (1823–92), provoked fury in conservative and clerical circles when it was published in 1863.

p.368 Monsieur Rouher: Eugène Rouher (1814–84) succeeded Billaut as Minister of State in 1863 (cf. note to cabinet minister, p. 218). He aligned himself firmly against Rome becoming the capital of a unified Italy. If this is one of the reasons for the imagined respect he earns from Monsieur Duveyrier, the latter also has considerable foresight. For Rouher would go on to a glittering career: he became Prime Minister in 1867; he had such power that he was referred to as 'vice-emperor' by opposition politicians keen to create jealousies in government ranks. He is one of the principal models for the figure of Eugène Rougon, the protagonist of Zola's most closely focused study of Second Empire politics, *Son Excellence Eugène Rougon* (1876).

The responses to *Pot-Bouille*, over more than a century, are inseparable from the larger patterns of Zola's own critical fortunes. During his lifetime, he was alternately hailed as the greatest European novelist of his generation or reviled as a writer wallowing in the baser appetites of humanity. But between his death, in 1902, and the early 1950s, his literary reputation faded to a point where his work was merely evoked in the context of a nineteenth-century realist tradition whose limits Zola himself exemplified. The few exceptions to this consensus occasionally cited *Pot-Bouille* as one of the novels responsible for their continuing admiration for the *Rougon-Macquart*. It was not until the modern revival of interest in Zola, however, that *Pot-Bouille* came under renewed scrutiny. And, even then, it was overshadowed: it seemed as if it could hardly compete for attention alongside belatedly acknowledged masterpieces such as *Germinal* or *La Terre*; for these have an epic sweep and imaginative power which serve to underline the apparently anomalous position of *Pot-Bouille* within Zola's series. It is often considered 'uncharacteristic', or 'in another key'. In that sense, there is a remarkable continuity between the response of its first readers and that of later critics. But to survey that contemporary and modern critical reception is also to be reminded of what is distinctive about *Pot-Bouille*, and of the ways in which successive re-readings of the novel have potentially enriched our own.

Two novels, in particular, changed a contemporary reading-public's view of Zola: *L'Assommoir*, serialised in the press in 1876 and published in volume form the next year, and *Nana*, which appeared in 1880. Both created a storm of protest: Zola was accused of exaggerating the miseries of working-class life, and his frank portrayal of sexuality provoked charges of obscenity. But both were also bestsellers, ensuring that, from then on, a new Zola novel always aroused massive interest. And that interest was deliberately enhanced by publicity mechanisms in which Zola himself had served an invaluable apprenticeship during his time at the publisher, Hachette, in the early 1860s. In the case of *Pot-Bouille*, these ensured an initial *succès de scandale*.

Certainly it was not by chance that, on 5 January 1882, *Le Gaulois* announced the forthcoming serialisation of *Pot-Bouille* in its columns in provocative terms. For it alerted readers who (at least in private) might have enjoyed Zola's depiction of working-class promiscuity that, in *Pot-Bouille*, the focus would now be turned on that of the middle-classes:

> M. Emile Zola, in *Pot-Bouille*, has studied the bourgeoisie, in the same way as he studied the proletariat in *L'Assommoir*. To the working-class house in the Rue de la Goutte d'Or, teeming with the instinctual shamelessness of misery, he has juxtaposed a bourgeois house in the Rue de Choiseul, behind the virtuous and respectable surfaces of which are to be found the hypocritical vices and degeneracy of a dominant class in the throes of decomposition. *Pot-Bouille* will thus be a novel of manners, or at least an unremitting picture, of the bourgeoisie, which will be the sequel to, or rather the counterpart of, *L'Assommoir*.

The article went on to spell out that the novel would be a study of middle-class adultery. *Pot-Bouille* was designed, in other words, as a conscious assault on the sensibilities and moral values of the majority of its readers. And the reaction to it was therefore unsurprising.

It explains why, hardly had the first instalment of *Pot-Bouille* appeared, the novel would benefit from further attention as a result of an incident beyond the wildest dreams of the most publicity-seeking of writers. For the figure of Duveyrier was originally named Duverdy, and a real Duverdy (a lawyer with an address within a stone's throw of the location of the fictional house in *Pot-Bouille*) successfully took Zola to court to force him to change the character's name. The affair, generating both serious debate and much hilarity, kept *Pot-Bouille* in the spotlight throughout February 1882, not least as other people came forward to claim that they too were the victims of defamation as a result of coincidences between themselves and particular

characters in the novel. Whatever else this tells us about the first
readers of *Pot-Bouille*, Zola had clearly touched a raw nerve!

This is equally evident in the vituperative campaign against
the novel orchestrated by the contemporary press. Familiar
charges were rehearsed: *Pot-Bouille* was 'immoral', 'infamous',
'disgusting', 'pornographic'. This was the vocabulary that had
also greeted *Nana*. But it was in the simultaneous defence of
bourgeois values that the impact of the novel's specific focus
can be gauged. Thus the literary critic of *Le Gil Blas* (6 February
1882), writing under the pseudonym of 'Colombine', could
explicitly encourage the bourgeois readers of *L'Assommoir* and
Nana to realise the errors of their ways in not being sufficiently
aware of Zola's treasonous opposition to everything they stood
for:

> So you are happy this time, you middle-class ladies and gentlemen
> responsible for M. Zola's success when he depicted the proletariat
> or the world of prostitution?
>
> Do you still believe in his so-called accuracy? Are you yourselves
> really such a grotesque bunch of imbeciles, sometimes monstrous
> but always revolting? Is the house in *Pot-Bouille* the one you live in,
> that madhouse filled with hysterical females, with its resident idiot,
> doddering old fool and soft-headed cretins?
>
> Ah! How I wish I had a more virile pen to defend the honour of
> that fine Parisian bourgeoisie slandered in this way, and made to
> look so ridiculous and hateful in the eyes of foreigners who will base
> their judgement on this abominable picture! Is there not a single
> patriotic writer, with a love of his country in his veins, who will
> come forward to praise the virtues of this part of society characteri-
> sed by energy and hard work, and made up of men and women of
> greater intelligence and probity than anywhere else?
>
> For the real truth is as follows: between the vice-ridden misery of
> the proletariat and the vice-ridden idleness of high society, the
> bourgeoisie itself is the class least vulnerable to corruption, repre-
> senting as it does all that is best and solid about the values of France.

What is so wonderfully ironic about reactions such as this is
that it resembles so closely the interventions in the heated
political debates of the assembled characters in *Pot-Bouille*
itself. There, the supposed historical context is the Second
Empire. But it is clear that Zola's critics detected a more
generalised perspective in remarks (notably in chapters 5 and

18) about the imminent collapse of bourgeois society. And, indeed, *Pot-Bouille* very precisely anticipates its own critical reception: the anonymous writer, living on the second floor, is accused by Monsieur Gourd of writing 'such scandalous novels . . . full of filth about decent folk' (p. 355) that he has come to the attention of the police; Léon Josserand, leafing through a copy of the *Revue des Deux Mondes*, decries 'yet another story of adultery' (p. 93); and the real *Gazette de France*, a copy of which is appropriately lying on Campardon's drawing-table, in the first chapter of the novel, would inevitably rise to the defence of its bourgeois subscribers.

In that newspaper, on 11 February, G. Dancourt adopted the now-familiar strategy of situating *Pot-Bouille* in relation to *L'Assommoir* and *Nana*:

> Compared to *Pot-Bouille*, *L'Assommoir* and *Nana* are lullabies for innocent little girls . . . What you find in this bourgeois house is a dance of death of rampant satyrs, from the concierge's lodge to the servants' quarters, and going through the middle floors inhabited by respectable tenants; just imagine for yourselves the most cynical and unbridled saraband of vice, and you'll have a pretty good idea of M. Zola's *Pot-Bouille*. Apparently that's what goes on in every middle-class building in Paris. I don't suppose you'll be in any doubt about it. But if, like me, you don't find it entirely credible, you should know that this has been confirmed by M. Zola, a so-called 'naturalist' novelist who therefore never gets these things wrong . . . On the other hand, M. Zola has never actually been inside a bourgeois home. Not that that prevents him from asserting that this is a place as unspeakably sordid as a working-class hovel in the slums. I'm quite sure that this writer has a very powerful imagination. But, as a 'naturalist' study, it does leave a lot to be desired.

What is interesting here is the critical move characteristic of much writing on Zola during his lifetime. In other words, the way in which recognition of imaginative or poetic gifts is used to devalue his work's quasi-scientific pretensions. It had been in response to charges of exaggeration, in *L'Assommoir* and *Nana*, that Zola had elaborated the theoretical tenets of Naturalism in essays published between 1879 and 1881. Collected in *Le Roman expérimental* (1879) and *Les Romanciers naturalistes* (1881), these established an analogy between the natural scientist and the Naturalist writer in so far as the working methods of both relied on direct observation and documentary material. For the hostile critic, not the least subtle way of dismissing such claims was to insist that Zola's work was testimony to the distance between inventiveness and truth.

Thus Henry Fouquier, in *Le Gil Blas* on 26/27 April 1882, could praise *Pot-Bouille*'s 'unity, at the level of both plot and style' before going on to list thirty-one instances of inaccuracy for which Zola's lack of direct observation of its social world was doubtless responsible. In a private letter to Fouquier, the same day, Zola went to the trouble of rejecting each and every objection, justifying the inclusion of various details on the basis of argument or supporting evidence.

But most of the reviewers discounting the verisimilitude of *Pot-Bouille* were far less specific. In an earlier piece in *Le Gil Blas* (4 April 1882), Émile Villemot stressed that he was far less concerned by the 'immorality' of the novel than by the fallacy of its mimetic ambitions:

> The author of *Pot-Bouille* is reproached for portraying the bourgeoisie in blacker tones and more vice-ridden than it really is; he is accused of a false naturalism . . .
>
> Let's leave aside the idiotic tactics of the moralists. All I want to say and prove is that M. Zola's naturalist inventions, whatever fine and superb ingredients they may contain, are far below the Truth. The novel cannot compete with history, and realism is the death of the novel. M. Zola is merely a cardboard naturalist incapable of capturing the dynamic realities of nature itself.

In *Le Figaro* of 22 April 1882, Albert Wolff's mixture of parodic incredulity and faint praise is similarly angled towards a militant Naturalism recently reinforced by a further volume of collected articles by Zola, *Une Campagne* (1882):

> In that extraordinary house in the Rue de Choiseul, its bourgeois inhabitants visit each other from morning till night. They're hardly ever in their own homes; they're always in somebody else's; they go from bed to bed, from the landing to the attic; it's a love nest; the concierge is never in her lodge; she's got to stand in her doorway saying to passers-by: 'we've got some lovely tenants here'. And if you leave this brothel in the Rue de Choiseul, that same concierge will ask you for forty sous in exchange for a pair of gloves to go out and about with. If adultery isn't consummated on the actual stair-

case, it's doubtless because it's too solemn; otherwise, somewhere between the lobby and the first floor, nobody would be at all surprised to come across a Parisian gentleman reading *Pot-Bouille* to a cook.

And as for those cooks! Yes, I know they're not all as great stylists as Mme de Sévigné . . . and I can well imagine that when such uneducated women let themselves go in the privacy of their kitchen, their language must be quite something. But do you really believe that a bourgeois house would tolerate such dreadful women insulting each other, from window to window and from kitchen to kitchen, calling each other sluts and pigs, throwing rubbish at each other while screaming at the top of their voices, without arousing the whole of the Rue de Choiseul and the surrounding neighbourhood? What a waste of time to devote so many volumes to the 'human document' and to write so many articles on naturalism (now under the collective title *Une Campagne*), only to produce this inauthentic and hypocritical book, with its calculated obscenities and filthy language; what a waste of so wonderful a talent for description to end up with this unrealistic portrayal of a bourgeois house and its inhabitants.

Yet Wolff's reference to *Pot-Bouille*'s 'obscenity' was relatively mild compared to the violence exemplified by Charles Laurent's article in *Paris* (10 February 1882):

This is the most shameless pornography, tempting the reader to swallow the most stupid and boring story. Like those habitués of vice weary of repeated pleasures and smutty tales, the author seems to have focused on rather special sorts of things and daring little inventions. He's in competition with the most obscene products of the literary underworld . . . Only naturalism has its own imperatives, and this latter-day M. de Sade puts an emphasis on precision.

From this pen, shaped for other kinds of works, there flows a soiled ink with which M. Zola imagines he's producing an analytical novel. He finds his bourgeosie in the heart of Paris; and he claims to be like Asmodeus, lifting up the roofs of our houses to display middle-class vices on every floor. But his imagination always proceeds in the same direction, conjuring up the same scene and the same filth.

From the ground floor to the top of the house, all the inhabitants are wallowing in hysteria and promiscuity.

All the women are racked by unhealthy desire; all his men are tormented by a vague and savage lust, ready to jump on anything at hand and then to be off again.

This former literary gent has gone mad, crazed by an entirely new genre in his onanistic inkwell.

Laurent's review was headed 'The Suicide of Naturalism'. In the *Journal des Gens de lettres belges* (1 March 1882), Ferdinand Loise entitled his 'The Gutter of Literature'. Such excess is all the more striking if one remembers that it was aimed merely at the serial version of *Pot-Bouille*; when it appeared in volume form at the end of April, the self-censoring cuts imposed by *Le Gaulois* were restored, allowing reviewers to both mock the newspaper's prudery and castigate the 'cynical eroticism' of so many of Zola's scenes now revealed behind elliptical dots and euphemistic blanks. The novel's reception abroad simply added to the presumed licentiousness of both Zola's writing and all things French: one American reviewer dubbed *Pot-Bouille* 'Zola's Stink-Pot' (*The Literary World*, 3 June 1882); another (in *The Critic*, 20 May 1882) summed up obloquy on both sides of the Atlantic: 'A Filthy Book'.

If such attitudes serve to remind us of the circumscribed literary context in which Zola was working, a less gratuitously insulting response to *Pot-Bouille* is to be found in Ferdinand Brunetière's assessment in the *Revue des Deux Mondes* (15 May 1882); penned by one of the most authoritative critics of the day, and coming as it does after the 'sound and fury' of the novel's immediate publication, Brunetiète's review prepares the ground for those twentieth-century readings of the text more alert to what it has in common with the rest of Zola's work. Brunetière is no less unsympathetic than other conservative critics more rabidly outraged by *Pot-Bouille*. But he is as scathing at the expense of those singling out the differences between this novel and its predecessors as he is at the new-found collective indignation provoked by it:

> What's all the fuss about? Is the language any filthier in this novel of so-called bourgeois manners than it was in the so-called novel of the working class? Is there anything more sordid in this *Pot-Bouille* than there was in *Nana*? Has M. Zola plunged into the disgusting as never before? I don't think so, whatever may have been said. The Boche couple, in *L'Assommoir*, are no better than M. et Mme Gourd, and I can't see how Uncle Bachelard or his nephew Gueulin

are any worse than the Marquis de Chouard or Count Muffat. If you're content to have M. Zola record, with his finest ink and pen, the conversation of wretches on the outer boulevards, you can't complain when he extends his 'philological studies' to what is said in an inner courtyard and on the back stairs ... *Pot-Bouille* and *Nana* can't be distinguished from each other; they're by the same hand; *L'Assommoir* and *Pot-Bouille* undoubtedly bear the same imprint and are similar products. M. Zola hasn't gone any further in his latest masterpiece; all he's done is repeat himself.

In this double-edged vein, Brunetière professed himself delighted with the excesses of *Pot-Bouille*, which seemed to justify his consistent refusal to ally himself with those voyeuristic admirers of *L'Assommoir* or *Nana* now receiving, in his view, their comeuppance.

It is also a measure of the antagonistic literary politics of the period that only Zola's close friends and associates voiced their appreciation of *Pot-Bouille*. The most long-standing and faithful of them all, Paul Alexis, complemented his recent authorised biography (*Emile Zola, notes d'un ami*, Paris: Charpentier, 1882) with an equally effusive article in *Le Réveil* (15 April 1882):

Pot-Bouille seems to me a sort of gigantic fresco worthy of Michaelangelo. It has to be understood and appreciated as such. With energetic brushstrokes reminiscent of the Last Judgement, many of its figures have been distorted, not so much above, but rather beyond nature. Reality, here and there, has been stretched. Within the series, *La Faute de l'Abbé Mouret*, as a sort of prose poem at the edge of the fantastic, already strikes a note of excess. In spite of their radically different styles, these two works have much in common. The former has its Paradou as a paradise of flowers and vegetation, of perfumes and colours, in riotous profusion. In *Pot-Bouille*, the house in the Rue de Choiseul is a terrible hell, a basin of the damned in which our chemist has stirred the stinking filth of an entire social class. Separated in the novel-cycle, each will find readers who prefer one rather than the other. But both demonstrate a stunning excess of contrasting qualities, expanding the range and enhancing the greatness of the writer.

Its own hagiographic excesses apart, what remains interesting here is the undogmatic subordination of strictly naturalist criteria to aspects of *Pot-Bouille* responsible for its continuing impact, notably a caricatural intensification at the limits of realism.

The most suggestive responses to *Pot-Bouille* were conveyed to Zola in private. In a letter to him of 16 April 1882, the novelist Joris-Karl Huysmans balanced his unease about the stilted quality of some of the novel's dialogues with his admiration for its textual economies and black humour:

> What strikes me, above all, is its structure, its beautifully engineered shape, with its simplicity matched by the effort you've made to keep the style simple. I find the descriptions, condensed into a few sentences, absolutely first-rate; so too the house: thanks to those same epithets, recurring in ritual fashion to insist on its characteristics, it comes across crystal-clear. You've exactly caught that kind of modern building, with its surface luxury and badly painted walls visible beneath its fake marble. The black courtyard, with its windows opening and slamming to the rhythm of slops being hurled out, is a brilliant idea. What a din! And how it stinks of grease and kitchen sinks! In terms of macabre comedy, I can't think of anything as savagely funny as those torrents of abuse. Except perhaps for that wonderfully horrific birth-scene. That note of black humour, but without malice, is unprecedented in your series. I was very struck by this entirely new dimension.

Céard, as a result of his involvement in the preparation of *Pot-Bouille* (see Introduction, p. xxii), published an article in *La Vie moderne* (1 July 1882) partly articulating its author's own analysis of bourgeois adultery. But he too had written to Zola, on 19 April, providing a commentary on his own reading of the novel more intelligent than most:

> I have just finished *Pot-Bouille*. What intuitive gifts you have! It's astonishing how much you've got exactly right. In what your characters say, either in trivial contexts or in moments of high passion, so often you reveal the secret workings of the bourgeoisie's heart and soul.
>
> What seems to be missing from the book, however, is quite enough atmosphere. It doesn't seem to me to be as fully immersed in the bourgeois world as *L'Assommoir* was in the working-class suburbs. I also find it mechanical in so far as its calculated precision is rather too visible, with its logical imperatives functioning at the

expense of subtlety. Of course, as far as the ideas are concerned, you have written a novel whose truth is not in doubt. But I wonder if ordinary life is as structured as your mathematical demonstration.

Your scenes at the Josserands are superb; so too is your description of old Vabre's death, as sinister as an episode out of Ben Jonson; and especially, and above all, that of Adèle giving birth. That, my dear Zola, is something very particular and new in your work, better than anything you've ever done before. It's a masterpiece: the tragedy of humanity, a dignified sadness and a technical austerity. You can't imagine how filled with emotion one is when reading that medical poetry resonant with pity for the suffering of the flesh and for the misery of the disinherited. What you have discovered there is a new form of literary beauty: you can feel it in the strange shiver in all our spines as we have read your book.

Céard is undoubtedly one of the most sensitive early readers of Zola. And what he foregrounds here are precisely the strengths and weaknesses of *Pot-Bouille* identified and developed in the modern era.

Not even the furore surrounding its publication could ensure *Pot-Bouille* matched the popular success of *L'Assommoir* and *Nana*, let alone sustain its position among Zola's bestsellers in the twentieth century. At the time of Zola's death, in 1902, it had sold 95,000 copies in France. By 1993, this had risen to 685,000, leaving it in roughly tenth place in a 'league table' based on such figures. By comparison, the 'market leaders', *L'Assommoir* and *Germinal*, are now over the 3 million mark. Between such sales and continuing critical attention there is only the crudest of correlations. But it remains broadly true that *Pot-Bouille* has only very recently been subject to the kind of fertile re-reading of Zola's better-known novels responsible for the modern revaluation of his literary achievement.

In the fifty years following his death, *Pot-Bouille* suffered much the same critical fate as the rest of Zola's work. Not even early Marxist analyses, in the 1920s and 1930s, cited the novel as further evidence of Zola's intuitive sense of the inevitable demise of bourgeois dominance. Critics like Henri Barbusse (*Zola*, Paris: Gallimard, 1932) preferred to dwell on a novel like *Germinal*, with its more explicit vision of working-class revolution.

But there was one writer who found in *Pot-Bouille* confirma-
tion of his own disgust with middle-class values and hypocrisy.
In his Journal entry for 17 January 1932, André Gide's appreciation of the novel's 'excesses' can be related to Alexis's half a
century earlier:

> I have just finished reading *Pot-Bouille*. It's an admirable book. I'm
> perfectly well aware of Zola's weaknesses; but, just like those of
> Balzac and many others, they're inseparable from his strengths; and,
> even at the expense of subtlety and delicacy, his portrayal has a
> savage power. What I so much enjoy in *Pot-Bouille* is, indeed, its
> excessive quality, its unflinching exploration of the sordid. There is
> much that is masterly and unforgettable: Octave and Berthe's rendez-
> vous in the maid's room, their soiled and miserable love affair
> swamped by the filthy commentary of the servants; Adèle secretly
> giving birth; the family scenes and Madame Josserand's rows with
> her daughters (though these are a bit repetitive like so many features
> of this book). The characters are over-simplified, but they're not just
> puppets, and their wonderful conversations catch exactly the right
> tone, which is far from always the case in Balzac. I think the current
> devaluation of Zola is an indictment of today's literary critics. There
> is no more personal or representative French novelist.

For those who did try to rehabilitate Zola's reputation, *Pot-
Bouille* nevertheless seemed something of an embarrassment.
The full title of Matthew Josephson's 1928 study is eloquent:
*Zola and his Time. A History of his Martial Career in Letters:
with an Account of his Circle of Friends, his Remarkable
Enemies, Cyclopean Labours, Public Campaigns, Trials, and
Ultimate Glory*; that did not excuse *Pot-Bouille*:

> *Pot-Bouille* was the drabbest book Zola ever wrote. Despite its
> successfully recognised reality, all the dark poetry which lived in
> Zola seems to have been for the time sold to the devil. It is
> photography, the stupid discoloured photography which succeeds
> the era of Daguerre. It is the *reductio ad absurdum* of Naturalism. It
> is Zola following the routine *train-train* of his little method, forget-
> ting himself for the time, as he yields to the most mediocre aspects
> of his nature.

That this book was published in New York is not beside the
point. Another Anglo-Saxon admirer, Henry James, had also
memorably distanced himself from 'the singular foulness of

Zola's imagination'. Josephson's deprecation, in *Pot-Bouille*, of the 'most mediocre aspects of his nature' speaks of residual Victorian attitudes, in the English-reading world, towards Zola's particular emphasis on sexuality. It is reflected in the first translation of *Pot-Bouille*, published by Vizetelly in 1885, not only bowdlerised in the shape of delicate circumlocution, but so truncated that the scene in which Adèle gives birth is omitted altogether. On the other hand, prurience dictated seductive titles subsequently overlaid on this version (originally published as *Piping Hot!*), such as *Lessons in Love*, even as late as 1953, thereby constraining serious assessment of a writer too often associated, in the public mind, with a titillating indecency.

That *Pot-Bouille* poses particular difficulties in this respect is underlined by the fact that, even in France (and even after the renewed interest in Zola from the 1950s onwards), the novel is sometimes treated with a suspicion reminiscent of the moral outrage of its contemporaries. For the eminent Catholic critic, Henri Guillemin (*Présentation des 'Rougon-Macquart'*, Paris: Gallimard, 1964): '*Pot-Bouille* is not Zola's best work. It is not even one of the best of the *Rougon-Macquart* ... It is so systematic that cinematographic adaptations have hardly had to rearrange it to produce a third-rate vaudeville.' Guillemin reveals his real agenda, however, when he singles out for praise the portrait of the Abbé Mauduit and wonders whether the sexual scenes of *Pot-Bouille* justify Monsieur Gourd's feeling that smut is itself the secret of the commercial success of the fictional writer living on the second floor.

Following Gide's ephemeral delight, it was another novelist who was instrumental in enlarging the critical debate about *Pot-Bouille*. Without ignoring the fact that 'entertaining, powerful though it is, the whole book is a little like a "witty French farce" scrawled on a lavatory wall', Angus Wilson was one of the first to direct its readers both to *Pot-Bouille*'s wider moral and social dimensions and to the underlying tensions generating so personal an attack on traditional conjugal values. In his pioneering *Emile Zola. An Introductory Study of his Novels* (London: Secker & Warburg, 1952), and in the Introduction to *Pot-Bouille* prefacing the reprinting of Pinkerton's translation in 1953 (London: Weidenfeld & Nicolson), Wilson highlighted features of the novel that remain no less pertinent today.

For he stresses that, in *Pot-Bouille*, Zola's attack on the bourgeoisie 'is more complete, more continuous, less hampered by any conventional consideration of good manners than in any of his other novels'. And he picks up Céard's response in alerting us not only to the novel's 'black humour', but also to its 'deep compassion' for the sterility and private suffering of the targets of his satire: 'Adèle is not the only innocent in this black world; many of the characters, notably M. Josserand are "good". But in the end, one feels, perhaps, that such arbitrary distinctions of "good" and "bad" are beside the point. There is a more complete humanity and compassion that embraces them all.' Wilson's explanation for this lies in the relationship he establishes between Zola's own 'sterile' marriage and the frustrations he depicts, and between private and collective repressions determined by the social codes and moral contradictions of the age.

Where Wilson is less discriminating, perhaps, is in his enthusiasm for the novel's compositional design:

> As a work of art or of entertainment, it is a remarkable novel. Rich in irony that merges into broad comedy, superb in melodrama, its most striking quality is the detexterity and ease with which Zola handles so many groups of characters and so many plots, carrying them along by flowing narrative, intertwining and untwining the various strands without confusing the reader.

But it was as a direct consequence of this (reviewing both Wilson's general study and his Introduction to the translation of *Pot-Bouille*, under the 'rather odd title' of *Restless House*) that Lionel Trilling, one of the most influential of post-war critics, lent his authority to readings of the novel liberated from both prudery and prurience.

Indeed, Trilling goes further than Wilson, describing *Pot-Bouille* as a 'masterpiece', with its 'gems of ironic poetry', and its device of the apartment building as the location of all its dramas 'not the mechanical trick it becomes for his followers', but rather 'organic and essential to his aesthetic effect', comparable to 'the limitation of space in one of Breughel's satiric fantasies' or 'Ben Johnson's claustral strictness of form'; seldom, in literary history, has *Pot-Bouille* found itself in such distinguished company:

> We do not ask whether Zola's representation of the bourgeoisie is accurate or even if it is justified. We read this book for the pleasure

of its fierce energy, for the strange pleasure we habitually derive from the indictment of human kind. The work has a reality beyond anything that might be proved of the Parisian class of 1882, it has the reality of the author's rage and disgust with human inadequacy. The book ... is in the great tradition of massive comic morality which I have tried to indicate by my mention of Breughel, Ben Jonson and Swift, to whom we may add Hogarth, and, nearer at hand, Heine, the later Dickens, and Flaubert. ('In Defence of Zola', *A Gathering of Fugitives*, London: Secker & Warburg, 1957, pp. 14–22)

Without suggesting that the novel precisely deserves those points of comparison, it is worth noting that Céard had alluded to Ben Jonson in his letter to Zola in 1882. With the wisdom of hindsight, we can see that what Trilling is doing is reinforcing the critical distinction (already evident in Alexis's complicitous eulogy) between the truths of realism and those of comic art. And it allows us to understand better the status afforded the novel by another modern critic, George Steiner, who claims that: '*Pot-Bouille* is one of the best novels of the nineteenth century – great in its comic ferocity and tightness of design' (*Tolstoy or Dostoevsky*, Harmondsworth: Penguin, 1967, p. 33).

The leading Zola scholar of this generation, F. W. J. Hemmings, adopts the broadly psychoanalytical perspective informing Angus Wilson's speculations on the bitterness and disgust running through *Pot-Bouille*:

The denunciation of moral looseness that runs through *Pot-Bouille* is a sign only of the uneasiness Zola felt when confronted with the sexual freedom that others permitted themselves but he recoiled from. *Pot-Bouille* and *Nana* are two differently angled exteriorisations of a still unresolved inner conflict. (*Émile Zola*, Oxford University Press, 2nd edition, 1966, p. 146)

For Hemmings, this itself explains the novel's moralising, but unconvincing, equation between promiscuity and social decomposition, organised as a demonstration of 'the eternal uniformity of lust' and barely supported by 'the ghost of a plot'. Yet, for all Hemmings's distaste for 'the tedious aridity of the book', characterised by the 'authentic greyness of realism', he is one of the first critics to argue that *Pot-Bouille* is less an anomaly within Zola's series than thematically consistent with its author's repeated, and ambiguous, explorations of human sexuality.

The subsequent application of the categories of psychoanalysis to literary texts, in the 1970s, took this radically further. Thus Jean Borie (*Zola et les mythes*, Paris: Seuil, 1971) finds in *Pot-Bouille* figurations patterning the whole of Zola's work. In particular, the building itself, with its intestinal passageways, is seen as an obsessive image of the body's functioning. Between its 'respectable' point of entry and the fetid orifice through which waste is evacuated, intersected by dramas of impotence and the penetration of spatial divisions, the house stages (in Borie's reading) an 'excremental vision' which is less unique to Zola as an individual than representative of the mental structures of nineteenth-century bourgeois experience. Such Freudian interpretations have not secured, of course, unqualified assent. But they have opened up critical perspectives foregrounding the symbolic register of *Pot-Bouille*, central to which is its preoccupation with the private and the public, articulated in the juxtaposed spaces of intimacy and social intercourse.

The most comprehensive and even-handed analysis of *Pot-Bouille* is that of Brian Nelson, integral to his study of *Zola and the Bourgeoisie* (London: MacMillan, 1983). He takes his distance from Trilling and Steiner's admiration for the novel, pointing to its 'stylistic weaknesses': 'a schematic rigidity, shrill overemphasis, didacticism'. But he also illuminates 'an assured and controlled art, revealing an unfamiliar Zola with no small talent for incisive satirical comedy':

> It is both harsh and funny; the narrative is full of rich and varied incident, including episodes of comic-opera extravagance. It has a compelling force, intensity and speed, which combine with repetition, recurring symbolic images and ironic use of décor to create a sense of the mechanical and the ritualistic. The novel is especially noteworthy for burlesque theatricality in comic elaboration of theme and situation, strengthened by comic-grotesque caricature, irony, verbal comedy and dramatic counterpoint.

Nelson rigorously plots the thematic continuities between *Pot-Bouille* and the rest of the *Rougon-Macquart* while engaging in a stimulatingly focused re-reading of the text itself. But it is precisely those textual details that underline the extent to which, as he says, 'to criticise *Pot-Bouille*, like most of the contemporary press, for its poor documentation and lack of "realism" is to miss the point that the essence of the novel is that it *is* a caricature and that it deliberately distorts reality in the creation of satiric fantasy.'

This has been developed in more recent studies extending the notion of caricature from the novel's subject to its form. In other words, as David Baguley puts it, 'it is a novel directed almost as much against bourgeois literature (or the literature favoured by the bourgeois reader) as it is against bourgeois morals' (*Naturalist Fiction: the Entropic Vision*, Cambridge University Press, 1990). In this light, *Pot-Bouille* can be read as 'an example of naturalist parody', parodying the conventions of the genre to which it only seems to subscribe. This perspective, but contextualised by a wider social crisis of patriarchal values, has been most fully articulated by Nicholas White:

> Parody is one way of having and not having the novel of adultery, and *Pot-Bouille* is therefore a fitting culmination to a cultural tradition, rather than a sudden break with the past . . . The novel of adultery is parodied in this way by Zola's use of the Don Juan figure who enjoys a double-edged relationship to the patriarchy that the novel of adultery subtends. As a sexual peripatetic, the Don Juan figure, Octave threatens husbands with the notorious uncertainty of paternity, and yet at the same time embodies a certain principle of virility (itself grounded in a crisis of masculinity and paternity). ('Carnal Knowledge in French Naturalist Fiction', in *Scarlet Letters. Fictions of Adultery from Antiquity to the 1990s*, ed. Nicholas White and Naomi Segal, London: Macmillan, 1997, pp. 127–8)

With its own emphasis on books and reading, it could also be argued that it leaves the modern critic unsure of the oblique relationship between the generic model ironised in *Pot-Bouille* and the pleasures of our own reading of this particular 'novel of adultery'. But what is certain is that such pleasures partly derive from the fact that, as in the novel's own concern with surface and depth, re-readings of *Pot-Bouille* since 1882 have confirmed that there is more to it than meets the eye.

SUGGESTIONS FOR FURTHER READING

The most reliable and readable account in English of Zola's life and work is *Émile Zola* by F. W. J. Hemmings (Oxford: Oxford University Press, 2nd edition, 1966).

As a supplement to this general critical biography, the following books and articles in English will be of interest to readers of *Pot-Bouille*:

Judith Armstrong, *The Novel of Adultery* (London: Macmillan, 1976) makes only passing reference to *Pot-Bouille*, but situates it in relation to the treatment of adultery in a wide range of novels both before and since.

Elliott Grant, 'The Political Scene in Zola's *Pot-Bouille*', *French Studies* (VIII, 1954) is a useful illumination of the novel's Second Empire background.

Sharon Marcus, 'Zola's Restless House', in *Apartment Stories* (Berkeley: University of California Press, 1999, pp. 166–98) is a brilliant recent essay on the relationship between the novel's spatial organisation and contemporary discourse on urban interiors.

Brian Nelson, *Zola and the Bourgeoisie* (London: Macmillan, 1983) puts *Pot-Bouille* in the context of Zola's treatment of bourgeois values throughout his career and devotes an entire chapter (*Pot-Bouille*: Black Comedy', pp. 129–57) to the structure and themes of the novel. This remains the best and most extended study of *Pot-Bouille* in any language.

Lionel Trilling, 'In Defence of Zola', in *A Gathering of Fugitives* (London: Secker & Warburg, 1957, pp. 14–22), is his 1953 review-essay of the Pinkerton translation of *Pot-Bouille* situating the novel within the major European comic tradition.

Nicholas White, 'Carnal Knowledge in French Naturalist Fiction', in his and Naomi Segal's (eds) *Scarlet Letters. Fictions of Adultery from Antiquity to the 1990s* (London: Macmillan, 1997, pp. 123–33). White insists that the parodic dimensions of *Pot-Bouille* exemplify a *fin-de-siècle* crisis of patriarchal values.

Thanks to its comprehensive indexing, David Baguley's *Bibliographie de la critique sur Émile Zola* (Toronto: University Press, 2 vols, 1976–82) will assist readers wishing to find their way through the huge amount of critical work on Zola. This is updated annually in the specialist Zola periodical, *Les Cahiers naturalistes*.

TEXT SUMMARY

Chapter 1

Octave Mouret arrives in Paris – he is welcomed to the apartment building in the Rue de Choiseul which is the setting for the novel – M. Campardon takes him on a guided tour and informs him about the other tenants – he is taken to 'Au Bonheur des Dames' and meets Mme Hédouin who offers him a job in this shop – he has dinner with the Campardon family.

Chapter 2

Mme Josserand walks her daughters home to the Rue de Choiseul after a party at which they have once again failed to find a husband – this leads to a furious row, during which M. Josserand is the victim of his wife's recriminations – Berthe Josserand is physically attacked by her mother, and comforted by Saturnin, her adoring brother.

Chapter 3

At a dinner party at the Josserands', the two daughters try to get money out of their Uncle Bachelard – Saturnin has a fit of rage and is locked out of sight – Octave learns more about the assembled inhabitants from Trublot – Berthe entertains the guests at the piano – Mme Josserand makes plans to marry off Berthe to Auguste Vabre.

Chapter 4

Octave lays plans to seduce Valérie – he dines at the Campardons' – the next day he is invited in to the Pichons' where he makes the acquaintance of Marie and her family – further meetings with Marie result in Octave lending her books – his advances having been refused by Valérie, he drops in on Marie and forces himself on her.

Chapter 5

Octave attends a musical evening at the Duveyriers' at which all the characters' situations and political opinions are revealed – Mme Duveyrier organises a collective rendering of the chorus from Meyerbeer's *Huguenots* – Octave finds himself attracted to Mme Hédouin – Berthe manoeuvres Auguste into a compromising position, thus assuring their marriage.

Chapter 6
On a visit to the attic the next morning, Octave discovers that Trublot is sleeping with one of the maids – he looks into the inner courtyard and is treated to the obscene commentary of the servants on their masters – he flirts with Mme Juzeur and has dinner with the Pichons, dallying with Marie while her husband sees out her parents.

Chapter 7
The Josserands have Bachelard to dinner to try to get out of him a dowry for Berthe – the next day they continue the campaign at his business premises in the Rue d'Enghien – Octave is taken by Bachelard to meet Fifi – from there, together with M. Josserand, they proceed to Clarisse's, Duveyrier's mistress – Berthe's marriage-contract is signed – Saturnin is sent to an asylum.

Chapter 8
At Berthe's wedding, Octave is accused, by Valérie's husband, of having an affair with her – during the wedding ball that evening, Valérie has a fainting fit in the midst of the continuing scandal of her alleged infidelity.

Chapter 9
Octave witnesses the formalisation of the Campardons' *ménage-à-trois* – he dreams of conquering Mme Hédouin – he takes the Pichon couple out to dinner – Mme Hédouin rejects his advances – he quits his job in her shop – he visits the church of Saint-Roch where the Abbé Mauduit shows him the restorations being undertaken by Campardon before joining him at the latter's apartment the same evening – Berthe and her new husband offer Octave employment.

Chapter 10
During a visit by Octave to Mme Duveyrier, old M. Vabre has an attack of apoplexy – meanwhile Bachelard is indulging in a gargantuan feast at the Café Anglais to which he had invited M. Duveyrier – when they go on to Clarisse's, they find she has decamped – Octave is sent there to bring him home to his father-in-law's bedside.

Chapter 11
Even before he is pronounced dead, old Vabre's condition generates much talk about the fortune his heirs are expected to share – his funeral takes place two days later – Octave tries to seduce Marie again, and

then moves on to Mme Juzeur who resists him too – outside the church, the characters engage in discussions about the political situation – after Vabre's burial, his family discover that their expected inheritance has disappeared.

Chapter 12
Saturnin is returned from the asylum – Berthe's marriage begins to disintegrate under the pressure of her extravagance – her husband demands from the Josserands the dowry which has still not been paid – with Saturnin's encouragement to protect her from her husband's violent reproaches, Octave starts buying presents for Berthe as part of a strategy to seduce her – he takes advantage of the increasing number of occasions when she turns to him for money and consolation by finally satisfying his desire.

Chapter 13
Octave's affair with Berthe proceeds ever more intermittently – it is threatened by the concierge's vigilance, nosey neighbours and the shame experienced by Berthe when she overhears the servants gossiping about her.

Chapter 14
Berthe finally agrees to meet Octave – after dinner at the Campardons', he goes upstairs to await her, calling in at Marie Pichon's – unable to resist her charms, he then spends most of the night hoping that Berthe will not come after all – when she does, they discover they have been betrayed by her maid – Auguste hammers at the lovers' door – Berthe takes refuge at the Campardons' – Auguste breaks in on Octave and challenges him to a duel.

Chapter 15
Auguste seeks Bachelard's help in finding Duveyrier to act as his second in the intended duel – they find him at Clarisse's new address – Auguste is dissuaded from going through with it – Octave catches Valérie at Saint-Roch with her lover – Saturnin threatens Auguste and is returned to the asylum.

Chapter 16
Berthe has to face the wrath of the Josserand family – Auguste arrives and accuses the family of fraud and deception – M. Josserand collapses.

Chapter 17
Several months later, preparations are being made for Octave's marriage to Mme Hédouin – a reconciliation, blessed by the Abbé Mauduit,

is effected between Berthe and her husband – Duveyrier returns to the marital home, having been shown the door by Clarisse – M. Josserand dies – Duveyrier tries to commit suicide.

Chapter 18
Eight months later, Adèle gives birth in her room – a dinner party at the Duveyriers' reassembles the inhabitants of the house – Mme Octave Mouret is joined by her husband – Mme Duveyrier organises another choral performance – life returns to normal.